DEDICATED TO THE MEMORY OF GIUSEPPE ZAMBONINI, 1942–90

CARLO SCARPA

ROBERT
McCARTER

INTRODUCTION
VERUM IPSUM FACTUM

i.1

i.2

Carlo Scarpa (1906–78) was a unique figure among second generation Modern architects, at once deeply embedded in the archaic and anachronistic culture of Venice, while also transforming the ancient city by weaving the most modern of spatial conceptions into its material fabric. To a degree unmatched by any other Modern architect, Scarpa stood in two worlds: the ancient and the modern – the particular historical place and the larger contemporary world. Through his work he forever joined these two worlds, constructing an entirely new interpretation of architectural preservation and renovation by producing works that integrate, engage and transform their place. *Time* – the way in which the rituals of everyday life act to inextricably intertwine the past, present and future within the charged context, and the *detail* – that condensation of the boundless whole into the precise part, the articulate joint, were fundamental to Scarpa's work. In addition to these attributes, the continued relevance of Scarpa's work lies in the fact that his architecture was determined and shaped by the experience of the inhabitant, as someone living in a particular place, to a degree rarely found anywhere else within Modern architecture. (i.1)

In his architecture, Scarpa redefined the concepts of 'preservation', 'conservation', 'restoration', 'renovation', 'intervention' and 'reconstitution', reinterpreting Modern architecture as constituting an integrated part of its historical place and culture. By re-engaging the traditional building methods and materials of the Veneto, Scarpa revived lost crafts, while at the same time introducing entirely new structures, constructions and materials into historic contexts. Scarpa deployed the articulate detail as a fundamental ordering idea, celebrating the joint in works that unfold the poetic and experiential richness of materials to a degree that was exceedingly rare in the twentieth century. Scarpa engaged modern culture in the Byzantine milieu of Venice by integrating concepts drawn from modern painting and sculpture in his contextually embedded works.

This book examines and explores Scarpa's architectural works, analyzing his design process and ordering ideas, particularly as these reflect his transformation of Modern architecture in relation to history, place and the experience of space. It also examines the construction methods and materials Scarpa employed, and how these reinforce his intention to ground his works in their local culture and context. Finally, an experiential 'walk-through' of the projects places particular emphasis on the interior – the articulation and construction of which Scarpa held to be of primary importance to achieving an appropriate Modern architecture. (i.2)

Due to the fact that Scarpa's design process, perhaps more than any other modern architect, was bound up with, and quite literally consumed by, the act of making, by decisions regarding the selection and crafting of materials, and the discoveries made during construction, the text's primary focus is on the experience of the space. At the beginning of construction, Scarpa's designs were only developed to a very schematic level; revelations uncovered in the existing buildings' fabric, together with insights inspired by the act of making and the engagement of craft, often altered the direction of the design process, both dramatically and subtly. While in his works there are repeated uses of constructive and formal elements, each project was also a new beginning, with the outcome often largely unforeseen at the outset. The early eighteenth-century Venetian philosopher Giambattista Vico's aphorism, *Verum Ipsum Factum*, 'truth is in the made', which can also be translated as 'we only know what we make', served as a guiding principle for Scarpa, who learnt through the process of making and building, and who, as he said, was able to see his designs only through the drawings he made of them.

Each of Scarpa's drawings is a complete, hermetic and self-referential 'archive', which rarely matches the built work precisely. Scarpa's drawings do not form a linear record of the process of design; rather, they are best described as both infolded and layered, making any definitive unravelling of the 'design process' virtually impossible. Assessing Scarpa's design process, which is literally embedded and inlaid in the finished construction, must involve the direct experience of the building, engaging the constructed fabric as the final 'documentation' of his design process. For this reason, among others, Scarpa's work has proven to be particularly difficult for scholars, as it is largely opaque

i.3

i.4

to traditional scholarly methods of assessment, relying on distanced mechanisms that have no way of grasping the 'corporeal imagination', grounded in the body of the inhabitant, and the nearness of things, in their sensorial richness, that forms the basis for Scarpa's architecture of experience. Scarpa's drawings are entirely engaged in the process of making and construction, and his buildings are, to an equal degree, engaged in experience. In our inhabitation of Scarpa's buildings, conception and construction are fused in our experience, bound so closely together as to be incapable of being unravelled in analysis. **(i.3)**

Scarpa's architecture is appropriately apprehended, understood and evaluated through experiential engagement. In this, we soon realize that his works are so densely layered and infinitely articulated as to make it impossible to remember, notice or experience every detail and joint, every material characteristic, every nuanced spatial moment, every shadow and reflection. There is a kind of excess of sensory stimulation, a labyrinthine density of historical layers and a compacted complexity of possible readings that we normally associate with very ancient places, where time, weather and interventions by generations of inhabitants have laminated things so thickly that, even if we visit every day, there will always be something new to experience: the angle of the sun striking a wall or the colour of the glass tile shining from the shadow. [1] For Scarpa, the Venetian, this density of experience is entirely natural and expected, but it is fair to say that it is a characteristic largely absent from most Modern architecture. **(i.4)**

The truly valuable qualities and characteristics of Scarpa's work are precisely those that cannot be summarized or captured in any descriptive or analytical text, no matter how empathetically written. This text is certainly no exception, and is not intended to represent, simulate or substitute the experience of the things themselves. This text is the result of many dozens of visits to Scarpa's buildings, standing in their spaces at all times of the day, all seasons and in every kind of weather and light. While touching, hearing, looking long and hard and repeatedly drawing, constitutes my primary research, this book is not intended to be any kind of conclusive summary, and makes no claims to comprehensiveness, something that is, in fact, impossible with Scarpa's work. Rather, this book is intended to be an invitation to its readers to visit Scarpa's buildings for themselves, to experience these unique spaces in the flesh – something that is perhaps more important for understanding Scarpa's work than for that of any other architect of the modern era. Scarpa's sketches and drawings often depict his buildings being inhabited by human figures, in groups and individually. For Scarpa, the ultimate measure of his work was the human figure – in its many sizes, in the precise positions of the eye, in what is within reach of the hand to be touched – and his architecture comes to life only when we inhabit its spaces.

i.1 PERIOD PHOTOGRAPH, 1978; CARLO SCARPA DURING THE CONSTRUCTION OF HIS *VALMARANA* TABLE, IN THE YEAR OF HIS DEATH

i.2 CARLO SCARPA, BRION CEMETERY, SAN VITO D'ALTIVOLE, 1969–77; THE FAMILY TOMB, THE BELL TOWER AND PARISH CHURCH OF SAN VITO D'ALTIVOLE AND THE DOLOMITE MOUNTAINS BEYOND

i.3 CARLO SCARPA, CORRER MUSEUM RENOVATIONS, VENICE, 1952–60; GOTHIC SCULPTURE SPACE, SCULPTURE OF THE DOGE

i.4 CARLO SCARPA, CA' FOSCARI RENOVATIONS, VENICE, 1955–6; AULA MAGNA, WOODEN PIERS AND BRACE BEAMS

CHAPTER 01
A MAN OF BYZANTIUM WHO CAME TO VENICE BY WAY OF GREECE

A MAN OF BYZANTIUM WHO CAME TO VENICE BY WAY OF GREECE

Carlo Alberto Scarpa was born on 2 June 1906 in Corte dell'Asio, Venice, near Campo Santa Margherita. He was the eldest of the three children of Antonio Scarpa, an elementary school teacher and headmaster in Venice, and Emma Novello, a fashion designer. In 1908 the family moved to Vicenza, a town in the Veneto region housing twenty-one buildings by Andrea Palladio, the great late Renaissance architect. In Vicenza, Scarpa's mother opened a fashion workshop, patronized by the local aristocracy, and his father commuted daily to teach in Venice. Antonio Scarpa imbued his children, Carlo, Luigi (Gigi) and Ida, with his idealistic spirit, reflected in his 1929 book, *How I Became a Teacher*, published by Libreria Emiliana Editrice. [1] His father encouraged young Carlo's drawing and design interests, which began around the age of seven.

'The town of Vicenza opens and closes the parabola of Scarpa's existence in ideal terms', as Giuseppe Mazzariol and Giuseppe Barbieri have observed. [2] Scarpa's early and late years were in Vicenza; his last studio occupied the Villa Valmarana's stables near Palladio's Villa Rotonda. Vicenza was founded as the Roman town of Vicetia, and later became part of the 'Breadbasket of Venice,' its *terra firma*, or firm (dry) land, providing the agricultural and manpower base for the maritime power of the Republic of Venice, which was built on islands in the lagoon on the coast of the Adriatic Sea. The *terra firma* cities, Vicenza, Verona, Padova, Treviso and others, were connected to Venice by a series of canals and dredged rivers, allowing supplies and traffic to be transported by watercraft to Venice; a city of canals and pedestrian passages and no vehicular streets. Two navigable rivers, the Bacchiglione and the Retrone, wind their way through Vicenza's centre and outskirts, giving boat access to both the town and the surrounding countryside villas.

As a boy, Scarpa played in Vicenza's spaces, including the Palazzo Chiericati's colonnade, Teatro Olympico and the Basilica's two-levelled colonnade in the main Piazza dei Signori – all designed in the sixteenth century by Palladio when Venice was at the height of its cultural influence. The Palazzo Chiericati's colonnade, where Scarpa played marbles, is raised on a plinth with stairs opening on three sides, and it overlooks the piazza at the city's eastern edge near the Bacchiglione River. **(1.1)** Viewed across the piazza is the Teatro Olympico, the oldest, continuously covered theatre space in the world and the first indoor theatre to revive the Roman tradition of providing a walled stage. Palladio designed the Teatro for the Accademia Olympico, founded by a group of Vicentine nobles and intellectuals in 1556. It was completed after Palladio's death by Vincenzo Scamozzi, who added the false perspective streetscapes that open behind Palladio's stage wall. [3] Continuously used since its construction, the theatre serves as the venue for music and theatre productions and for political and cultural meetings. **(1.2)**

Formally known as the Palazzo della Ragione, the Basilica is formed by a medieval brick building, with shops on the ground floor and a large barrel-vaulted hall on the upper floor, around the whole of which Palladio wrapped a two-level, stone arcade of large columns, between which are arched openings carried on smaller columns. Knitting together the city's primary central public spaces, the Basilica's arcade may be entered from the Piazza dei Signori to the north, the Piazza della Erbe to the south and the small Piazza Palladio to the west. **(1.3)** The Piazza Palladio includes a statue of Palladio himself, gazing up at the Basilica's open corner. Serving as the city's major gathering place, the upper level's large vaulted hall is surrounded by Palladio's arcade, providing views into the surrounding squares and along the streets leading to the main square. Today, this upper arcade, elevated 10 metres (32 ft 9 in), remains one of Italy's greatest public spaces, inviting children to play and adults to promenade while enjoying the view.

1.1

1.1 ANDREA PALLADIO, PALAZZO CHIERICATI, VICENZA, 1550–1680; SOUTHWESTERN PORTICO

1.2 ANDREA PALLADIO AND VINCENZO SCAMOZZI, TEATRO OLYMPICO, VICENZA,1580–1585; INTERIOR VIEW OF THE STAGE

1.3 ANDREA PALLADIO, LOGGE DEL PALAZZO DELLA RAGIONE, VICENZA, 1546–9; WESTERN AND NORTHERN FACADES FROM THE PIAZZA DEI SIGNORI

1.2

1.3

1.4

During summers and holidays Scarpa lived in the Veneto countryside around Vicenza, famous for its Palladian villas. He spent most of his time at the eighteenth-century villa owned by the Count Tacchi family, his godparents, where his aunt was the housekeeper. Built for the wealthy families of the *terra firma* cities and Venice, Veneto's villas combined palatial homes with agricultural structures, for each villa was also a working farm. In his designs for the villas' facades, Palladio employed the pediment carried on columns of the Roman temple front, a form heretofore reserved for churches. Palladio's most influential design, the Villa Almerico (later Valmarana), called 'La Rotonda', is a short walk south from Vicenza's centre across the Retrone River, past the Roman Berga Theatre and along the ridge east of Monte Berico overlooking the Bacchiglione River. **(1.4)** The Villa Rotonda, as its name implies, is centred on a circular room covered by a semi-spherical dome, opening to the sky through an oculus, into which the rain originally fell as at the Pantheon in Rome. Palladio's unprecedented and ingenious idea for the Villa Rotonda was to place entry porticos and stairs on all four sides of the square plan, making four equal front facades. One can enter the villa from any side and, standing under the oculus, look out to four different landscapes.

After completing primary school in Vicenza, Scarpa, with his father's support, enrolled at the Technical High School, studying design and drawing. Scarpa's mother died when he was 13 years of age, and a few months later his family moved back to Venice. Despite his youth, Scarpa took the Royal Academy of Fine Arts' admissions exam, but he was unsuccessful. With his father's encouragement he applied the following year and, in 1920, at age 14, was admitted to the Academy, where he intended to study art. **'I had not considered architecture – for me, the Academy was a school of art where you became an artist. I soon developed a passion for architectural design and painting'**, Scarpa recounted in a late interview. Noting the deep impression made on him by his first exposure to Greek art, **'Our studies at the Academy were mainly directed towards classical Italian art. I was stunned one day when I saw a Greek statue in the school. Questions, issues about art I had not understood before became clear in my mind.'**

Scarpa also recalled the impression made by a fellow student, Morgens Brandstrug, **'I distinctly remember the tremendous influence a Danish painter had on me ... He made me see what was new and different in the modern world, much more than our teachers, whom we thought modern but were not, in fact ... He was the first person who made me look at things.'** [4] This idea of learning to **'look at things'** would prove to be of utmost importance to Scarpa and is directly related to his later connection of seeing to drawing. It also parallels contemporary pedagogical developments at the Bauhaus in the teaching of first, Paul Klee and later, Josef Albers; both believed that teaching students *to see* was the modern design school's primary task. At the Academy, Scarpa became friends with Carlo Maschietto, who later became an engineer and Scarpa's regular collaborator on architectural projects, and the painter Mario De Luigi, who became his life-long collaborator for plaster colouring and tile-work design.

Scarpa was very fond of his professor, Guido Cirilli, who, according to Scarpa, had been the favourite pupil of Giuseppe Sacconi, the architect of the Vittorio Emanuele II monument in Rome. **'So you might say I am a product of the tradition that produced that *bête blanche* of modern architecture'**, Scarpa stated late in life, referring to the criticism heaped upon what was called the 'wedding cake of Rome' by generations of modernists. [5] Cirilli was the Academy's chair of architecture from 1913–26 and was the director of the School of Architecture at the University of Venice (Instituto Universitario di Architettura, Venezia; IUAV) from 1929–43. In his own work, Cirilli employed classical and Renaissance precedents and had little interest in the then-emerging modern architecture. Despite this stance by his favourite teacher, Scarpa noted, **'I have always believed in the modern movement'**. While still a student, Scarpa was given a copy of Le Corbusier's *Vers une architecture*, first published in 1923. For Scarpa, reading this book was a **'great breakthrough'** and it **'produced a cultural reaction in me'**. [6]

1.5

From 1922–4, while still in school, Scarpa worked as assistant to the architect Vincenzo Rinaldo, mostly supervising the construction of church buildings. He would later marry Rinaldo's granddaughter, Onorina Lazzari, in 1934. In 1925, he received his first independent architectural commission: a small addition to an eighteenth-century villa on the Brenta River at Dolo, near Venice. He was also commissioned by Cappellin, the Murano glass manufacturer, to oversee several industrial buildings' construction, including the glass kilns, and to restore the Palazzo Da Mula, all on the island of Murano. In autumn 1926, age 20, Scarpa presented a design for an embassy building as his diploma project, receiving his degree as a teacher of architectural drawing and began teaching that same year at the newly founded IUAV, remaining there for the rest of his life. For the first three years he was an assistant lecturer to Professor Cirilli, who also began teaching at the IUAV that year.

1.4 ANDREA PALLADIO, VILLA ALMERICO 'LA ROTONDA', *C.* 1570

1.5 VITTORE CARPACCIO, *MIRACLE OF THE TRUE CROSS*, 1494; OIL ON CANVAS, 36 X 38 CM (14 X 15 IN), GALLERIE DELL' ACCADEMIA, VENICE

During his six years as an Academy student, Scarpa immersed himself in the history, culture and architecture of Venice. He developed a strong identification with Venice's Byzantine foundations, its connections to the East and West, its painters – Giorgione, Tiziano, Tiepolo, Guardi and Canaletto – and its crafts, particularly printing, bookmaking and glass. Scarpa himself later noted his propensity for 'a relentless analysis of detail', which he felt came from being a Venetian. 'When I visited Florence for the first time, I was immediately aware of the enormous architectural difference between the two cities. I cannot deny that I am impressed by Tuscan architecture, but such precision, such certainty are not part of my being. I am a true son of my region and have a strong feeling for my roots.' [7]

'Any story of Scarpa's life is a *story of places* before all else. And they are physical, concrete, unrepeatable', as Mazzariol and Barbieri have noted, '[for Scarpa], place meant the space where some rite was made manifest'. [8] Venice and the Veneto provided the context for almost all of Scarpa's work; rarely in modern architecture has a city and its rituals shaped an architect's work the way Venice shaped Scarpa's architecture. Scarpa's work, like all great architecture, can only be truly understood through visiting it 'in the flesh', in its Venetian and Veneto setting. **(1.5)**

1.6

The Venetian Republic lasted from 1081 until 1797, when Napoleon became the first foreign ruler to conquer the city-state. During that remarkably long period, Venice was truly unique among nations, being governed by a constitution that emphasized trading and manufacturing, it developed one of the most effective naval military forces and extensive diplomatic corps in modern history. While its military power declined after 1481, its cultural influence and political importance actually increased from that date until 1669, after which it slowly declined, culminating in its abdication to Napoleon. Due to its supremacy in maritime trading, Venice always looked both East and West, connecting the Catholic and Protestant countries to the Islamic, Greek Orthodox and Chinese civilizations, its trade routes linking the Silk Route to the Mediterranean.[9] It was a Venetian, Marco Polo, who in the thirteenth and fourteenth centuries travelled extensively in today's China, India and the Middle East and whose book documenting his travels makes him one of that period's only individuals **'of whom everyone today has heard'**.[10]

For the seventy years following 1797, Venice was dominated alternately by the French and Austrians. During this period, starting in 1817, the Venetian Republic's archives were organized by the Austrians, stored at the former Convent of the Franciscans at the Frari, where they remain today. When first collected the Republic's records filled 300 large rooms and galleries; today they fill 8 kilometres (5 miles) of shelves, with approximately twelve million volumes and document bundles. Among the records are extensive maritime navigational maps, world maps and numerous maps of the Veneto, some up to 6 x 6 metres (20 x 20 feet), showing the *terra firma's* extensive drainage and irrigation system. Due to the Venetian ambassadors' diligence, the archives contain information regarding all of Europe, Russia and the Middle East. As John Premble noted:

> **'The Republic had matched the sophistication of its bureaucracy with the percipience of its diplomacy. It had eyes and ears everywhere and the making of modern European history had been witnessed by its perspicacious envoys. During nearly four centuries the Venetian ambassadors had been famous for their skills at observation, inquiry, understanding and reporting; above all, of reporting.'**[11]

The Archives of Venice is considered the most comprehensive historical documentation of its kind and, as it was for Scarpa, it is every Venetian's birthright. **(1.6)**

In 1866 the Austrians withdrew from Venice and it became part of the new Kingdom of Italy. Previously only accessed by water, Venice was linked to Vicenza by a train viaduct constructed across the lagoon in 1846. In 1857, the train link was extended to Milan, further connecting to England, France and Germany; Henry James recalls seeing a tourist group in the city in 1881.

Before 1870, Venice had been a favourite of foreign poets and writers, including Lord G. G. Byron, Percy Shelley, Fennimore Cooper and George Sand. After 1870, a new generation of writers began to set their works in Venice, including James, Gabriele d'Annunzio, Thomas Mann and Marcel Proust. As James noted, **'It is a fact that almost everyone interesting, appealing, melancholy, memorable, odd, seems to have gravitated to Venice.'**[12] Yet, while they used it as the setting for contemporary events in their writings, Venice remained a place apart. Throughout its rise and fall, Venice remained a city of carnival, where people from all civilizations could meet on neutral ground, and a city of craft, where things were made using techniques passed down through generations. Marking the city's rise as a modern international cultural centre, the first Biennale for Art was held in the Giardini in 1895; the Venice Biennale is today the largest international art exhibition in the world.

In describing this island city's unique spatial structure, it is important to understand that Venice's sunlight does not usually come from the side, but from the sky above and reflected from the water below. The buildings, pedestrian passageways and plazas, rather than standing on solid earth, are lifted just above the water's surface by submerged wooden pile foundations. Venice's canals and pedestrian passageways, tightly held between tall walls, only intersect at the many bridges and *campi*, Venetian for plazas. Together, these elements form overlapping labyrinthine lines of movement, whose tight twists and turns can only be confidently navigated by daily users.

The primary means of movement in Venice has always been by boat, originally by gondola, a long narrow vessel that is manoeuvred by a long oar set into the elegantly carved wooden *forchetta*. Every major building in Venice has two entries, the important canal-side entrance reached by gondola and the service entrance accessed from the passageway, *campo* or, more rarely, across a bridge. In a similar way, a *campo* fronts on to the canal, with pedestrian passages considered secondary, often entering the *campo* at its corners. A church opens on to almost every *campo*, giving it its name, and its front usually faces the canal edge's steps. The typical *campo's* original, bare earth floor was later paved over to assist in the collection of rainwater, held in cisterns beneath, and retrieved from a well that stood at its centre. Today, there are also drains in the *campi's* pavement directing rain water into the canals. **(1.7)**

The water level of the canals and surrounding lagoon fluctuates with the tide and the dramatic, seasonal *acqua alta*, or high water. Starting each November, this flooding is the result of winds coming off the Adriatic, pushing seawater into the lagoon, often combined with excessive rainwater runoff entering from the rivers. During the *acqua alta* season, the lagoon water will emerge from the *campi* drains, rising above the canals' edges, flooding the passageways and *campi* and driving away all but the hardiest tourists. Yet, in *acqua alta*, the buildings of Venice appear to emerge directly from the water's surface; the heavy stone city appearing to float above its mirrored reflection. (see c.1) It is hardly surprising that this season has always been a favourite time for many to visit Venice, including the poet Joseph Brodsky, whose book of reminiscences of winters spent in Venice is titled *Watermark*. [13] (1.8, 1.9)

1.7

1.8

1.9

1.6 SCUOLA GRANDE DI SAN ROCCO, VENICE, 1515–60; THE CHAPTER HALL, FIRST FLOOR

1.7 CA' D'ORO, VENICE, *C.* 1420–30; GRAND CANAL FACADE

1.8 CA' FOSCARI (R), 1452–3, AND THE PALAZZI GIUSTINIANI (L), LATE FIFTEENTH CENTURY, VENICE; GRAND CANAL FACADES

1.9 PALAZZO DUCALE, VENICE, SOUTHERN LAGOON FACADE, BUILT IN THE FOURTEENTH AND FIFTEENTH CENTURIES, WITH SOME CAPITALS, AND THE DOGE'S SCULPTURE, REPLACED IN THE NINETEENTH CENTURY

1.10

1.11

1.12

Venice's architecture is unlike any other in the world. Rather than attempt to reduce its astonishing variety to a general set of characteristics, it would be better to examine one of Scarpa's favourite buildings, Santa Maria dei Miracoli, built from 1481–8 by Pietro Lombardo.

The very small church is known for its rich marble cladding and for its highly refined surface patterns and subtle colourations. **(1.10)** This is also one of Venice's only churches that has one side directly on a canal. This long, taut sidewall, only viewed in its entirety at an acute angle, is framed by two sets of twelve shallow pilasters, one above the other. **(1.11)** At the bottom of the wall, the pilasters stand on slightly projecting bases supported in turn by pilaster capitals that emerge from the water. This unique detail suggests that another set of columns is hidden beneath the water's surface. The entire wall is reflected in the canal's surface and the stone-clad church appears to float, as if it was weightless.

Walking around the apse and along the southern side's narrow passageway we are able to touch the marble's smooth surface on the other sidewall. Between each pair of white Istrian stone pilasters is a double-square panel with a grey marble frame. At its centre is a reddish Verona Prun stone cross surrounded by four rectangles of white veined marble. **(1.12)** In feeling the weathered stone surfaces, we note the smooth, cracked and flaked Prun stone and the gritty, matte white marble. We also observe that the Istrian stone is bright white where it receives sunlight while the areas receiving no direct sunlight appear almost black, like a permanent shadow. The combination of the taut marble skin and the sunlit, glowing stone makes this church's exterior wall appear thin and translucent, giving the sense the interior space is pressing outwards from beneath its surface.

1.10 PIETRO LOMBARDO, SANTA MARIA DEI MIRACOLI, VENICE, 1481–8; WESTERN FACADE

1.11 SANTA MARIA DEI MIRACOLI; NORTHERN CANAL FACADE

1.12 SANTA MARIA DEI MIRACOLI; WESTERN FACADE, DETAIL

1.13 PIAZZA SAN MARCO, VENICE; VIEW EAST ACROSS THE PIAZZA TO THE CAMPANILE DI SAN MARCO (REBUILT IN 1912) AND THE THIRTEENTH-CENTURY FACADE OF THE BASILICA DI SAN MARCO

Inside, the church's barrel-vaulted, coffered ceiling is made of wood. The floor, made of the same coloured marbles used in the exterior walls, is laid in a square woven pattern, each frame enclosing a rotated, central white square. The high altar has an even more remarkable floor, made of the same coloured marbles laid in a complex trapezoidal, interlacing pattern with inset triangles, depicting three-dimensional, cubic, shadowed volumes within the floor's surface. These woven stone floors, their smooth surfaces polished by centuries of wear, reflect the weak light in uneven, wave-like patterns, reminding us of the paradoxical impression we received outside: that this heavy stone building floats on water.

Yet, on the inside and outside of this church, it is the walls that are the most sensuously fabricated surfaces. The interior walls are composed of panels of intensely white marble with black veining set in a book-match rhythm: each pair of slabs is cut and folded open, like opening a book, so the veining patterns are mirrored across the centre joint. At the upper level, a window is opened between each pair of panels and, from inside, we can clearly see the small circular, convex glass discs, each set in a delicate metal frame and stacked in horizontal and vertical rows. From outside, these windows appear dark, like the canal water, but within, these glass discs admit the most ethereal light, shining with **'the very translucence of water'**, as Adrian Stokes has written. Yet the glass, like the marbles that surround it, came from the earth. Stokes writes that in Venice, **'the lives of generations have made exteriors, acceptable between sky and water, marbles inhabited by emotion, feelings turned to marble'**. In Venice, **'light and shade are recorded, abstracted, intensified, solidified. Matter is dramatized in stone'**. [14]

1.13

While *acqua alta* floods Venice every winter, it has been known for some time that the city is also slowly sinking into the water. This became apparent soon after the end of the Republic, as Premble noted, **'In 1810, French engineers excavating the *broglio*, or patricians' promenade, in the lower arcade of the Doge's Palace, discovered that the missing bases of the columns were below the level of the pavement, which had been raised by some 38 centimetres [1 ft 3 in] over a period of five centuries to compensate for subsistence of the soil.'** [15] For the first time a discussion began, both inside and outside Venice, of whether and how to preserve its physical fabric. During the nineteenth century, a heated debate took place between those following Eugène-Emmanuel Viollet-le-Duc, who believed that buildings should be **'restored'** back to the style consistent with the time of their origin – even if they never existed in that ideal condition and even if it was restored using modern construction materials and methods; and those, such as John Ruskin in his *The Stones of Venice*, who believed that the buildings' decayed and ruined conditions reflected the history of their inhabitation, and should not be made to appear as new through 'restoration'. **(1.13)**

Siding with Ruskin, the novelist Victor Hugo argued that a building was only complete when time, weather and wear had left their imprint on it and Benjamin Constant argued, **'Modern buildings are silent; but ruins speak'**. [16] Giacomo Boni, who in 1888 was appointed head of the Italian government agency charged with caring for ancient buildings, stated, **'The ruin evoked the idea of the antiquity of the building; antiquity expressed in the corrosion of the marbles and in the delicate amber colouring and surface polish, produced by the alteration of sunshine and rain.'** [17] These opposing definitions: our ability to determine the age of a building by the patterns of weathering and wear of its original materials, versus our being able to 'date' a building by means of the historic style it presents on its surface, irrespective of the age of the materials, have split the discipline of architectural preservation since that time, and remains an unsettled question. In this context, it is interesting to note that in his writings from the 1880s the Venetian Camillo Boito, who has been called the father of Italian restoration, argued for a middle path, holding that **'a restoration project should respect and reveal all the historical layers involved, even those less successful, and that whatever was new should complement them ... For Boito, the question of an architectural intervention was not an either – or matter, but a moderate acknowledgement of both sides, an interweaving of fabric that supported both the new and the old.'** [18] **(1.16)**

The uniqueness of Venice with regard to this issue of the preservation of its historic fabric, and how during the last two centuries the world has sought to involve itself in these decisions, was highlighted by the events of 14 July 1902. On that day, the Campanile in Piazza San Marco collapsed – miraculously, without the loss of life. Venice's *Sindaco*, Count Filippo Grimani, argued that the world, which saw Venice as its common heritage, would not accept a Venice without the old Campanile and announced that it would be rebuilt as it had been and where it had been, **'come era e dove era'**. In fact, the Campanile was rebuilt only to *look* as it did before. Clad in brick to look like the original masonry tower, the Campanile we can visit today incorporates modern steel construction, and even has a lift. The international community almost unanimously opposed this **'sham born of the idea of "restoration"'**, which proposed making a modern building look like an historic one, holding that the original Campanile was a product of the most advanced construction technology of its time and that its replacement should reflect, with equal accuracy, 1902 construction technology. A newspaper editorial explained, **'In any previous period, if an important building fell down, the immediate desire would have been not to "restore" it, but to erect something better and finer in its place.'** [19] Despite this opposition, which was particularly strong from the English, **'backed up by the moralistic doctrines of John Ruskin'**, as Colin Rowe has noted, this would in fact prove to be a defining moment for modern preservation and an early example of **'a populist solution to preservation – make a *reproduction*'**. [20]

Scarpa would engage these exact issues in the vast majority of his projects, which were renovations and additions to historic structures. Yet, it is important to remember that the buildings of Venice and the Veneto have often experienced forms of deterioration in addition to normal wear and weathering and decidedly abnormal sinking. In February 1918, one year before Scarpa and his family moved to Venice from Vicenza, three hundred bombs were dropped by the Austrians on Venice, part of forty-two separate bombing raids from 1915–8, with one thousand bombs total dropped on Venice during the First World War. As we shall see, a number of the structures Scarpa was asked to work on during his career had suffered such more extreme forms of damage.

GLASS DESIGNS

MURANO, 1926–1947

In 1926, the same year Scarpa began teaching at the newly opened IUAV, he initiated a parallel second career as a glass designer working in Murano, first with M.V.M. Cappellin from 1926–31 and then with Paolo Venini from 1932–47. Scarpa became an acknowledged master in glass design well before his architectural works began to receive substantial recognition, and many of his glass designs are still in production today. Glass manufacturing is an ancient craft tracing back to Roman times; a tradition that has been practised at the highest levels in Venice from the time of the Republic to today, it is in many ways inextricably linked to the city. Stokes wrote that glass had the same importance as limestone in the constructed character of the city, 'If in fantasy the stones of Venice appear as the waves' petrification, then Venetian glass, compost of sand and water, expresses the taut curvature of the cold undersea, the slow, oppressed yet brittle curves of dimly translucent water.' [21]

As mentioned, Cappellin had been the client for one of Scarpa's first independent architectural commissions in 1925, the year the company was founded. The next year Scarpa began to work as a designer at the company and in 1927, Scarpa replaced the firm's lead designer, Vittorio Zecchin. Scarpa's brother, Gigi, recalls this early period at Cappellin:

> 'I still remember well the enthusiasm with which [Scarpa] spoke of the fabulous vase adorning, in solemn central position, Paolo Veronese's *L'Annunciazione* in the Accademia Gallery, and of Cappellin's desire to produce works equally transparent, equally colourful with the same perfection ... These pieces are the fruit of the characteristic, fundamental to Carlo Scarpa's art, which springs from his search for perfection. His unceasing, studied attention to even the smallest detail, and his noted inability to be contented in the quest for perfect results, craftsmanship included, were well known.' [22] (see pp. 4–5)

Over Scarpa's twenty-plus year career as a glass designer he spent innumerable hours with the glass-blowers and craftsmen at the kilns, first learning common techniques, then reviving lost or abandoned techniques and eventually inventing new ones, many of which remain in use today. As Carla Sonego noted, Scarpa 'acquired a singular knowledge of glass as a material thanks to the fact that the best craftsmen of the time worked in the [Cappellin] kiln house: glass-blowers who were renowned for their technical skills and, above all, for the extraordinary colours they were capable of creating.' [23] While a number of Scarpa's designs were produced, he paid little attention to the concept of serial production. Many of his designs were one of a kind, either due to the extreme difficulty of the craft required in its production or to the fact that he employed the unique remains of that day's materials left at the bottom of the mixing tub. In his glass designs, Scarpa exhibited a deep understanding of the traditional glass-blowing, colouration and finishing techniques of Murano.

1.15

1.16

Scarpa's first glassworks may be identified by their cone-shaped foot, which was his invention, and the consistent use of pure geometric forms. Scarpa understood from earlier glass-making generations that glass could be distinguished from other materials, like porcelain, primarily by its transparency. **(1.15)** Thus, his earliest works involved making transparent pieces including his *reticello* glass pieces, lined with strongly coloured thin filigrees. Scarpa's *lattimi*, or milk glass pieces, are opaque, therefore breaking from Murano tradition. **(1.16)** He also made pieces using the *millefiori* technique, which involved pieces of coloured *murrine* glass being fused into the *lattimi* milk glass vase's surface. Additionally, Scarpa employed gold and silver leaves, applying it to the still-soft glass in various ways and sometimes refiring it so as to oxidize the metal. **(1.14)** In the five years Scarpa worked at Cappellin, 141 separate glass objects were fabricated to his designs.

1.14 *NERO ARGENTATO*, 1930; GLOBE-SHAPED BLACK VASE WITH RED *RETORTOLI* CANES AND OXIDIZED SILVER LEAF, M.V.M. CAPPELLIN & C.

1.15 *VASO TRASPARENTE*, 1926; GLOBE-SHAPED CLEAR VASE WITH BLUE TRUNCATED CONE BASE, M.V.M. CAPPELLIN & C.

1.16 *VASO FENICIO*, *C.* 1930, H: 21.5 CM (8.5 IN); CONICAL *LATTIMI* GLASS WITH BLUE *FENICIO* DESIGN, M.V.M. CAPPELLIN & C.

1.17

1.18

1.19

1.20

After Cappellin's bankruptcy in 1931 during the Great Depression, Scarpa began to work with Venini and C., a collaboration that would be of unprecedented productivity over the next ten years in particular. With little interference from Paolo Venini, Scarpa enjoyed an extraordinary freedom to explore new forms and techniques. The result was the unprecedented number of 283 glass objects made to Scarpa's designs. Venini and Scarpa set out to revive lost techniques and materials, including the half-filigree, involving filaments of coloured and transparent canes shaped into simple geometric forms. **(1.17)** Another example included the Roman *murrine*, made of cold slices of glass canes, called tesserae, placed in a mould and fused to form a single element; rather than being polished smooth, the tesserae were often left with a rough, irregular surface. Scarpa also perfected the tiny bubbles technique, *a bollicine*, **(1.21)** involving a chemical additive, and the submerged *a bollicine* technique, where a glass piece is submerged in crystal, enclosing and coating the coloured nucleus. **(1.22)** Additionally, Scarpa invented the *corrosi*, or corroded technique, dipping a vase in hydrofluoric acid then embedding it in sawdust. **(1.18)** These were sometimes characterized by *bugue*, or bumps, applied hot to the piece's outer face, which was then corroded. At the 1934 Milan Triennale, Scarpa was awarded the *diploma d'onore* for his glassware designs made with Venini. **(1.19)**

At the 1938 Venice Biennale, Scarpa showed a series of new techniques, including: 'dots and stripes', brightly coloured spots floating within the transparent glass; 'rings and bands', a brightly-coloured, simple spiral running continuously around the piece's entire surface; 'variegated knurled', a lace-like, scalloped variation of coloured and clear glass in wave-like patterns; and the bicoloured *a incalmo*, two differently-coloured glass hemispheres joined together and moulded. **(1.20)** In 1940, the Venice Biennale reserved an entire room for Venini, displaying exclusively Scarpa's designs. Marina Barovier described the exhibit:

> 'The capacity for self-renewal exhibited by Scarpa – every two years at the famous exhibitions he presented astonishing new pieces – was the fruit of his vast knowledge of glass and its infinite combinations. Fabrics could be transparent or opaque, shiny or satin, smooth or rough, thin or thick, colourless or polychrome. The light falling on them could mutate the shape, change and become imprisoned, give depth to, or highlight, a colour, emphasize the incisions or at the same time appear to emanate from within the glass itself.' [24]

(1.23)

1.17 *MURRINE OPACHE*, 1936–40, H: 25 CM (10 IN); BLACK, CORAL AND RED *LATTIMO MURRINE* ELEMENTS ARRANGED IN DIAGONAL ROWS AND ALTERNATING COLOURS, VENINI & C.

1.18 *CORROSI*, C. 1936, H: 33 CM (13 IN); ORANGE-SHADED (*ARANCIATO*) *CORROSO* GLASS WITH APPLIED COIL AND IRIDIZED SURFACE, VENINI & C.

1.19 *IRIDATI*, C. 1940, H: 24 CM (9.5 IN); SMOKE-GREY (FUMÉ) GLASS OVERLAID WITH CLEAR GLASS LAYERS OF DIFFERENT COLOURS AND HOT-APPLIED *BUGNE*, AN INTENSE SUPERFICIAL IRIDIZATION, VENINI & C.

1.20 *BATTUTI*, C. 1940, H: 11 CM 94.25 IN); TWO-COLOUR VASE IN GREENISH (*VERDOGNOLO*) AND KAISER RED (*ROSSO KAISER*) GLASS WITH DEEP HONEYCOMB GRINDING MASKS AND LIGHT VELATO FINISH. THE LOWER PORTION OF THE VASE IS SET WITH LAMP-WORK BEADS, VENINI & C.

1.21 *A BOLLICINE*, C. 1934, H: 15 CM (6 IN); VENINI & C.

1.22 *SOMMERSI*, C. 1934, H: 21 CM (8.25 IN); RUBY AND AMETHYST *SOMMERSO* GLASS WITH TWISTED RIBBING, VENINI & C.

1.21

1.22

1.23 *VASI BATTUTI*, 1940–6; VENINI & C.

1.24

1.24 *VASO TESSUTO*, 1940; CLEAR GLASS WITH GREEN, BLACK AND PINK VERTICAL CANES, VENINI & C.

1.25 *PIATTO SERPENTE*, 1940; BLACK AND RED *LATTIMO MURRINE* GLASS WITH SNAKE PATTERN, VENINI & C.

1.26 *VASO INCISO*, 1940; CYLINDRICAL GLASS WITH WAVED ENGRAVINGS, VENINI & C.

1.26

1.25

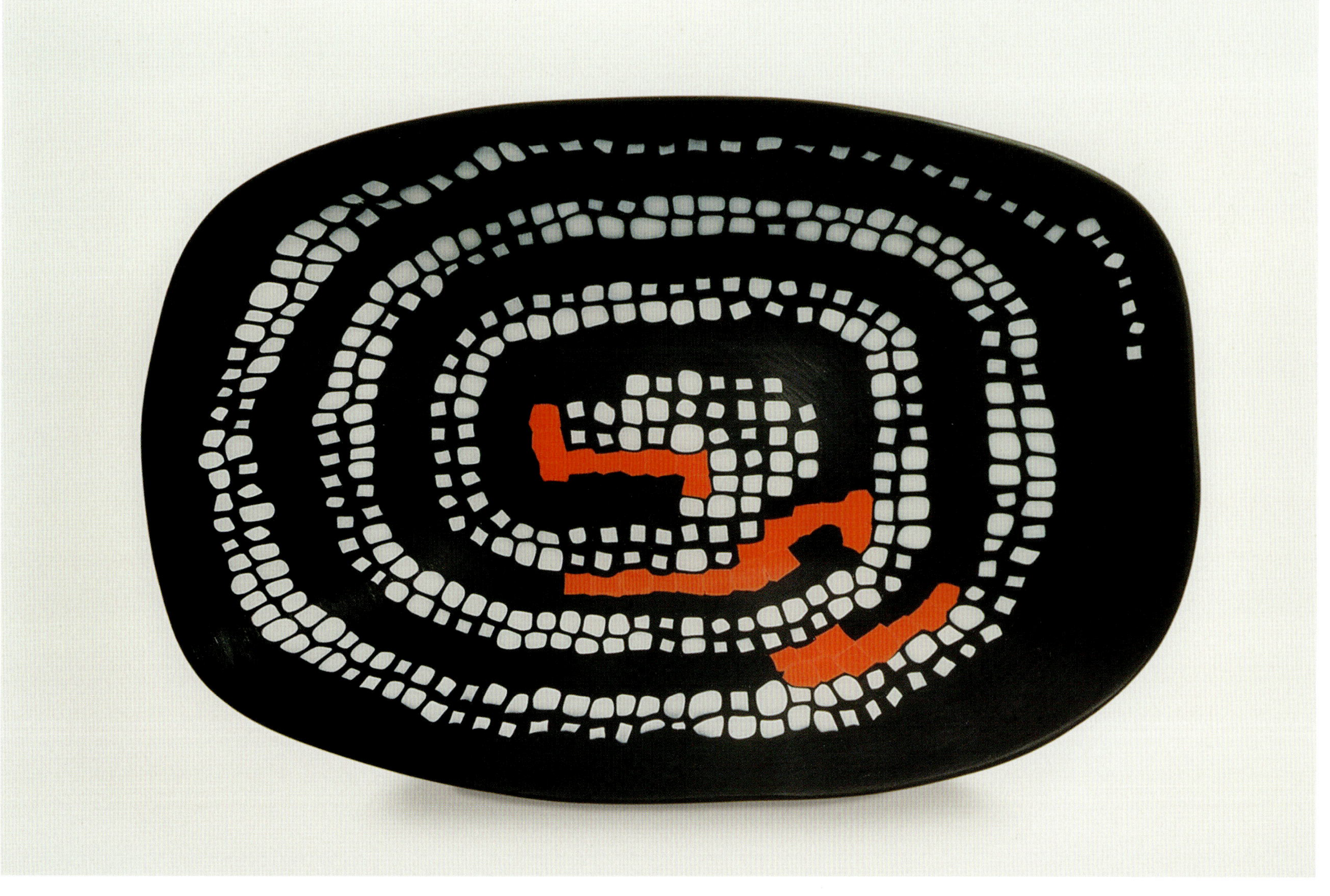

1.27 *VASO INCISO*, 1940; CLEAR GLASS WITH TRANSLUCENT, ENGRAVED BANDS, VENINI & C.

1.28 *CIOTOLA A FILI*, 1942; TURQUOISE BOWL WITH 'PASTA VITREA' THREAD, VENINI & C.

1.29 *VASO A PENNELLATE*, 1942; CLEAR GLASS WITH RED AND ORANGE *PENNELLATE*, OR BRUSH-STROKED PIECES, VENINI & C.

1.30 *CIOTOLA MURRINE*, 1936; TRANSPARENT GLASS BOWL WITH YELLOW AND BLACK GLASS TESSERAE, VENINI & C.

1.27

1.28

1.29

1.30

This exhibit also included pieces using: the *granulari*, or granulated technique, which were rough-surfaced and made by including *conterie*, glass beads or nodules of opal; *battutie velati*, or hammered glass, ground to produce deep carving, dimpled or veiled (lightly ground) surfaces; 'ribboned', or *tessuti* glass, where multicoloured thin glass canes are hot-fused and shaped into the final piece; so-called *nuovo murrine*, where polychrome slices of glass canes are arranged in irregular motifs, fired and ground perfectly smooth – this includes Scarpa's famous individually unique *serpente* bowls; and the uniquely made *incise*, or engraved pieces, comprising clear glass engraved with figural or abstract designs, where the engraved glass becomes translucent, although sometimes ground smooth and made transparent again. **(1.24, 1.25, 1.26, 1.27, 1.28)** These pieces were also included in the 1942 Venice Biennale, the last time Scarpa presented as a glass designer. Alongside them, Scarpa showed an extraordinary series of *pennellate*, or brush-stroked glass pieces, involving the hot application of blown pieces of threads, bands and other coloured glass marks dragged around the piece. Scarpa said these pieces presented **'marks of torn colour'**.[25] **(1.29)**

During the Second World War, Venini's operations were reduced to producing light bulbs. Shortly after the war ended in 1947, Scarpa ended his relationship with Venini, at his wife's insistence, devoting himself fulltime to architecture. A postscript to this history of Scarpa's glass designs and an indication of their remarkable quality is an event that took place during Frank Lloyd Wright's 1951 visit to Venice. Wright visited the Venini glassworks showroom on Murano, where he became enamoured with a *murrine* bowl of clear, yellow and black glass. **(1.30)** He asked to purchase it and was deeply disappointed to be told that the bowl, designed by Scarpa, was one-of-a-kind and not for sale. When directed to the Venini pieces available for purchase, Wright selected six glass vases, all designed by Scarpa.

This immersion in one of the oldest Venetian cultural traditions, the Murano glass-making 'guilds' dating back to Roman times, and Scarpa's reading of works by the early eighteenth-century Venetian philosopher Giambattista Vico, who held that **'we can only know that which we and our kind have made'**, is typical of one side of Scarpa's approach to design. This is the part of Scarpa that is, as he said, inextricably bound up with Venice and the Veneto region, engaging in the making of glass as a way of knowing his place in the world. **'Any history of Scarpa is a history of materials and of the work of the hand'**, as Mazzariol and Barbieri have said.[26] The characteristics and qualities of materials, the manner in which they captured and reflected light and how they could be worked, was of critical importance both to Scarpa's designs and to his contemporary Adrian Stokes' perceptive reading of Venice's architecture:

'Apart from glass utensils and ornaments, at Venice, probably for the first time in Europe, glass was used as window-panes. The very translucence of water was fixed to palaces affronting the sea.'[27]

Yet, in Scarpa's work, this attentive approach to his place and acute sensitivity to its history of built form is paradoxically combined with a fierce dedication to the emerging modern art and culture of his time, a truly international development untethered to any single place in the world. Scarpa's complex personality and extraordinary range of references, his devotion to his Venetian culture and its pivotal position historically and contemporarily, between the East and the West, between ancient and modern, between classical and vernacular, is alluded to in an anecdote told by a client and travelling companion, Aldo Businaro, who recalls Scarpa quoting a passage from a poem by Eugenio Montale, entitled *We Never Know How We Will Turn Out*:[28]

'...and then, one day,
these words with no sound
that we derived from you,
fed on weariness and silence,
will come to a brotherly heart
well-seasoned with the salt of Greece.'

Scarpa then said,
'When my time comes, cover me with these words, because I am a man of Byzantium who came to Venice by way of Greece.'[29]

CHAPTER 02

NOTHING COMES FROM NOTHING

2.1

A number of Scarpa's early architectural commissions were for the Murano-based Cappellin and Venini glass companies. These first projects, exhibitions, showrooms and company offices, involved primarily interior renovations – as would be the case for the majority of his career's works. These early works demonstrate the extensive knowledge Scarpa already possessed about contemporary Modern architecture and art from around the world.

In 1930, Scarpa designed the Cappellin room at the 4th International Exhibition of Modern Decorative Arts in Monza, Italy. **(2.1)** Along one wall of this long narrow room, Scarpa placed a series of tall thin wooden display stands, each of which had its central spine split in two – perhaps Scarpa's earliest use of the double vertical, the number 11. From these spines the shelves cantilevered on alternating sides as they rose, creating a dynamically balanced asymmetry closely related to the contemporary works of both Frank Lloyd Wright and Paul Klee. [1] At the end of the room, folding around the corner, is a large stained glass window composed of a series of irregularly sized, rectangular coloured glass panels, serving as the background for a series of abstract figures. The pattern of the stained glass, divided by the caming's dark lines, is close in spirit to the contemporary paintings of Piet Mondrian and Theo van Doesburg, of the Dutch De Stijl movement. Another rarely noticed feature of this early design are the wall-mounted light fixtures made of horizontal metal brackets carrying cantilevered, slightly forward-tilted sheets of rectangular glass samples of Cappelin's available range of colours, patterns and finishes. Besides illuminating the room, these lights presented the raw material of the finished vases and bowls on display below.

In the unrealized glass mosaic artists' studio, designed for Cappellin in 1930 for a Paris building, Scarpa designed all six surfaces of the rectangular space as a folded composition of coloured surfaces moving from floor to wall to ceiling. Three walls are made of different forms of glass: frosted rectangular panels to the left near the staircase, an opalescent white wall ahead and a four-panelled, stained-glass window to the right, in which isometric figures float against an irregularly gridded background. The smooth plaster ceiling has a T-shaped panel that projects slightly forwards of a U-shaped surround, from which two long pendant lights are hung asymmetrically. Two strips of darker stone at the floor's edges frame the central surface, which is made of large rectangular slabs of polished, light-coloured stone, reflecting the Scarpa-designed, abstract rectangular furniture. There is nothing resembling classical moulding or details; the surfaces meet cleanly and sharply in this elegant but restrained composition. The design is similar to projects by Mondrian, such as his 1926 *Salon de Madame B.*, Dresden and the 1923 *Colour Composition for an Exhibition*, Berlin by Vilmos Huzar and Gerrit Rietveld, both three-dimensional interior projects by members of De Stijl. [2]

Scarpa made a similar three-dimensional interior for the 1936 Venini exhibition, at the 6th Triennale in Milan, where his glass designs were prominently displayed. **(2.2)** A dark floor and ceiling were separated by a white folding wall with an inset shelf on its left side, illuminated by a horizontal light below eye level. On the right, the ceiling and wall were linked by a full-height, black-walled display case, illuminated by a frosted-glass ceiling. The room's ceiling had a series of rectangular and cylindrical openings, with white-painted inner surfaces, from the centre of which hung Venini chandeliers.

For the 22nd Venice Biennale in 1940, where Venini was given an entire room, Scarpa constructed an ephemeral, room-sized glass display case that stood within the large room. **(2.3)** A thin steel frame of four corner posts, with horizontals at the bottom and above eye level, stood on a low black base and rose to the ceiling. This delicate frame held four very large sheets of plate glass on its long sides, each aligned to the next with small circular clips, and with large sheets of frosted glass above, from the header to the ceiling. Out of this cloud-like, upper volume hung a chandelier, above which the ceiling lights shown down on to the glass pieces arrayed on three levels of thin, clear glass shelves. The white lines on the steel frame's interior, combined with the black base beneath, made it appear that the display case was floating in the centre of the room, as if hung from the ceiling. Similarly, the coloured glass pieces within appear to float within the black and white composition of the display case.

NOTHING COMES FROM NOTHING

2.2

Scarpa's other designs of this early period also indicate his exposure to a broad spectrum of contemporary architecture. The built-in wood furniture Scarpa designed in 1932 for the antique dealer Ferruccio Asta in Venice, with its horizontal black-and-white lacquer striping and its interlocking corners, was informed by Scarpa's knowledge of both the De Stijl and the work of the Austrian Secessionists Josef Maria Olbrich and Josef Hoffmann. **(2.4)** Hoffmann's designs, from furniture to buildings, emphasized their surfaces through the moulding or trim that he applied to the corners, acting to deny the materials' weight and implying a uniform thinness. Late in life, Scarpa spoke of the influence of Hoffmann at that time:

> 'Of course, the artist we knew and loved best, one who was able to publish most in German reviews – *Moderne Bauforum*, *Wasmuth*, etc. come to mind – was Josef Hoffmann. And Josef Hoffmann had a great sense or feeling for decoration ... (one has to recall, as Ruskin said, that art is decoration). This fact includes a very basic orientation for us both: I am a Byzantine at heart, and in Hoffmann, you will find something of an Oriental too: like a European looking towards the Orient. This may be a difficult way to explain the phenomenon, though those who know this architect's expressive forms will have to agree intuitively with what I say.' [3]

2.1 CARLO SCARPA, CAPPELLIN EXHIBITION DESIGN, 4TH INTERNATIONAL EXHIBITION OF MODERN DECORATIVE ARTS, MONZA, 1930; SCARPA DESIGNED DISPLAY UNITS, LIGHTING AND GLASSWARE

2.2 CARLO SCARPA, VENINI EXHIBITION, 6TH TRIENNALE, MILAN, 1936; INTERIOR

2.3

Scarpa's design for the interior of the Café Lavena in Venice, built in 1931, had polished, vertical dark wood panelled walls, a smooth, white plaster ceiling, a square-gridded terrazzo floor and a large curving bar, white above and black below. **(2.5)** The design indicated Scarpa's knowledge of works by the Viennese architect Adolf Loos and Vienna's contemporary culture. This included the writings of Loos and the cultural critic Karl Kraus and the paintings of Gustav Klimt, which would hold particular fascination for Scarpa throughout his career.

During the early years of Scarpa's career he was able to meet a number of artists at the Biennales, including the Italian Futurist painter Carlo Carra and the sculptor Arturo Martini, who became a lifelong friend. Through his friendship with Mario De Luigi, Scarpa also met the Italian Futurists Gino Severini and Giacomo Balla, among others. Scarpa joined a group of intellectuals who met at Florian's Café and at *Il Campanile* bookshop, both on Piazza San Marco. This group included the artists and critics Aldo Camerino – a Jew whom Scarpa later gave shelter to during the Fascist regime – Vincenzo Cardarelli, Carlo Izzo, Diego Valeri, Giuseppe Ungaretti and Massimo Bontempelli.[4]

2.4

2.5

Many of this same group met regularly at the Palazzo dei Piombi as part of *Il Circolo Artistico*. It was here that Scarpa came to know the artist Bice Lazzari, granddaughter of his early employer Vincenzo Ranaldo and the older sister of Scarpa's future wife, Onorina Lazzari. The relationship between Scarpa and Bice Lazzari, an early abstract artist whose works include paintings, collages, weavings, fabrics, rugs and floor mosaics, has rarely, if ever, been examined. Yet, from the time they first met in 1926, and continuing for their lifetime, the artist and the architect were well aware of each other's works, which included their first respective abstract designs made in Venice before she moved to Rome in 1935. Similarly to how Scarpa's works developed in parallel with those of his artist friends, Lazzari's art was influenced by the work of her architect friends and she would later marry the Roman architect Diego Rosa. Scarpa and Lazzari shared a strong interest in textile-based patterns and numerical ordering measures and several parallels can be drawn between their decorative and abstract compositions of surfaces from the 1930s through the 1970s. Due to her close relation to the Scarpa family, extending to her lifelong friendships with Scarpa's sister Ida and brother Gigi, Lazzari was a regular guest in the Scarpa house and at Scarpa's weekly dinners with artists in Venice.[5]

The owner of the *Il Campanile* bookshop, where Scarpa spent much time with his artist and intellectual friends, was the anarchist Ravenna, who introduced Scarpa to a number of art books that were either unpublished in Italy or banned by the regime. For his own library, Scarpa had his brother-in-law, a ship purser, obtain some of these otherwise unavailable books when he was abroad.[6] In 1934, after Scarpa married Onorina Lazzari, they moved from the Fondamenta degli Eremiti to a house on Rio Marin, also in Venice. As their new house lacked a garden, Scarpa rented one in an adjacent building. He felt that it was essential to have a garden and a tree that would grow even in his absence. This garden became his secluded place for reading, which he tried to do every day while sitting under the tree.[7]

Scarpa's personal library tells us quite a lot about him. By the end of his life, Scarpa's library contained 4,052 volumes and 620 issues of 184 different periodicals. Among the periodicals were architecture and art journals from Europe and elsewhere in the world, indicating that Scarpa was well informed about these fields' developments, as is also evidenced in the range of influences seen in his projects. His collection included 376 books on architecture, mostly Modern, with twenty-one books on Frank Lloyd Wright, sixteen on Le Corbusier, a number on both Antonio Gaudí and Palladio. There were also 187 books on architectural history (including the works of E. E. Viollet-le-Duc, John Ruskin and Camillo Boito), 347 books on painting, 1,088 books of fiction, 241 books of poetry, 217 books on geography and guidebooks, seventy-eight books on general history and 630 books of philosophy and essays.[8]

In this last section, there were ten books by the Spanish philosopher, José Ortega y Gasset, whose 1914 *Meditations on Quixote* is a remarkably early investigation into the idea of surface and depth, a key concept for the Cubist painters' thinking, which would have particular meaning for Scarpa's work. Also included were the writings of the Venetian philosopher Giambattista Vico, whose concepts of **'corporeal imagination'**, or an imagination that resides in the body, and *Verum Ipsum Factum*, meaning **'we can only learn from what we, and others like us, have made'**, would underlie Scarpa's work. There were also nine volumes by Benedetto Croce, whose 1901 *Aesthetic, As Science of Expression and General Linguistic* developed Vico's ideas into a fully articulated theory of art and architecture, emphasizing the importance of intuition and the idea that theory comes from practice. Scarpa also read the writings of the French philosopher Gaston Bachelard, whose concept of **'material imagination'** held that materials directly effect our imagination and experience and whose 1942 *Water and Dreams: An Essay on the Imagination of Matter* has particular pertinence for Venetians. Finally, this library contained a number of books by the French poet and essayist Paul Valéry, including his *Cahiers*, or notebooks, a lifelong examination of the working of the human mind in which Valéry argues the importance of **'finding the right combination of things'**, and *Eupalinos, or The Architect*, a debate on the nature of architecture in the style of Plato's dialogues, which Scarpa counted among the most important books he had ever read.

'It was not just a library made up of books, but of relationships lived with friends, with conversations and exchanges of ideas and arguments with artists and men of letters, colleagues and friends, who used to drop by, and for whom his house and library were open at all times and to everyone', as Scarpa's brother Gigi recalls.[9] In the introduction to the 1892 book *Architecture, Mysticism and Myth* (a copy of which was in Scarpa's library), W. R. Lethaby, the English Arts and Crafts architect, defined invention as **'a new combination of those images that have previously gathered and deposited in the memory: nothing comes from nothing. [The architect] who has laid up no materials can produce no combinations.'**[10] From early in his career, the depth and breadth of Scarpa's deposit of images is truly striking, indicating his extensive studies of the architecture, art, poetry, prose and history of both contemporary and ancient cultures, as well as his position at the cultural and historical crossroads that is Venice.

2.3 CARLO SCARPA, CAPELLIN SHOWROOM, 22ND VENICE BIENNALE, VENICE, 1940; INTERIOR WITH ROOM-SIZED GLASS DISPLAY CASE

2.4 CARLO SCARPA, ASTA HOUSE, VENICE, 1932; SCARPA DESIGNED BUILT-IN WOOD FURNITURE

2.5 CARLO SCARPA, CAFÉ LAVENA, VENICE, 1931; INTERIOR

The renovation of the Ca' Foscari, an historic building housing the University of Venice's School of Economics and Commerce, was Scarpa's first architectural work that brought him attention in Italy. Commissioned when Scarpa was just 29 years of age, it was undertaken from 1935–7. The entire building was renovated, starting at the ground floor where the vertical stone, structural columns were freed of infill and large sheets of glass were set between the columns facing the courtyard and behind the columns at the Grand Canal entrance. Here, Scarpa also made a second, inner glass door that reflects the rippling light bouncing off the canal's surface.

Scarpa designed the first floor conference room and chancellor's office, along with their furnishings and fittings, and installed new guard and handrails on the main central staircase. On the second floor, Scarpa renovated the great hall, or 'Aula Magna', placing a tribune along one wall, with a dais, on which are set two oval columns originally carrying busts of the king and Mussolini. **(2.6)** The columns stand in front of a slightly projecting, stone wall panel, and on the plaster wall above is a fresco painted by Italian Futurist Mario Sironi. On the floor in front of the dais were faculty seats, and along the wall to the tribune's left were elevated tiers of wooden student's seating. The entire wall to the tribune's right was opened by eight large, multi-lancet gothic stone windows. Scarpa's innovative and unprecedented glazing method was later widely employed in ancient Venetian palazzi renovations. He set the new glazing entirely behind, or inside, the original stone windows, making the new window frame independent of the original structure – a true 'window wall'. The window wall's steel mullions were given a rectilinear proportioning and set at a wider and slightly irregular spacing with respect to the original Gothic openings. The six, thicker mullions of the lower section's new glazing framed three horizontal windows, with two square windows between, while the upper portion's thin mullions framed six equal sets of three horizontal glass panes, stacked above one another. Scarpa's glazing design allowed new (inside) and old (outside) to be clearly legible, while also integrating the two in our experience of looking out through the window layers to the Grand Canal.

2.6

2.6 CA' FOSCARI RENOVATIONS, VENICE, 1935–7; PERIOD PHOTOGRAPH, VIEW ACROSS THE GREAT HALL, OR AULA MAGNA, TO THE 'WINDOW WALL' AND MARIO SIRONI'S FRESCO.

2.7 CA' FOSCARI RENOVATIONS; CARLO SCARPA, PERSPECTIVE DRAWING, 1955, AULA MAGNA ENTRY FOYER

2.8 CA' FOSCARI RENOVATIONS; AULA MAGNA, WESTERN ELEVATED GLASS WALL WITH WOODEN CEILING, AS SEEN FROM INSIDE THE GALLERY

CA' FOSCARI RENOVATIONS
VENICE, 1935–1937, 1955–1956

Twenty years later, in 1955–6, Scarpa was commissioned to convert the Aula Magna into a lecture theatre. The difference between Scarpa's earlier and later designs rests largely on the influence exercised on Scarpa in the intervening years by the works of Frank Lloyd Wright. Scarpa replaced the tiered wooden seating with a single-storey structure serving as an entry foyer for the Aula Magna, accessed through the doors at both ends, and an interior gallery running along that side of the room, allowing people to pass without disturbing the events taking place in the room. Scarpa designed the new volume as a freestanding, elevated glass wall with a wooden ceiling. **(2.7)** This glass wall hovers above a new wooden floor that meets the main room's stone floor at the point where the previous tiered seating terminated, stopping 1 metre (3 ft 3 in) inside the new volume where a single step transitions down to a stone floor.

Seen from inside the gallery, the recessed wooden piers supporting the glass wall stand on the slightly elevated wooden platform formed by the flooring. **(2.8)** These six piers are made of differently coloured hardwoods, salvaged from the previous wooden seats, and they support pairs of pivoting panels that may be closed to block the view into and out of the Aula Magna. **(2.9, 2.10)** The piers are supported at the wooden floor by small steel bases in the form of a pair of square posts with double V-shaped brackets that receive the matching V-shaped wooden pier footings. From the bottom of each pier, a separate pair of brace beams projects up and out towards the main space at a 45-degree-angle, carrying the angled wooden skirt panels, below which a 15 centimetre (6 in) piece of glass, set 90 degrees to the skirt panel, provides a slice of light at the floor. When seen from the Aula Magna, outside the gallery, this glass line gives the appearance that the entire structure is floating above the floor. Near the top of each pier, a brace beam projects down and out towards the main space, where it meets the double support post rising from the floor's brace beam. Steel brackets project from near the top of this post to brace the wood-framed glass wall, meeting every second glass panel's midpoint. The piers and vertical glass frames are not aligned and, as a result, the glass wall and piers appear to be sliding past one another.

2.7

2.8

2.9

2.9 CA' FOSCARI RENOVATIONS; ELEVATED GLASS WALL WITH PIVOTING DOORS OPEN AND A VIEW OF THE AULA MAGNA

2.10 CA' FOSCARI RENOVATIONS; ELEVATED GLASS WALL WITH PIVOTING DOORS CLOSED

2.10

At their tops, the recessed piers fork to form 45-degree angle bracing arms, above which the ceiling rises, opening into a thick wooden lattice. At the top, the lifted glass wall folds to form a butt-glazed corner where two sheets of frameless glass meet, then running horizontally to join the raised ceiling. It has been noted that these piers, with their 45-degree-angle bracing arms opening like tree limbs, bear a striking resemblance to the wooden roof supports of Wright's 1932 drafting room at Taliesin in Spring Green, Wisconsin, and has quite rightly been taken to be a gesture of homage from Scarpa to the American master. **(see i.4)**

Looking out through the delicately scaled, wood-framed, lifted glass panels to the elegantly thin, steel-framed curtain wall and the curving stone, Gothic window frames beyond, ending at the Grand Canal, we are made aware of the relation between Scarpa's elegant woodwork and Venetian canal boats. **(2.11)** This is true both in the multi-coloured strips of wood bundled together to make each pier, reminiscent of the gondola's woodwork, and in the framing of the all-wood ceiling. The ceiling's pattern is composed of pairs of slats that pivot slightly downwards to form a V-shaped space between, with square slats on either side, running parallel to the glass wall. This dark wood ceiling is set within a frame of lighter wood boards that run both parallel and perpendicular near the glass wall, but which become all perpendicular, more closely spaced and deeper as they move away from it. Near the plaster wall at the back, the dark wood is divided into T-shaped panels, between which rectangular apertures open in the ceiling, which illuminate the back of the gallery and allow us to view the angled wooden truss supporting the ceiling from above. The overall impression is like seeing the structural frame and wooden shell of an overturned boat. This nautical impression is subtly reinforced by the 45-degree skirting panels at the bottom of the glass wall, similar to the sides of a boat; by the floor's glass strip, making the wall literally appear to float; and by the interior's flickering light, reflecting off the canal's surface.

The reflections in the two walls of glass that face each other across the Aula Magna, those of Scarpa's 1935 window wall and those of his 1955 wood-framed gallery, remind us that glass, which is linked both to Venice and to modern architecture, shares its reflective surface with water. It is hardly coincidental that Scarpa believed that Venice was able to absorb and accept the thin, lightweight forms of modern architecture better than other Italian cities because of the way buildings are reflected in, and made to float above the water that is its datum, its liquid ground plane.

In the years that saw the rise of Fascism in Italy, Frank Lloyd Wright's work exerted an ever-increasing influence, largely due to the belief among Italian architects that his work was representative of true democracy. After the Second World War, the Italians would play a pivotal role in the concept for the last international exhibition of Wright's work, 'Frank Lloyd Wright: Sixty Years of Living Architecture'. The idea for this exhibition was conceived at the American Embassy in Rome, where the American ambassador, Clare Booth Luce, playwright and wife of publisher Henry Luce, and Arthur Kaufmann, of Gimbel Brothers department store in Pittsburgh, had been discussing ways to counteract the rise of communism in post-war Italian politics. After the idea of an exhibit of creative works by Americans was proposed, Italian cultural figures were asked to suggest whose work should be selected, unanimously they answered **'Wright'**.[11]

This was partly due to the influence of Bruno Zevi, the architectural historian and author of *Towards an Organic Architecture* of 1945, the first post-war architectural book whose one and only illustration, on the cover, was of Wright's Fallingwater. That same year Zevi was also the founder of the 'Association for an Organic Architecture', with chapters in the nine major Italian cities. Wright's selection for the exhibit also indicates the manner in which his work had, for some years, been seen by Italians as diametrically opposed to fascism. This began with Edoardo Persico's lecture in January 1935 in Turin, wherein he argued that Wright's work represented the best of the Modern movement, embodying as it did the aspects of freedom, individuality and diversity in society. The anti-Fascist movement in Italian architecture, led by Persico and Giuseppe Pagano, editor of *Casabella*, who died in a Nazi concentration camp, had come to see Wright's organic architecture as an idealized vision of life in a free society. Thus it is hardly coincidental that the primary organizer of Wright's exhibit in Italy was the art historian and close friend of Scarpa, Carlo Ludovico Ragghianti, a legendary resistance fighter. In 1944, in order to maintain contact between the resistance forces in the city and the Allied troops on the other side of the Arno River, Ragghianti crossed Florence's Ponte Vecchio in the dark of night, threading his way through the upper level, called 'Vasari's Corridor', which had been mined with explosives by the Germans.[12]

2.11

2.12

In 1951, Wright travelled to Italy, arriving in Florence, the exhibition's first venue, which was installed in the Palazzo Strozzi. During Wright's review of the installation, Scarpa was able to meet Wright for the first time. Wright then travelled to Venice, where, in the Palazzo Ducale, he was to receive an honorary degree from the University of Venice, as well as the Star of Solidarity, one of Italy's highest awards. Wright was met at the aeroplane by the official architects' committee of Venice, of which the unlicensed architect Scarpa was not a member. Refusing to acknowledge the presence of the official committee members, and preferring to select his own escort, Wright's first words were, **'Which one of you is Scarpa?'** [13] Accompanied by Scarpa and Zevi, Wright's tour of Venice was met by crowds of architecture students, as his work was of the utmost importance to the school of architecture, then directed by Giuseppe Samona, whose faculty included: Scarpa, Luigi Piccinato, Ludovico Belgiosio, Franco Albini, Ignazio Gardella, Mario De Luigi, Giancarlo De Carlo, Mazzariol, Barbieri and Zevi. [14] **(2.12)** Zevi recalled, **'When Wright walked in the *calli* or through the *piazzette*, or when he travelled by gondola, Venetians of all social strata recognized, greeted and applauded him.'** [15] During this trip, in addition to purchasing the Scarpa-designed vases from Venini, Wright received the commission for a house near Venice's Grand Canal for Angelo Masieri, Scarpa's former student and associate. From Wright, Scarpa received a signed copy of *The Life Work of the American Architect Frank Lloyd Wright*, a 1925 special edition of the Dutch journal *Wendingen*, and Scarpa would wear the turquoise ring, given to him by Wright's wife, Oglivanna, for the rest of his life.

Among the related designs from this period is Scarpa's 1944–6 renovation of a building close to Venice's Santi Apostoli. Designed for Vittorio Belloto, a fabric merchant, the structure comprises the owner's shop, a first-floor office and an apartment on the second and third floors. An oval staircase at the plan's centre is lit by the atrium's glass-block wall and topped by overlapping twin circles cut into the ceiling – likely Scarpa's first use of this form. The living and dining rooms open on either side of the central hall; each includes a large sliding door with fourteen tiny square portals in horizontal rows of five, four and five. The hall's sidewalls are made of plasterboard divided by dark wooden battens into a Mondrian-like pattern and painted with rectangular figures that overlap with the battens. **(2.13)** The central hall's floor is Venetian terrazzo, with a white edge band and a central field of black stones, into which Scarpa placed white stones in an even but random pattern; the whole floor is polished to a highly reflective finish. Scarpa placed two glass layers at the end of the hall. **(2.14)** The first, a double layer of windows with two operable windows above and one below, is set on the low sill just behind the three original arched stone windows; the second is a full-height window wall, with offset doors set a few feet inside, creating a winter garden. This narrow space's ceiling and walls are faced with thin wood boards, their varnished surfaces joining with those of the hall's ceiling and floor to reflect the light off the canal.

2.13

2.14

2.11 CA' FOSCARI RENOVATIONS; ELEVATED GLASS WALL, VIEW FROM FROM AULA MAGNA

2.12 PERIOD PHOTOGRAPH, 1951; CARLO SCARPA (L) AND FRANK LLOYD WRIGHT (C) IN PIAZZA SAN MARCO

2.13 BELLOTTO HOUSE, VENICE, 1944–6; HALLWAY, PLASTERBOARD SIDEWALL

2.14 BELLOTTO HOUSE; VIEW FROM HALLWAY THROUGH WINDOW WALL TO THE WINTER GARDEN

2.15

Two unrealized apartment buildings show the direct influence of Wright's work on Scarpa. In the 1947 project for a 75 metre (246 ft) tall mixed programme building in Piazza Spalato in Padova, Scarpa interlaced the vertical columns and horizontal floor slabs. **(2.15)** The floors projected at the base, creating an arcade housing shops, a restaurant and bar, and cantilevered at the floors above to form the apartments' garden terraces. The interweaving of the horizontal and vertical rectangular masses is close to several of Wright's designs. Scarpa's 1949 project for a six-storey apartment building in Feltre bears a striking relationship to Wright's unrealized 1929 Noble Apartments in Los Angeles. **(2.16)** The vertical concrete walls, horizontal stonework, slightly outward-stepping cantilevered balcony walls and the cantilevered, perforated concrete slab at the roof of Scarpa's design are all derived from Wright's work of the period that included Fallingwater of 1936 and the Usonian Houses from 1935 onwards.

2.16

2.17

2.18

Scarpa was asked by his former student Angelo Masieri to collaborate with him on the design of the Banca Cattolica del Veneto in Tarvisio, near Udine of 1947–9. Scarpa gave this building a flat roof, to contain the snow, while its standing seam metal cladding wrapped down to meet the building's horizontal stone wall base. **(2.17)** Both the roof and base wall are shaped into horizontal L-shapes, opening at the corner to form the entrance. Between the metal roof and the stone base, a white plaster-faced balcony is cantilevered at the corner, separated from the roof by a band of horizontal windows. The whole structure is characterized by a compressed dynamism and can be understood as an urbanized interpretation of Wright's Fallingwater.

The overall massing and form of the 1952 house designed by Masieri in Udine for Italo Romanelli bears a striking resemblance to Wright's 1953 Boomer House in Phoenix, indicating how closely the young Italian architect followed Wright's work. That summer Masieri was killed during a trip to America and Scarpa completed the house together with the architect Bruno Morassutti, whom had spent time in Wright's studio from 1949–50. [16] The house's plan is composed of a two-storey rectangular, plaster-faced masonry volume, which is rotated 30 degrees off the site boundary and intersected at the top by a large cantilevered, wood-clad roof, perforated with square skylights, and at the first floor level by a cantilevered concrete balcony, both of which run parallel to the site's edge. **(2.18)** The overlapping vertical and horizontal volumes allow interior and exterior spaces to interpenetrate, while the elegantly detailed woodwork of the windows, soffits, shelving and cabinetry that Scarpa laced through the building between the white plastered piers ties the wood-clad roof down even as the piers rise up to meet it. This interlocking of the wood roof and window frames, which come down from the sky, with masonry piers rising from the ground, is the typical tectonic structure of many of Wright's works.

The 1951 Veritti Tomb, in the Cemetery of San Vito, Udine, was also designed by Scarpa in collaboration with Masieri. Organized as a walled garden court, this family crypt is entered through a circular gateway, similar to Chinese gardens' gateways. **(see pp. 26–7)** An asymmetrical brass gate, hinged on a thin metal post at the left, opens to a rectangular landing notched into the bottom of the gateway. A shallow hemispherical vase holder is set into and cantilevered off the wall at the right of the entrance. Inside, the Botticino stone-walled, pebble-floored room is partially open to the sky and partially covered by a circular disc roof that floats above the top of the wall. This circular ceiling is made of rectangular panels of oxidized bronze, edged in steel, and is supported from below by two brass pins rising out of the wall, and from above, suspended from a steel beam crossing above the space to bear on the entrance wall. The gateway is set to the right of the rectangular tomb's centre while the circular roof is set to the left, so from the entrance we are drawn diagonally across the space to reach the small altar, set beneath the central axis of the circular bronze disc overhead.

2.15 MIXED PROGRAMME BUILDING DESIGN, PADOVA, 1947; EXTERIOR PERSPECTIVE DRAWING

2.16 FELTRE APARTMENT DESIGN, FELTRE, 1949; EXTERIOR PERSPECTIVE DRAWINGS

2.17 BANCA CATTOLICA DEL VENETO, TARAVISO, 1947–9; SOUTHERN AND EASTERN FACADE

2.18 ROMANELLI HOUSE, UDINE, 1952; WESTERN FACADE WITH LARGE CANTILEVERED WOOD-CLAD ROOF

2.19

2.19 VENICE BIENNALE BOOK PAVILION, 26TH VENICE BIENNALE, 1950; FAN-SHAPED 'TAIL' END

2.20 VENICE BIENNALE BOOK PAVILION; SEMI-CYLINDIRICAL NORTHEASTERN WALL WITH *VESICA PISCIS*-SHAPED WINDOWS

BOOK PAVILION, ENTRANCE AND ITALIAN PAVILION COURTYARD

BIENNALE, VENICE, 1950–2

2.20

In the 1942 Biennale, the last under the Fascist regime, Scarpa was commissioned to design the exhibition of his friend, the sculptor, Arturo Martini's work; this was the beginning of Scarpa's long relationship with the Biennale.[17] In 1950 Scarpa was commissioned to design the Art Book Pavilion for the *Il Cavallino* modern art gallery, built just to the right of the Italian pavilion's entrance. In this design, Scarpa employed the 30-60-90 degree triangular geometries and wood-frame construction language of Wright's 1929 Ocatilla Camp and 1937–40 Taliesin West. This wood and glass structure was composed, in both plan and section, of triangulated frames lifted above the ground. At the Italian pavilion end, Scarpa made a series of nested triangles in plan, projecting vertically into a straight-walled section. Near the gardens at the other end, a long, slowly opening fan-shaped 'tail' extended from the triangular 'head', composed in section of a trapezoid with two sides parallel to the ground, and a 30-60-90 degree triangle, the whole structured by interlocking triangular wood frames. **(2.19)**

Inside, Scarpa employed, possibly for the first time, the *vesica piscis*, an eye shape created by the intersection of two circles, in the form of windows inserted into the long, northeastern wall. **(2.20)** Scarpa placed two glass sheets with curved outer edges, facing and folding outwards, and straight inner edges, facing and folding inwards, where they were joined in a frameless 90-degree edge. Embedded in the white, semi-cylindrical wall, these vitrine-like windows projected into the room and protruded out through the wall, appearing as independent glass volumes when viewed from inside and outside. Each window was matched to a triangular, glass-topped display case, notched to create a V-shaped re-entrant corner that received the window's inwardly projecting edge. On the opposite, lower southwestern wall, past a display wall of books, a series of wood-framed Masonite panels pivoted open between each triangular wood truss double post. At the southeastern end, where the triangular frame reached its largest size as it opened to the gardens, the roof, floor and frame projected out forming a covered porch. The floor was sandblasted concrete while the ceiling, between the wood truss beams, was clad in bright yellow panels. The remarkably open and loosely jointed building felt like an open air shelter and provided panoramic views of the surrounding gardens.[18]

2.21

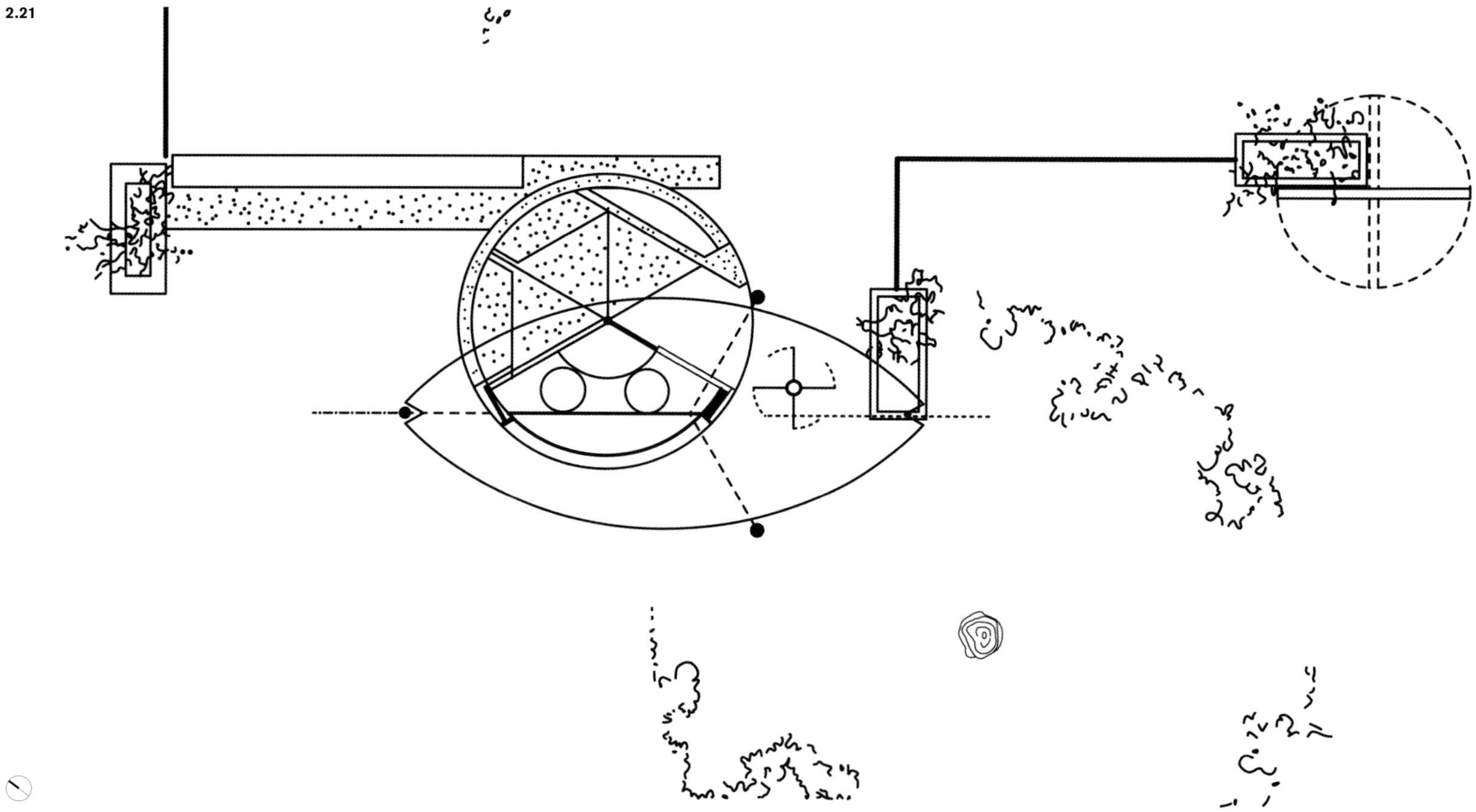

In 1951–2, Scarpa designed and constructed the Biennale's new ticket office and entrance pavilion in the Giardini di Castello. A low, concrete broken wall wraps the edge of the site, its washed surface revealing its stone aggregate. The straight, curved, thicker and thinner sections of the wall are staggered along the Giardini's edge, standing in no apparent geometric relation, as if they were fragments of some ancient ruin. With large planters at both ends and near the middle, this wall anchors the freestanding entrance and ticket office to its site, physically and spatially, so that it is read less as an object, and more as part of a larger landscape pattern. A low, cylindrical wall houses the ticket office in one third of its volume; the remaining section is divided into triangular floor sections, with hexagonal walls behind. The ticket office's concrete floor is raised and a full-height wall of black, steel-framed wire glass is set along the two straight lines radiating from the circle's centre. The entrance door pivots on a post set at the circle's centre point, making its own matching inner arc when it opens. The low wall at the front is set back on the right side so that the wire glass meets the circle and begins to follow its curve. The curved concrete wall at the front is lowered to receive the ticket counter's thick slab, a laminate of thin, variously coloured horizontal hardwood bands. The clear, curved glass above the counter is framed in thin black steel, through which the ticket agents are visible. **(2.21)**

The ticket office, the space in front of it and to the right where we enter through a turnstile, are covered by a freestanding roof, which takes the form of a *vesica piscis* in plan, with V-shaped re-entrant corners at its ends. This lenticular structure, whose top curves up and bottom down in section as it spans, is edged all around in a T-shaped steel plate, with bent ash wood spring beams top and bottom, held apart by thin steel posts at its centre. On this structure Scarpa stretched a canvas skin top and bottom, securing it at the edges by hooks and grommets and opening it along the *vesica piscis*' central axis where tensioning ropes are laced to stitch it together. Three columns, one at the left-hand end, standing in the V-shaped re-entrant corner, the others located one-third of the way around the curved edge on either side from the far corner, support the roof, which is hung from a Y-shaped steel frame connecting the three columns above the roof. Each of the columns is made of three steel flange plates welded into a Y shape, their outer edges tapering out slightly from the base to the midpoint, and then tapering back in as they rise to the top. This provides the columns the maximum moment resistance at the midpoints, where it is required. The three columns are clad in vertical strips of various coloured hardwoods, whose polished and varnished surfaces follow the curving taper of the flanges, stopping a few inches from the ground and approximately 30 centimetres (1 ft) from the roof. These columns' structurally strengthened midsection detail is reminiscent of boat masts, which, combined with the sail-like canvas roof, secured with ropes and hooks, once again links Scarpa's architecture to Venice's boat-building traditions. **(2.22)**

2.22

2.21 VENICE BIENNALE TICKET OFFICE, 1951–2; PLAN (REDRAWN)

2.22 VENICE BIENNALE TICKET OFFICE; EXTERIOR VIEW

2.23

2.24

2.23 ITALIAN PAVILION COURTYARD, VENICE BIENNALE, 1951–2; CONCRETE CANOPY, SUPPORTED BY THREE PLASTER-FACED CONCRETE PILLARS

2.24 ITALIAN PAVILION COURTYARD; POOLS OF VARYING DEPTHS WITH WATER SPOUTS SURROUNDED BY COPPER DISCS

2.25 ITALIAN PAVILION COURTYARD; PERIOD PHOTOGRAPH (1951)

2.25

In 1950–2, Scarpa was also commissioned to make changes to the main, and largest, Biennale building, the Italian pavilion. Creating a new rectangular courtyard within the existing building, Scarpa removed some of the previously built smaller rooms to make a new transition space where visitors could relax in the garden-court between exhibits. He stripped off the brick walls' plaster, providing a consistent outer wall for his freestanding canopy structure, which provides sheltering cover for those passing between the two doorways. This hovering, 46 centimetre (18 in) thick concrete slab does not touch the outer walls, allowing sunlight to wash them. The canopy is carved into by three arcs of differing diameter, a small semi circle at the centre, with two quarter-circles at either end. The dramatically curving canopy is banded by a steel plate at its edge and supported by three pink-coloured, rough plaster-faced concrete pillars, as wide as they are tall; each forms a *vesica piscis* in plan, with two small, V-shaped re-entrant corners, and stand in three different orientations within the garden-court. Each pillar stands only halfway under the edge of the canopy; the actual load bearing is carried through a small steel sphere that rests on a pyramidal stand set atop each pillar, inset from the edge. The plants growing from the top of the pillars obscure these supports, so that the massive roof canopy appears to hover just above the load-bearing pillars. **(2.23)**

The space is layered with increasing intensity from the top down: starting where the uppermost brick bounding wall frames the sky and continuing to the heavy hovering canopy overhead, to the varying heights of the brick sculpture bases, to the brick planters doubling as seating areas, to the two levels of paving, to the surface of the water in the pools and finally to the varying pool depths. With its use of shifting rectangular surfaces of stone, plantings, grass and water, set at various heights to create an ambiguous ground plane, this was Scarpa's first example of what would become his typical garden-court designs. He created a landscape of paved surfaces, elevated planting beds, reflecting pools, submerged planes and curving shadows, with sculptures placed both on land and water. The garden-court's ground plane was ordered on a square grid, the large, pebble-faced, washed concrete paving slabs, either square or divided in half in a non-repeating pattern. The concrete paving slabs overhang the pools so that the water disappears into shadows beneath, suggesting that the entire court is flooded and that the water's surface is the true ground plane. This is reinforced by several paving slabs placed within the pools, hovering just above the water's surface. Although the water level in the four pools is set at the same height, the pools have varying depths, from just below 2.5 centimetres (1 in), where the bottom is clearly visible, to 1 metre (3 ft 3 in), where the bottom is lost in blackness. The deepest and shallowest pools are set side-by-side along one side of the garden-court, giving the sense that there are multiple ground planes in this small space, with as many planes submerged below the water as there are above. The four pools appear to take up the same amount of space as the concrete paving, so that we experience the space as half-land, half-water, and thus in this way reconnecting this inner court to Venice, even when the city is not visible. A rarely noted feature of this garden-court is the small fountains in the pools, in which a spout, surrounded by a copper disc, is set close to the water's surface. When the thin stream of water rises from the spouts and then falls back to strike the copper disc, it fills the garden-court with gentle, soothing sounds like little cymbals or chimes. **(2.24, 2.25)**

CHAPTER 03

BEAUTY, ART, WONDER

From the beginning of his career, exhibition design and museum restoration would form a central part of Scarpa's work as an architect. While the exhibition designs were temporary, surviving today only in photographs and drawings, his museum work would transform our definition of museum display and a collection's relationship to its architectural context. For Scarpa, both works of art, and the architecture housing them, were living things, and the design of museums was an act of bringing this history to life, engaging it in our contemporary experience of place. To a degree rarely matched, Scarpa endeavoured to understand the character of each piece in an exhibition, entering into a dialogue with it which largely determined how he had it sequenced, positioned and lit. Scarpa intended the museum visitor to form a sense of intimacy with, and nearness to, the artefacts, fostering a direct emotional and intellectual relationship between the artwork and the observer. This approach is directly related to Giambattista Vico's statement, *Verum Ipsum Factum*, the belief that we can only learn from what we, or others like us, have made, and that our shared history only exists in the artefacts, places and actions that are the result of that making.

Scarpa described his museum designs by saying:

> 'I have a great passion for works of art, as you know. I have always taken the trouble to learn, to know, to understand, and, it seems to me, to have a real critical awareness. I would not be able to write, to produce a critical article; but I have a lively sense of critical values, and they move me. Indeed, I would rather, on the whole, build museums than skyscrapers – though logic might say otherwise, since the former may perhaps be creative, while the latter requires one to adapt and subordinate oneself to things as they are … It can be very important for the presenter of works of art to have a critical appreciation of them, because presentation can be a form of interpretation, of drawing attention to collocation – to the advantage of the works, naturally, not to the advantage of the presentation itself.' [1]

It was these museum designs where Scarpa first began to evolve a new definition of architectural preservation, one that accepted and made present in contemporary experience *all* historical layers found within a building and its site, including the modern interventions. This was a radical break from the accepted definition of 'restoration', based on E. E. Viollet-le-Duc's theories, maintaining that a building should be restored to a specific period of greatest historical significance, even if this required removing later additions and 'completing' it in a manner true neither to the structure's history, nor to contemporary construction methods. Neither does Scarpa's approach follow the teachings of the Venice observer and preservation advocate, John Ruskin, who argued for leaving a building in its state of picturesque decay, as its restoration would confuse the original building fabric with later repairs. In Scarpa's view, the ability to inhabit buildings that contained construction elements, or layers, from all periods of that site's occupation, was both necessary for us to understand the site's human history and critical to establishing our contemporary sense of identity in place and time.

Most of Scarpa's projects employed various forms of Venetian polished plaster. Scarpa's lifelong plasterwork collaborator, Eugenio De Luigi, noted that both stucco *alla veneziana* and *marmorino*, techniques dating back to Roman times, involve the hand application of hydrated lime and either sand (*calce*) or crushed clay tiles and bricks (*cotto*) as base layers, with finishing layers of hydrated lime and fine sand, to which marble dust and coloured pigments are added. Each layer is hand worked on to the wall using steel trowels, through the application of intense pressure, with a hot iron employed for the *marmorino*'s final finish, achieving a water-resistant, highly polished, reflective surface finish similar to polished marble or lacquer. [2] Due to its labour-intensive demands, polished plaster was a traditional Venetian technique largely abandoned before Scarpa employed it in his works, effectively reviving this ancient handcraft. As Kenneth Frampton noted, rather than lying on the surface, **'the colour in polished plaster appears to emanate from the interior of the rendering'**, [3] giving the polished plaster a depth that glows beneath its reflective surface.

BEAUTY, ART, WONDER

3.1

In Scarpa's designs for the Accademia, one of Italy's great art collections, he engaged an extraordinarily charged set of architectural spaces, including the gothic church of S. Maria della Carita, the attached Palladio-designed convent and the *Scuola*, or school. The Accademia's director, Vittorio Moschini, first consulted Scarpa during the Second World War when the artworks were in storage and the Accademia had suffered bomb damage. Completed by 1948, Scarpa's first renovation involved a dramatic alteration of the existing galleries, bringing them into line with contemporary exhibition criteria. Scarpa oversaw the removal of the draperies, decorative work, wallpaper and dark paint; the walls were painted in lighter shades and paintings were positioned in chronological and thematic order. Also critical to the final experience were Scarpa's display panels, stands and frames, with handcrafted metal connectors, allowing works to float free of the walls and floors, surrounded by space and light. Irrespective of the ceilings' height, Scarpa had the artworks positioned at eye level, in contrast to their typically higher location, bringing the artwork and the observer into an intimate, direct relation.

From the *campo* at the end of the Accademia Bridge, we enter the Accademia through the Scarpa-designed entrance doors of 1952. The new entryway is set inside the stone portal of the historic Scuola della Carita, appearing freestanding, the new frame is spaced away from the masonry piers and beams by narrow glass panes, allowing light to wash on to the walls and ceiling, connecting interior and exterior spaces. Like all the windows and doors Scarpa designed for the Accademia, this frame is made of steel on the outside and wood on the inside, with glass set between. The entryway is a masterpiece of doubling, beginning with the trapezoidal shape of the identical entrance and exit vestibules, allowing us to recognize the nonorthogonal shape of the existing room. The elements of the composition are doubled throughout; including the clerestory window over the entrance, split into two large glass panes, on either side of a narrow pane, and framed by two thin wood bands. Inside the vestibule, two ceiling windows, one above the entrance door outside and one above the exit door inside, sit diagonally across from one another. On both the vestibule's exterior and interior faces, a wide, double wooden post separates the two doors at the centre, while at its four open, outer corners, the glass is frameless. **(3.1)**

Climbing the existing stairs, we enter the main room of the Scuola della Carita, with its beautifully patterned floor of white, black, grey, and light and dark pink stones. **(3.3)** A black steel band separates the floor from the white plaster walls, held away from the walls on small cylindrical steel posts, Scarpa's first use of this detail. Passing through the Scarpa-designed iron turnstiles, composed of numerous pairs of steel bars, we move among the large freestanding panels, raised on steel legs. The panels, which have paintings mounted to both sides, are banded with wood, narrow at top and bottom, wider on the sides, and their surfaces are pale yellow in colour to set off the paintings' gold leaf backgrounds. The paintings have been removed from their frames, unless they were original, and each is set forward of the surface of the panel by a steel frame below and two small clips on the side. Each panel carries a group of paintings that are directly related to each other, and each panel is set a discrete distance from the others, in order to allow us to concentrate on one group of paintings at a time. At the end of the hall, a large freestanding wall panel is set forward from the wall and stands on a stone base, with stone piers projecting slightly forward at either end. Slightly angled stairs descend on both sides of this wall panel. **(3.4)**

This is the first of a series of freestanding stone staircases, each of different design, that weave the museum's diverse rooms together, block the view from one room to the next and precisely position the visitor to receive carefully calibrated views into upcoming rooms. Walking around the end of this freestanding wall to ascend the stairs, we see a doorway opening into the next room with two more steps set into its threshold. The landing behind the wall panel acts as a vestibule between the two rooms, not allowing direct views from one room to another. Entering the altarpiece room, which has a black terrazzo floor into which tiny white flecks are set, we find a massive block of complexly interlocked, light-coloured stones set against the wall to our left, at the top of which is a tall doorway. On one side of the stone mass a vertical, steel fin grille is set into an opening, while on the other side, a large stone has been shifted outwards, seemingly floating above the floor, both done to accommodate the radiator set within. In this stonework, as well as other Accademia stairs, Scarpa is close to the construction characteristics found in Romanesque churches in the way various-sized, stacked rectangular stones, all set flush, create a highly charged surface. In Venice, the city of reflections, Scarpa created fainter echoes in stone, shifted as if to record and make present the history buried beneath the surface: reflections, registering the depths below, the stirrings within coming to the surface, touching but not breaking it. That this dynamic composition of polished, white and grey stones is in fact a staircase is not revealed until we have traversed the room to inspect the artwork, and then turn to leave. **(3.2)**

3.2

GALLERIE DELL'ACCADEMIA RENOVATIONS
VENICE, 1945–1959

3.3

3.4

3.1 PREVIOUS PAGE > GALLERIE DELL'ACCADEMIA RENOVATIONS, VENICE, 1945–59; NEW ENTRANCE VESTIBULE, SEEN FROM THE INTERIOR

3.2 GALLERIE DELL'ACCADEMIA RENOVATIONS; ALTAR PIECE ROOM, STONE STAIRCASE WITH INSET RADIATOR

3.3 GALLERIE DELL'ACCADEMIA RENOVATIONS; MAIN ROOM, SCUOLA DELLA CARITA

3.4 GALLERIE DELL'ACCADEMIA RENOVATIONS; MAIN ROOM, SCUOLA DELLA CARITA, STAIR DETAIL

3.5

3.6

The 'small masterpiece' room is one of the most diminutive rooms in the museum; Scarpa divided it in half with a freestanding wall panel, making the room feel even smaller while bringing us into close and intimate contact with the paintings. This large, white, frameless wall panel stands on four double feet, made from pairs of steel twin bars, with a V-shaped notch bearing on the shared V-shaped base; a thin, steel double beam braces the panel against the sidewalls. **(3.5, 3.6)** To accommodate the large and small paintings set into cavities carved into the panel's surface, an off-centre joint splits it into two uneven sections. On the other side, the panel is split in half, and this symmetrical composition is matched by the two freestanding, slightly angled panels, set in the corners of the wall behind, each carrying a single painting. The strong light from the rooflights is filtered by silk fabric hangings, and the floor is reddish-hued terrazzo. This room's paintings are hung against off-white fabrics with the exception of Giorgione's *The Tempest*, the masterpiece of the collection, displayed against a brown velvet background. This careful positioning and mounting allows us to feel alone with each painting, existing on its own wall and given its own space.

3.7

3.8

Ascending to the rooms accommodating the large paintings, where Scarpa's more extensive designs remain unrealized, we can appreciate his brilliant decision to lower the large paintings to eye level, near these tall rooms' floors. The paintings' almost lifesize figures feel as if they are in the room with us. In the windowless galleries, as these are, Scarpa opened large rectangular rooflights fitted with frosted glass filters. Scarpa located the black-painted, cast iron radiators in these room's centres, so as not to be seen with the artworks. Walking down the long arcade of Palladio's convent, with his stone spiral staircase at the end, we enter the space of S. Maria della Carita, a church dating from Gothic times. This space, with a massive wood truss overhead, was given six larch-framed rooflights, four on one side and two on the other, each lined with jute fabric. The large freestanding wall panels, set parallel and perpendicular to the church's walls, are informally placed in the room, giving the layout **'the look of a temporary exhibit, more in keeping with the historic and architectural importance of the vast space.'**[4]

Sitting in the room housing the *Miracles of the Cross*, by Mansueti, and works by Gentile Bellini, all large paintings depicting scenes in Venice, we feel as if we have been momentarily transported back in time to inhabit the city during these historic events. **(3.7)** The cool grey plastered walls fold gently up to meet the ceiling's large roof light, its frosted glass filters set in pairs of thin double-square wood frames, each rotated by 90 degrees with respect to those on all sides. Again, these larch-framed paintings are brought down to within 46 centimetres (18 in) of the terrazzo floor, their bottoms aligning with the thin, black steel guard rail running around the room's perimeter. These guard rails, used in a number of the museum's rooms, are fixed in place and supported by L-shaped legs, reaching back to connect to the wall in the small space below the plastered surface.

In the room housing the multiple painting cycle of *The Legend of Saint Ursula*, Carpaccio's masterwork, Scarpa plastered the ceiling black and the walls off-white, while the terrazzo floor is a reddish-brown. **(3.8)** The same wood used to make the paintings' thin frames is also attached to the guard rails, merging the frames and guard rails into a single horizontal line as, from a seated position, we follow the cycle of the Saint's life around the room. This room's specially designed benches, like the others in the museum, are made of wood with leather cushions, but in this room Scarpa bevelled the two benches' corners, allowing people to sit and look diagonally across the room rather than only at the opposite wall. Scarpa placed the cycle's last painting, *The Funeral of Saint Ursula*, to the door's right, thus behind you when you enter the room. It was this painting – in which the body of Ursula is carried into the church, lifted high above the crowd's heads on an ornate litter (or bed) – seen during a 1963 tour of the Accademia, that inspired Le Corbusier to place the patients on high platforms set beneath the top floor clerestory windows in his great, unrealized 1964 Venice Hospital design.[5]

3.5 GALLERIE DELL'ACCADEMIA RENOVATIONS; MASTERPIECE ROOM, WITH A FREESTANDING WALL PANEL

3.6 GALLERIE DELL'ACCADEMIA RENOVATIONS; DESIGN FOR THE FREESTANDING WALL PANEL, COLOURED PENCIL ON PAPER

3.7 GALLERIE DELL'ACCADEMIA RENOVATIONS; ROOM HOUSING THE *MIRACLES OF THE CROSS*, BY MANSUETI, AND WORKS BY GENTILE BELLINI

3.8 GALLERIE DELL'ACCADEMIA RENOVATIONS; ROOM HOUSING THE MULTIPLE PAINTING CYCLE OF *THE LEGEND OF SAINT URSULA* BY CARPACCIO

3.9

3.10

3.11

Among this period's related exhibition design projects, one that would prove to be of particular importance for Scarpa was the 1948 exhibition, 'Paul Klee 1879–1940', for the 24th Venice Biennale.[6] **(3.9)** As he had done with the works of the Accademia, Scarpa studied each of Klee's six oil paintings and twelve watercolours to be exhibited, making careful drawings with measurements and his own analysis of their formal structure. Scarpa developed an appropriate line of movement through the space, establishing the correct relationship between the paintings and their respective positions, which Klee defined as **'the problem of proportions'**.[7] In determining the position of each painting, Scarpa gave pre-eminence to the painting titled *EMACHT*. He also appears to have derived the plan's angles from the folded planes shown in Klee's exhibited painting, *Geöffnet*, as seen in one of his sketches.[8]

The paintings Scarpa felt to be more distinct as individuals were given their own panels, while others were grouped together. The individual or group panels, in white or black, were carefully sized to provide a ground for the small figures of the paintings. Many panels were pivoted at different angles, allowing visitors to approach them frontally, one at a time. All of the panels floated slightly off the floor; the horizontal panels along the back wall and at either end were elevated. Discrete clips on either side secured the vertical panels, while clips at the bottom held the horizontal panels. Scarpa positioned the paintings with what he considered their compositional centres at standing eye level, 1.6 metres (5 ft 3 in) off the floor. The grey walls ran up behind the backlit, white stretched fabric ceiling. Scarpa's attention to detail is evident in the invisibility of the majority of the support structure, imparting to the whole assemblage a sense of floating without anchorage, and the complementary strong but enigmatic presence of the four thin, pier-like verticals that run from floor to ceiling, made of laminated strips of hardwoods of different lengths and colours, reminiscent of Venetian boatbuilding. Scarpa considered this modest work, part of which he paid for, his **'first spatial statement, unitary and homogeneous'**.[9]

At the same 1948 Biennale, Scarpa designed the exhibition, 'Arturo Martini; Three Metaphysical Painters from 1910 to 1920' in the Italian Pavilion, which included paintings by De Chirico, Campigli and De Pisis and sculptures by Scarpa's friend Martini. In this exhibit Scarpa first made use of a technique he would repeatedly employ later: stretching draped white fabric at an angle from the ceiling to either the floor, or the top of low display walls, creating inward-angling, vertical-ribbed surfaces that erased the architectural enclosure. This brought the scale of the tall room down to the paintings' and sculptures' more intimate, human scale. In the Pavilion's central room, Scarpa brought four walls out from the sides to divide the room into three spaces, wrapping their vertical upper portions with the same fabric. Indirect light evenly illuminated the space from rooflights above the fabric ceiling. **(3.10)** At the same Biennale, Scarpa also designed the exhibition of the Peggy Guggenheim Collection in the Greek pavilion. The Collection, which Guggenheim would permanently house in the Palazzo Venier dei Leoni on the Grand Canal the next year, included works by the Cubists, Abstractionists (including Mondrian and Albers), Surrealists and newly emerging Abstract Expressionists, allowing Scarpa an unparalleled opportunity to study some of the most important modern art in the world.

Scarpa's 1950 exhibition design, 'The *Fauves*, Four Masters of Cubism', also set in the central space of the Biennale's Italian Pavilion, was structured similarly to the Martini exhibition. Only, here, Scarpa organized everything rectilinearly to reflect the Cubists' work; draped fabric hung straight down to form two diaphanous, suspended planes, creating a basilica-like space. Scarpa placed freestanding wall panels, lifted off the floor and supported by thin piers, half-out and half-in the central space, the hanging fabric planes just touching the panels' centre points. The tall central area's ceiling was again made of white stretched fabric, through which light from the rooflights filtered. The resulting space shared with the Cubist canvases the characteristics of overlapping, layering, folding and interpenetrating. **(3.11)**

3.9 'PAUL KLEE 1879–1940' EXHIBITION, 24TH VENICE BIENNALE, 1948; INTERIOR, BLACK AND WHITE PIVOTED PANELS

3.10 'ARTURO MARTINI; THREE METAPHYSICAL PAINTERS FROM 1910 TO 1920' EXHIBITION, 24TH VENICE BIENNALE, 1948; INTERIOR, ANGLED STRETCHED WHITE FABRIC WALLS

3.11 'THE "FAUVES", FOUR MASTERS OF CUBISM' EXHIBITION, 25TH VENICE BIENNALE, 1950; INTERIOR, VERTICAL STRETCHED WHITE FABRIC WALLS

3.12 TELVE TELEPHONE CENTRE, VENICE, 1950; INTERIOR VIEW

3.13 TELVE TELEPHONE CENTRE; CEILING OF TEAK BANDS AND FROSTED GLASS

In addition to Klee, Scarpa was increasingly influenced by Piet Mondrian, whose works were included in the 1948 Guggenheim Collection exhibition. This is clearly evidenced in a 1950 work built by Scarpa in Venice, and sadly now demolished. The Telve Society's public telephone centre was a small space into which Scarpa placed six phone booths, a waiting area and staff desk. (3.12) The brass-framed, glass front door was pushed a few inches into the space, its projection matched by a recess in the back wall. The space's surfaces were ordered on a series of De Stijl-like grids. The floor was made of differently sized, rectangular, grey granite slabs whose joint lines did not directly connect from wall to wall. The booths had teak wood and leather floors, full height doors with thin steel-framed, clear glass, and their plastic panelled back walls lined with olive-grey felt, each with an eye-level, opaque-white Plexiglas screen, providing visual privacy from the adjacent booths. Each of the booths had its own plastic pyramidal ceiling with a light set at its peak.

The main space's ceiling was structured by a symmetrical pattern of polished teak bands derived from Mondrian's paintings, but with Scarpa's touch of being centred by a double band, with a second pair of bands set to either side. Teak bands crossed this central spine, running left and right, with spaces between filled with frosted glass, two pieces of pink glass and four pieces of black marble. (3.13) Neon tubes set above the translucent ceiling lit the space. The staff desk at the end was composed of three vertical slabs, two of polished black marble, the other thin plate glass, which were shifted along the central axis with respect to one another; a plate glass tabletop spanned from the desk front to the wall of the room. The room's back and left sidewalls were made of grey-lacquered, plastic panels and secured with brass clips, while a painting by Mario De Luigi obscured the coat stand in the back corner.[10] The long left wall across from the booths supported two large mirrors just above eye level. These mirrors reflected the ceiling, doubling the room's size, similar to the high-set mirrors in Adolf Loos's 1908 American Bar. Scarpa's space felt both compressed and expanded, as the reflective surfaces generated dense, overlapping three-dimensional layers while the ceiling's dark lines interlaced across the narrow room.

The Austrian architect Peter Noever recalls an incident from 1974:

'One of my first encounters with Carlo Scarpa was in the American Bar in Vienna by Adolf Loos. We had hardly entered when he began to express his passionate admiration for what he saw. Gradually his eyes wandered from the ceiling – which had caught his attention first – into the room itself. He noticed the women who were sitting at the bar, approached them, and bowed with a smile. At once he found himself the centre of a group of people who quite obviously were interested in everything but architecture. Scarpa ordered champagne for them and a measuring tape for himself. He was fascinated by Adolf Loos and his architecture. He joked with the guests as he surveyed every detail of the room with his eyes and hands. He assumed unexpected positions, and eventually started – with the aid of the ladies – to take exact measurements of the *Loos* bar. He was inspired by the proportions and details and wanted to know the diameter of the bar rail down to the last millimetre. He finally proclaimed the room a place of "singular spiritual and emotional quality".'[11]

3.12

3.13

In 1952, Scarpa was commissioned to renovate and reorder the collection of the Correr Museum, the main museum of Venetian art and history. Since the 1920s, the Correr has been housed in the Procuratie Nuove buildings along the south side of Piazza S. Marco. Scarpa worked from 1952–3 on the first floor historical collection and renovated the second floor painting galleries from 1957–60.

After ascending the monumental double staircase in the Napoleonic Wing at the Piazza's western end, we enter the museum, moving along a series of large rooms with north-facing windows opening onto the Piazza. On the first floor, Scarpa left the period carved-wood ceilings and Venetian terrazzo floors in place, plastering and painting the walls an off-white to form a quiet background for the paintings, etchings, maps, banners and other historical artefacts. The historic collection is remarkable for its variety of unique, piece-specific displays. In one room, a painting, occupying the entire wall, is set on two supports, each a square steel bar cantilevered from the wall, clad with two pieces of L-shaped wood wrapping the side and top, leaving a small joint between, with a steel plate attached to the top to accept the weight. In another room, six rows of tilted cases hold open books, with wood sides and bottoms and glass tops; two rows of these cases are set against the walls, while two double cases stand in the room's centre. The cases' wood pieces are complex compositions of 30- and 60-degree angles; the double cases are supported at the outer edges by four cylindrical wooden legs and at the centre by double steel tubes, bending near the floor to brace the legs.

The display case holding a large boat model is particularly ingenious, the model being held in a six-sided glass case set within a steel frame at its base, with small steel and brass clips reaching out to hold the glass. As a result, the glass case and boat appear to float in space before us. One room includes a built-in display case, its glass, with frameless corners, projects out from a recessed slot in the wall, resting on a cantilevered wooden base and forming a three-dimensional glass volume quite similar to Scarpa's windows in the 1973–8 Banca Popolare di Verona. To the right of this case a narrow, gold-leafed passage leads to the Bucintoro room, housing the arms collection. A large galley ship lamp is mounted on a stand that is composed of pairs of double steel plates, secured with pairs of brass pins. A group of rifles are displayed on individual, anthropomorphic stands, with splayed legs, appearing ready to break ranks and rush forward. **(3.14)** Nearby, five pairs of shields are mounted on five lightly coated, white plaster panels, stacked one above the other and hung on two steel bars, each secured at the ceiling and near the floor by a double steel piece cantilevered from the wall, to which the bar is attached by a large brass pin.

Arriving at the second floor, we enter a small room housing the early Venetian paintings, which is behind a thick wall made of vertical and horizontal wood boards with dark and light streaks, into which a carved slot, running from the top, terminates in a square display case. **(3.16)** In this and most of the upper level's rooms, a black steel band is attached to the white plaster walls just above the terrazzo floor, as at the Accademia. Nearby, a dozen small cubic vitrines are cantilevered off the wall; each differently sized vitrine has three walls of glass, a wood bottom and top and a light above, which casts a uniform glow on to the small sculptural figures. **(3.15)** Placed on the wall in a line, like three-dimensional music notes moving up and down and in and out, the vitrines form a dynamic rhythm.

3.14

3.15

CORRER MUSEUM RENOVATIONS
VENICE, 1952–1960

3.16

3.14 CORRER MUSEUM RENOVATIONS, VENICE, 1952–60; FIRST FLOOR, BUCINTORO ROOM

3.15 CORRER MUSEUM RENOVATIONS; SECOND FLOOR, ROOM CONTAINING SCULPTURAL FIGURES, VIEW OF SMALL CUBIC VITRINES

3.16 CORRER MUSEUM RENOVATIONS; SECOND FLOOR, ROOM HOUSING EARLY VENETIAN PAINTINGS, WOOD DISPLAY WALL

3.17

3.18

3.17 CORRER MUSEUM RENOVATIONS; FIFTEENTH-CENTURY SCULPTURE SPACE, BLACK BUST (C) AND GOTHIC CARVED STONE BANISTER PIECES (L)

3.18 CORRER MUSEUM RENOVATIONS; GOTHIC SCULPTURE SPACE WITH SMALL SCULPTURE OF THE DOGE (R)

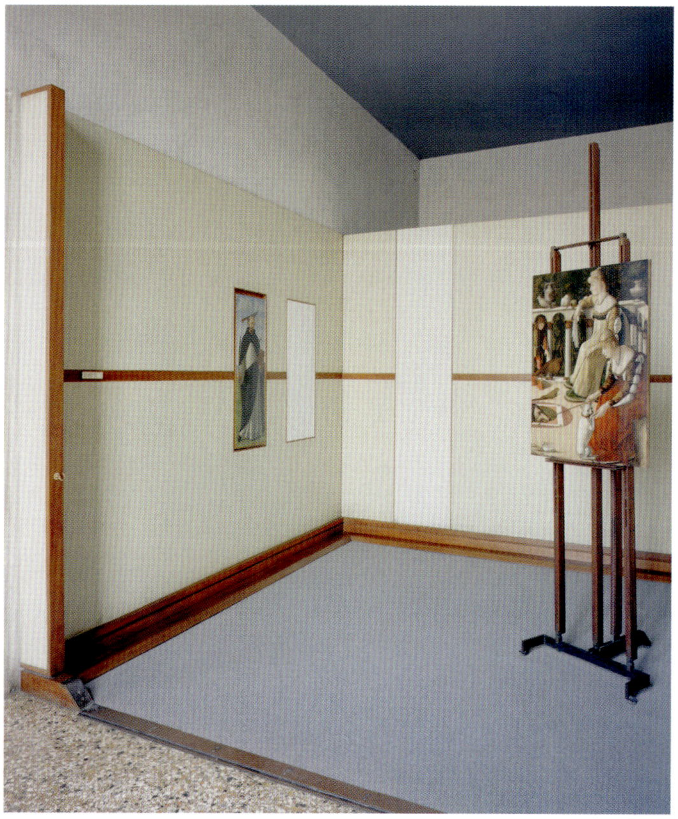

3.19

3.20

3.21

The room housing sculptures was originally divided by a wall, which Scarpa removed, creating a pair of ambiguously related spaces. The Gothic sculptures are placed in the smaller, southern space, with the fifteenth-century sculptures placed in the larger, northern space. Lacking direct natural light, the Gothic sculpture space's dark grey, low plaster ceiling folds down, with a steel-framed, frosted glass partition set beneath. **(3.18)** The small statue of the doge, Tommaso Mocenigo, is mounted near the back wall, held out a short way into the room, turned to face the light. Standing on a small stone block, the sculpture is supported by a cantilevered steel bar projecting from a steel post tied to the wall by a steel bar. **(see i.3)** Lit by two large windows, the high ceilinged, fifteenth-century sculpture space to the north includes a wall that comes down to meet the lower edge of the southern space. Positioned in front of two frosted-glass wall panels is a black bust projecting slightly forward from its stand; it faces the light coming in through the windows. **(3.17)** The bust rests on a gently curved piece of white stone, which in turn is supported by double steel upstands turned 90 degrees to one another to form a T-shape in plan. All sculptural figures are placed at eye level, with generous space around them, so that we approach each piece as an individual. Next to the frosted glass panels, two low pieces of a Gothic carved stone banister are positioned in a staggered line, blocking our passage to the southern half of the space. We pass through the double sculpture room twice during the exhibition circuit, once on either side of the banister that divides the room into two galleries; from the southern gallery we can see but not move into the northern gallery, and vice versa. This is one of many examples in Scarpa's work where the path of the eye differs from the path of the body.

We now walk through a series of aligned doorways opening into the large rooms along the north wall. Each room has two Piazza-facing windows and two small paintings placed on Scarpa-designed wood, steel and bronze easels; on entering the room, we find ourselves facing a painting receiving a strong sidelight from the window. **(3.20)** These easels, which Scarpa would employ throughout his career, have a T-shaped steel foot, above which rises a low back post tied to a crossbar behind the painting, two high legs tied together above the painting and a central mast-like spine. All four vertical elements are made of double wood pieces, joined by brass pins and hinge-like caps; the entire easel is adjustable. Each of these easel-held paintings is displayed at eye level, allowing us to have an intimate conversation with it while standing in the middle of the room.

3.22

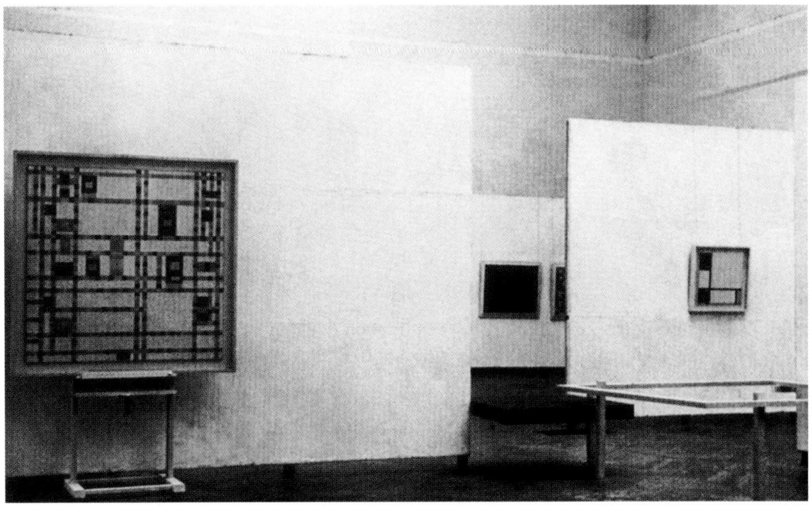

The north-facing rooms' walls are covered with smooth, white plaster panels separated from the floor, ceiling and each other by wooden boards, matching the easels' wood; on each a single painting is hung. The exhibited artefacts are generously spaced, allowing us to move from one distinct experience to the next. The paintings have been positioned to both receive the best light and to enter into relationships with nearby paintings, as if the figures they depict were conversing. A small, wood-framed room within the larger masonry and terrazzo space houses the Carpaccio paintings. **(3.19)** The room's inner walls, which reach just above head height, well below the ceiling, are wood-framed panels of the smoothest plaster, with a wooden band running at eye level all around, into which paintings are incised. Carpaccio's *Dame Veneziana*, a painting of two sisters, is presented to us on an angled easel in the centre. In the Antonello da Messina room, a new inner wall, set forward from the existing wall, is made of sandblasted travertine panels, on which paintings are mounted. **(3.21)** This wall is lifted off the floor by steel clips and held at the top by Y-shaped, steel key-like bars, fitting into Y-shaped notches cut into the travertine panels' tops. The bottom of each Y-shaped cut ends in a small circular hole, larger than the cut, which has been drilled through the travertine; this was Scarpa's typical way of terminating an incision into a material, as evidenced in the brass joints of the easels. In the centre of this room, Antonello's *Pietà* is presented on a steel stand inclined slightly towards us, so that we sense the weight of Christ's slumping body.

At the end of the Correr Museum circuit, we come to a large, frosted glass wall suspended slightly above the floor and framed in teak wood boards, hiding service elements. This composition is clearly related to Mondrian's paintings, and was likely designed at the same time that Scarpa was installing the 1956–7 Piet Mondrian exhibition in Rome's Galleria Nazionale d'Arte Moderna. For this exceptional exhibition, including works from throughout Mondrian's career, Scarpa stripped the gallery's walls and constructed freestanding, white cloth-covered panels lifted above the floor by small steel posts. Presented in chronological order, each painting was carefully positioned off-centre on a single panel, responding to each piece's centre of gravity. Only the *Broadway Boogie Woogie*, one of Mondrian's last two paintings, was presented on a white wood frame, freestanding like an easel, as it had stood in Mondrian's New York studio. To bring down the scale at the portal between two of the largest rooms, Scarpa made a rectangular ceiling panel of layered wood strips set 90 degrees to each other, forming a lattice screen. **(3.22)**

3.19 CORRER MUSEUM RENOVATIONS; SMALL, WOOD-FRAMED SPACE WITH SMOOTH PLASTER WALLS, HOUSING CARPACCIO PAINTINGS

3.20 CORRER MUSEUM RENOVATIONS; PAINTINGS DISPLAYED ON SCARPA-DESIGNED EASELS

3.21 CORRER MUSEUM RENOVATIONS; ANTONELLO DA MESSINA ROOM

3.22 PIET MONDRIAN EXHIBITION, GALLERIA NAZIONALE D'ARTE MODERNA, ROME, 1956–7; *BROADWAY BOOGIE WOOGIE* DISPLAYED ON A WOOD FRAME-LIKE EASEL

3.23 / 3.24

In 1953, Scarpa designed the 'Antonello da Messina e la pittura del "400 in Sicili"' exhibition in the Palazzo Zanca in Messina. In the main room, Scarpa made a lattice-like weave of wide bands of fabric at the ceiling's centre, through the openings of which blackness could be seen above. Draped fabric was hung from the ceiling's rectangular edges, forming a diaphanous, vertically ribbed wall that inclined inwards as it rose from the floor. From behind draped fabric, light filtered into the room from windows on two sides, while paintings were displayed on free-standing panels set at varying angles to the room's walls. Tall portals, also lined with fabric, opened into smaller similarly draped adjacent rooms, where the paintings were displayed at eye level against the walls, either on stands or floating in front of the fabric surface. **(3.23)**

This exhibition was widely praised in Messina, and that same year the professor and architect Roberto Calandra visited the recently completed historical section of the Correr Museum. This resulted in Scarpa being commissioned, with Calandra as his assistant, to renovate the Palazzo Abatellis in Palermo into the Galleria Regionale della Sicilia.[12] Constructed to the designs of Matteo Carnilivari in 1490–5, the building was heavily damaged by bombing in 1943 when the arcade and loggia on the courtyard's southern side were destroyed. The client required that the renovation be completed in one year, during which Scarpa resided on site.

Entering through the western wall's broad arched opening, the new courtyard floor opens out before us. **(3.25)** A rectilinear grid of five by five bands of square paving stones fills the space. The outer sections are paved with tightly set river-washed stones, while nine inner sections are filled with grass; the entire courtyard is crossed by diagonal stone bands. The walls on three sides have been finished with smooth stucco plaster, held back from the stone frames of the original windows and doors. Thin joints inscribed into the stucco subtly divide the walls into large rectangular sections, emphasizing the historical windows' irregular pattern while giving the wall surface a distinctly modern character. Thus, the old windows appear to be displayed on the wall as part of the museum collection, suggesting that the building's elements are as much a part of the museum experience as the art.

To our right, the reconstructed, two-storey arcade's floor is made of brick set in a herringbone pattern set flush with the courtyard. On the wall behind the arcade, windows and doors are incised directly into the stucco surface, identified as new by their lack of frames. The doors are made of a square wood lattice, with solids and voids of equal size, the horizontal and vertical pieces attached by single screw, the slot aligned vertically, at each intersection. Where the arcade meets the far courtyard wall stands a magnificent stone staircase, its solid banister rising from projecting mouldings that follow the serrated profile of the stairs behind.

We enter the museum through a doorway on the wall to the left, opposite the arcade, on the palazzo's northern side. We come first to the chapel whose apse exhibits the collection's largest artefact, the fifteenth-century fresco *Triumph of Death*. The fresco is exactly as wide as the square apse, and slots carved into both sidewalls' back corners, creating a truncated T-shape in plan, extend the rear wall's surface, allowing it to accommodate the piece. As we stand and look at the fresco, which projects slightly forward from the rear wall, we cannot see the corners of the space, which, as a result, expands to either side. The lantern in the cupola above washes the white walls with strong daylight, emphasizing the side shadows, making the fresco appear to float in the light. **(3.24)**

PALAZZO ABATELLIS RENOVATIONS
PALERMO, 1953–1954

3.25

3.23 'ANTONELLO DA MESSINA E LA PITTURA DEL "400 IN SICILI"' EXHIBITION, PALAZZO ZANCA, MESSINA, 1953; LATTICE WEAVE FABRIC CEILING AND DRAPES

3.24 PALAZZO ABATELLIS RENOVATIONS; PERIOD PHOTOGRAPH, C. 1954, CHAPEL APSE WITH THE FIFTEENTH-CENTURY FRESCO, *TRIUMPH OF DEATH*

3.25 PALAZZO ABATELLIS RENOVATIONS, PALERMO, 1953–4; VIEW OF ENTRANCE COURTYARD THROUGH THE WESTERN WALL'S BROAD ARCHED OPENING

3.26

3.26 PALAZZO ABATELLIS RENOVATIONS; CORNER ROOM, *ELEONORA OF ARAGON* BY FRANCESCO LAURANA

3.27 PALAZZO ABATELLIS RENOVATIONS; CORNER ROOM, MARBLE HEAD OF A WOMAN, FRANCESCO LAURANA

3.27

3.28

3.29

We pass through a room opening to the courtyard in which the large *Vase of Malaga* is displayed, hovering above a steel stand, with three double-plate legs, and braced at the top by a steel rod. Through a doorway, we see a small corner room containing the works of Francesco Laurana, including the marble bust of *Eleonora of Aragon*, facing to the right, illuminated by the window's light. **(3.26)** The white marble is seen against the deep green, Venetian polished plaster panels mounted on the wall and wrapping around the corner. Its weight received by a pair of brass pins and a small piece of lead, the bust floats above a curved ebony wood base, carried on a thin, square steel post projecting from the floor. Stepping into the room, in the left-hand corner, backed by green panels, we see the bust of a young boy supported by four rectangular pieces of wood wrapping a steel post with four blades, a pinwheel in plan, each face presenting narrower and wider wood pieces. On the wall behind us, a horizontal wood band divides a violet-coloured plaster panel, in front of which is cantilevered the marble head of a woman, set on a wood base, cut at the sculpture's angle, and supported by a horizontal steel plate projecting from a slot in the plaster panel. **(3.27)**

In the next room sculptures of the Gagini family are displayed. Facing us to our right, a Madonna and Child statue stands on a cubic stone base, receiving light from the windows, while ahead of us, a smaller Madonna and Child statue is positioned high up with her back to us, gazing through the door into the next room. As we move to the front of the sculpture, we see that its tall, rectangular stand is made of four thick panels of laminated vertical hardwood boards, ranging from almost black to brown to red to an orange-yellow, joined with contrasting wood-coloured dowels. Looking up at the *Madonna and Child,* we meet their downward gazes. Behind us, framed in the doorway we just passed, the window-lit *Eleonora of Aragon* is now facing us, floating against a dark green field, illuminated by light from the window. Turning, we see a page's marble head, displayed on a rotating wood and steel stand identical to the bust of the young boy. **(3.29)** Looking at this sculpture from the side, the light white-grey marble is seen against a green, wood-framed vertical wall panel, the profile of the head, delicately outlined by the light, is clearly revealed.

Against the next room's far wall, a new staircase rises to a doorway halfway up the wall. The hexagonal stone treads appear to float next to the wall, supported by a steel beam set back beneath, and the staircase is given no handrail. As we walk towards the large stone landing, we pass by a display of column bases set on the floor, with matching capitals lifted above head height on narrow, three-legged steel stands. **(3.30)** This positioning allows us to see the base and capital in their correct architectural relationship. Stepping on to the landing, we turn and, through the doorway in the far corner, we see Gagini's *Madonna and Child* and Laurana's *Eleonora of Aragon*, both facing us, and both brilliantly illuminated by adjacent windows. **(3.28)**

At the top of this staircase we arrive at the landing of the ancient stone staircase we saw in the courtyard; ascending it we reach the first floor loggia. On this upper level, the floors are new, made of light red-brown terracotta tiles set in a herringbone pattern, differing from the ground floor's original stone and terracotta. At the end of the loggia, a doorway leads into the 'Room of the Crosses', one of the museum's largest spaces. **(3.31)** The Gothic, three-columned stone windows on the room's sidewalls have new wood-framed windows set behind, divided into two horizontal panes at the bottom, four vertical panes in the middle and three panes above (narrow-wide-narrow). The new windows' thin mullions do not align with nor obstruct the Gothic columns. Together the enclosure's two layers, at the wall's outer and inner surface, make a syncopated pattern that constantly changes as we move. Stone window seats carved into the walls beneath these windows allow two people to sit facing one another. The end walls, against which altarpieces are displayed, are white plaster, and a band of this same material runs the length of the sidewalls, below the windowsill, above which the frescos are displayed on the newly exposed stone masonry of the wall structure. Standing in the centre of the room, two large crosses, painted on both sides, are supported by brass and steel frames. The smaller cross stands on a black stone cube, the other stands on two horizontal, light grey stone slabs.

3.28 PALAZZO ABATELLIS RENOVATIONS; VIEW OF GAGINI'S *MADONNA AND CHILD* AND LAURANA'S *ELEONORA OF ARAGON*

3.29 PALAZZO ABATELLIS RENOVATIONS; SCULPTURES OF THE GAGINI FAMILY, A PAGE'S MARBLE HEAD

3.30 PALAZZO ABATELLIS RENOVATIONS; COLUMN BASES AND CAPITALS DISPLAYED ON STEEL STANDS BEFORE A RISING STAIRCASE WITH HEXAGONAL TREADS

3.30

3.31 PALAZZO ABATELLIS RENOVATIONS; 'ROOM OF THE CROSSES'

3.32 / 3.33

A door in the corner leads into the room housing Antonello da Messina's works. Vertical panels of teak wood, secured at their joints by brass and steel clips to the steel frame behind, are folded to enclose a small room within the larger room. Upon entering, set at an angle and facing the door, we first see Antonello's *Annunciation*, in which the Madonna wears a celestial blue shawl, displayed on a freestanding, white-plastered, teak-framed panel. Inset into the panel, the painting is surrounded by a background of red-brown velvet, found during the building's renovation. On the right wall, each of Antonello's *Three Saints* are placed on similar, although smaller, panels, their right sides hung on brass hinge rods set in front of the panels' surface. The paintings can be turned to catch the light coming through the window behind us, and to allow us to examine each individually, before stepping back to see them as a group. **(3.32, 3.33)**

Finally, we move into the church's mezzanine, where the sixteenth-century paintings are displayed beneath the groin-vaulted ceiling. New openings, carefully detailed to reveal the original stonework, allow views into adjacent rooms, while large vertical slots cut into the inner walls reveal the new, structural-steel columns embedded into the walls to stabilize the building. Carved marble artefacts are mounted on the wall, supported by cantilevered double steel bars, with precisely shaped wood and brass elements fitted to each piece's profile to provide a secure anchorage. Standing at the room's edge, we overlook the chapel below and are provided a second, elevated view of the *Triumph of Death*, floating in the brilliantly illuminated apse. **(3.34)** Throughout the museum, each artefact has its own individual and unique mode of being presented to us, which seems exactly right for that particular object. Yet, we also note that the brackets, wooden panels, pivoting supports, frames, stands and bases share a common formal, material and detailing language – giving the whole experience a strong sense of unity.

3.34

Two closely related commissions were for the renovation of the first six rooms of Florence's war-damaged Gallerie degli Uffizi, undertaken from 1953–6 with Ignazio Gardella and Giovanni Michelucci, and the renovation of the Drawing and Print Room in the Uffizi, undertaken from 1957–60 with Scarpa's friend and repeat collaborator Edoardo Detti. Dedicated to Italian painting from Giotto to the Renaissance, the six rooms' artefacts again are given an individually unique mode of presentation, while also sharing the double steel members, in L-shapes and T-shapes, of their bases and frames. Giotto's large cross is supported by an L-shaped, double steel base set on a large, greystone slab, which acts to keep us from approaching too close. **(3.35)** Two thin steel rods tie the arms of the cross to the wall behind, and the cross is inclined towards us; looking up at the painting, we sense the weight of Christ's body. Scarpa was also responsible for the steel tensioning ties in the ceiling's wood trusses, the thin, elegantly staggered rooflight frames; the spatial connection of the rooms by narrow vertical slot-like openings; and the continuous band of black steel sharply separating the white plaster wall from the dark red terrazzo floor. **(3.36)**

3.35

3.32, 3.33 PALAZZO ABATELLIS RENOVATIONS; ROOM HOUSING WORKS OF ANTONELLO DA MESSINA

3.34 PALAZZO ABATELLIS RENOVATIONS; CHURCH MEZZANINE LEVEL, AN ELEVATED VIEW OF THE *TRIUMPH OF DEATH*

3.35 GALLERIE DEGLI UFFIZI RENOVATIONS, FLORENCE, 1953–6; LARGE CROSS BY GIOTTO

3.36 GALLERIE DEGLI UFFIZI RENOVATIONS, 1953–6; STAGGERED ROOFLIGHTS

3.37 GALLERIE DEGLI UFFIZI RENOVATIONS, 1957–60; DRAWING AND PRINT ROOMS

3.37

In the Drawing and Print Rooms, a band of wall display panels runs at eye level around the room's perimeter, while stands, with four display panels on each side, are placed in the room's centre. **(3.37)** The floor is dark-red terrazzo, while the ceiling is made of terra cotta-coloured polished-plaster panels, separated by metal joints, and into which linear lights are recessed behind frosted glass, forming a Mondrian-like pattern. The wall panels are supported, top and bottom, by two horizontal black steel bars, with vertical steel struts set between each panel to form a truss; the panels stand forward of the off-white plaster walls. The stands' frames are formed of complexly interlocked sets of thin steel pieces. A steel truss, similar to the one used in the wall panels, runs down the stands' centres, welded to a steel bar at either end, which in turn is anchored between the pair of steel bars that compose the double legs at either end. The frame is braced at its midpoints by two wider bars that run from side to side beneath the display panels, a horizontal one over a vertical one, and by two vertical rods running up through the centre. All panels are square, with a field of dark red-brown linen into which the drawing or print is placed; the whole is covered with a glass sheet. Held in a brass frame, the panels are spaced away from each other by the truss' steel strut; the four corners of each panel are notched at 45-degree angles, allowing the brass clip and large set pin to secure the panel to the steel frame. The display panels' finely grained details focus our attention on the prints and drawings, and the meticulous craft that has gone into the panels' design and fabrication heightens our sensitivity to the exquisitely thin lines and subtly modulated shading shown in the handmade works they hold.

3.36

CHAPTER 04

ARCHITECTURE DETERMINED NOT BY THE WHOLE BUT BY THE PART

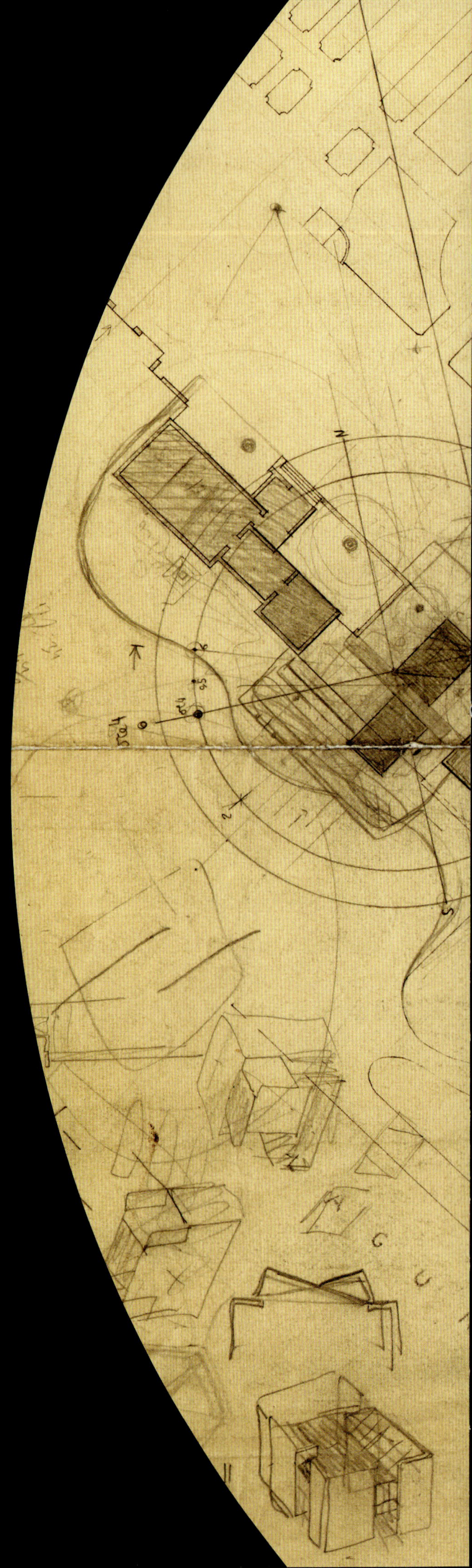

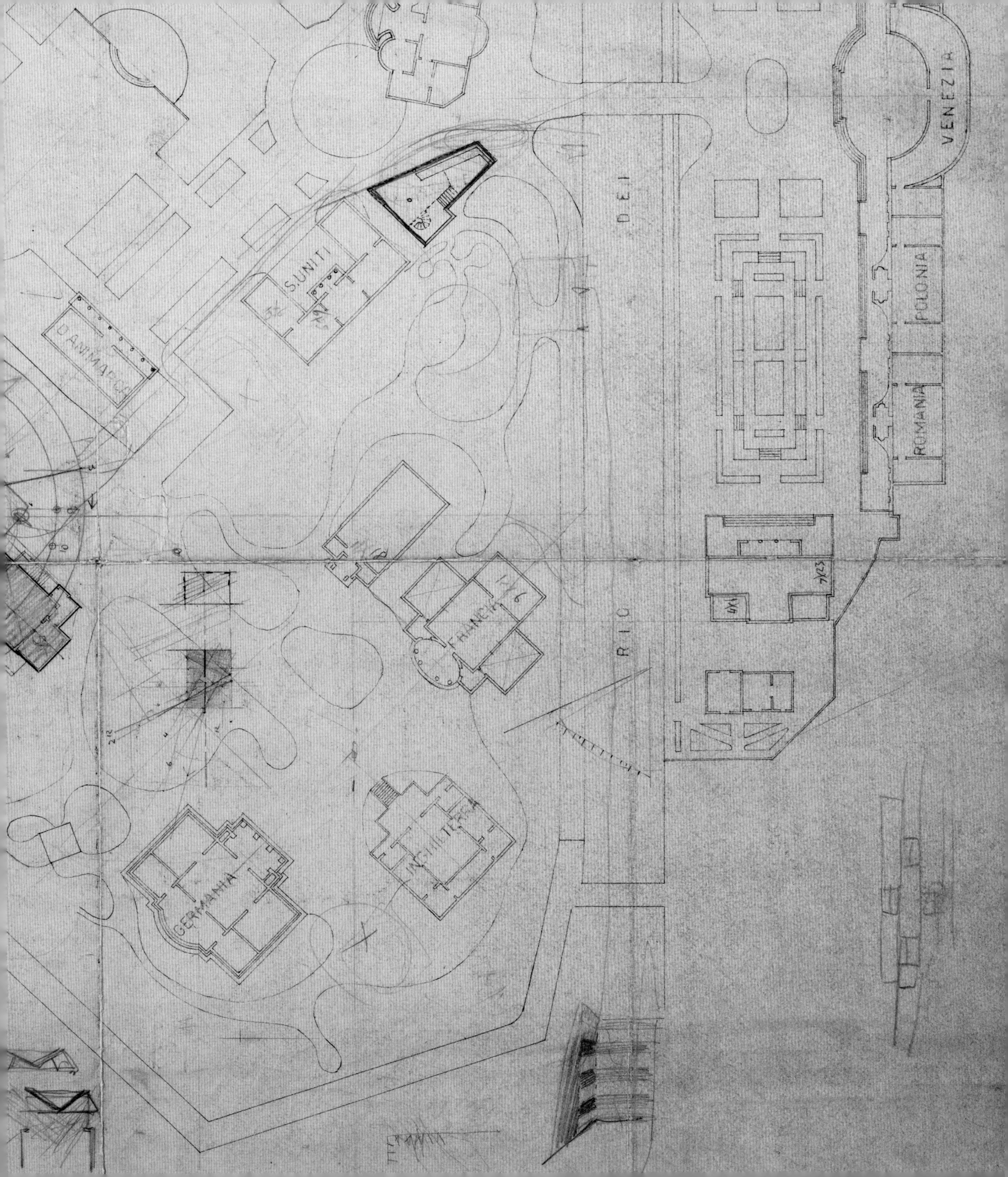
VENEZIA
POLONIA
ROMANIA
DEI
RIO
S.UNITI
DANIMARCA
FRANCIA
GERMANIA
INGHILTERRA

During the 1950s we can discern a layering and fusion of Scarpa's various formal and spatial sources, combined with the ever-increasing importance of the work of Swiss Bauhaus painter, Paul Klee, whose works Scarpa installed in the 24th Biennale in 1948. The process of designing this installation enabled Scarpa to get to know Klee's work intimately. Scarpa's employment of Klee's formal and colour patterns was likely less important than the fact that they shared an acute sensitivity to: the passage of time – the insight that, in our experiences, time and space are not present in a logical, linear sequence; the understanding of the way in which our knowledge and experience of real places and events excludes unitary interpretations or singular points of view; the belief that experience consists in moving through an itinerary of related fragments and articulate details; and the idea that tactile and material experience are intimately tied to emotion, memory and the simultaneity of human time.

In 1914, Klee wrote, **'I should like to create an order out of feeling and, going still further, from motion.'** Scarpa's works shared this conception of motion motivated by emotion, as well as the idea of the importance of the tactile quality of materials and how our perception of time is changed by tactile experiences. Klee noted, **'Things that one has touched firmly, desultory things, are attached by a strong line and made into one … Distance is time, whereas a surface is apprehended more in terms of the moment.'** In Scarpa's work we are brought into a more intimate relationship with things, but equally important is the relationship between things, the possibility that our experience of something changes due to its proximity to something else; collocation. Of the positioning of things, Klee wrote, **'Whenever we bring different things together, the question of proportion comes up, the relation between things and their position. Proportion is not only a question of actual measurements, but also of the forces at work in the measurements. It can be extended to produce local density, simplicity, or complexity.'** (4.1)

In a definition that applied to all modern art and architecture, Klee stated, **'One of the artist's basic problems is how to enlarge space. We do it by means of overlapping planes … interpenetrating, so that here even boundaries are spatial.'** In Scarpa's work, the boundary, as both threshold and horizon, is critical to our experience. Klee notes that, **'the passage of time brings with it a movement of the ground plane'**, and Scarpa's works are characterized by a layered topographic datum that serves to anchor our movement across its surface. Klee's paintings developed a structural tension by alternately emphasizing the erratically gridded field and the articulate fragment. Scarpa's work is similarly composed of highly articulated details set within a more ambiguously defined spatial field. Klee wrote, **'we assemble objects, but the relationships we create between them can be plausibly experienced only in fragments.'** Klee believed that a work of art is assembled or constructed from articulate details, fragments and elements, and that **'this formation is arrived at by a successive singling out of parts of the total form'**, a phrase that aptly describes the experience of moving through Scarpa's architecture. How we engage Scarpa's architecture is largely dependent upon our empathic experience of it. Klee refers to empathy as beginning with our experience of gravity, **'Our own physical-human dependence on this earth force [gravity] helps us to draw inferences about our fellow sufferer, the building, the physical object.'**

Klee believed in the importance of drawing, not to represent the world but to understand it, **'Art does not reproduce the visible, but makes visible.'** Scarpa was even more emphatic in this regard, **'I want to see things, I don't trust anything else. I place things in front of me, on the paper, so I can see them. I want to see, therefore I draw. I can see an image only if I draw it.'** [1] For Scarpa, drawing and making were intertwined completely, and he never made construction drawings in the normal sense of the word. Scarpa simultaneously engaged conception and construction, so that his drawings were only 'finished' when the building's construction was completed.

4.1

4.2

ARCHITECTURE DETERMINED NOT BY THE WHOLE BUT BY THE PART

As Marco Frascari has noted, 'In Scarpa's works the relationships between the whole and the parts, and the relationships between craftsmanship and draftsmanship, allow a direct substantiating *in copore vili* of the identity of the processes of perception and production, that is, the union of the construction with the construing in the making and use of details.' [2] Scarpa's design process fuses construing and constructing, thinking and making, so that we may rightly consider him as much of a craftsman as an architect. **(4.2)**

Klee also emphasized the importance of how a thing is made and argued that: our ability to understand the act of making was more critical to our experience than the final form's appearance; rather than the form representing something, the form should be a presentation of making; and art should accentuate 'the processes leading to the form'. Scarpa shared these concerns, and Kenneth Frampton has written about how in Scarpa's design process, we see 'the gestural impulse passing almost without a break from the act of drafting to the act of making.' [3] The relationship between materials and making, and the relationship of materials to our experience of what is made, was crucial in both Klee's and Scarpa's thinking. Klee defined the creative process as essentially an engagement with the materials of making, '[Creativity] must make itself known through the familiar kinds of matter and be at one with them in function. Merged with matter, it must enter into a form that is alive and real. And it is thus that matter takes on life and order.' The capacity of materials, ordered in articulate details, to construct our experience is part of what Klee considered the language of form. The fragments, out of which both Klee and Scarpa constructed their experiential events, are not the result of complexity and multiplicity, but of layering, lamination and polishing of the surface to reveal the depths within. Klee stated, 'The truly creative person works with the lapidary quality of language, not with its multiplicity.' [4]

The architectural historian and critic Manfredo Tafuri has noted the close bond between what he called Scarpa's 'complex and many-layered webs' and Klee's 'semblance-haunted labyrinths':

> 'The extension of memory and the contraction of experience into choices that are necessarily definite yet open to concatenation become translated [in Klee's work] into enigmatic forms … in order to permit a dialogue with future experiences, to enable interpretation, to create *breaks* in the continuity of space-time: not even the expressive metaphor of the labyrinth wholly expresses the disseminative process achieved by Klee in his "voyages". It is this very point that links Scarpa with the Swiss artist. The deviations, the broken phrases, the "figures" that crop up in work after work [by Scarpa] appears as a kind of ocean populated by elements that are recognizable but lend themselves to an endless process of deciphering – these all speak of time as made up of always open possibilities and multiple co-presences, crystallized into spatial allusions that are *waiting*. The invitation is not to unravel this centreless web, but … to abandon one-track approaches … The slowing down of the time of reading, the expansion of the instant imposed by his work on forms and materials implies an arrest of the nihilistic succession of "measurable" time and space … Perhaps Ernst Bloch might have been able to read in Scarpa's details answers to his appeal for the recovery of *experience*.' [5] **(4.3)**

4.3

In their shared obsession with merging Modern geometry and archaic symbolism, contemporary theories of space and ancient images of the cosmos, Modernist conceptions of experience and timeless rituals, Scarpa found in Klee an almost identical temperament to his own. Frampton has noted, 'Scarpa, following [the Venetian architect and disciple of Vico] Lodoli, was committed to the idea of analogy at every level in his work, that is to say, to a deductive argumentation that does not proceed from the whole to the part but rather moves homologically from part to part.' Scarpa's was 'an architecture of the disjunctive narrative in which what is is always accompanied by what has been and what might have been'. Scarpa's details, like the figures in Klee's paintings, are strangely familiar, yet never fully decipherable, as Frampton notes, 'At once critical and celebratory, Scarpa saw such cryptic, micro-tectonic inscriptions as somehow capable of transcending the ruinations of time.' [6]

4.1 PAUL KLEE, *EMACHT*, 1932; OIL ON CANVAS, 50 X 64 CM (19.75 X 25.25 IN), KUNSTMUSEUM, BERN

4.2 PAUL KLEE, *GEÖFFNET [OPENED]*, 1933; WATERCOLOUR, PEN AND PENCIL ON PRIMED MUSLIN ON PLYWOOD, 40.5 X 55 CM (16 X 21.75 IN), PRIVATE COLLECTION, ZENTRUM PAUL KLEE, BERN

4.3 PAUL KLEE, *LAGUNENSTADT [LAGOON CITY]*, 1932; WATERCOLOUR AND PEN ON CARDBOARD, 48.6 X 28.8 CM (19.25 X 11.25 IN), ROSENGART FOUNDATION, LUCERNE

4.4

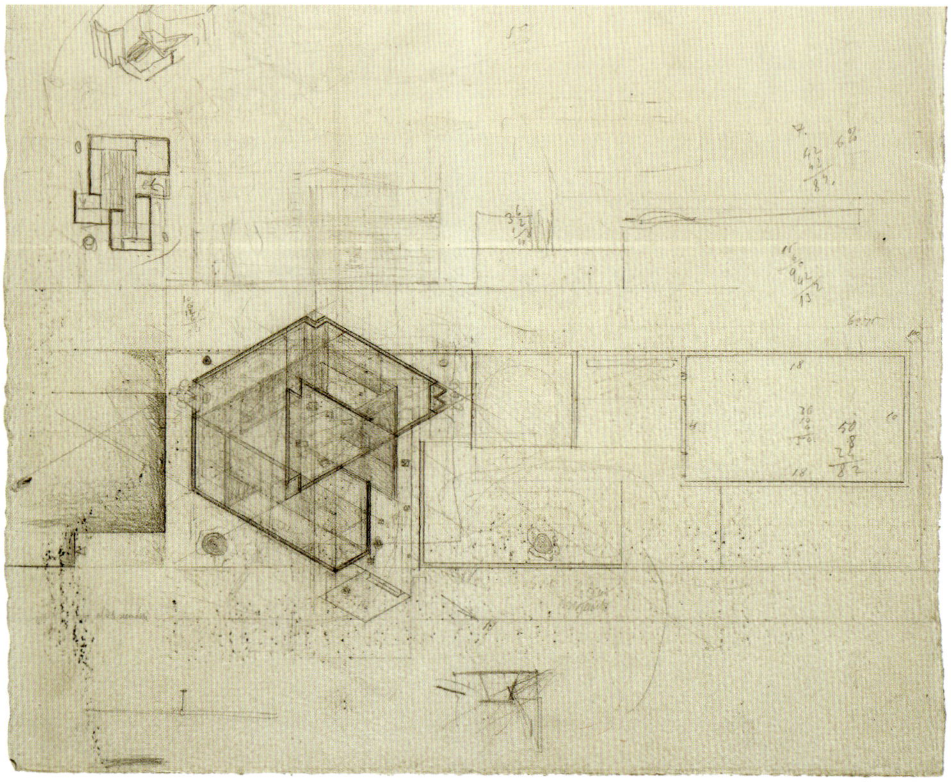

4.5

The Venezuelan Pavilion was part of the Biennale's expansion in the Castello Gardens; initiated in 1951, this intended to provide pavilions for several countries lacking dedicated exhibition spaces. In 1953, Scarpa's former student, Graziano Gasparini, an Italian painter and architect living in Venezuela, recommended he be commissioned to design the new Pavilion.[7] The site, which had three existing trees, is located between the Russian and Swiss pavilions on the garden's southwestern-most avenue, adjacent to the lagoon. Rather than beginning with an existing building, as he had done with most of his earlier built works, this was one of the relatively few freestanding new buildings realized to Scarpa's designs.

Scarpa's initial design, a series of interlocked triangles and hexagons in plan, was quite close in spirit and form to the work of Frank Lloyd Wright, for whom the equilateral triangle planning grid was a favoured device for the Usonian Houses; the 1936 Hanna House in Palo Alto, California, being perhaps the most widely published example. In Scarpa's first design, the building had a three-sided, tetrahedral roof rising above the centre of a lower, horizontal roof plane. What appears to be Scarpa's second design emerges in a small sketch in the corner of a larger floor plan of the first scheme, and shows a group of rectangular volumes rotating, or pinwheeling, around a large, court-like central space. **(4.4)** This plan is developed on another drawing, showing Scarpa carrying a version of the now four-sided, or pyramidal roof, forward to this scheme. **(4.5)** The section shows beams at either edge of the angled roof running down to the ground, intersecting smaller angled beams about 1 metre (3 ft 3in) off the floor, which together form small triangles standing on the floor and larger triangles reaching up to support the horizontal ceiling plane, with the two sets of triangles meeting at their points. This section is similar to several of Wright's designs, including the Beth Sholom Synagogue, then under construction in Elkins Park, Pennsylvania, and the triangular column piers are remarkably similar to those the American architect, Louis Kahn, was proposing at almost the same time for the unrealized Adath Jeshurun Synagogue, also in Elkins Park.

4.4 VENEZUELAN PAVILION, VENICE, 1953–6; PRIMARY SCHEME PLAN WITH SECONDARY SCHEME SKETCH PLAN SHOWN TOP LEFT, PENCIL ON CARDBOARD, 58 X 39 CM (22.75 X 15.25 IN)

4.5 VENEZUELAN PAVILION; SECONDARY SCHEME SKETCH PLAN AND SECTION, PENCIL ON PAPER, 44 X 74 CM (17.25 X 29.25 IN)

VENEZUELAN PAVILION
BIENNALE GARDENS, VENICE, 1953–1956

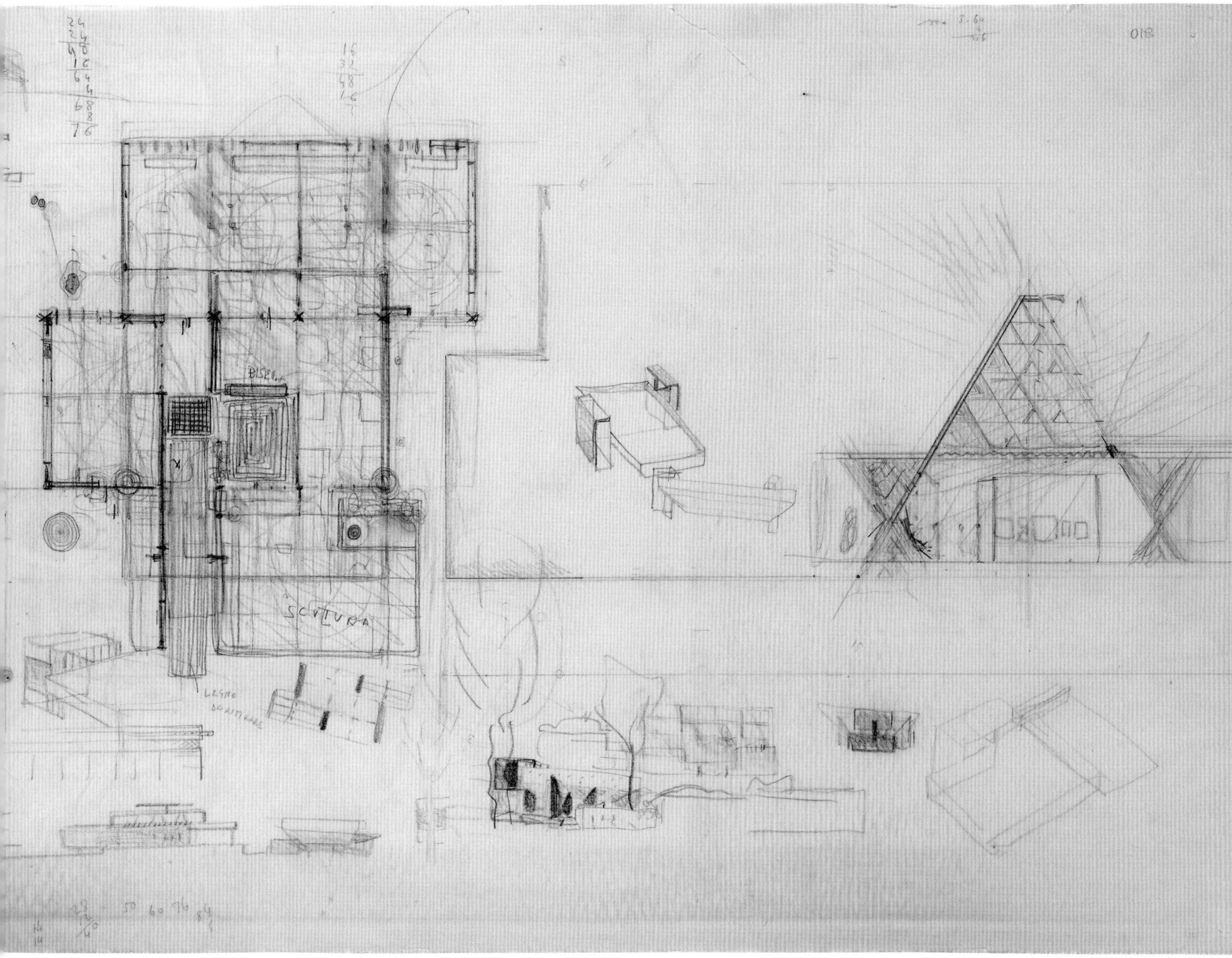

The second scheme's plan is closely related to the nearby Dutch Pavilion, designed by Gerrit Rietveld in 1953, composed of four rectangular volumes set into the corners of a square plan, forming a pinwheel around a large central room; a plan form used on some of the busts' wood and steel bases in the Palazzo Abatellis. Scarpa had intriguingly presaged the large and small masses resulting from the pinwheel plan, and the plaster-mass and glazed void, in the elevation of his 1950 Art Book Pavilion facing the Italian Pavilion, literally a few steps from Rietveld's building. Scarpa further developed this plan in two directions, the first a more compacted, square plan, similar to Rietveld's, where four pinwheeling square volumes set into the corners of a larger square plan are separated by circulation zones. The inner walls dividing these four volumes are this plan's only elements that still pinwheel around the centre, which is no longer a large void, but a small, almost solid cruciform of four structural piers. Secondly, on the same drawing, Scarpa further developed this scheme in smaller plans: anchoring the four inner corners of the four main spaces with columns; setting smaller square rooms at the outer corners, notching into the main spaces; and connecting the outer corners to the central columns with diagonal roof beams. These smaller plans are close to both Wright's 1906 Unity Temple and Kahn's contemporary Trenton Jewish Community Center Bath House. **(4.6)**

Yet these plans, with their bilateral symmetry, central axes and geometric massing, possessed a purity of overall form that we rarely find in Scarpa's realized designs, where he tended to accentuate the site's pre-existing conditions and local irregularities through the positioning of independent spaces and elements in a much looser arrangement. In his next two schemes, which are close to the final plan, Scarpa returned to a variation on Rietveld's pinwheel plan, but with only three rectangular volumes set around a smaller, L-shaped central space. In the second of these plans, the central space became a spine-like hallway running across the plan. Setting the building away from the classical Russian Pavilion on the left, Scarpa closely engaged the modern Swiss Pavilion's offset masonry walls to the right, pushing a volume into the small space at the rear of the Pavilion, taking advantage of the site's slight L-shape. In both plans, all three rectangular volumes, the two running perpendicularly to the avenue and the one running parallel to it, were shown in elevation as being enclosed by solid walls striated from top to bottom with vertical joints, and narrow vertical windows opening continuously across the tops of the walls.

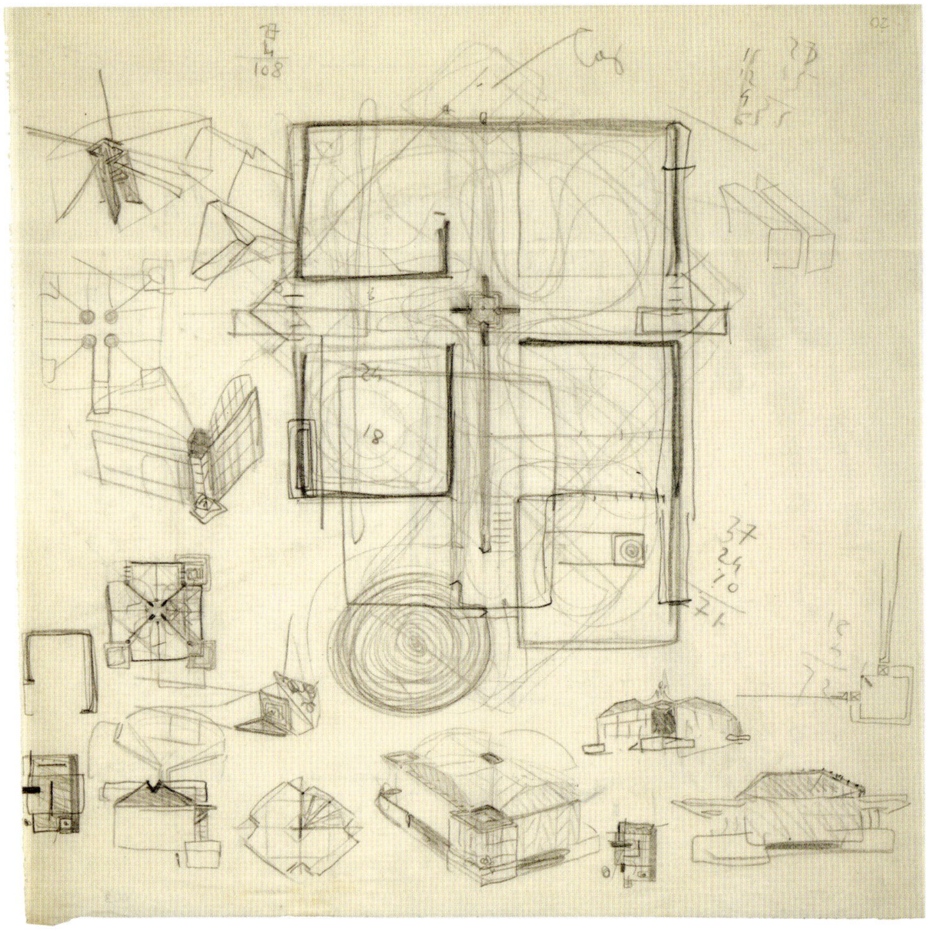

4.6

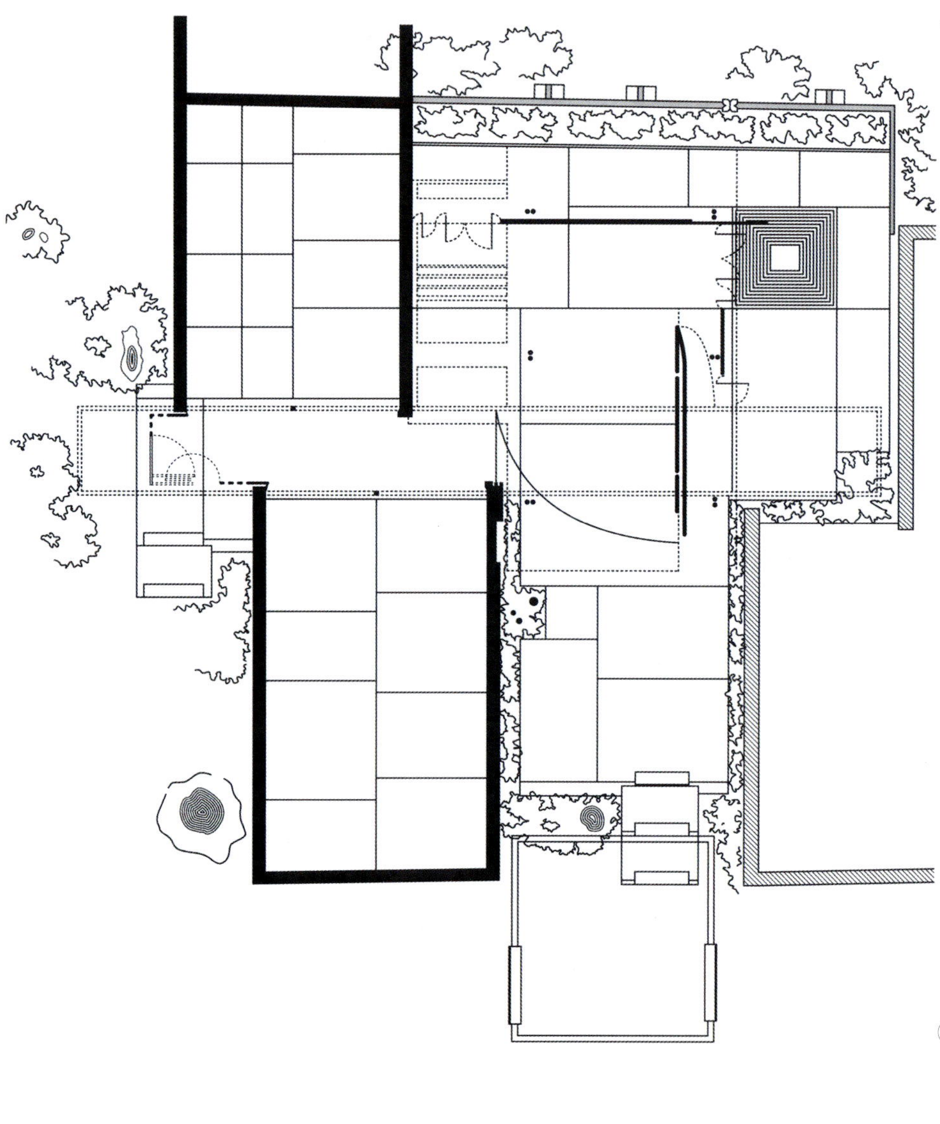

4.7

4.6 VENEZUELAN PAVILION; SKETCH PLAN, SECTION AND ISOMETRIC DRAWINGS, PENCIL ON PAPER, 37 X 37 CM (14.25 X 14.25 IN)

4.7 VENEZUELAN PAVILION; PLAN (REDRAWN)

4.8 VENEZUELAN PAVILION; SITE PLAN OF PAVILION WITHIN BIENNALE GARDENS, WITH ISOMETRIC DRAWINGS OF GERRIT RIETVELD'S DUTCH PAVILION, ALVAR AALTO'S FINNISH PAVILION AND SCARPA'S ITALIAN PAVILION COURTYARD AND BOOK PAVILION, BROWNPRINT

PENCIL ON PAPER, 73 X 54 CM (28.75 X 21.25 IN)

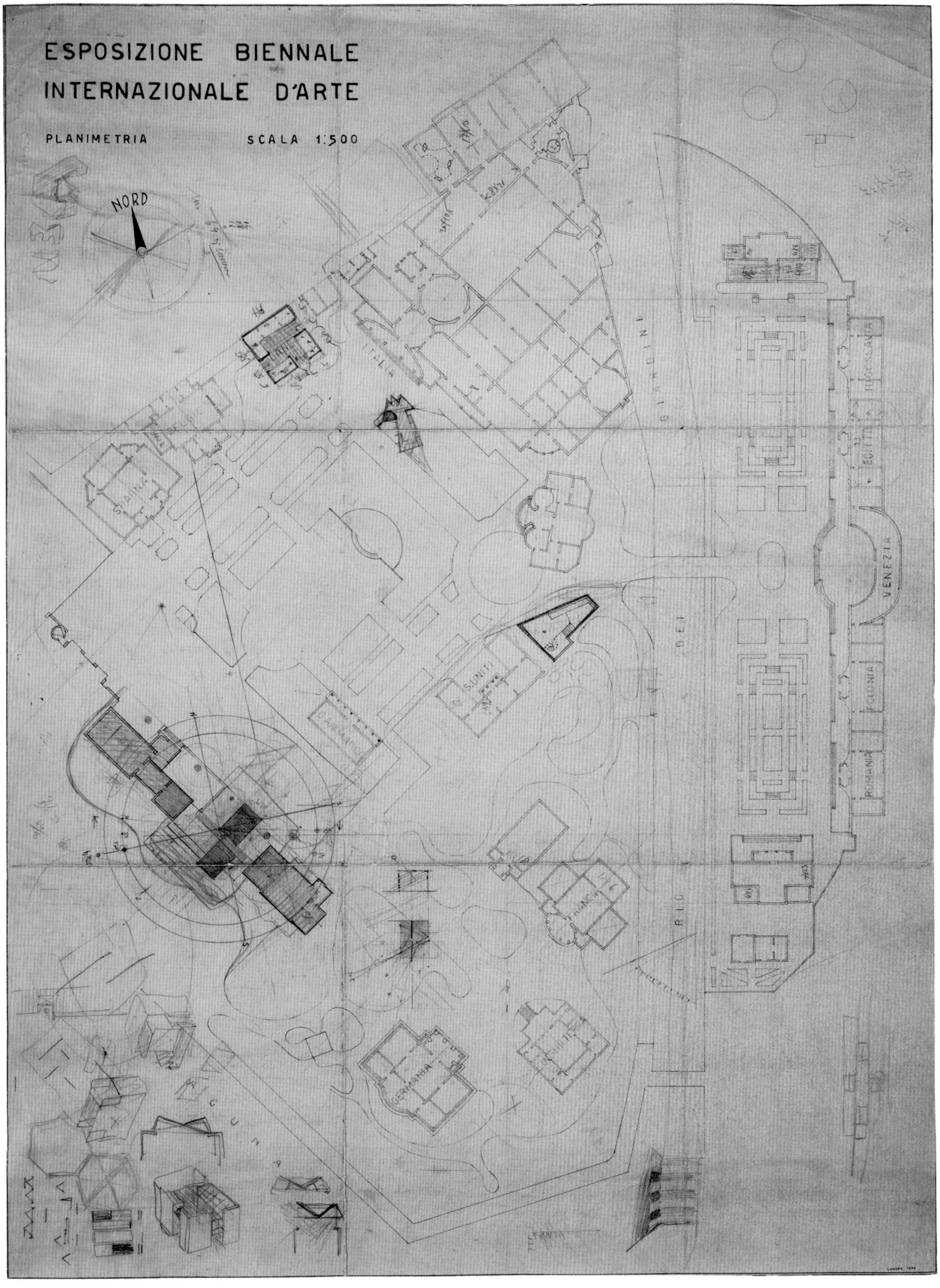
ESPOSIZIONE BIENNALE
INTERNAZIONALE D'ARTE
PLANIMETRIA
SCALA 1:500
NORD
ITALIA
GIARDINI
DEI
RIO
JUGOSLAVIA
EGITTO
VENEZIA
POLONIA
ROMANIA
GERMANIA
S.UNITI

4.8

4.9

4.9 VENEZUELAN PAVILION; FRONT ELEVATION FROM THE GARDEN AVENUE, SHOWING BUILDING'S CURRENT DEGRADED CONDITION

The final plan's precisely inked, presentation drawing was required by the authorities for design approval. Two large rectangular volumes with solid walls on three sides are set perpendicularly to the avenue; their open sides face inwards. Slightly offset from one another, the two volumes' shearing, or sliding, relationship retains a hint of the pinwheel configuration. These two volumes are separated by a narrow hallway defined not by walls, but by an overhead plane. The third volume's previous location, at the back of the site running parallel to the road partially behind the Swiss Pavilion's existing wall, is now occupied by a covered terrace, its floor merging with the entrance. **(4.7)**

Scarpa drew this final scheme's site plan on to the existing Biennale Gardens' plan, and the carefully positioned pair of off-set volumes in his scheme counterpoint the larger volumes of the Russian and Swiss pavilions, indicating how, within the constrained site, he created a dynamic spatial composition. **(4.8)** On this same site plan, Scarpa darkened in the plans of Rietveld's Pavilion, Scarpa's own Art Book Pavilion and the Finnish Pavilion's fan-shaped plan designed by Alvar Aalto in 1955. In the lower left corner, Scarpa made a small isometric drawing of Rietveld's pavilion and several sketches of Aalto's bow-tie-shaped roof and rooflight structure, Aalto's first use of this form. Scarpa met both Rietveld and Aalto during the construction period of their respective Biennale Pavilions. Aalto and Scarpa later visited their pavilions together at the opening of the 1956 Biennale – Aalto said Scarpa's Venezuelan Pavilion was **'most interesting,'** – and they also visited the recently opened Peggy Guggenheim Collection in the Palazzo Venier Leoni. [8] Aalto's influence on Scarpa can be discerned in Scarpa's unrealized project for the Olivetti Colony at Brusson of the same year, with its series of fan-shaped spaces.

From the garden avenue the Venezuelan Pavilion appears as a vertical, cast concrete cubic mass, to the right of which, set towards the back of the site, a low horizontal roof projects towards the Swiss Pavilion's low, buff-coloured brick walls. [9] **(4.9)** The upper half of Scarpa's building is opened in a series of tall, vertical windows, separated by narrow white-plastered vertical piers, the only place where the white colour of the interior is brought on to the exterior. At the roof, the windows meet rooflights, of the same width, in a frameless, 90-degree corner, allowing us to look through the corner to see the sky beyond. At the top of the solid sidewall, projecting triangles, set between triangular recesses, step up at a 45-degree angle at the corner, with rough, board-formed concrete below and smooth stucco plaster above. Projecting forward between the two pavilions, the large square, bevel-edged concrete landing slightly floats off the ground. To the right of the large tree, three steps lead up to the covered terrace, with hexagonally profiled wooden treads inset into, and cantilevering out of, the concrete slabs and terrace floor, which incline backwards. The terrace floor is made of various sized, concrete slabs with exposed river-washed pebble aggregate, and extends to left and right as we enter under the shade of the low ceiling. **(4.11)**

This terrace gallery has two layers of enclosure, the inner boundary under the ceiling is formed by a complex series of pivoting and fixed walls, faced in vertical wooden slats, pivoting glass doors and gridded wooden screens. Framed in steel, they all hover off the floor and just below the ceiling and, with two exceptions, can be opened and closed. The exceptions are the central portions of the back and front wood slat walls, which have a second wall layer of white polished plaster applied to their inside faces, allowing artworks to be displayed in the open air. Beyond the low ceiling's edge, the terrace space's outer boundary is formed by the Venezuelan Pavilion's concrete wall to the left, the Swiss Pavilion's brick wall to the right and a low, smooth concrete wall at the back. This back wall is lifted off the ground, its bottom edge aligning with the concrete terrace's surface on which we stand, allowing the garden's ground plane to enter into the space. The wall has diamond-shaped openings above the structural buttresses on the backside, while a large V-shaped notch gives a view through to the lagoon.

A series of parallel, rib-like ridges project from the low ceiling's concrete surface, crisscrossing back and forth overhead, into which black metal discs, in sets of six, have been cast in a repeating linear pattern. Together these ridges and staccato metal accents give the ceiling a strong but subtle presence, a woven character that belies its weight, and the more active ceiling and quieter floor, both made of concrete, shape the space. **(4.12)** The ceiling is supported by thin cylindrical steel columns set in pairs perpendicular or parallel to our direction of movement. Each pair is connected by a small collar, made of alternating thin plates of brass and steel and joined by two brass pins, set between the two columns at head height. When the large pivoting door is closed, we can see two double columns, one perpendicular on the left and one parallel on the right; when the door is open we see four double columns set in a pinwheeling pattern. The concrete roof is supported by six pairs of columns, the final two set beyond the wood wall running along the back; from inside, only their tops and bottoms can be seen. In the terrace gallery's right corner, glass doors open on to a square pool and fountain, the gridded wooden screen behind the back wall extends partway over the pool, further blurring the reading of inside and outside. **(4.10)**

Beneath the concrete surface, a narrow, oak-board ceiling, set between two thin flitch beams, each made of a steel plate placed between two layers of laminated wood, crosses the terrace gallery from right to left, starting outside near the Swiss Pavilion's walls, where a flagpole rises through an opening at the end, and continuing through the entrance door into the Venezuelan Pavilion's interior. At the centre of the concrete ceiling, the oak ceiling briefly opens providing a view of the ribbed concrete surface above. As we walk through the Pavilion doorway, the lower, oak-board ceiling carries through the two exhibition galleries and out the other side, covering a small back terrace seen through a gridded wooden screen.

When the pavilion is in use, and the pivoting partitions are opened, this central hallway is defined only by the low oak-wood board ceiling, the outer edges of which bevel down at a 45-degree angle, aligning with the V-shaped beams' bottoms. Enclosed only by the roof, this hallway's sides are entirely open, while the two galleries are enclosed up to the passageway's height by solid walls, opened above with windows on two sides. The two double-height galleries, opening to the left and right, are of slightly different size and height, and are spatially joined by the transverse hallway that connects them at the centre. The two galleries are fused together by the S-shaped circulation path repeatedly weaving back and forth across the hallway, going from one gallery to another.

4.10

4.11

4.12

4.13

4.14

Emerging from beneath the hallway's low, darker wooden ceiling, we enter the tall, brighter, white, polished-plaster walled galleries, with their coloured, polished-plaster ceilings – blue in the larger space and yellow in the smaller – and our eyes rise to the tall windows, through which we see the garden's trees. **(4.13)** Occupying the upper half of the gallery's outer wall and wrapping the corner between wall and ceiling, the windows' rhythmic vertical voids push slightly out of the space, while the plastered wall and ceiling surfaces are set slightly into the space. This effect is accentuated by the fact that the inner faces of the pier-like strips of wall between these wall-ceiling corner windows are finished in grey concrete, as on the building's exterior, reminding us that we earlier saw their outer faces, which were finished in the white plaster of the interior. To either side of these windows, the white plaster inner wall surfaces step down to form a serrated, bevelled corner, revealing a recessed layer of the exterior's grey concrete as if the corners have been eroded by sunlight. The interior and exterior finishes have, in effect, been exchanged, heightening the feeling that these unusual corner windows are both inside and outside.

Moving into the galleries, we look back and see an identical set of wall-ceiling windows opening above the low, wood-ceilinged hallway, generously illuminating the galleries. **(4.14)** This view towards the hallway reveals the dramatic contrast between the solid, massive outer walls we saw when entering and these almost completely perforated inner walls at the building's centre. The inaccessible space above the hallway's wooden ceiling, into which both galleries' windows open, appears as a kind of elevated courtyard garden, filled with the vertical forms of the pier-like walls and trees of the garden. While Wright had used frameless corner windows in his designs as early as 1923, his windows always turned the corner from wall to wall. The Venezuelan Pavilion windows, which turn the corner from wall to ceiling, are a form of aperture uniquely Scarpa's own, and he would employ them again in later projects.

4.10 VENEZUELAN PAVILION; PERIOD PHOTOGRAPH, *C.* 1956, GLASS DOORS AND GRIDDED WOODEN SCREEN SEEN FROM THE EXTERIOR SQUARE POOL. SCARPA AND PHOTOGRAPHER, FERRUCCIO LEISS, VISIBLE IN THE GLASS REFLECTION

4.11 VENEZUELAN PAVILION; PERIOD PHOTOGRAPH, *C.* 1956, ENTRANCE UNDER LOW CEILING WITH PIVOTING WOOD-SLAT WALL RUNNING ADJACENT FROM PAVILION SIDE WALL

4.12 VENEZUELAN PAVILION; PERIOD PHOTOGRAPH, *C.* 1956, TERRACE GALLERY, PIVOTING WALL CLOSED

4.13 VENEZUELAN PAVILION; PERIOD PHOTOGRAPH, *C.* 1956, LARGER INTERIOR GALLERY SEEN FROM THE CENTRAL HALLWAY

4.14 VENEZUELAN PAVILION; PERIOD PHOTOGRAPH, *C.* 1956, LARGER, INTERIOR GALLERY LOOKING BACK TOWARDS THE CENTRAL HALLWAY

4.15

Scarpa was commissioned to design this house by the solicitor Luciano Veritti, whom he had met during the Veritti family tomb's construction, designed together with Angelo Masieri, Veritti's second cousin. Scarpa's only other single-family, freestanding house would be for the Ottolenghi family, twenty years later. Veritti originally wanted to build on a site at the edge of the city, but Scarpa convinced him to build closer to the city centre. The rectangular site measures 27 x 50 metres (88 ft 6 in x 164 ft), with its long sides to the north and south, and is set back from the road, accessed by a narrow lane. All of this project's schemes involved cylindrical volumes; the two early schemes separated the living and sleeping into two volumes, while the final scheme organized the house's primary volumes within one circular form. To the north is a two-storey, largely solid, semi-cylindrical, plastered masonry-walled volume, while to the south a two-storey, largely open, rotated square, wood-framed glass-walled, prow-shaped volume cantilevers out over a semi circular pool of water. **(4.15)** The living spaces, including the doubleheight portion of the living room behind the angled glass prow, are on the ground floor, along with the winter garden, a smaller rotated square in plan, which extends out to the west. On the first floor are the bedrooms, including the main bedroom overlooking the two-storey portion of the living room, while at the roof, a penthouse contains a small study and terrace. **(4.16)**

We approach the house along the narrow lane at the site's southern edge; a low concrete wall on our right wraps around the site. The rough-plastered, semi-cylindrical wall curves away from view on the right, while to the left we see the large, prow-like form of the living room's wood-framed glass projecting out over the pool. **(4.17)** Behind this, we can see the winter garden's diamond-shaped – in plan and section – projection, concrete below and glass above. Approaching the entry portico, carved out of the semi-cylindrical wall's near

VERITTI HOUSE
UDINE, 1955–1961

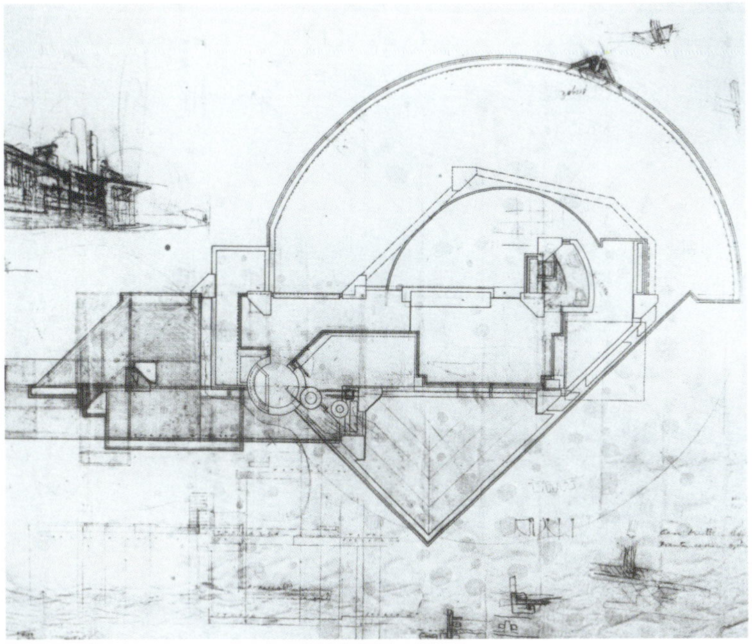

4.16

4.17

4.18

corner, we see a first floor, triangular-plan balcony cantilevering out over the pool, beneath which is a recessed terrace. Directly above the entry portico, a wood-framed window projects out at a 45-degree angle, one of the house's many prow-like forms. Stepping up on to the entry bridge, a concrete slab running beneath the overhanging first floor and alongside the pool to the left, we grasp the handrails running along the bridges both sides. These handrails, matching the balcony above, are supported by vertical double steel bars, with a lower horizontal steel tube structure that holds, by offset bent steel bars, a higher horizontal steel bar, on to which semi-cylindrical wood pieces have been attached to form a cylindrical handrail. [10] The handrails' steel elements are painted a red-orange colour, indicating Wright's influence, but the combination of structural steel, cold to the touch, and wood-clad handrails, warm to the touch, is something Scarpa shared with Alvar Aalto.

Passing through the small vestibule, we arrive in the entry foyer, its floor made of square white stones set in a stepping pattern; and its smooth white plaster ceiling continuing into the living room beyond. Directly ahead is one of the structural piers that punctuate the plan of this house, shaped, in plan, as a 45-45-90-degree triangle with truncated outer corners. **(4.18)** Turning to look back, we see two small triangular windows of the same shape in the red polished plaster entry door. The piers are made of L-shaped precast concrete elements, stacked and then bonded together by reinforcing steel and concrete placed into their inner voids. The concrete elements' horizontal joints are clearly legible, while on their longer, inside faces, small precast concrete blocks with prismatic projections of varying lengths, close the space between the L-shaped pier's legs to house the heating pipes. To the right is the landing of the main staircase, which has open wood treads, mahogany wall panelling and a sky blue, polished-plaster panel ceiling.

Looking directly ahead, across the living room's back wall we see an angled window on the far side, opening into one of the several vertical shafts connecting the basement below to the main floor and the upper floor, visually and acoustically integrating the house's spaces. Moving into the living room, passing between the two concrete piers, we step down on to the terracotta floor, made of rectangular tiles of the same length but varying widths, set in a nonrepeating pattern. To the right is a cabinet composed of vertical, light-coloured pinewood panels edged in dark mahogany bands, stepping up and down. **(4.19)** The panels' vertical rhythm is complemented by the horizontal mahogany shelves with 45-degree angled, bevelled edges; the whole is sheltered beneath a thin, cantilevered mahogany soffit. Diagonally across the living room from the entrance, set in the far corner, is a low fireplace, with a bevelled, plastered concrete hood. At the outer edge of the living room, the white plaster ceiling ends in a band of wooden trim, and the entire space opens upwards behind the prow-shaped, double-height Douglas fir-framed glass wall.

4.15 VERITTI HOUSE, UDINE, 1955–61; SOUTHEASTERN FACADE

4.16 VERITTI HOUSE; ROOFTOP, PENTHOUSE PLAN, PENCIL ON PAPER, 73.4 X 53 CM (29 X 21 IN)

4.17 VERITTI HOUSE; EASTERN APPROACH AND ENTRY PORTICO

4.18 VERITTI HOUSE; ENTRY FOYER WITH STRUCTURAL PIER

4.19

4.20

ends in a gentle counter-curve to the outer plaster wall; and, above this soffit, recessed lighting washes the main ceiling, which is a plane of white polished plaster. **(4.22)** In the room's three corners, the wooden wall panels pivot or slide open, giving access to the kitchen at the right, and opening to the left into the vertical light-well we saw from the entryway. Standing at the vertical shaft's edge and looking up, following the delicate shadow patterns of the concrete pier's prismatic projections, we see the ceiling of the bedrooms above; looking down, through a set of interlocked wood-framed windows, we see the basement below.

The winter garden has a northwest facing full-height wall of small square glass panes, set in a thin concrete frame. On the south side, a band of high clerestories is opened above the diamond-shaped, prow-like projection, with solid concrete walls below and glass clerestories and rooflights above. **(4.23)** Two of the precast concrete piers stand inside the humid winter garden, and in contrast to those inside the house, appear aged and weathered, their surfaces mottled with mould and mildew. The first floor bedrooms have mahogany flooring and white polished plaster ceilings. Set above the living room, the main bedroom can be opened or closed by a sliding wall of glass and wood; the room's walls are almost entirely made in wood, with full-height built-in cabinetry. **(4.24)** Through windows, with wood mullions abstracted from the piers' prismatic patterns, opened in a wood-panelled wall, the main bedroom overlooks the triangular double-height living room, enjoying views out through the upper portion of the wood framed glass wall to the pool and landscape beyond. From this elevated vantage point, just beneath the horizontal roof which projects out beyond the glass wall, our awareness of the sweeping horizontal enclosure of the house's spaces by the circular walls of the pool and the house is even more pronounced. But this emphasis on the horizon is balanced and integrated by the vertical shafts that perforate the floors, which, combined with the patterned piers rising from the foundations and projecting above the roof, act to stitch the interior spaces into place between earth and sky.

Stepping into this double-height space, triangular in plan, we have moved out of the house's masonry mass and are cantilevered out over the pool running under the floor beneath our feet. The space's wood-framed glass wall can be almost completely opened, connecting outside and inside. **(4.20)** The right side's lower section, a large, single, horizontal panel, pivots open, as do vertical wood-framed windows to the left and right, which rise to the cantilevered roof eave and each include smaller vertical ventilation bottom sections. These tall windows do not reach the floor, but stand above narrow horizontal slots of glass framed in steel; the steel verticals are much thinner than those of the wood above, so that the wood frames appear to float off the floor, drawing our gaze to the horizontal pool surface beyond. Open or closed, the glass wall allows us to hover over the pool so that the surface of the water becomes the datum, the most important horizontal plane defining the space we inhabit, and we feel the space of the house is bounded as strongly by the pool's curved edge before us as by the massive curved plastered masonry wall behind us.

Opposite the angled glass wall are the double pivoting wood panel doors opening into the dining room. The far wall of the dining room is part of the house's semi-cylindrical outer wall and is faced in white polished plaster. The only window to the exterior is a prow-like, rectangular, wood-framed glass-walled and glass-topped volume, projecting from the curved wall's centre and rising past the ceiling to the first floor windowsills (precisely presaging Scarpa's Gipsoteca corner windows). **(4.21)** Windows opening in the two straight sidewalls, made of pine and mahogany vertical panelling, give views between rooms. The terracotta floor carries in from the living room, and the ceiling of the dining room is in three layers; above the double door it is a triangle of red-brown polished plaster, set at the same height as the living room ceiling, and into which lights are recessed in narrow slots; further in, a slightly lower soffit, made of a thin plane of light green-coloured highly polished plaster, runs across the two wood-panelled sidewalls and

4.21

4.19 VERITTI HOUSE; VIEW ALONG BACK WALL OF THE LIVING ROOM LOOKING TOWARDS THE ENTRY FOYER

4.20 VERITTI HOUSE; LIVING ROOM, DOUBLE-HEIGHT, WOOD-FRAMED GLASS WALL OPENING TO THE GARDEN

4.21 VERITTI HOUSE; DINING ROOM, VIEW UP THROUGH THE PROW-SHAPED WINDOW

4.22 VERITTI HOUSE; VIEW OF DINING ROOM (L) AND VERTICAL LIGHT-WELL (R)

4.22

4.23

4.24

4.23 VERITTI HOUSE; VIEW OF THE PROW-LIKE WINTER GARDEN ON THE WESTERN FACADE

4.24 VERITTI HOUSE; FIRST-FLOOR MAIN BEDROOM

4.25

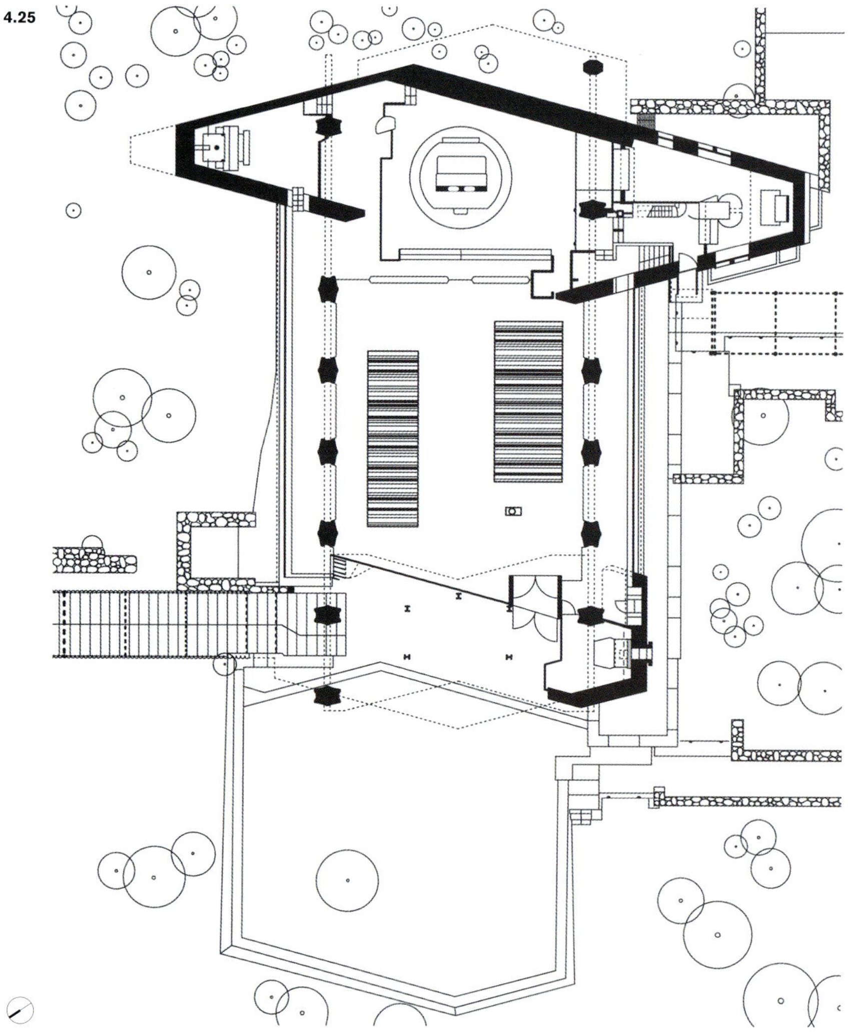

4.26

The Church at Corte di Cadore, which Scarpa designed and realized in association with Edoardo Gellner from 1956–61, again highlights Scarpa's propensity for collaborating with other architects.[11] Gellner, Scarpa's student at the IUAV during the 1940s, was hired to design the church in the Dolomite Mountains as part of new tourist facilities in the village of Corte di Cadore. When Gellner invited Scarpa to collaborate, the general character of the site plan, the building position and the steeply pitched sanctuary roof had already been set. As a result Scarpa's designs were largely directed towards developing the details of the building's fabric, and here we can see Scarpa's hand everywhere, including in the asymmetrical plan, with its use of 30-degree angled, truncated triangular forms. **(4.25)** Despite the rectilinear overall form dictated by the roof structure, the entry wall is pivoted back at a 15-degree angle, and the smaller chapel and larger sacristy and baptistery, projecting to left and right of the altar respectively, are housed in low, truncated triangular concrete masses shifted to match the pivoting entry wall.

Approaching the church, we see that the thick copper shingles of the steeply sloped roof come almost to the ground on either side. **(4.26)** A continuous narrow, horizontal window separates the bottom edge of the roof from the cast-concrete foundation's sloping wall, so that the massive roof appears to float above the ground. In contrast, the sloped foundation wall continues beneath the ground and is set within a trench-like excavation, the surrounding earth retained by a low wall (exactly as seen later in Scarpa's Brion Cemetery). We enter under a low, gently sloped canopy with a wood slat ceiling and copper roof and edges, supported by black-painted steel columns, H-shaped in plan and set in a rotating pattern (as Scarpa would do again in the Gipsoteca Canoviana Plaster Gallery). A vertical, wood slat wall runs most of the way across this open-air narthex, with the main entry vestibule on the right, its heavy double doors clad in copper sheets and stitched together with lines of bolts. The vestibule's sidewalls are massive, hammer-finished slabs of pink-coloured, Verona Prun stone, the concrete ceiling overhead displays an intricate pattern of square cast ribs and the floor is a recessed fibre mat. Inside, the ceiling soars over our heads, a steeply angled surface of wood boards, in front of which rise a series of vertical concrete structural pier-beams, standing in black steel bases and woven together with black steel rods that form an X-shape as they cross the space. **(4.27)**

CHURCH AT CORTE DI CADORE
1956–1961

4.27

4.25 CHURCH AT CORTE DI CADORE, 1956–61; PLAN (REDRAWN)

4.26 CHURCH AT CORTE DI CADORE; VIEW ACROSS WESTERN FACADE AND CANOPY TO THE MAIN ACCESS RAMP

4.27 CHURCH AT CORTE DI CADORE; CHURCH NAVE, LOOKING SOUTHEAST TOWARDS THE APSE

4.28

4.29

4.30 / 4.31

The entire roof seems to float above horizontal lines of strong sunlight that run at eye level down both sides of the church. A series of large columns runs beneath an angled wooden soffit at either edge of the sanctuary, and behind them, under the horizontal window, we see the outer foundation wall's angled inner face. The floor between the columns, under the pews in the room's centre and at the altar, is made of stone slabs raised 15 centimetres (6 in) above the floor on which we walk. This lower floor is made of circular sections of tree trunks that have been cast into the concrete floor; the polished wood seems to have been petrified. The hexagonal columns, with slightly angled inner and outer faces, are clad in thick, rough-faced slabs of light pink-coloured Prun stone. The columns' sides reveal their massive cast-in-place concrete structure, recessed behind the stone slabs' projecting edges, while at eye height we see the large steel clips attaching the stone cladding to the concrete structure. **(4.28, 4.29)**

The thick-walled wooden pews are set upon raised, red marble slabs. The pews' seatbacks project through a notch at the top, its seat cantilevers behind the sidewall at the middle while the kneeling board projects out at the bottom, turning to merge with the wooden floorboards inset into the red stone floor. The lifted floors between and behind the columns are made of white stone slabs, and the concrete wall beneath the outer window band is carved to receive a continuous flat wooden bench. The chancel floor is also raised, with a broad white stone lower landing and a red marble front edge into which wooden kneeling boards are set to the left and right, while a square red marble slab is centrally inset. Three red marble stairs run continuously across the front of the sanctuary, forming the elevated plinth on which two massive, white marble circular discs are set, serving as the altar floor. Two red marble steps lead up to the top of the second circular stone disc. The T-shaped altar is composed of a base that is a double hexagon in plan with a bevel-edged slab of red marble set around its sides and back, forming the elevated floor where the priest stands. On the double base is set a white marble altar top with a curved front edge, separated from the dolphin-curved bottom by a deep horizontal joint, from which six rectangular candle holders rise. **(4.30)**

The double pulpit is made of vertical slabs of red Prun stone in the front pulpit, and of white marble in the rear pulpit; all the slabs are joined at their tops by brass double-cylinder connectors inset into drilled holes on either side of the stone slabs' joints. In the red pulpit's front face the edges of the two slabs of stone forming the central joint are notched with 11 centimetre (4.25 in) square holes alternating back and forth from one slab to the other across the line of the joint; the pulpit stones appear stitched together by these square, shadowed voids. The baptistery, housed in the concrete-walled truncated triangular volume behind the double pulpits, has a polished red marble square baptismal font supported by black steel legs on three sides, with the carved semi-spherical bowl set towards the fourth edge, near the entry. The sacristy, crypt and organ loft, located behind the baptistery and accessed by an exterior door, are composed of a layering of black steel plates, grilles and rods, gridded wooden screens, wooden walls and wood-trimmed white-plaster panels. **(4.31)**

Walking back towards the entrance, we see that the slats run horizontally on the inside of the narthex's wooden wall; light entering through these vertical exterior and horizontal interior slats form a square-gridded screen, similar to versions to be found in virtually all of Scarpa's works. On the other hand, the church's consistently massive scale and heavy detailing, as well as materials such as the cast tree trunk floor, seem quite different from Scarpa's typical designs and should be understood as the result of Gellner and Scarpa's efforts to respond appropriately to the rustic mountain context.

4.28 CHURCH AT CORTE DI CADORE; SOUTHERN CHURCH AISLE, VIEW NORTHEAST ACROSS THE ENTRANCE TO THE NORTHERN AISLE

4.29 CHURCH AT CORTE DI CADORE; NORTHERN CHURCH AISLE, VIEW TOWARDS ALTAR

4.30 CHURCH AT CORTE DI CADORE; VIEW OF THE APSE AND WHITE MARBLE ALTAR

4.31 CHURCH AT CORTE DI CADORE; VIEW INTO BAPTISTRY, WITH SACRISTY, CRYPT AND ORGAN LOFT BEYOND

CHAPTER 05
EDIFICATION AS THE FOSTERING OF EMOTIONS

Antonio Canova, a celebrated neo-classical sculptor from the late eighteenth and early nineteenth centuries, was born in the small Veneto town of Possagno, at the foot of Monte Grappa. Canova's house is a rectangular volume running east-west along the mountainside's sloping southern face, with Canova's personal studio at the top of a tower at the eastern end, the whole opening to a south-facing terraced garden, looking away from the city. Upon Canova's death in 1822, the materials used in the design and fabrication of his sculptures were brought from his Rome studio to Possagno where some of them were housed in an 1836 museum designed by Francesco Lazzari.[1] Built as a freestanding structure in the form of a symmetrical basilica, behind and west of the Canova house, its three-part interior volume is covered by a coffered, barrel-vaulted ceiling and lit by large rooflights, with its central axis running from a northern colonnaded entry to the southern apse. In 1955, with the bicentenary of Canova's birth approaching, the Soperintendenza alle Gallerie e alle Opera d'Arte for Venice and the Veneto hired Scarpa to enlarge the Canova Museum. Scarpa received this commission because of his ongoing work with the superintendent, Moschini, on the Accademia Gallery in Venice.

Located to the west of the 1836 museum, this site sits tight against a small lane running down the hill to the south, with stables to the north. Several of the site's buildings were demolished to accommodate the addition, but, due to property lines, Scarpa was required to work within their footprints. Scarpa was challenged by the fact that the existing museum separated his new addition from Canova's house and garden, but he also wanted to minimize major changes to these existing structures, while also creating something that would fit into the site and, equally important, the surrounding, small-scaled Possagno buildings. Only a few of Scarpa's original design drawings remain, but copies and photographs of some of his missing drawings allow us to discern some aspects of his design process.

An extremely important drawing, the original of which is lost, has an aerial view at its centre looking from the southwest at the existing basilica volume, with its semi-cylindrical apse and pitched clay-tile roof. **(5.1)** Scarpa has drawn in the new addition's massing, almost exactly as it would be built, with a taller, cubic volume rising at the basilica's northern end, the lower, horizontal volume placed along the basilica's western edge and a small walled garden at the southern end. The drawing shows four clerestory windows notched into the corners of the taller cubic volume, as well as the clerestory windows at each of the points where the roof of the gallery steps downhill. On this same drawing there are separate studies of wall-roof corner windows, similar to those of Scarpa's Venezuelan Pavilion, as well as a perspective view of the narrow exterior space he proposed between his new gallery and the basilica's exterior wall, at the end of which is a view across the valley.

The most important sketch on this sheet appears in the upper right corner, where Scarpa drew an elevation of the entire complex, as if from across the valley. The basilica, with its semi-cylindrical apse, projects forward at the left and Scarpa's smaller addition is shown, the low garden wall boldly rendered, and the larger cubic volume, drawn faintly in the distance, rises above the foreground's lower volumes. To the left is an existing building, and to the right the terraced garden's wall incorporates a gate flanked by trees, with vineyards running down the slope below. The house's main, horizontal rectangular mass rises behind the garden wall; Scarpa denotes the windows with short vertical lines repeated across the facade. Attracting our attention, because Scarpa carefully drew in the large, south-facing window, is the tower room projecting above the house's eastern end. This is Canova's personal studio, a space that has heretofore never been mentioned in any study on Scarpa's Possagno building. Yet, it is clear from the way Scarpa has drawn it in this sketch that this space was of considerable importance in his thinking about the project, despite the studio's distant location, in both plan and section, from his own addition. This drawing indicates that, for Scarpa, there was a clear relationship between Canova's personal studio, at the house's upper eastern edge, and his own addition at the lower western edge of the complex.

Climbing the staircase in the house's eastern end, running north-south with each landing offering views over the valley below, we enter Canova's personal studio by ascending a half-flight of wooden stairs to the east, looking up at the room's far corner. **(5.2)** This room, measuring 5.5 x 7.3 metres (18 x 24 ft) and 5.5 metres (18 ft) tall, has a wooden floor and off-white plaster walls. Three large wood-framed windows set as high as possible in the centre of the northern, eastern and southern walls immediately draw our attention. The northern and eastern windows are square, while the southern window is a longer rectangle; all three windows are set flush with the thick wall's interior edge. The windows have two layers of glass with the two tall vertical hinged windows set to either side of, and pushed into the room with respect to, the larger central pane. When opened, the hinged windows project into the room perpendicular to the fixed central window, the whole prismatic composition set just beneath the ceiling.

GIPSOTECA CANOVIANA ADDITION
POSSAGNO, 1955–1957

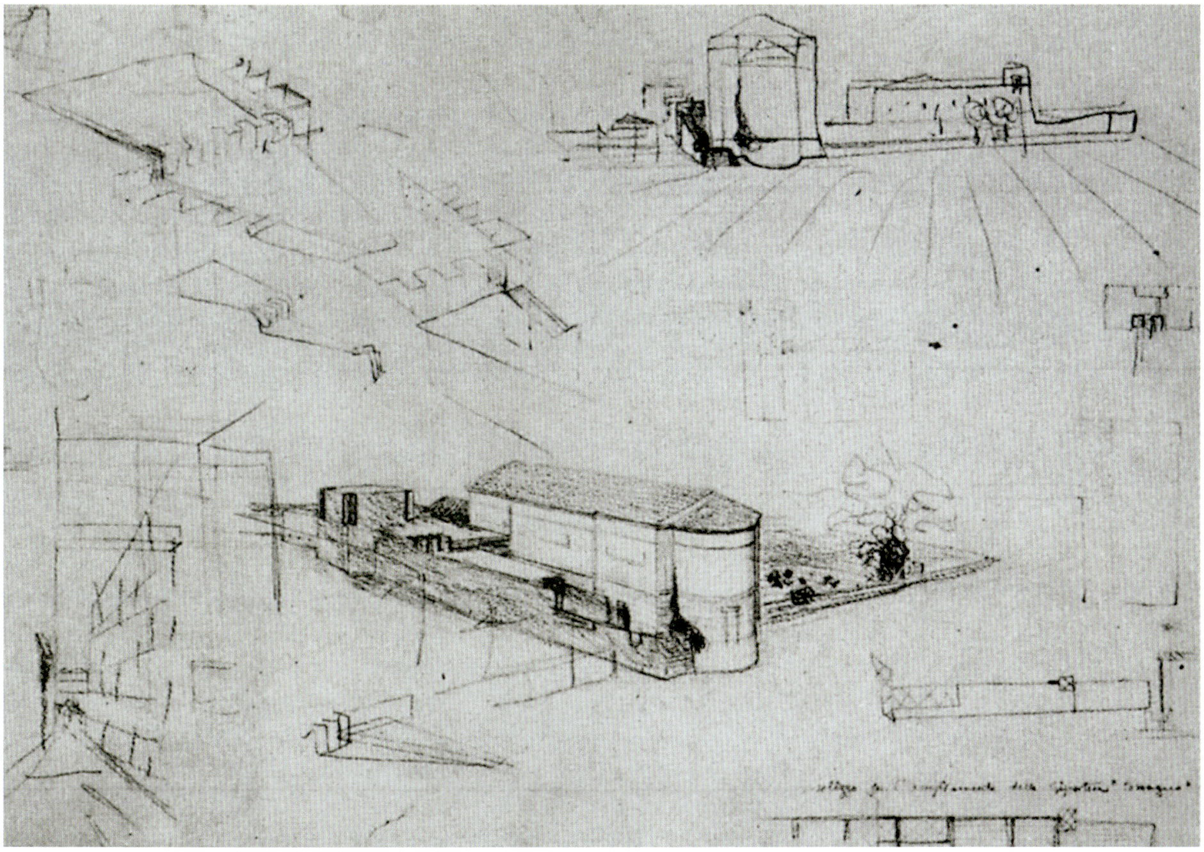

5.1

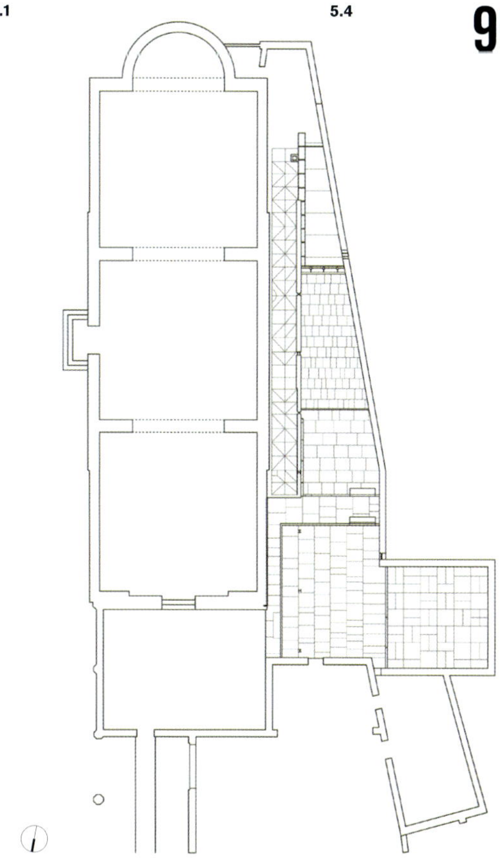

5.4

5.2

5.3

5.1 CARLO SCARPA, GIPSOTECA CANOVIANA ADDITION, POSSAGNO, 1955–7; SKETCHES: AERIAL VIEW (C), CLERESTORY DETAILS (L), EXTERIOR VIEW OF SPACE BETWEEN ADDITION AND THE BASILICA WALL (BL) AND ELEVATION FROM THE VALLEY (TR)

5.2 MUSEO CANOVA, 1822; CANOVA'S PERSONAL STUDIO

5.3 MUSEO CANOVA; ARCHED PORTAL ENTRANCE FROM THE MAIN EAST-WEST ROAD RUNNING THROUGH POSSAGNO

5.4 MUSEO CANOVA AND GIPSOTECA CANOVIANA ADDITION; PLAN (REDRAWN)

5.5

5.6

These three high windows offer sky views while washing the studio's walls and floor with strong even light throughout the day. Only the western wall, through which we entered, and set against the roof, lacks a window. On the eastern wall, a double-wood door, with windows in the upper halves of its panels, opens to hoist large pieces in and out, obviating the need to use the stairs. The room is ringed by built-in, open-backed wooden shelves, revealing the plaster wall behind, on which plaster casts are set. A large worktable stands in the centre of the room, while the northern and southern walls have small square windows, below standing eye level, in front of which are built-in angled drawing tables. These windows look down to the south-facing garden, and to the house's entry court to the north. Sitting on a stool at the table on the southern wall, the drawing before us illuminated by daylight, we are given the most delightful framed view of the valley beyond. Canova made his preparatory sketches at this drawing table, and the studio is where he made his clay model studies, the first steps in his creative process. In the same way that Scarpa carefully studied each museum artefact before designing a place for them, it is clear from the Gipsoteca's final design that Scarpa closely studied this studio and we will find a number of direct references throughout.

The Gipsoteca e Museo Canoviana's arched portal opens off a narrow paved forecourt sitting just below the main east-west road running through Possagno. **(5.3)** Passing through the wide archway, the original horse-drawn carriage entrance, we enter the covered portico and walk down a sloping, smooth-paving slab pathway edged by river-washed stone paving bands. Moving through a second archway we see the house's large gardens opening to the left, through a pair of octagonal columns. At the end of this portico, we pass into the entrance hall through the double door opening on to the portico's central axis. **(5.4)** Standing in this Scarpa-renovated space, it is hard to define precisely where his addition begins; there is no clear demarcation of old and new, entrance and gallery. The entrance hall, which is entered off centre, was made by enclosing the portico's last two bays, its width identical is to the 1836 museum's basilica space. The floor is made of pale-pink and white square stone pavers, set in a 45-degree diamond pattern, and the ceiling has a curved cove between wall and ceiling, marking them as older. **(5.5)** The wall's corners, base and top, and the arched doorway into the old museum, lack trim, forming abstract planes of white plaster, in contrast to the classically ornamented walls and arched openings seen within the basilica-like space. Marbles, plasters and bas-relief panels are displayed in this room, standing on cream-coloured stone bases and cantilevered off the walls on black steel supports; Canova's *Adonis Crowned by Venus* stands centrally, illuminated by rooflights. Ahead, we can see down the vaulted basilica space's central axis, its white and tan-coloured stone floor set in a square and hexagonal pattern, while plasters are formally arrayed on either side of the large arched openings.

To the right, the corner of the room appears to delaminate, opening into a series of layered horizontal and vertical planes, allowing a view to the west into a brightly lit gallery space where we can only see two walls and no ceiling, making it difficult to discern the room's height and width. **(5.6)** On this opening's right side, the gallery's sidewall forms a 90-degree corner with the wall of the entrance hall, and the gallery sidewall's thickness is revealed by the vertical joint opening between them The opening's left side is formed by the basilica building's outer corner, cut back at the top beneath the coved ceiling, to reveal a classical moulding that turns the corner and dies into the thickness of the new plaster wall. Beyond the coved ceiling's base, a plaster ceiling carries 1.8 metres (6 ft) up into the gallery, where it meets an elevated, screen-like wall supported by a white-painted, H-section steel beam at its bottom. The beam is supported by a single, white-painted H-section steel column set away from the right wall. The elevated wall is separated from the thick sidewall on the right by a narrow vertical slot, allowing us to perceive the open space behind. On the left, the elevated wall and beam disappear around the old museum's outer corner. At the floor, a polished, white Clauzetto marble landing-like step runs continuously across this ambiguous opening and around the corner to the left. A low wall, of the same marble, rises from this first step, its top notched above the marble stair tread hovering in front of the low wall. **(5.7)** These horizontal layers of marble flooring and treads seem to levitate off the entrance hall's floor; the horizontal reveals carved into the treads' edges make them appear to be three stacked layers of marble, each the thickness of the floor.

5.5 MUSEO CANOVA AND GIPSOTECA CANOVIANA ADDITION; ENTRANCE HALL WITH VIEW SOUTH THROUGH TO LAZZARI'S VAULTED BASILICA SPACE

5.6 MUSEO CANOVA AND GIPSOTECA CANOVIANA ADDITION; VIEW WEST FROM ENTRANCE HALL THROUGH TO SCARPA'S GALLERIES

5.7 GIPSOTECA CANOVIANA ADDITION; OPENING FROM ENTRANCE HALL WITH VIEW THROUGH TO SPATIAL JOINT BETWEEN FOUR INTERSECTING SPACES

5.7

5.8

5.9

Near the wall to the right, set on a base of two rectangular blocks of light tan-coloured stone separated by a wide joint, is a large, male torso plaster looking into the space to the left, around the corner. Climbing these three stairs, we find ourselves in a spatial joint where four spaces intersect and are woven together. While the four spaces' floors, walls and ceilings are uniformly white, fusing the Gipsoteca into a singular place, they are strikingly different in their spatial characteristics. Behind us is the entrance hall; ahead of us the lower ceiling stops and a taller, vertical space rises beyond, into which bright sunlight pours from unseen sources above; to our left, a long, more dimly lit, low-ceilinged, horizontal gallery space telescopes out to the south, the floor and ceiling stepping down the slope; the space in which we are standing, a narrow, 1.8 metre (6 ft) wide space, defined by the old museum's thick masonry wall to the left, and the new gallery's thinner, steel-framed wall to the right, which continues out through a full-height glass wall to a narrow exterior garden – its floor formed of black and white pebbles set in a triangular pattern, beyond which a view is given through the tree branches and across the valley. **(5.8, 5.9)**

5.8 GIPSOTECA CANOVIANA ADDITION; VIEW FROM HIGH-CEILINGED WESTERN GALLERY TOWARDS THE ENTRANCE HALL AND OLD MUSEUM'S MASONRY WALL

5.9 GIPSOTECA CANOVIANA ADDITION; VIEW FROM SPATIAL JOINT TO THE TOP-LIT, HIGH-CEILINGED WESTERN GALLERY

5.10 GIPSOTECA CANOVIANA ADDITION; VIEW SOUTH THROUGH THE SOUTHERN GALLERY, WITH FOUR FROSTED CORNER WINDOWS WHERE THE CEILING STEPS IN SECTION

5.11 GIPSOTECA CANOVIANA ADDITION; VIEW SOUTH FROM THE SPATIAL JOINT ALONG THE INTERIOR TRENCH AND LONG SOUTHERN GALLERY

5.10

5.11

This narrow space, open to, but dramatically different from, the other gallery spaces, is defined by the old museum's smoothly rusticated plaster wall on the left, on to which are mounted bas-reliefs, and the thin elevated wall to the right, the steel beam at its bottom carried on three steel, H-section columns. The columns, rotated 90-degrees with respect to each other, face perpendicular, parallel and then perpendicular to the wall surface, suggesting a subtle rotation of space at this location where the three new gallery spaces interpenetrate with the entrance hall and old museum.[2] Overhead, two sets of four deep grey concrete beams run from the old museum's wall, slightly above the moulding, to the elevated wall; two large rooflights, one placed above each set of concrete beams, illuminate the space and the wall-mounted bas-reliefs. These beams are the only part of the Gipsoteca structural fabric not coloured white. On the floor, the lower, landing-like step carries along the old museum's wall, turning the corner in front of the full-height glass to run across the low stepping gallery, as does the marble curb at the edge of the higher floor on which we stand. Together, these form a narrow, trench-like space along room's two edges, a typical detail in many of Scarpa's buildings whereby the floor and wall are separated, allowing for the *acqua alta*, reminding us that although we are in the foothills, we remain in the Veneto. This reference to seasonal flooding, combined with the rooflights illuminating the old museum's exterior wall, the narrow garden wedged between the two buildings and the distant valley views, allow us to read this space as both being inside and outside. **(5.11)**

This complexly overlapping threshold space is the Gipsoteca's most dynamic spatial joint, and moving through the gallery we find that the tensions generated here are resolved at the terminations of the long, horizontal southern gallery and the tall, vertical western gallery. We first move into the lower, more dimly lit southern gallery, extending to the south, where, on the left, the bed of Canova's plaster *Recumbent Magdalena* is placed on a low, thin stone slab on an iron frame with four feet, hovering only inches from the floor. The floor steps down to subtly divide this long gallery into three terraced planes. The gallery's floor is made of rectangular slabs of white marble of the same length but differing widths, with the aligned joints running north-south at the top level and east-west at the middle and lower levels. The white polished plastered ceiling dramatically steps down at this gallery's exact midpoint, measured from the northern stable wall to the southern vertical glass wall. At this step, in section, four frosted glass wall-ceiling corner windows are opened, pouring pure white light inwards while not allowing views outwards. **(5.10)** Two of the wall-ceiling corner windows are set directly against the sidewalls, so that light washes the wall in a line precisely marking the sun's angle.

5.12

5.12 GIPSOTECA CANOVIANA ADDITION; VIEW NORTH THROUGH THE SOUTHERN GALLERY, WITH THE ENTRANCE HALL AND BASILICA MASONRY WALL (R) AND HIGH-CEILINGED WESTERN GALLERY (L). THE HEADLESS DIRCE PLASTER SITS IN THE FOREGROUND

5.13 GIPSOTECA CANOVIANA ADDITION; CANOVA'S *THREE GRACES* SCULPTURE AT THE END OF THE LONG SOUTHERN GALLERY, WITH A VIEW OUT TO THE POOL

Before reaching the edge of the upper floor level, we see that the tall, vertical gallery's southern wall, to the right, is separated from the horizontal gallery's sidewall by a 30 centimetre (1 ft) wide vertical slot of clear glass running from floor to ceiling, set in a thin, black-steel frame. Through this slot we see the difference between the interior walls, made of white, smooth plaster, mixed with powdered marble, and the exterior walls' grey, rough *graniglia* cement stucco finish. The base, a black steel band that projects slightly forward of the walls on small steel tube spacers and screw housings, separates the walls from the floor and allows us to clearly read the five different levels of floors – these black bases **'outline the space as if by drawn line'**.[3] At the top of this slot window the structural concrete's rough exposed aggregate sits just below the white polished plaster ceiling.

Small, fired-clay figures are held in a series of freestanding cases set along the long gallery's eastern and western sidewalls. Each case is a rectangular glass-walled volume with a wooden bottom, thin wood corner mullions and a butt-glazed top, supported by double, thin black steel bars, bearing on paired feet. These cases become progressively larger, yet also lighter and more transparent as they rise from the floor, culminating in the all-glass top, which the bright light seems to dissolve. We walk down two steps to reach the lower, trench-like level that runs around the gallery to the entrance, and then down two further steps to reach the long gallery's middle level, the floor of which is made of wide, rectangular slabs of polished white marble. (5.12) To the left, a wall of large, wood-framed windows is set on a low marble faced wall, rising to the sidewall's white steel beam. These large wood-framed windows provide a view of the old museum's rusticated plaster wall 1.8 metres (6 ft) away, off which bright yet soft sunlight is bounced into the gallery. Partway into this space, beneath the four wall-ceiling windows, the ceiling steps down to meet the steel beam. At this same point the white plastered wall on the right bends inwards, narrowing the space ahead and transitioning from horizontal to vertical in proportion.

The floor steps down a final time, and we reach the end of the gallery where the plaster of Canova's famous *Three Graces* stands, slightly elevated on a light grey-coloured stone base, allowing us to look up at their faces. This is the Gipsoteca's lowest and most compressed space, and the floor is made of the gallery's smallest and narrowest slabs of polished white marble. (see pp. 96–7) To the left, at the point where the last step meets the wall, the wood-framed glass windows stop and a wall made of square blocks of *pietra tenera*, a white stone from Vicenza, is set into the square frame of the white steel beams and columns, floating just above the white marble floor, which runs up under it. Ten small, square glazed windows are opened in the wall, in an apparently random pattern, like the coloured squares in Klee's gridded watercolours. These apertures allow us to perceive the thickness of the solid stone wall, as well as to see the old museum's exterior wall. This white stone wall, with its scattered squares of light, forms one of two backgrounds against which we view the *Three Graces*, the second being the reflecting pool, extending to the south, surrounded by the sunlit leaves of the trees beyond. This pool which forms the foreground of this, our only view of the surrounding landscape from within the Gipsoteca, reflects the blue sky and bounces the sunlight up off its rippling surface, providing the plaster of the *Three Graces* a shimmering light from below that complements the strong southern light falling through the large window at the end of the room.

5.13

At the end of the room, the marble floor stops and the low curb runs from the shadows beneath the stone wall on the left to the right wall's black steel base. Beyond this curb, a wall of vertical glass panes, held only in vertical steel frames, appears to rise from the reflecting pool and run up past the edge of the ceiling overhead, where they meet matching horizontal rooflights. Scarpa later noted that he had made these windows larger than the longest glass sheets then available, so they are broken by horizontal butt joints, sanded to form a frosted white line, to match the gallery's other materials.[4] Both the white stone and white plaster wall are carried out past the glass wall and along the sides of the wedge-shaped reflecting pool. Standing at the end of this gallery, bathed in the sunshine that illuminates the *Three Graces*, seeing the blue sky overhead and the rippling pattern of the sunlight on the ceiling, reflected from the surface of the pool, we are as much outside as inside. (5.13) The line separating interior and exterior, almost erased in the thin steel and glass joint between, is paradoxically emphasized by the marked difference of the interior's pure white stone and polished plaster and the exterior's mottled, discoloured, eroded surfaces just outside the glass, where they have been subjected to weathering. The placement of what are normally interior finishes on the building's exterior acts to interweave inside and outside; this registration of the weathering and ageing of materials was important to Scarpa as a means of marking the passage of time.

5.14 / 5.15

Turning to walk back up to the taller, brightly lit western gallery, we are presented with a very different view than what we were given as we descended. Moving towards the *Three Graces*, strong light sources punctuated our field of vision, coming from behind the plasters and emphasizing their profiles. Now, with the light coming from behind us, complemented by the strong, even light bouncing off the old museum's wall to the right, we see the plasters illuminated from the front, literally placing them in an entirely new light, emphasizing their richly shadowed surfaces. On the middle level, the headless Dirce plaster reclines on a low stone platform and steel frame, while the small fired-clay figures in the glass-topped cases are bathed in light from above. Stepping on to the top level, we see that the old stables' wall, with a gridded wooden door on the right, pushing slightly into the space ahead. At the left edge, the stables' wall turns and disappears at an angle through a floor-to-ceiling slot, through which we glimpse more plasters on display. To our right, the rooflights in the narrow zone illuminate the bas-reliefs on the old museum's exterior wall, while, to our left, light falls into the tall gallery from above. In fact, in the long terraced gallery behind us, light mostly enters horizontally, while in the three spaces at the northern end, light enters vertically from above. The line of afternoon sunlight that the floor-to-ceiling slot of glass casts across the gallery forms the joint between these two types of light.

Turning left towards the brightest light, we enter the tall vertical gallery, its floor raised one step above the main level, and its ceiling lifting higher than any of the others in the Gipsoteca. This astonishing room, 5.5 metres (18 ft) square in plan with its ceiling 7.3 metres (24 ft) above us, is lit by four remarkable windows at its four upper corners; similar windows to those found in the Veritti dining room, but here set into the corners of a cubic space. Resting in openings cut away from both walls and the roof to form three-sided re-entrant corner apertures, the glazing of the two taller windows, on the full-height western wall, projects into the room, while the glazing of the two smaller, cubic windows, on the raised eastern wall, under which we entered, projects out of the room. **(5.14, 5.16)** Each of the taller western windows has a thin plastered, L-shaped sill-frame set beneath the two walls of glass, which opens at its centre to let the corner of the wall carry up into the light. These windows' inner corner is framed by a double line of thin, vertical, black steel bars, tied together by small paired horizontal steel pieces, with a thin piece of bevelled glass set between the steel verticals. The white plaster L-shapes at the base of these windows merge with the plastered walls, obscuring the window's bottom steel frame, while the steel frame at the top of the window is clearly visible at the ceiling, making the window appear to float in the corner of the room. Each of the cubic eastern windows have a shallow plaster sill that projects in at the two lower edges, undercut to cast a thin line of shadow, the windows' other four sides cut cleanly through the walls and ceiling. Looking through this opening we see only a thin vertical mullion of steel rising at the far corner, while the horizontal top of this glass cube is butt-glazed to the two vertical plates of glass, a detail clearly related to the display cases in the gallery below. The manner in which these two types of windows are detailed makes the taller windows appear to be suspended, hanging from the ceiling, while the cubic windows appear to project, cantilevering up out of the walls. The white polished plaster walls stop just short of the ceiling, separated by a narrow shadowed joint. The white plaster ceiling disappears into this joint and appears to hover above the walls.

With space pushing both in and out, this extraordinary room seems to breathe, and the play of light within is constantly changing, magically marking the passing time. The walls are washed with light from these four apertures at all times of the day, with direct and bounced light forming geometric patterns that are in constant motion, creating the most activated of backgrounds against which to view the plasters. The room's triple light – direct, bounced off the wall, and double-bounced by being reflected off the glass – seems to come from all directions at once. Typical windows opened in the wall's centre, create a strong bright central glare surrounded by dark, shadowed wall, with light falling on to the floor. But, as seen in the Vermeer's paintings, when a window is set against a wall, the light bounces off the wall, washing the wall with light, eliminating glare and spreading the light more evenly through the space. These rectangular windows open the space and pour light into the corners – the places where a space is usually the most solid and dark – allowing the blue of the sky to enter the room from all sides in a totally unprecedented way. Referring to this remarkable effect, in a 1970 interview, Scarpa said, **'The day of the official opening, there was a very fine blue sky; and since the glazing was well polished and very transparent, the sky looked as though it had been sliced into blocks.'** [5] **(5.15)**

5.16

5.14 GIPSOTECA CANOVIANA ADDITION; SMALLER CUBIC WINDOW ON THE RAISED EASTERN WALL OF THE WESTERN GALLERY

5.15 GIPSOTECA CANOVIANA ADDITION; WESTERN GALLERY CEILING, WITH FOUR CORNER WINDOWS

5.16 GIPSOTECA CANOVIANA ADDITION; WESTERN GALLERY WITH TWO INWARDLY PROJECTING, STEEL-FRAMED WINDOWS. CANOVA'S *SLEEPING NYMPH* LIES IN THE FOREGROUND (R), WITH GEORGE WASHINGTON IN ROMAN ATTIRE (L)

5.17

5.18

On our right as we enter the tall gallery, Canova's plaster, *Sleeping Nymph*, lies on her plaster bed, its low, horizontal stone and steel-framed base extending slightly past the step up into the room, effectively joining the two spaces and crossing the threshold with us. The *Sleeping Nymph* is turned towards the right-hand wall, where a plaster Napoleon bust stands on a cantilevered black steel base. To the left, in the room's centre, resting on a pinwheel-in-plan base made of four large slabs of white *pietra tenera* stone, is a plaster of George Washington clothed in a Roman general's attire. The figure of Washington, pen in hand, looks up from his writing and gazes towards the plaster bust of Canova himself, standing on a black steel base projecting from the western wall. **(5.17)** Behind Washington, towards the left corner, the plaster of *Naiads* reclines on her low stone and steel base, while, in the right-hand corner, the plaster of *Amore and Psyche with Butterfly* stands on a cylindrical grey stone base. The plasters are presented in an informal yet dynamic space, replete with multiple overlapping viewpoints, all bathed in a constantly changing natural light coming from every direction. The main cubic gallery, with its inward and outward pushing corner windows, is strikingly similar to Klee's transparent perspectival volumes and floating figures. Here, Scarpa has set up 'conversations' among the plasters, and between the plasters and the visitors, all taking place within an astonishing play of light and shadow.

It is precisely the whiteness of the walls, floors and ceilings that allow the natural light to bring out the soft, warm and fragile nature of the plaster material, as well as the subtly different characters of the individual plasters. It therefore comes as a surprise to learn that when Scarpa began work on the Gipsoteca, the old museum was painted a dark grey to contrast with and set off the white plasters, as was typical at the time. As Scarpa recalled:

> 'When the moment came for me to decide on the colour of the walls I consulted the officials. So, of course, when you have something white, like a plaster cast for example, you would need to use a dark background to make it stand out – it's natural to think this way. Instead, not because I want to argue with traditional reason, but out of a sudden intuition, I thought it would be better to have a white background because in the other gallery, the larger one, they had chosen ash-grey colours … to make the statues stand out. What sort of colour would I have? Black? Impossible, it doesn't reflect at all. Then dark colours, but you have to be careful here because you can't have a completely dark room in order to get a very emphatic and therefore very banal effect. I thought white was best …'[6] **(5.18)**

As its name implies, the Canova Plaster Gallery contains none of Canova's finished marble sculptures, which are housed in the great museums of Europe; rather, it contains plaster works, full size mock-ups made by Canova and used by marble carvers to execute the final product in their remote workshops. Scarpa notes, **'Canova's casts are of two kinds: some are copies and some are true originals; these have the lead stitches that are used for translation into marble.'**[7] Most of these plasters are covered with small lead pins, organized in a three-dimensional grid, to facilitate the transfer of the form to the marble in the workshop. The assistants who made these transfers from plasters to marble blocks left a 'veil', or thin layer of marble on the surface, and Canova did the final marble work, producing the lustrous, translucent, diaphanous finish on the marbles for which he was famous. Scarpa believed the plasters were, if anything, of greater interest than the marble masterpieces for which they served as models. The plasters, with their metal pins and dull, pocked surfaces, made by instruments used to transfer measurements, have all the marks of *making*, of both conception and construction, which were so carefully polished from the final marbles.

Scarpa's display design articulates the difference between these plasters and their marble twins; unlike the 1836 gallery, Scarpa does not place these plasters in a space at all reminiscent of classical galleries. Throughout the three overlapping gallery spaces, Scarpa displays the plaster casts, each on an individually designed pedestal, platform or bracket, as if they were in transition, moving from the studio to the workshop. Several of the pieces occupy two spaces, two floor levels or two walls at once, their simple stone bases made of the same material as the floors and walls, often merging with them. We occupy the space, as do the plasters, and the easy informality of the display allows an entirely different experience than that typical of almost any art gallery. In this it is important to note that the Gipsoteca is an entirely interior experience. In fact, it proves difficult to gain a view of the building's exterior: we can glimpse the vertical gallery rooflights from the stables' courtyard, but the building's exterior can only be seen upon leaving the Canova complex and walking down the narrow lane on the western side. **(5.20)**

5.17 GIPSOTECA CANOVIANA ADDITION; WESTERN GALLERY WITH CANOVA'S *SLEEPING NYMPH* IN THE FOREGROUND AND GEORGE WASHINGTON IN ROMAN ATTIRE BEHIND

5.18 GIPSOTECA CANOVIANA ADDITION; STRONG ANGLED LIGHT ACROSS THE WESTERN GALLERY'S WALL

5.19

5.20

In this project, there are numerous ways in which Scarpa weaves his new design into its historic context, and the most compelling are those that have been least noticed. The most astonishing, because it is the most striking to anyone who visits both Scarpa's gallery and Canova's studio, is the way Scarpa formed the taller gallery, the western-most space in the complex, as an intentional echo of Canova's studio, the eastern-most space. In fact, they form a precise point and counter-point, a dialogue between the studio, the place of initial creative conception, and the gallery, the place of display of the fabricated products of that conception. Both rooms are vertical, tower-like volumes set at the high points of their respective parts of the overall complex, and the two rooms share dimensions – precisely. Canova's studio is 5.5 x 7.3 metres (18 x 24 ft) in plan (a Palladian proportion of 3 to 4), and is 5.5 metres (18 ft) tall. Scarpa's gallery is 5.5 x 5.5 metres (18 x 18 ft) in plan, and 7.3 metres (24 ft) tall, so that besides sharing its Palladian proportions, the gallery is, quite literally, Canova's studio tilted up on its end. Both rooms display the plasters against a white plaster wall, directly in Scarpa's Gipsoteca and through the open-backed wooden shelves in Canova's studio. Most remarkable is the reciprocal relation between the two rooms' windows, for while both rooms share the highly unusual feature of having their windows set at the very top of their walls, against the ceiling, those in the gallery are set in the four corners, while the studio's are set in the very centre of each wall. In this way, Scarpa overcomes the physical separation of his addition from the Canova house and studio, caused by the 1836 museum, and joins the two parts, old and new, through our experience of their two principal spaces. **(5.19)**

5.19 GIPSOTECA CANOVIANA ADDITION; EXTERIOR DETAIL OF ONE OF THE INWARDLY PROJECTING WESTERN GALLERY WINDOWS

5.20 GIPSOTECA CANOVIANA ADDITION; EXTERIOR VIEW OF THE SOUTHERN FACADES OF SCARPA'S MUSEUM ADDITIONS. CANOVA'S *THREE GRACES* IS VISIBLE THROUGH THE FULL-HEIGHT GLAZING AT THE END OF THE SOUTHERN GALLERY

CHAPTER 06

GIVING PRESENCE TO THE ELEMENTS

olivetti

OLIVETTI SHOWROOM
PIAZZA SAN MARCO, VENICE, 1957–1958

In the 1950s and 1960s, the Olivetti Company was one of the world's leading industrial design firms, perhaps best known for the high-quality design of their typewriters. The company's founder, Adriano Olivetti, created the Olivetti Prize in the early 1950s to recognize design excellence in architecture. In 1956, at the urging of Bruno Zevi, Scarpa received this prize, and the next year Olivetti hired him to design their new showroom on Piazza San Marco, Venice's most important public space. The corner site's narrow front opened on to the ground floor portico of the Procuratie Vecchie on the piazza's northern side across from the Correr Museum's windows; its longer side ran along the Sottoportico del Cavalletto, a passageway running under the building's first floor leading to a bridge over the Rio del Cavalletto canal. This site is perhaps the most severely circumscribed context in which Scarpa ever worked, embedded in both the most important fabric of the historical city and a popular tourist site. Yet, like Michelangelo, who apparently was unable to conceive a statue's form before seeing the stone block from which it was to be carved, Scarpa believed that the freedom to make form and space only came from the imposition of strict limitations. Nearly all Scarpa's designs were made for complex, densely layered historical contexts, yet, rather than making the design more difficult, he paradoxically believed the opposite to be true, **'When the context is fixed, perhaps it makes the work easier.'** [1]

A former shop, this new showroom had two south-facing bays on the Piazza San Marco, beneath the portico's vaulted ceiling; two large western bays opening under the *sottoportico's* vaulted ceiling and, further north, an arched entryway flanked by two narrower windows also facing the *sottoportico*, which opens to the sky in this middle section. This space was 21 metres (68 ft) long and 5 metres (16 ft) wide at the front and narrower in the rear third where the *sottoportico* bent to the right; at 4 metres (13 ft) tall, it was not quite tall enough to fit two full floors. **(6.1)** The initial work, once the previous shop's nonbearing walls and fittings were removed, involved reinforcing the structure supporting the floor above, undertaken with the assistance of Scarpa's lifelong collaborator, the engineer Carlo Maschietto.The bottom flanges of the new double steel beams embedded in the ceiling are clearly legible in the completed project.

Scarpa's unparalleled ability to create a generous sense of space within the tightest confines is demonstrated by his making an open mezzanine at the 4 metre (13 ft) tall space's midpoint, almost doubling the floor area while still allowing the space to be experienced as a single room. Scarpa closed the Sottoportico del Cavalletto facade's central arched entryway, and recessed the showroom's entrance in the right bay facing the Piazza San Marco, so that one enters into the narrow end of the long space rather than at the centre of the long side. This presented the problem of where to place the stairs, as Scarpa noted:

> **'You had to go to the floor above; there were spaces you could not change, a central pillar, two windows – where should the stairs go? I decided to put it wherever I could gain elbowroom. I even had to violate things; by putting it in the most difficult point, I could throw something out – and I was interested in getting rid of things. In this way I could make better use of the length. Once the problem is grasped you get to work ... Things come to me slowly, if there is something to start me off. The conclusion should be to find rational, inescapable reasons, which, however, have nothing to do with rationalism and functionalism. It is a really expensive staircase, but Olivetti can afford it ... And then the theme was "A visiting card in Piazza San Marco".'** [2]

As we approach through the Procuratie Vecchie's historical colonnade, the largely glass showroom wall, turning the corner into the *sottoportico*, does not, at first glance, stand out from its neighbours. The three large, square glass windows, running from the base to the beam between the original stone piers, allow us an unobstructed view into the showroom, and we perceive its unusual depth. On the longer side, beneath each of the two large windows, a low concrete base, with exposed pebble aggregate, rises from the stone pavement supporting an Istrian stone band aligning with the top of the base of the piers on either side. Above the windows, a teak board runs between the columns, overlapping the original stone beam. On the teak band's right end, at the arcades' corner, the company name appears in brass, the individual letters attached over a double horizontal band of black ebony countersunk into the teak band. Designed by Scarpa for this project, the Olivetti signs' lowercase lettering style was subsequently adopted by the company and used on all its literature and signage. **(6.2)**

6.1

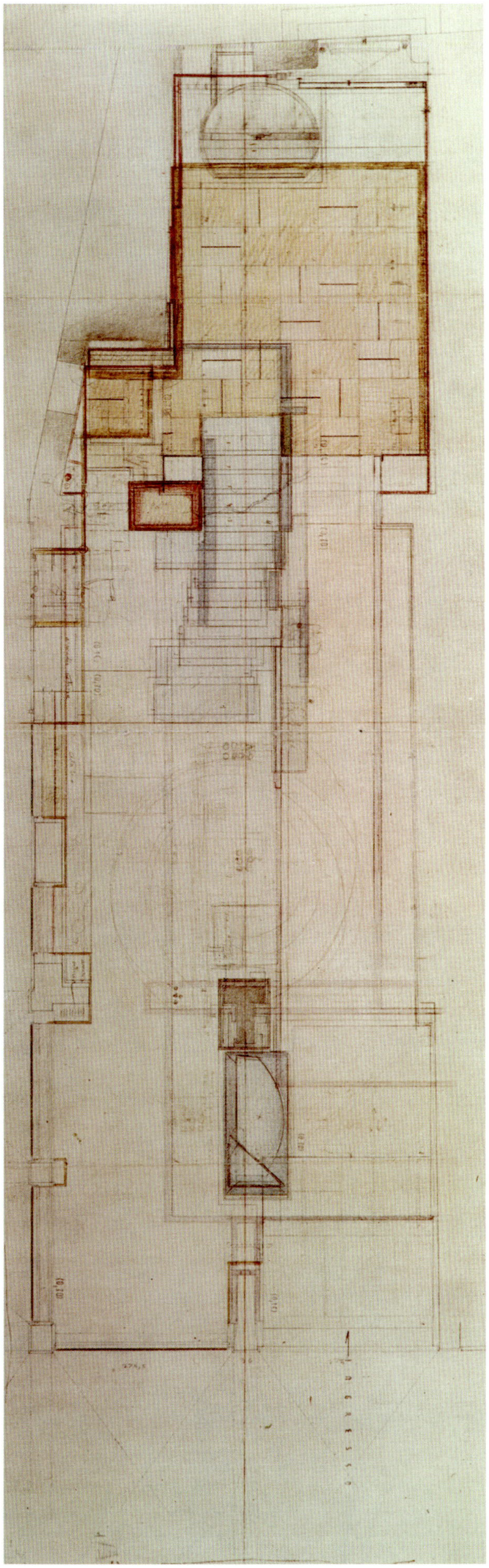

Above the beam, the original classical moulding runs between the pier capitals, while beneath the vaulted ceiling, solid plaster walls fill in the arcade's arches. Running floor to ceiling, the two large windows are held in brass frames, the chamfered edge of the 14 millimetre (0.55 in) thick glass sits just forward of the frames' front face. The edge sections of the window frames interlock with the corners, bevelled at 45-degree angles, connected by pairs of steel fasteners with small soldered cylindrical caps covering their heads. Looking through the glass, we see that the brass frames are secured to the piers by pairs of exposed clips made of small brass bars and cylindrical steel pins.

Beyond the third stone pier, at the point where the *sottoportico's* roof opens to the sky, the pre-existing openings become increasingly altered. Above the classical moulding, the central, semicircular arched opening and the two adjacent rectangular openings have been closed, with solid plaster surfaces recessed just inside the original stone frames. These stone frames' regular rhythm registers the changes that have occurred on the wall beneath. Below the moulding, the teak band runs continuously across, its sections joined and secured to the wall by double pairs of steel fasteners covered by ebony dowel caps. Beneath the teak band, Istrian stone panels clad the wall; the majority are smooth-faced with small recessed edge bands. A vertical, full-height window opens on the far right, and a smaller, square window sits below the central arch's right edge, in what was the original doorway. **(see pp. 112–3)** Both windows have the same brass frames as the larger windows at the front. Below the square window, on its centreline, two stone panels meet at an open joint, as if pulled apart, revealing a roughly textured recessed band. This, combined with the fact that the two panels are of slightly different heights and lifted off the sloping pavement, reveals that the Istrian stone panels are a thin, skin-like cladding, rather than full-depth masonry.

To the square window's left, the facade is entirely solid, made of rectangular slabs of various-sized Istrian stone. Equal in size, the complexly carved Istrian stone panel on the square window's left side has a roughly textured field crossed by thin vertical and horizontal smooth-faced bands. A wide, horizontal, smooth-faced band carries the Scarpa-designed Olivetti name, the letters projecting well forward of the other stone panels. To the left of this panel, the square, spiral Olivetti logo is carved into two Istrian stone panels, with gold leaf pressed into its recessed surface. The three Istrian stone panels at the wall's left-hand edge make an irregular, seemingly unfinished edge at the point where the *sottoportico* angles back, its vaulted ceiling returns, and the classical mouldings and piers of the ancient building come to a halt. This combines with the facade's various-sized, off-centred windows and stone panels to impart a paradoxical sense of thinness and dynamism, as if the surface is shifting or breaking apart the further it gets from the Piazza.

6.1 CARLO SCARPA, OLIVETTI SHOWROOM, VENICE, 1957–8; COMPOSITE GROUND-FLOOR AND MEZZANINE PLAN, COLOURED PENCIL ON PAPER

6.2 OVERLEAF > OLIVETTI SHOWROOM; VIEW OF THE GLAZED SHOWROOM WALL BENEATH PIAZZA SAN MARCO'S NORTHERN COLONNADE

olive

olivetti

6.3

6.4

The fragmented quality of this stone skin is confirmed in a rather startling way when we discover that the large, vertical Istrian stone panel, its top-right corner carrying part of the gold-leafed spiral logo, is hinged and can be opened as a secondary access and service entrance. In this stone doorway, Scarpa combines a modern transformation of traditional materials with an homage to one of the most ancient buildings in the Venetian lagoon, the Basilica Santa Maria Assunta in Torcello, the windows of which have hinged shutters made of thin stone slabs.

Returning to the front of the showroom in the arcade opening into the Piazza, each of the arched bays beneath the vaulted roof displays a round-topped, wood-framed window projecting 30 centimetres (1 ft) out from the wall, with glass on its front face as well as its sides and bottom. While quite similar to the projecting windows on Scarpa's late Banca Popolare di Verona, these windows were part of the arcade's historically regulated appearance, limiting Scarpa to work only within or behind the pre-existing windows. Beneath these windows, the teak band carries across the showroom's two bays, and at the right hand edge of the glazed bay, the Olivetti name is again set in brass letters.

Through the large front window, we can see that the floor inside is raised, lifted 30 centimetres (1 ft) above Piazza San Marco's paved floor, famous for its regular flooding during *acqua alta*. Above, a low ceiling, formed of teak boards, aligns with the top of the large windows. Just behind these windows, wide teak shelves hover above the finely patterned, polished floor to display Olivetti typewriters. **(6.3)** These display shelves are supported at the front by two thin steel and brass legs that emerge from beneath the wood, angled towards us at 45-degrees, pinning into the angled stone sill beneath the window. The shelves are supported at the back by a single, thin brass rod hanging from the teak ceiling. A rectangular ebony light fixture cantilevers off of the brass rod, placing each typewriter in a bright pool of light.

Located in the right-hand bay facing the Piazza, the entrance can be closed at night by a gate made of thick bands of black steel woven to form a tartan grid; the bands alternate between narrower and wider spacing both horizontally and vertically. **(6.4)** The woven steel bands' intersections, clustered in sets of four, are secured with circular brass fasteners. At the top and bottom, the gate is framed by pairs of black steel sections, while at the hinge points, single black steel sections stand to either side of the two teak vertical posts. Suspended from a steel track with brass outer facing, the gate is hung beneath the ceiling by a U-shaped black steel bracket attached to the track with a large brass pin. The entrance can be opened by folding the gate back and inserting it into a recess in the deep central pier on the left. The entrance vestibule is one step up from the arcade's pavement, and the central section of the Istrian stone tread is slightly raised above the outer edges. The floor of the vestibule is made of narrow Istrian stone slabs, each given a different finish, rough to smooth, and the floor is recessed one step in from the portico's face. Overhead, the teak ceiling's wide boards come out to cover the vestibule; the boards run in the same direction as the Istrian stone slabs underfoot, from the Piazza to the showroom.

When folded, the steel gate's pattern forms the vestibule's left wall; the right wall is made of Istrian stone slabs, set in a pinwheeling pattern, their surfaces smooth except for the rough-faced slab at the lower left. Carved into these stone panels is a recessed square, with carved bands running out to meet the narrow, recessed edge bands to the sides and top; gold leaf is pressed into the square's and bands' inner surfaces. Pieces of teak, faced with brass plate, forming the square spiral Olivetti logo, are set into the square recess, held forward of the stone's surface by steel pins. **(6.5)** The gold-leafed stone has a matte surface, while the brass surface is reflective so that, during the day, the spiral logo catches the light, appearing to float forward of the wall. After dark, the opposite effect is created when the spiral logo is backlit by small neon tubes set behind, and the light glows off the gold-leafed stone beneath.

At the vestibule's inner face, the full height, steel and teak-framed glass doors pivot open, standing away from the walls to either side. Entering, the low teak ceiling gives way to the polished plaster ceiling, rising 4 metres (13 ft) overhead. **(6.6)** Now, the space's three primary elements are immediately made present. The first is the space's remarkable masonry and plaster encasement, largely constituted by the double skin of the plaster panel walls, with their thin vertical inset lights running to the top of the double-height space. The second element is the tessellated, polished terrazzo floor, inlaid with glass mosaic pieces, at the centre of which stands the remarkable staircase, a series of massive suspended stone slabs shifting in and out of alignment as they rise. The stone staircase leads to the third element, the mezzanine floating just above overhead: two narrow, suspended, wood-bottomed and polished plaster-walled volumes running down the space's long outer walls.

The Istrian stone flooring is carried 1 metre (3 ft 3 in) into the showroom to meet a low Istrian stone curb, at the top of which the showroom floor opens out before us. This celebrated floor was made using Scarpa's own unique variation on traditional Venetian terrazzo: a light grey-white cement bed into which rectangular mosaic tesserae of Murano glass paste, of four different colours and sizes, were hand-placed in a pattern of horizontal rows, each alternately shifted with respect to adjacent rows.[3] After setting, the floor surface was ground smooth and polished, and the depth of the lustrous, highly reflective surfaces of the mosaic glass tesserae, as George Ranalli notes, **'make the floor appear to ripple and undulate like moving water.'**[4]

6.3 OLIVETTI SHOWROOM; GROUND-FLOOR SHOWROOM WITH TEAK DISPLAY SHELVES AND FULL-HEIGHT GLAZING. WOODEN GRILLES COVER A RADIATOR SET AGAINST THE PIER BEHIND

6.4 OLIVETTI SHOWROOM; EXTERIOR GATE DETAIL SHOWING THE STEEL GRID, FRAME AND A VERTICAL TEAK POST, SUSPENDED FROM A BRASS-FACED STEEL TRACK AND HUNG BENEATH THE CEILING BY A U-SHAPED BRACKET

6.5

6.5 OLIVETTI SHOWROOM; PINWHEEL OLIVETTI LOGO, FORMED OF REFLECTIVE BRASS AND MATTE GOLD PIECES RECESSED INTO THE VESTIBULE'S ISTRIAN STONE WALL

6.6 OLIVETTI SHOWROOM; VIEW OF GROUND-FLOOR SHOWROOM FROM THE ENTRY VESTIBULE WITH BLACK MARBLE BASIN AND SMALL AURISINA MARBLE FOUNTAIN IN THE LEFT FOREGROUND

6.6

6.7

6.8

Immediately to our left, the curving, gilded bronze surface of Alberto Viani's 1956 statue, *Nudo al Sole*, hovers just above a rectangular basin of black Belgium marble, filled with water. While the statue is reflected in the shallow water's surface, beneath it we can barely discern the curving and triangular forms cut into the basin's bottom. Stepping up on to this open foyer's red mosaic glass tesserae floor, on our left we see a massive rectangular pillar, standing centrally in the space, rising to the ceiling between the two mezzanines. The pillar is clad in vertical slabs of putty-coloured Aurisina marble set, in plan, in a pinwheel pattern around the pillar, the direction alternating with each of the three successive vertical levels of panelling; between each level is a thin horizontal brass joint. The marble slabs hover just above the floor and do not reach the ceiling. The pillar's marble cladding is polished smooth on all faces except one narrow end, which has a rough-hewn, hammered finish. The stone cladding is loosely fitted around the pillar, and each stone panel has a small, square hole, a 'finger-pull', suggesting the stone cladding is able to be opened like cabinetry doors. **(6.8)**

At the thin stone joint between the red and the white mosaic glass tesserae floors, running between the marble-clad pillar's centre and the plaster-panelled wall's first inward step to the right, is a small fountain made of Aurisina marble. The fountain's bevelled edge, sliced apart at its centre by a thin cut, hovers over the end of the Viani sculpture's black marble basin. An 'O', in Scarpa's typeface, and the spiral company logo are carved in shallow relief into the fountain's top face. A keyhole-shaped opening is cut through the fountain's top and its undercut-bevelled edges make the marble surface appear to have no thickness. The keyhole-shaped opening – a central, slightly stretched circle with a slot running back towards the pillar – likely references similar, keyhole-shaped fountains in the pool of the Court of the Myrtles at the Alhambra, Grenada, Spain.

We move forwards beneath the mezzanine's low teak ceiling, set away from the full-height wall to the right. Above a concrete base, this wall is formed of vertical, white polished-plaster panels, with thin teak edge-bands at top and bottom. At their sides, the panels are separated by vertical, teak edge-bands set flush with the plaster's front face and then stepping back. Recessed between the pairs of teak edge-bands are thin brass plates, secured to the frame behind by pairs of brass screws. Between some of the plaster wall panels, single or double vertical electric lights are inset with frosted glass faceplates covering recessed fluorescent bulbs. The lights, running from floor to ceiling, are framed in bands of trim boards, alternating light Brazilian rosewood and dark teak wood; at the joints, the edges of the glass and wood are notched at a 45-degree angle to form a V-shape. The glass faceplates' horizontal joints align with the light and dark wood piece joints, and the wood board is secured to the frame behind by pairs of fasteners, their heads covered by ebony caps. Where the lights are paired, they are separated by double wood bands, which alternate colours, both above and below and side to side.

Wrapping the walls and piers of the showroom's two long sides, and the pier next to the staircase, these plaster-panel walls are set forward of the masonry walls behind, stopping short of the floor and ceiling. The loose fit of these new plaster-panel clad walls forms a second inner skin set in front of the masonry and concrete walls and piers. In Venice, the buildings' ground floor walls and piers tend to wick moisture up out of the water-saturated ground. The new inner skin formed by the plaster panels allows the walls to 'breathe' and remain dry by permitting air movement in the airspace between the inner and outer walls, thus removing moisture. **(6.7)**

The mezzanines float above our heads with no immediately discernable supporting elements, the closest one separated from the outer plaster-panelled wall by a narrow slot of space. In fact, the mezzanines are suspended from the ceiling and pinned at the side to the outer walls and marble-clad pillar in the room's centre. At first glance, the mezzanines' matching teak ceilings appear to hover the same distance from the terrazzo floor; but in fact, the mezzanine on the left aligns with the tops of the large windows and is higher than the mezzanine under which we stand. The teak boards running down the mezzanines' outer edges, where the horizontal teak ceiling meets the vertical plaster sidewalls, are angled down at a 45-degree angle, forming a bevelled lip similar to the wood beam detail at the edge of the lowered ceiling running through the Venezuelan Biennale Pavilion's centre.

To our left, beneath the mezzanine's teak ceiling, a concrete pier is clad in teak-edged, white polished-plaster panels. Set into two faces of these plaster panels are wooden grilles, connected with a brass corner clasp, their outer faces finished in white polished plaster, while, on their inner edges, the darker wood is exposed; the two grilles allow heat to escape the radiator set against the pier. Beyond the pier, the square window we saw outside has a radiator set beneath it, covered with a slab of Aurisina marble, into which two offset rows of dentil openings have been cut, projecting and receding squares. This dentil pattern, which is also carved into the planter's marble wall, pressed with gold leaf, is a more precise variation of the floor's offset mosaic glass tesserae pattern.

Beyond this window, the floor steps down, the colour of the tesserae changes to deep blue, and the outer wall, made of interlocked teak panels, conceals the stone door. On the showroom's right side, the mezzanine's teak ceiling meets a slightly lower stone ceiling, the floor steps down and the tesserae changes to yellow. A massive marble planter, a truncated circle in plan, stands in the back corner, behind the staircase. From the canal outside, dim daylight is filtered through a screen running up the back wall's full 4 metre (13 ft) height, made of a densely interlaced, complexly gridded pattern of thin teak and Brazilian rosewood slats.

6.7 OLIVETTI SHOWROOM; GROUND-FLOOR SHOWROOM WITH MARBLE-SLAB STAIRCASE, ALBERTO CAROLO'S SCULPTURE *CRESCITA* IS SET ON TO THE LOW MARBLE WALL AND AN INNER SKIN OF PLASTER PANELS WRAP THE WALLS

6.8 OLIVETTI SHOWROOM; ALBERTO VIANI'S GILDED BRONZE STATUE, *NUDO AL SOLE*, SET ABOVE THE BLACK, BELGIUM MARBLE BASIN

6.9

6.10

The staircase stands at the showroom's centre, pushing its way up between the two mezzanines, and literally dividing the upper level in two. The staircase is made of massive L-shaped slabs of polished Aurisina marble, the thicker blocks set to the back, where recessed concrete bases provide primary support, with the thinner planes projecting forwards as treads. Each identical tread is lifted 5 centimetres (2 in) above the one below, supported only by a deeply recessed, cylindrical brass pin. Approaching the staircase, these small brass cylinders, shining from within the shadows under each cantilevered tread, seem to be their only means of support, yet appear incapable of holding their massive weight. The floating effect this engenders is heightened by the fact that the treads are of differing lengths and are cantilevered varying distances to the staircase's right and left. Standing before the staircase, we notice that the brass cylinders are not placed beneath each stone's centre of gravity, but rather are aligned with the showroom's central axis. The shadowed spaces between the suspended marble slabs allow them to maintain their independence from each other, accentuating the fragmentary nature of the overall composition. This spectacular staircase has rightly been compared to the sculptural staircase designed by Michelangelo at the Laurentian Library in Florence,[5] sharing both its dynamic character and the quality of dominating the small room in which it is set; the staircase can also be related to the neo-Plastic De Stijl sculptural compositions of Rietveld, Vantongerloo and others.

The staircase's dynamic sculptural composition begins at the low marble wall that extends forward on the right, its leading edged notched – the only slab in this composition with this detail. Set on to the top of this low wall, a marble slab cantilevering dramatically to the right, without immediately visible support, forms a low table on to which typewriters are displayed. For a time, this table-like slab also formed the base for the metal sculpture, *Crescita,* by Alberto Carolo, a diamond shape, composed of dozens of cubes, which stood on its point. The first tread is a broad, wide landing hovering above the floor and extending forward and to the left, wrapping around the side of the staircase. The only tread given two brass pin supports, it is composed of two slabs, set one behind the other; its ends turn up into thick curbs at the front right and at the back left. This diagonally inflected first step acts to pull the four steps above it towards the left, so that the entire staircase cascades towards the showroom's glazed outer corner. Above this landing-like tread, the third marble slab projects to the right, resting on the low wall and merging with the table-like slab, while the seventh tread cantilevers dramatically to the left to form a platform floating in front of the plaster-panel clad pillar. **(6.9, 6.10)**

On the staircase's right side, just behind the projecting third tread, are two vertical marble slabs, which are followed by a large, square marble wall-slab. These vertical slabs progressively step outwards from the staircase; the largest slab stops 25 millimetres (1 in) below the edge of the right-hand mezzanine's teak ceiling, with which it aligns. **(6.11)** Climbing the staircase, our eye comes level with the thin slot of space between the marble wall's top and mezzanine's bottom, where a delicate joint connects them. Small black steel pieces are inserted into a carved slot in the top of the marble wall and a brass-lined recess in the mezzanine's edge above; two brass pins lock them together, while also allowing for the wood and stone's differential movement. While this joint helps support the mezzanine's weight and braces the two structures, it draws our attention to the precision of craft required to construct this narrow gap between the stone wall rising from the floor and the wood mezzanine hanging from the ceiling and cantilevered from the wall.

6.9 OLIVETTI SHOWROOM; STONE STAIRCASE, VIEWED FROM ABOVE, SHOWING THE TREADS' SHIFT TO THE SHOWROOM'S OUTER CORNER

6.10 OLIVETTI SHOWROOM; SUSPENDED STONE STAIRCASE, VIEWED FROM THE SIDE

6.11 OLIVETTI SHOWROOM; VIEW OF THE STONE SLABS BORDERING THE STAIRCASE'S RIGHT SIDE AND THROUGH TO THE FULL-HEIGHT GRIDDED SCREEN ALONG THE BACK WALL

6.12 OLIVETTI SHOWROOM; VIEW DOWN THE BRIDGE-LIKE, LEFT-HAND MEZZANINE TOWARDS THE FRONT OF THE SHOWROOM

6.11

6.12

Arriving at the top of the staircase, the same Aurisina marble becomes the floor of the small office at the back of the showroom. Made of square and split-square marble slabs, the latter's joints set in a nonrepeating, rotating pattern, the floor runs out to a low Istrian stone curb. At the back, the teak and Brazilian rosewood screen we saw below rises up, with a double, vertical inset light fixture at its centre. On the back left-hand side of this double-height space, the semi-cylindrical marble planter also rises up from below. The two sidewalls are reciprocally related: the right-hand wall is a series of horizontal bands of white polished plaster, double brass bands, wood panelling and a continuous horizontal inset light fixture, trimmed with teak; the left-hand wall is made of three vertical trimless, white polished-plaster panels stepping inwards, with a double, vertical inset light fixture at the edge closest to us. Both sidewalls stop short of the smooth, polished plaster ceiling.

Turning towards the front of the showroom and the Piazza, the mezzanine directly ahead of us seems to float down the room's left-hand side. **(6.12)** The independence of this lightweight, teak floored and teak veneer-walled, bridge-like volume from the white polished-plaster wall is established by a continuous narrow slot of space and by the wooden handrails running along both the inside, next to the central opening, and along the outside, next to the wall. The vertical, frosted glass-faced, teak-trimmed light fixtures inset into the wall on the left rise from below, while on the outer wall, at the mezzanine to the right, similar light fixtures, only horizontally orientated, run continuously between the piers, their bottoms set at handrail height. The sidewalls' and piers' plaster panels stop short of the polished plaster ceiling, allowing the double steel beams to run across this space. The steel beams are partially embedded into the ceiling and partially encased in concrete, with only the last 25 millimetres (1 in) of the web and the bottom flanges exposed, and, unlike the showroom's other steel elements, they are painted white, matching and merging with the ceiling.

The mezzanine to the left runs out to the marble-clad pillar, where it turns left, providing access to a small room located above the neighbouring shop, while the mezzanine to the right runs to the front wall, where it also turns left, forming the ceiling over the entry vestibule. Stepping on to the left-side mezzanine's teak floor, we hear the wood creak and feel it give at bit as it flexes with our weight – this in marked contrast to the rigid hardness of the solid terrazzo floor and massive marble slabs of the staircase and office landing. The wood floor is set level with the office's marble floor, and the side-walls are of differing heights; the outer wall is lower, with teak display shelves projecting into the narrow space rising from below, while the inner wall is higher, matching the wall height of the other mezzanine, whose floor is two steps higher. At its end, the inner wall bends down at a 45-degree angle, its lower edge matching the height of the outer wall.

In accessing the mezzanine on the right, we move around the plaster-panel clad pier and past a wall of built-in, teak-faced wooden cabinet doors. We then step up on to the teak floor, set between the teak veneer-lined inner wall and the plaster-panelled outer wall, down which runs a continuous horizontal light fixture, banded with teak of alternating colour. Below the light fixture are teak display tables, each supported by a single brass rod leg and anchored to the wall behind. We come alongside the central, marble-clad pillar, where the mezzanine's inside wall has been cut open and a lower wood wall frames a matching opening in the floor. The inside wall's two ends, on either side of the opening, are clad in brass cover plates and caps, wrapping around on to the wall's outer and inner faces, with bevelled corners at the tops, reminiscent of boat detailing. Looking down through the central void of the double-steel beam that emerges from the pillar to support the mezzanine, we see the terrazzo floor below. **(6.13)**

The only readily visible support for each mezzanine is a black, double-steel bar hanger set just inside the left-hand mezzanine wall's inner teak face and just outside the right-hand mezzanine's outer plaster face. These are anchored into the slot between the double-steel beams in the ceiling by intricately interlocking black steel and brass joints, set just above eye level, allowing for close inspection from the mezzanine. The wood caps' details on the mezzanine handrails are similar to the inset light fixtures' wood trim; sections alternate between light Brazilian rosewood and dark teak wood, and the three pieces of wood forming the solid wall cap and handrail are elegantly jointed with T-shaped and L-shaped intersections, secured with fasteners whose countersunk heads are covered with wood dowels in contrasting colours. Standing on the floor of these wood decked, walled and bottomed vessels, grasping the varnished handrails with brass fittings, while suspended above the rippling, water-like floor under the reflective polished-plaster ceiling – in its materials, details and experience, the whole is reminiscent of the traditional Venetian gondolas.

At the far end of the longer, right-hand mezzanine, a brass-edged joint in the floor marks the turn of the mezzanine and the transition in the direction of the teak floorboards, set perpendicular to the nearest outer wall. In the polished-plaster panelled outer walls on either side of the central column, two horizontal, *vesica piscis*-shaped windows overlook the Piazza's arcade. Each wall is divided horizontally at its middle into two plaster panels, with narrow teak edge bands at the ceiling and floor, and a wider double teak edge-band at the middle, divided by a recessed brass band. At each walls' centre the teak banding merges with the *vesica piscis*-shaped aperture's curving teak frame, its edges secured with pairs of wood-capped fasteners above and double pairs below. Vertical teak boards with bevelled top and bottom edges, projecting forward of the teak frame's face, form this aperture's outer edges. The window frames' upper and lower curves match; mimicking, but not aligning with, the round-topped historic window beyond. A set of gridded screens, similar to those at the back wall overlooking the canal, and also made of teak and Brazilian rosewood, can be slid behind the plaster sidewalls, opening and closing the *oculi*, or eye-like apertures, to provide the upper level's only views out. [6] **(6.14)**

While Scarpa's discovery of, fascination with, and engagement of the *vesica piscis* shape has been traced to many different sources, from the mundane, including a Chinese cigarette packet and a small inlaid wood box, to the sacred, Scarpa made this shape, and its generative geometry of two interlocked circles, his own by deploying it in almost all his works. Late in life, when an assistant inquired about the meaning of the *vesica piscis* form for Scarpa, he replied, enigmatically, **'It is the leit-motif of my life'.** [7] It can also be argued that this form, like so many other things, came to Scarpa from Palladio. Kurt Forster noted that the portico's double columns in the Palazzo Chiericati in Vicenza, where Scarpa played as a child, form an interlocked double circle in plan, their overlapped solid forming a *vesica piscis.* [8] As Kenneth Frampton noted, **'While the interlocking version of this icon is reminiscent of the oriental yin-yang symbol, it also represents the opposition between solar universality and lunar empiricism',** [9] to which may be added the archetypal and the sensible, unchanging and changing, unification and pluralism – all resolved within the overlapping *vesica piscis* as balance, proportionality and mediation. Late in life, Scarpa said he became aware of the important part this *vesica piscis* form, and its generative two overlapping circles, played in the work of baroque architects, in particular the oval churches of Francesco Borromini, whose *vesica piscis* shapes were structured by a *mandola* geometry of two facing equilateral triangles, which Scarpa felt to be its purest expression. [10] It is also intriguing to note that the late baroque architect Guarino Guarini, whose work was closely related to that of Borromini, built Santa Maria d'Aracoeli, an oval church whose plan is generated by overlapping circles, in Vicenza in 1680.

Scarpa also had an equally strong fascination with, and use of, the double figure, particularly the number 11. As Marco Frascari wrote, **'The understanding of the peculiarity of the usage of eleven in Scarpa's architecture must begin with the consideration of two Byzantine occurrences. On the one hand, there is the bizarre fact that a total of eleven letters composes the name ... Carlo Scarpa. On the other hand, in the Italian tradition of construction, the thickness of a standard hollow tile partition wall is approximately 11 cm.'** [11] This can only be called a creative obsession on Scarpa's part; he endeavoured to apply the double, and the possible variations of the number 11, to every aspect of his work, most notably in the numerous double forms – particularly the double column, which reads as a literal figure '11', and the employment of 11 centimetres as a module of measurement. This involved: the division of 11 in half to produce 5.5; the multiples of 11: 22, 33, 44, 55, 66, 77, 88, 99; and larger dimensions such as 15 x 11, equalling 165. Scarpa, whose two names are made of five and six letters, employed dimensions such as 56 centimetres and 65 centimetres as variations on this general theme. One of many examples can be seen in the design for the three wood rails that cross the 1974–6 Memorial to the Victims of the Terrorist Massacre in Piazza della Loggia, Brescia, where Scarpa made double vertical steel end posts, forming the figure '11'. Cantilevered off each one is a small stainless steel arm, from which is hung a double brass connector, joined by double steel pins, carrying three cylindrical wooden rails, measuring 33, 44 and 55 millimetres in diameter, respectively. **(6.15)**

6.13

6.14

6.13 OLIVETTI SHOWROOM; VIEW DOWN THE RIGHT-HAND MEZZANINE, FROM THE FRONT OF THE SHOWROOM WITH THE BRASS-CAPPED OPENING ALONG THE RIGHT WALL IN LINE WITH THE CENTRAL PILLAR

6.14 OLIVETTI SHOWROOM; A BLACK, DOUBLE-STEEL BAR HANGER SUPPORTS THE RIGHT-HAND MEZZANINE, AS SEEN IN FRONT OF TWO *VESICA PISCIS*-SHAPED WINDOWS

6.15

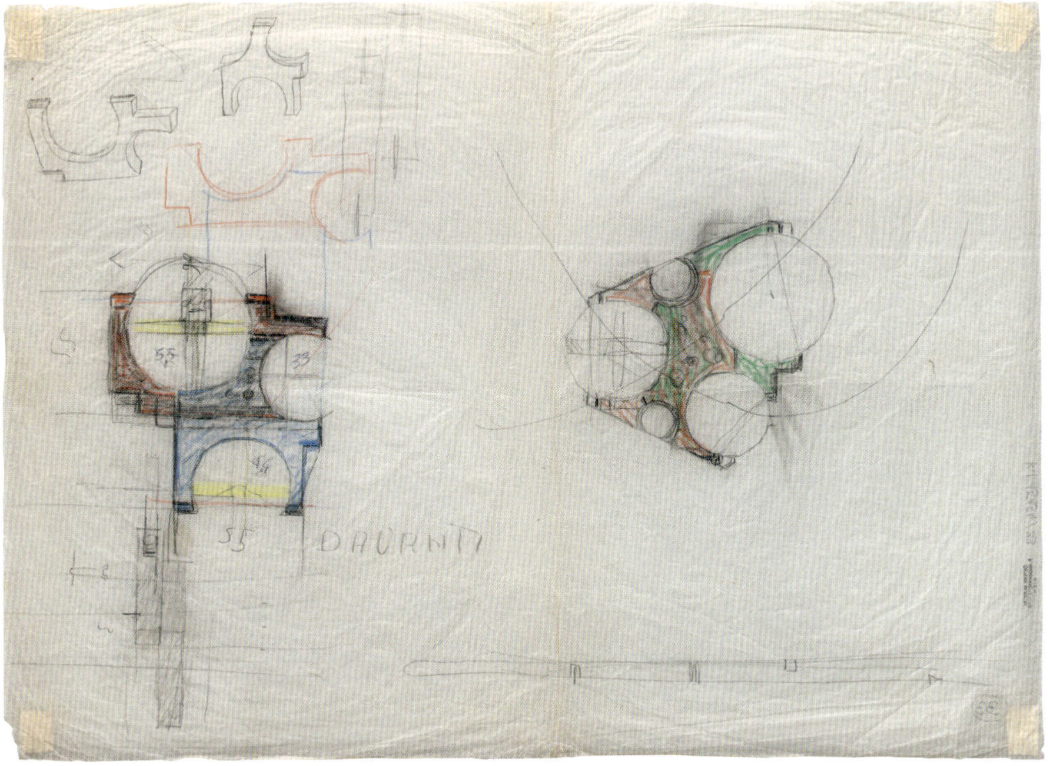

6.15 CARLO SCARPA, MEMORIAL TO THE VICTIMS OF THE TERRORIST MASSACRE, BRESCIA, 1974–6; DETAIL SECTION OF THE BRASS CONNECTOR HOLDING THREE CYLINDRICAL WOODEN RAILS, GRAPHITE AND COLOURED PENCIL ON TRACING PAPER, 32.5 X 45 CM (12.75 X 17.75 IN)

6.16 CARLO SCARPA, MANLIO CAPITOLO COURTROOM, VENICE, 1955–7; MAHOGANY-VENEER PLYWOOD WALL AND DOOR SET FORWARD FROM THE OLD WHITE PLASTER WALL

6.17 MANLIO CAPITOLO COURTROOM; MAHOGANY-VENEER VERTICAL PLYWOOD PANEL WALLS FRAME THE SEMI-CIRCULAR MAHOGANY MAGISTRATES'S BENCH, TWIN MAHOGANY LAWYERS' BENCHES AND ASYMMETRICAL MAHOGANY-VENEER PLYWOOD PUBLIC SEATS

6.18 CARLO SCARPA, 'VITALITY OF ART' EXHIBITION, PALAZZO GRASSI, VENICE, 1959

6.19 CARLO SCARPA, FRANK LLOYD WRIGHT EXHIBITION, 12TH TRIENNALE, MILAN, 1960

6.16 / 6.17

6.18

6.19

Among Scarpa's other works from this period, the 1955–7 Manlio Capitolo courtroom, built for the Tribunale of Venice, is particularly noteworthy. Located on the second floor of the sixteenth-century Fabbriche Vecchie, overlooking the Rialto market, the courtroom's entrance is at the intersection of two wide hallways. The new door is part of a square, mahogany-veneer plywood wall set forward of the old building's white plaster wall. **(6.16)** This wood wall is divided vertically into three unequal panels, the largest, at the centre, being the door, its midpoint divided by a horizontal joint, below which a rectangular window offers interior views. At the wood wall's geometric centre, a double-steel bar post runs from floor to just below the ceiling and the door pivots open when the steel handle on the right edge is pushed. Mahogany-veneer vertical plywood panels line the small courtroom's front wall and half of both sidewalls, stopping short of the polished plaster ceiling to expose the polished plaster walls, and are secured to the frame behind by copper nails set in vertical rows 11 centimetres (4.25 in) apart. **(6.17)** The courtroom's rear wall and the back half of the sidewalls are faced in red-brown polished plaster, complementing the mahogany. The room's front corners are bevelled at a 45-degree angle, while a T-shaped notch houses a double-steel bar truncated cross, painted deep red, in the wall at the front. In the right corner, a Greek marble plaque is held in a steel frame, secured to the wall with brass pins. Three rectangular ceiling lights, partially recessed and partly projected, each a double square with frosted glass fronts and red-painted steel surrounds, are set in a T-shaped formation.

The semicircular, mahogany magistrates' bench is placed at the room's end on a wooden floor, raised above the red Veronese marble courtroom floor. This bench has an elevated table top, beneath which the solid cabinetry takes a slightly different shape. The bench's central, three-quarter cylinder is formed by a thin layer of the mahogany veneer panelling, which folds to become straight, extends towards the door, and aligns with the central aisle. This keyhole-shaped space allows people to approach the bench for *sotto voce* conversations. For the lawyers, twin mahogany benches are set to either side of the central aisle, each with double table tops elevated above the main cabinet. The public's asymmetrical seats are each made of three pieces of bent-formed mahogany veneer plywood, with curved corners and bright yellow-stained edges. The three parts are made up of: a single piece that makes the low left side, rises up to form the taller back and turns the corner to form the equally tall right side; a gently upward-curved square seat; and a T-shaped piece that is folded across the right side's top to form the writing table and arm. The effect of the whole space, and its furnishings' remarkable craftsmanship, is at once intimate and dignified, imparting a deep respect for the traditions represented by the institution.

'By strange coincidence, Scarpa worked on this courtroom in the same period he was appearing in it as defendant, having been accused of exercising his profession without qualification', as Beltramini and Zannier noted.[12] Following his receiving the Olivetti Prize, the Venice Order of Architects charged Scarpa with not holding a license to practise architecture. Other architects brought charges against Scarpa based on the fact that his Royal Academy of Fine Arts degree was in architectural drawing. The lawsuits were eventually settled in Scarpa's favour, but after this experience he understandably remained embittered towards the profession.

In the 1959 'Vitality of Art' exhibition in Venice's Palazzo Grassi, Scarpa presented sculptures on elevated floors and platforms, with spaces divided by large diaphanous screen walls, all set beneath hovering ceilings. **(6.18)** This created a layered composition that flowed through and around the existing spaces and walls of the Palazzo Grassi, transforming the massive building's spaces into a series of floating coloured planes. The exhibition's entrance occurred beneath a lowered, gold-leafed ceiling plane. For the 1960 Frank Lloyd Wright Exhibition at the 12th Triennale in Milan, the year after Wright's death, Scarpa created a series of hovering and interwoven walls, all organized beneath a tent-like ceiling made of white drapery fabric hanging from the ceiling and wrapping beneath a thin frame set just above the display panels' tops. At the exhibition's entrance, Scarpa placed a floating, backlit wall with a large semicircular opening, a similar shape to Scarpa's roof forms in the 1952 Biennale Courtyard. **(6.19)**

GAVINA SHOWROOM
BOLOGNA, 1961–1963

6.20

The Gavina Showroom was built into the ground floor of a three-storey structure on via Altabella in Bologna. An entirely new facade, made of one massive concrete slab, was placed across the entire shop's width. **(6.23)** Hovering just above the pavement, this concrete wall, its four corners cut at 45-degree angles, projects slightly forward of the old wall into which it is set. Cast in horizontal board-formed concrete, its surface has been chiselled to remove its wood-grain pattern. At the centre, the inverted L-shaped open entryway has three smooth-faced, gold leaf-pressed recessed bands running from its corners to the left edge, to the top and to the concrete wall's right-hand edge. These recessed bands terminate in tube-like brass pieces in the shape of three-quarter squares with a corner removed; cast into the concrete they form small openings at the doorway's corners. The wider band on the left has the Gavina name cast in slightly projecting letters. The concrete facade's three openings occur at the points where the original apertures existed, but have been entirely reworked. The right side's large, circular window dips below the floor line inside, while, on the left, two large circles interlock. Both windows have their curved, plate-glass sheets set flush with the wall's outer face, pressed against the steel frames inside by brass and steel clips, carrying the form of two interlocked cylinders.

The entryway gate is made of a series of vertical, cylindrical, turned walnut rods with brass caps, joined by horizontal, collar-like steel sections, and it stands above a single elevated concrete step projecting out from the building's face. Stepping up into the entrance, large floor-to-ceiling windows reveal the shop's interior, its glass set in thin steel frames, clad with vertical, multicoloured hardwood bands. The entryway's cage-like frame stops just short of the plaster ceiling above, returning over our heads to meet the front facade. At the small vestibule's right end is the Japanese spruce and padouk wood entrance door into which two pieces of glass are set, each with a square end at the top and bottom, respectively, and a semi-circular curved end set at the door's centre, forming an H-shape with an inward-curving horizontal midsection. **(6.20)**

The shop's main space is roughly a square in plan, with two arms extending to the left around the projecting escape staircase, and a small office space in the upper right corner. **(6.21)** Four structural pillars are scattered in an irregular pattern through the interior, to which Scarpa added a fifth pillar and made them all massive rectangular blocks, so that the pillars merge with each other and the surrounding walls to create a complexly layered space. **(6.22)** Two of the pillars are faced in hammered concrete, one in cobalt-blue polished plaster, one in white polished plaster mixed with silver foil and the nonstructural pier is faced in glossy-black plastic laminate panels mounted on particle board, with teak banding secured by double brass pins. **(6.24)** Two sets of interlocked double cylindrical wood-lined holes, one with the cylinders set side-by-side and one with the cylinders stacked one above the other, pass all the way through the depth of this pillar, forming an opening in each face. The golden-coloured plaster ceiling is sculpted into projecting and receding rectangular masses that do not align with the pillars' edges, and the brown tile floor is spaced away from the white, limewashed plaster walls and pillars by a recessed white stone gutter-like band.

The office, concealed behind a wall, opens into the main shop space through a narrow, full-height slot at the back corner, as well as by a small horizontal eye-level opening with inward-bevelling wood edges and a large clerestory opening at the top, given an L-shaped wooden frame made of narrow bands of different coloured hardwoods. **(6.25)** Behind the street-facing, double-circle window, a dropped ceiling soffit, out of which a large curve has been cut, (like those in the Biennale Courtyard), hovers above a similarly curved, red-polished plaster wall panel and three interlocked teak veneer panels, concealing the service door, which have a three-quarter square brass piece, forming an aperture at their intersection. **(6.26)** In the left back corner is a concrete-walled pool and fountain; the red stone slab's scalloped opening discharges water from the upper to the lower pool, both triangle-shaped. This stepped pool stands on the floor beneath a square, deeply recessed rooflight, which is framed in thin hardwood bands. On the back wall and partway around the corner on to the sidewall, a square, multicoloured vitreous tile mosaic, designed by Scarpa and made by Mario De Luigi, is set in an irregular stepping shape against the plaster wall, the inside corners enlarged by three-quarter square cut-outs. **(6.27)**

The experience of this thick-walled, carved-out space of the Gavina Showroom, its small entrance cut through the massive concrete facade and its interior filled with large pillar blocks standing beneath the rising and falling ceiling volumes, could not be more different from the thin, floating, layered experience of the Olivetti Showroom; clearly indicating the difference between the deeply shadowed, regular rhythm of Bologna's arcaded streets and the shimmering, reflective surfaces of the labyrinthine Venetian canals.

6.21

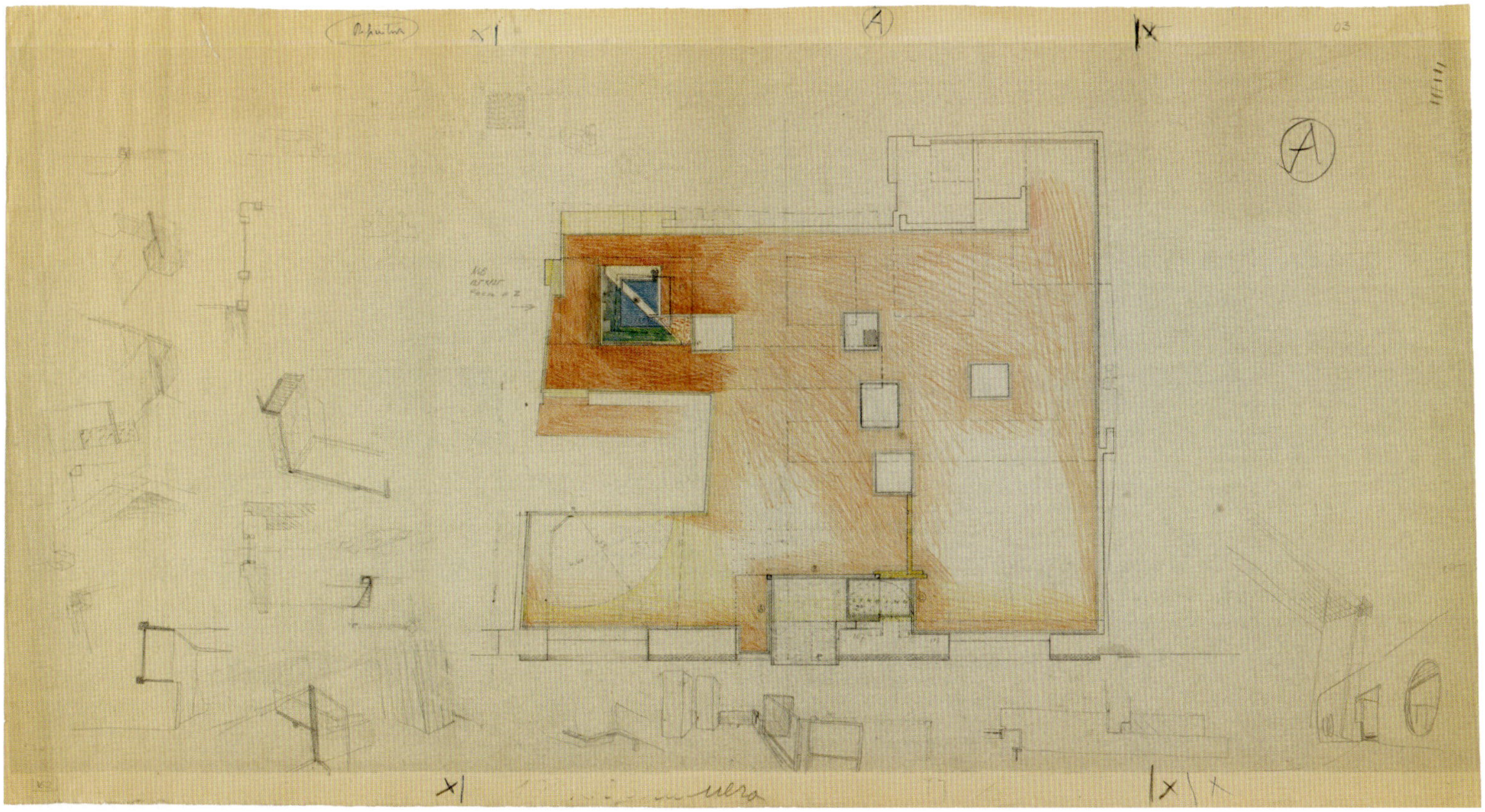

6.22

6.20 GAVINA SHOWROOM; ENTRANCE VESTIBULE WITH VERTICAL WALNUT-ROD GATE AND SPRUCE AND PADOUK WOOD DOOR

6.21 GAVINA SHOWROOM; PLAN, GRAPHITE ON PAPER

6.22 GAVINA SHOWROOM; VIEW ACROSS CENTRAL INTERIOR, THROUGH FIVE PIERS, FROM THE PROJECTING ESCAPE STAIRCASE

6.23 OVERLEAF > CARLO SCARPA, GAVINA SHOWROOM, BOLOGNA, 1961–3; STREET FACADE FROM VIA ALTABELLA

6.23

6.24

6.26

6.25

6.24 GAVINA SHOWROOM; DETAIL OF THE NONSTRUCTURAL PIER FACED IN BLACK PLASTIC LAMINATE WITH DEEP, DOUBLE-CIRCLE HOLES AND TEAK BANDING

6.25 GAVINA SHOWROOM; BACK WALL OF THE MAIN INTERIOR SPACE CONCEALING THE OFFICE, WHICH IS VISIBLE THROUGH THE FULL-HEIGHT SLOT, HORIZONTAL EYE-LEVEL OPENING AND A LARGE CLERESTORY OPENING

6.26 GAVINA SHOWROOM; VIEW INTO SPACE BEHIND DOUBLE-CIRCLE WINDOW, CURVED SOFFIT AND WALL PANEL, WITH TEAK VENEER PANELS CONCEALING THE SERVICE DOOR

6.27 GAVINA SHOWROOM; CONCRETE-WALLED POOL AND FOUNTAIN WITH MULTICOLOURED VITREOUS TILE MOSAIC

6.27

CHAPTER 07

WORKING WITH TRACES OF THE PAST AND EXPECTATIONS OF FUTURE MEANING

CASTELVECCHIO MUSEUM RENOVATIONS
VERONA, 1957–1975

7.1

Scarpa was commissioned to work on the Castelvecchio Museum in 1957 by the museum's new director, the art historian Licisco Magagnato, beginning with the installation of the 'From Altichiero to Pisanello' exhibition. As Magagnato recalled, the Castelvecchio designs were conceived **'by Scarpa right from the start as a radical restoration of the castle.'**[1] Verona's Castelvecchio, or old castle, divided by a twelfth-century city wall when the city was a free republic, or Commune, was enlarged to its present dimensions in 1354 to serve as the palace, Reggia, and the protective fortress of the ruling nobility, the Scaligeri family. Located on the Adige River's southern bank, the castle walls and battlements were turned to face the city, as it was not intended as a place of refuge for Verona's citizens, but for the Scaligeri during popular uprisings. The Reggia lies to the west, with the castle battlements to the east, originally creating a large garden or courtyard opening to the river. Between them is the Torre del Mastio and, built along the medieval Commune city wall, the fortified bridge crossing to the Adige's northern side, where the territory was controlled by Scaligeri's allies. The eponymous bridge was the Scaligeri escape route in case of insurrection by the city's populous.

From 1802–6, during the Napoleonic occupation of Venice and Verona, the French built a thick defensive wall along the castle courtyard's northern side, at the river's edge, with bevelled slot openings for guns aimed at the Austrian forces occupying the other side. Additionally, barracks for the French troops were built behind this new riverfront wall and along the courtyard's eastern side; a staircase leading to the top of the battlements was built on the courtyard's western side, against the Commune wall. In 1923, Antonio Avena, the director of Verona's art museums, persuaded the municipal leaders to bring the city's collections together into one central museum in the Castelvecchio. From 1924–6, with the architect Forlati, Avena 'restored' the Castelvecchio's interior to a Renaissance style, including false wood beamed ceilings. The barracks' facades on the courtyard's northern and eastern sides were reconstructed to form a historical 'mask', the rectangular grid of Napoleonic apertures replaced with symmetrically composed groupings of Venetian Gothic and Renaissance windows salvaged from the Adige flood of 1882. The museum's new entrance was through the three-arched loggia placed centrally on the longer, south-facing facade.[2]

From the beginning Magagnato intended to organize the museum so that the Castelvecchio's historic fabric, in all its complex layers, would be again revealed:

> **'In reality, commissioning Scarpa to design the exhibition installations was a way of deliberately involving him in the restoration of a castle that had suffered from mistreatment; for he was the person who first, instinctively but lucidly, tackled the problem of enabling ancient and modern to coexist in terms of urban planning, and this at the very time when the problems of defending and developing historic Italian inner city areas were being given a basis in theory.'**[3]

Scarpa worked on the Castelvecchio from 1957–75, a long and complex process of many stages, often involving unexpected discoveries of new historical layers, each of which was honoured in the final fabric. Scarpa's approach when making this 'radical restoration of the castle' was at once subtle and aggressive, accepting and working with certain previous renovations, but also removing sections of historical fabric and making modern constructions throughout. The initial and most extensive work was accomplished between 1957 and 1964, when the museum was reopened to the public, with work on the library coming between 1968–9, and the final exhibition space in the sequence, the Avena room, completed in 1973–5. In 1967, Magagnato purchased over 500 drawings made by Scarpa for the Castelvecchio's first phase of work, ostensibly as a way of paying Scarpa's fee. This trove of drawings, though not dated or definitively ordered, offers unusual insight into Scarpa's design process over its seven-year construction period.[4]

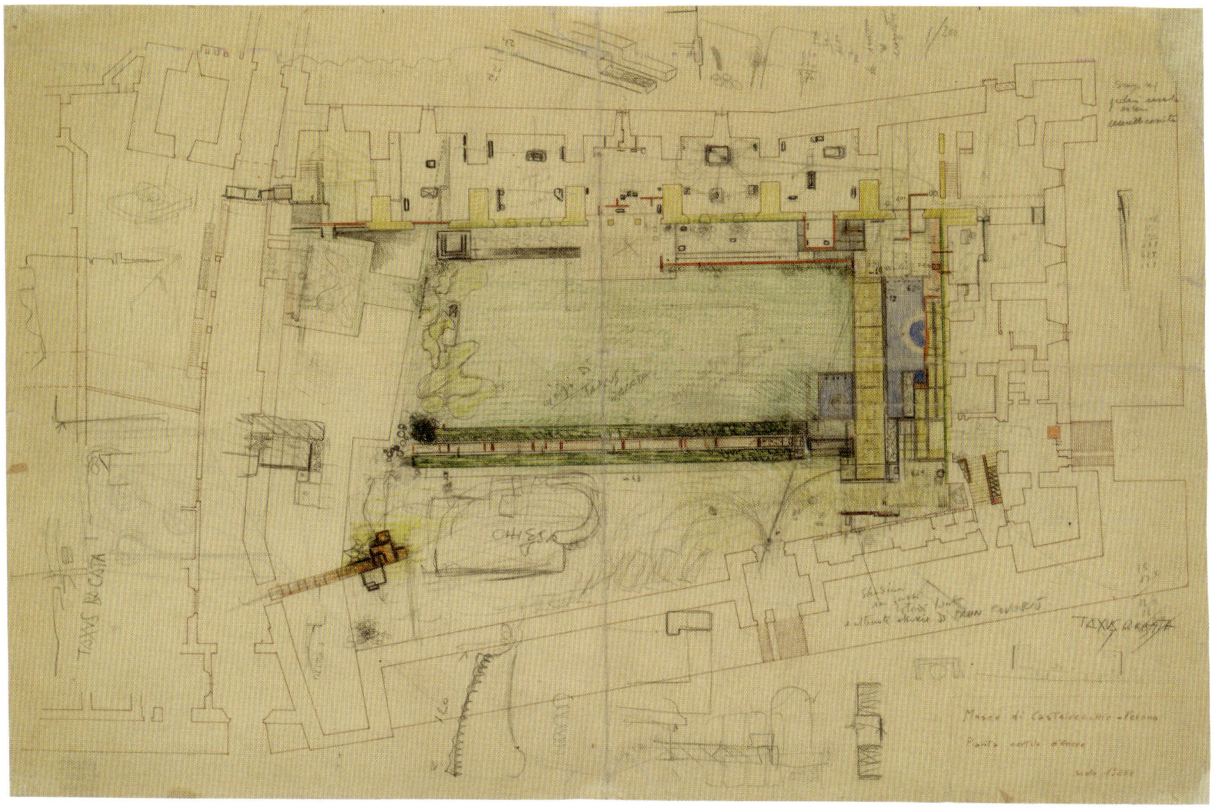

7.2

7.3

7.1 CASTELVECCHIO MUSEUM, VERONA; WITH THE ADIGE RIVER AND SCALIGERO BRIDGE IN THE FOREGROUND AND ROMAN AMPHITHEATRE IN THE BACKGROUND

7.2 CARLO SCARPA, CASTELVECCHIO MUSEUM RENOVATIONS, VERONA, 1957–75; GROUND-FLOOR AND GARDEN PLAN, GRAPHITE AND COLOURED PASTEL ON PAPER, 43.8 X 65 CM (17.25 X 25.5 IN)

7.3 CASTELVECCHIO MUSEUM RENOVATIONS; STUCCO-FACED NORTHERN WALL OF COURTYARD

7.4

During the Castelvecchio's major work, undertaken with his assistant Arrigo Rudi and structural engineer Maschietto, Scarpa would work evenings in his Castelvecchio draughting room, followed by a late dinner with Magagnato and others, after which he and his wife would stay overnight in Verona at the d'Oro Columba hotel. [6] As with other projects, Scarpa was on the construction site daily, often returning after dark to focus on the details. As Frascari noted:

> 'Scarpa's detailing is the result of interfacing of design and craftsmanship on the site and of the constant "sensorial verification" of details during the assembly of the building. Scarpa made a practice of visiting the building site during the night for verification with a flashlight, thereby controlling the execution and the expression of the details. In normal daylight it would indeed be impossible to focus on details in such a selective manner ... Another Veneto architect, Piranesi, used the same technique in visiting the sites of the buildings he was going to survey and represent in his etchings of the *Antichita Romane*. To single out the "expression of the fragments", that is, the details, he used the light of a candle.' [7]

Approaching the massive, stone-walled Castelvecchio from the south, we see its three main towers, all facing the city along the moat's edge, itself surrounding the castle's eastern, southern and western sides; their crenellated tops covered with hipped roofs. To the east, the reconstructed Arco dei Gavi, a Roman triumphal arch from the time of Augustus, stands in a small park overlooking the river. (7.1) We enter the building by crossing the wood-floored double drawbridge at the central tower's base, passing through the small, stone-floored chamber within, and stepping out on to the courtyard's gravel floor. (7.2) Across from the entrance is the Gallery's light grey-coloured, stucco-faced southern wall, with its marble-framed, pointed-arched Gothic windows and doors. Revealing the facade as an invented historical 'mask', the modern, steel-framed glazed interior volumes project out of some openings, while garden space has been pulled into others. (7.3) To the right is the similarly stuccoed east wing wall, with its row of round-arched Renaissance windows opening into the first floor Sala Boggian, while round-arched doorways give access to the museum's ground floor offices. Across the courtyard to the left, and enclosing it, is the masonry Commune city wall; the Scaligeri-era moat, immediately in front of it, was discovered during construction and re-excavated by Scarpa. Through a small doorway near the southwest corner, where the Commune wall meets the Scaligeri wall, a new steel bridge gives access from the street crossing the Scaligeri Bridge.

From 1957–64, the earliest work, after the 'From Altichiero to Pisanello' exhibition, was on the Reggia's first and second floors, with later work on the ground and first floors of the former barracks' larger spaces, called the Gallery. In both cases, Scarpa elected to remove and replace all the flooring, which was generally terracotta paving; in the Gallery he removed the structure supporting the first floor. Referring to the Gallery's series of square rooms, the former barracks, running between the thick masonry wall at the river and the courtyard wall with the Gothic windows, Scarpa said:

> 'The rooms were laid out in rows, between two walls distant and distinct from each other. They were the two facades of the castle. The more ancient of the two walls is solid, almost without apertures. It opened towards the river, on the outside. The other, more recent wall one was less massive and opened on to the garden. You see how the building retains its identity in time: it's a basic principle. In earlier restorations lots of small beams had been set between the two walls. They didn't serve any structural purpose, they were dummies, but they helped define the geometry of the spaces and connected the ceilings visually. I could have inserted a simple ceiling, leaving it in the gloom, since I didn't need to emphasize the load-bearing elements. But something would have been missing. That hall needs to have a geometry stressed.' [5]

7.5

7.6

In front of us, a double row of hedges runs across the courtyard. When trimmed as Scarpa requested, the double hedge forms an eye-level, horizontal line that compensates for the ground's slight slope to the left, while blocking our view of the courtyard floor between the hedge and the museum's wall, which appears to rise above this inner horizon line.[8] The two offset hedges, the northern one running further to the right and the southern running further to the left, create a corridor-like space that aligns with the doorways from the courtyard and the Arco dei Gavi, accessing the stairs up to the Sala Boggian. The gravel-floored parking area in which we stand, between the Scaligeri walls and hedge, narrows towards the right, where stone paving extends outwards, indicating the direction to the museum's entrance.

However, we pause, for our eyes are drawn to the northwest corner where the museum's stucco-faced wall comes to an abrupt halt, as if carved in a stepped line, and the roof appears delaminated, a layer of patinaed copper emerging from beneath the terracotta tiles. The roof does not reach the bridge's wall on the left, whose top masonry layer is removed to reveal the Commune city wall's original stones. Cantilevered into this covered gap, between the stucco-walled Gallery and the stone-walled bridge, is the Cangrande equestrian statue, the museum's most important artefact. **(7.4)** Originally located above the church of Santa Maria Antica's transept door in Verona, the statue was replaced by a copy in 1876 and stored in the Castelvecchio. In 1924, Avena located the Cangrande in a recess next to the Torre del Mastio in the small court south of the Reggia. After considering five different locations, including the northeast corner and the current entrance, Scarpa finally placed the Cangrande in the northwest corner, in the space he opened between the Napoleonic barracks, bridge and Reggia. As Scarpa later noted, **'The most challenging item was the location of the Cangrande, the equestrian statue. It wasn't easy to work that one out. Even set where it is, up in the air, it is related to movement and conditions it, stressing one of the most important historical connections between the different parts of the castle.'**[9] Acting as a pivot or hinge for our entire Castelvecchio experience, the Cangrande statue is encountered on three occasions and seen from three different vantage points, forming a threshold between the building's primary spatial components.

Walking east, we see the first of a series of low concrete walls set forward from the southern and eastern building walls, each fronting a doorway landing, and together forming a broken, delaminated layer at the walls' base, suggesting that the main entry does not lie that way. Across from the first of these, a slightly elevated, wide, bridge-like walkway of large polished and bush-hammered Prun stone slabs projects into the gravel from behind the hedge. Approaching the end of the walkway, a landing made of three Veronese red marble slabs extends towards us. We step up off the gravel on to the entry walkway made with locally quarried stones, Prun and Veronese red marble, historically used in Verona.

This walkway runs parallel to the courtyard's eastern wall. On the right, narrow flowerbeds separate the broad walkway from an irregular series of rectangular concrete slabs with Prun stone edges extending various distances into the gravel, forming a shifting surface that accesses the eastern wall's doorways. On the left, an ancient circular marble fountain, at the centre of a square, shallow pool curbed in Prun stone, appears to float on water, which runs beneath its base. A single rough, quarry-faced Prun stepping stone is set out into this pool, its bottom also Prun stone. Across the stone pathway, a larger, equally shallow pool opens on the right, and because both pools' edges align, the water appears to run under the pathway on which we are walking. The right, larger pool extends to the entry forecourt, and an ancient semicircular fountain projects out into the pool from a horizontally banded concrete wall with rough-faced Prun stone trim. To our left, a grass lawn extends to the moat at the courtyard's far end. The ground planes of water, stone, concrete and grass are close to the same level and the joints are strongly emphasized; the whole surface appears to shift and realign around us as we walk, its composition forming a carefully choreographed, laminated entry sequence. **(7.5, 7.6)**

7.4 CASTELVECCHIO MUSEUM RENOVATIONS; NORTHWEST CORNER OF COURTYARD WITH THE CANGRANDE STATUE

7.5 CASTELVECCHIO MUSEUM RENOVATIONS; STONE ENTRANCE WALKWAY ALONG EASTERN WALL

7.6 CASTELVECCHIO MUSEUM RENOVATIONS; CIRCULAR MARBLE FOUNTAIN ABOVE A SHALLOW POOL

7.7

7.8

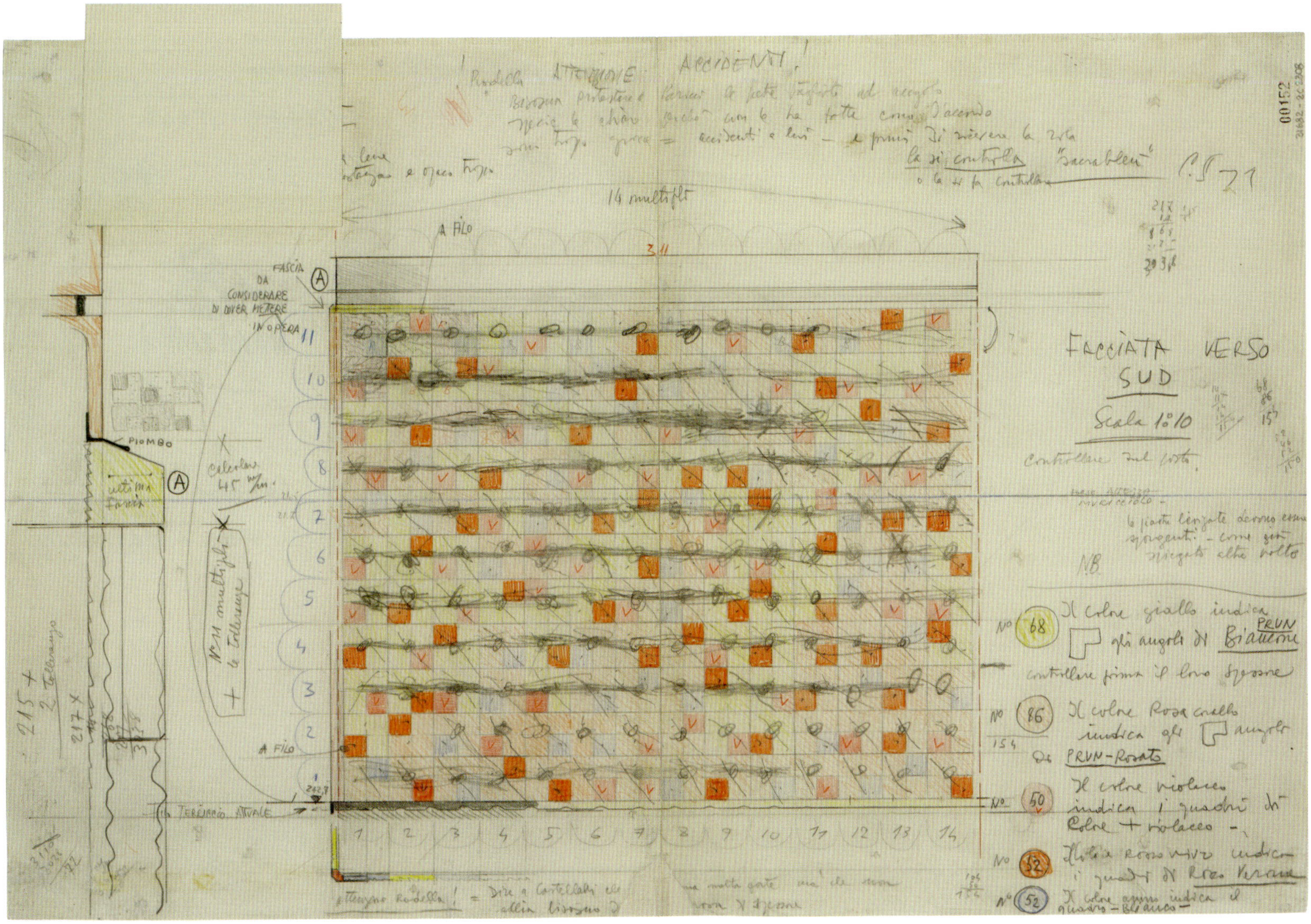

The large stone slab walkway ends at the forecourt, paved with much smaller Prun stones set in bands of the same length but varying widths. To our left, a chest-high, black steel-edged concrete wall, horizontally banded with exposed pebble aggregate, its upper half leaning away from the building, is set parallel to the northern wall, running across to the old entrance's raised platform. Behind this wall, the stone floor stops against a steel edge, and a three-tiered, shallowly recessing concrete floor, each tier held by a steel edge, steps down from the museum's wall. Standing on this concrete floor is a large, lidless Prun stone sarcophagus on a steel base, and a cubic, stone-walled volume, the Sacello (shrine-like place), projects out from the existing doorway. **(7.7)** Deeply recessed glazing is set into the arched opening above, and the stone walls and black steel-banded top of the Sacello do not touch the stone frames of the doorway, but emerge from shadowed recesses. The intricate stone mosaic pattern of the Sacello's exterior, made of white Prun stone, Broccato di S. Ambrogio and Veronese red marble, takes the form of rough-faced, L-shaped, three-quarter square stone pieces, made by removing one quarter from a square block and replacing it with a polished, square stone. [10] Scarpa carefully designed these three walls' complex pattern, using two colours of larger L-shapes and three colours of smaller squares to produce a nonrepeating rhythm based on the larger squares' grid; these are set in 11 horizontal rows. **(7.8)** While similarities between this and the patterns in Klee's and Mondrian's gridded paintings have been noted, closer study reveals that this pattern of squares, subdivided to form L-shapes, which Scarpa would employ in subsequent projects is, in fact, unique to his work. **(see pp. 136–7)**

7.7 CASTELVECCHIO MUSEUM RENOVATIONS; ENTRANCE FORECOURT WITH BLACK STEEL-EDGED CONCRETE WALL, PRUN STONE SARCOPHAGUS AND MOSAIC STONE-WALLED SACELLO BENEATH DEEPLY RECESSED GLAZING

7.8 CASTELVECCHIO MUSEUM RENOVATIONS; FRONT ELEVATION DETAIL OF THE SACELLO, WITH 11 ROWS MARKED OUT, GRAPHITE, COLOURED PENCIL AND PEN ON CARDBOARD, 43.2 X 63.2 CM (17 X 25 IN)

An ancient circular sundial, made of the Prun stone and Veronese red marble, held in a steel frame, is mounted on the stucco wall adjacent to the museum entrance. The entrance is through the last Gothic arch, into which the glazed wall and doors are deeply recessed, and out of which an L-shaped wall projects. **(7.10)** This lime plaster-faced concrete wall, splitting the portal in two and separating the entrance and exit doors, is edge-banded in black steel with a grey-coloured inner face and a black-coloured outer face. The museum's rough stuccoed exterior wall contrasts with the projecting wall's smooth textured lime plaster. Rough-faced bands of Prun stone paving run from the wall out to the entry forecourt's edges, dividing the surface into narrow bands at entrance and exit, with a larger central space between.

Opening the glass entrance door, we find the dividing wall continues into the entrance hall, stepping down to align with the built-in cabinetry's top. The entrance hall floor's Prun stone paving pattern, interspersed with bronzetto slabs, matches the exterior forecourt's paving, fusing the two spaces. To the right, a large black-painted radiator aligns with the entrance wall, separating entrance and exit movement. Next to the radiator is the large, black steel-edged, thin-walled, board-formed concrete ticket desk, lifted off the floor on steel feet; above which floats a thin top of Brazilian rosewood. **(7.9)** The entrance hall walls are a rough-finished white plaster, with the largest opening on the left, an arched doorway leading to the sculpture galleries. Ahead, a small, L-shaped, black steel-edged opening, with a semi-cylindrical, cantilevered black-steel edged concrete step, gives access to a black plaster walled, bevelled niche in the thick masonry wall, from which a wood-framed window overlooks the Adige River. When open the sound of the rushing river water enters the room, amplified by the massive bevelled walls.

In front of the back wall of the entry hall, a large concrete wall, with a black steel beam at its lower edge, descends from the ceiling, concealing the gallery exit stairs. The wall's surface has three receding layers, the largest and thickest at the top, with a smooth, bush-hammered finish, while the thinnest bottom layer has a pitted, pick-hammered surface. At the wall's centre, a small inverted T-shaped opening stands above the thin slot separating the two steel beams. On the right wall, in the corner beneath the concrete wall and exit staircase, a low opening leads to the library, while in the other corner, the gallery exit emerges through a taller, vertical opening. At the top of this opening, three concrete planes form an inverted T-shaped header standing on a black steel beam, which, set at the same level as the beam at the bottom of the concrete wall screening the exit staircase, connects the two elements in the gallery exit sequence.

Just below the apricot-coloured plaster ceiling, a double black steel beam runs across the entrance hall from east to west, disappearing into a recess above the large arched doorway opening into the galleries. Through this doorway, we can see through the five arched openings joining the five sculpture gallery rooms to the entrance hall. The doorway, deeper than it is wide, reveals the walls' massive thickness. At the openings' faces, arched beams frame the barrel vault-like ceiling finished with rough-textured plaster. Below the arched ceiling, single large slabs of rough, quarry-faced pink Prun stone cover the sidewalls. At the doorway's floor, between the entrance hall and the first sculpture gallery, three shallow tiers of white Prun stone curbing form an overlapping, layered threshold. A wide stone band frames the bristle mat, set level with the entrance hall paving, a thin stone band frames the concrete trench-like recess at the wall's edge, and a second thin stone band frames the *in situ* concrete floor above, which extends from the gallery floor. **(7.11)**

7.9

7.9 CASTELVECCHIO MUSEUM RENOVATIONS; ENTRANCE HALL

7.10 CASTELVECCHIO MUSEUM RENOVATIONS; ENTRANCE ARCH WITH DEEPLY RECESSED GLAZED DOOR AND PROJECTING L-SHAPED WALL

7.10

7.11

7.12

The first sculpture gallery floor, a room sized square of shimmering, dark-grey concrete framed by white stone, forms a slightly elevated platform separated from the surrounding, irregular castle walls by a stepped Prun stone band, with a dark concrete lower surface between the edge band and the white rough-plastered wall. The floor has irregularly spaced single and double white Prun stone bands running north-south, crossing our direction of travel, with dark-grey cast concrete between. The elevated concrete floor was levelled by tamping with a wooden rod while still wet, leaving the surface striated with thin lines running parallel to the stone bands. The concrete was then lightly polished, giving it a shimmering, slightly reflective surface. Scarpa later noted that this idea came from the water that once filled the surrounding moats, 'The paving is one of the key surfaces defining the geometry of a space. I had to solve the problem of the dihedron-shaped seam between the wall, which is a luminous vertical surface, and the dark, horizontal floor ... Thinking of the water flowing round the walls of the castle, I got the idea of creating a version in negative,'[11] a dry moat surrounding a lifted plane of water. As would be typical in many of Scarpa's later works, this curb and trench-like edge detail also subtly alludes to the Venetian habit of raising the floor above the periodic inundations of the *acqua alta*.

The sculpture gallery room's ceilings are each made of four quadrants of cement brick faced in grey plaster, their direction of span pinwheeling around the centre. These sections are supported by a cross-shaped pair of board-formed reinforced concrete beams. Two C-channel beams of black steel, set back to back with a space between, run down the centre of the room, just below one of the concrete beams. The steel beam disappears into the deep niches cut into the top of the walls directly over the arched doorways. At the centre of the ceiling, where the concrete beams cross, a small, upside-down T-shaped steel bearing post sits on the top of the steel beam and cradles the semi-cylindrical steel piece that is welded to the square steel plate cast into the bottom of the concrete beams. (7.12) The steel beams run continuously down the axis of the arched door openings, tying the ground floor's six rooms together. These rooms' white plaster walls stop short of the ceiling, its grey plaster surfaces passing above the walls into the shadow of the reveal, reinforcing the ceiling planes' apparent continuity as suggested by the aligned steel beams. This effect is contrasted by the square, island-like, concrete floors, precisely defining each room as a separate place. As Scarpa noted, 'the floor of every room is individuated, as if they were a series of platforms.'[12]

The new ceilings of the ground floor galleries are the result of Scarpa's demolition of the existing Avena restoration, of which he said:

> 'I wanted to preserve the originality, the character of every room, but I didn't want to use the wooden beams of the earlier restoration. Since the rooms were square, I set a paired steel beam to support the point where the two reinforced concrete beams crossed, so indicating the main lines of the building's formal structure. Where they crossed the importance of that square was emphasized because the crossing of the two beams in the centre implies the pillar, which helps to define the square ... This is the visual logic I wanted to use as a frame of reference. The way the beams were made also brings out the visual logic, but only in the details. I could have used the steel profiles already on the market, but it would have been an engineering solution without any visual emphasis. I thought it would be more interesting to take the profiles and make a composition out of them. The new joints reveal the structure of the element and the new functions.'[13]

While the five sculpture gallery rooms share concrete and steel ceiling structures, white rough-plastered walls and raised black reflective concrete floors, each room has its own distinct character. In the first room, the brightly lit Sacello projects outwards, while above, the large, black steel-framed glazing sits slightly forward of the wall's inside face, giving views of the Scaligeri battlements and tower through its curve-topped window. (7.13) Inside the Sacello, the small Longobardic tomb pieces are displayed against the bottle green-coloured polished-plaster walls, illuminated by the large rooflight running along the back wall. The ceiling is a thin grey plaster-faced concrete slab, edged in black steel, forming the sill of the large window above. The Sacello's slightly elevated floor is made of smooth red-brown terracotta tiles set within black steel frames that divide the floor into two sections, and to which the pedestals' and display case's thin steel legs are secured. The long, horizontal Iroko wood-walled display case projects slightly out of the Sacello and into the main room, acting as a threshold between the two spaces. Across from the Sacello, the sarcophagus of SS. Sergio and Bacco is supported by a pair of L-shaped blocks of white Biancone di Vicenza stone, while the stone tomb lid, its surface carved with inscriptions, is set in a black steel frame and lifted off the floor by a hidden support.

7.11 CASTELVECCHIO MUSEUM RENOVATIONS; VIEW FROM THE ENTRANCE HALL THROUGH FIVE DEEP ARCHES CONNECTING THE SCULPTURE GALLERIES

7.12 CASTELVECCHIO MUSEUM RENOVATIONS; DOUBLE STEEL CHANNEL BEAMS SUPPORTING CONCRETE CEILING BEAMS AT MIDPOINT OF GALLERY CEILING

7.13

7.13 CASTELVECCHIO MUSEUM RENOVATIONS; VIEW FROM THE FIRST ROOM OF THE SCULPTURE GALLERIES INTO THE SACELLO

7.14 CASTELVECCHIO MUSEUM RENOVATIONS; SCULPTURE GALLERIES' SECOND ROOM WITH LARGE MEDIEVAL STATUES ON POLISHED PLASTER-FACED CONCRETE SLABS

7.15 CASTELVECCHIO MUSEUM RENOVATIONS; PERIOD PHOTOGRAPH, 1965, CARLO SCARPA IN THE SECOND ROOM OF THE SCULPTURE GALLERIES

7.14

7.15

7.16

7.17

In the sculpture gallery's second room, large medieval statues, placed on low polished plaster-faced concrete slabs, edged in black steel, hover just above the floor. **(7.14)** The statues are lit by the southern wall's three windows: a large square central window and two small, square, bevel-edged windows set high in the wall. Entering this room, we feel that we have interrupted a conversation among the pieces, their faces dramatically lit from the side or front. A photograph of Scarpa looking up at one of the statues, both figures illuminated by daylight, suggests the care with which he placed each artefact.[14] **(7.15)** Scarpa, who believed strongly in displaying sculpture only in natural light, provided only a few artificial light fixtures, each a steel pipe with three thin steel legs and a bare bulb mounted on top.

The third room, the museum's former entrance, is the most complex in this sequence. On the outside wall, next to the river, a half-height, black steel-edged wall projects partway into the room, its longer right-side faced in Pompeian red polished plaster, its left side and return faced in light-grey polished plaster. Small marbles are presented on this wall, each in its own folded steel bracket designed to bring out the piece's individual character. **(see c.2)** Doors behind this wall lead to the cleverly inserted toilets, set on either side of a partition placed within the bevel-walled window niche in the outer wall, where the roar of the river below fills the small space. Opposite, a complex projecting and receding wall of steel, plaster-faced panels and glass is set behind the three central Gothic-arched openings. A steel-edged concrete slab ceiling divides the upper zone, behind the pointed arches, from a lower zone behind the columns. Glazing running across the top is ordered on a syncopated, nonrepeating pattern of narrow vertical panels, while at the floor, two black plaster-faced panels are separated by three vertical frameless glass panes, set in a receding stepped formation. **(7.17)** At the right edge, a pivoting glass door opens on to the square terrace, its Prun stone-edged, dark-grey concrete floor matching the gallery inside. Between the central columns, against the black polished plaster wall, a small sculpture of three figures, set within three arched openings, stands on a pedestal made of two L-shaped black steel pieces, set back-to-back with a narrow vertical slot between. **(7.16)**

7.16 CASTELVECCHIO MUSEUM RENOVATIONS; EXTERNAL TERRACE OFF THE SCULPTURE GALLERIES' THIRD ROOM

7.17 CASTELVECCHIO MUSEUM RENOVATIONS; THE SCULPTURE GALLERIES' THIRD ROOM, LOOKING BACK TOWARDS THE ENTRANCE

7.18

7.19

7.20

In the fourth room's far left corner stands Tomba's *Crucifixion* and *Saints*, illuminated by three windows in the southern wall. **(7.18)** The two saints, looking left and right respectively, are set on cubic steel pedestals, formed by two C-shaped frames. Between them, the Christ figure hangs on a Y-shaped cross mounted on a T-shaped, black polished plaster-faced, black steel-framed back stand floating just above the floor; a small, square notch cut at the centre of the stand's top emphasizes the sagging figure and Y-shaped cross. Walking behind these sculptures we see that the notch continues down the back as a steel-edged slot, separating the T-shape into two L-shapes, into which attaches the black, stepping, double-steel bar frame supporting the entire stand and sculpture.

A small sculpture of a seated pope looks towards the window in the fifth room, while behind, a large, tomb lid is set in a black steel frame next to the bevel-walled window niche overlooking the river. A glazed recessed window in this room's floor reveals the Scaligeri moat running beneath the building. This window is protected by four cylindrical Iroko wood rails with steel end caps, held by four pairs of black steel L-shaped posts attached to the window's steel frame below the floor, where they hold small brass cylinders that secure the glass from above, **'as if the whole assembly had been lowered as a single unit into the void'.** [15] The rails, hung from the steel posts by brass rings set in circular brass castings, swing gently in their mountings when touched. Along this room's far wall, the floor steps down, changing from dark-grey concrete to small, white Prun stone slabs, as in the entrance hall. This wall's glazed arched opening includes a glass door, set to the right of centre, with a sliding, woven black steel gate that, like the Olivetti gate, secures the doorway after hours. **(7.19)** Grasping the door handle, a vertical wood cylinder pinned between steel brackets, we notice that the door frame, a black steel T-section with its longer central leg set to the outside and aligned with the glass edge, appears as an unusually thin plane of glass and steel.

Through the door we enter the open-air, covered space between the Napoleonic barracks and the bridge wall. **(7.20)** To the right, the rough-plastered riverfront wall continues across, closing the space, with a bevel-walled window niche overlooking the river through woven steel grating. Ahead, three stairs lead down to a complexly layered set of Prun stone-paved platforms slowly winding their way down to a double, outer and inner archway at the bottom of the bridge wall. The various-sized, rectangular Prun stones are a mixture of rough- and smooth-faced slabs; their constantly changing orientations interlock in a puzzle-like composition set parallel to the interior's flooring. The stone platforms' edges are set away from the surrounding walls and lifted above the ground; guard rails are made of vertical and horizontal, double black steel bars. To the left the gallery's white rough-plastered outer wall extends beyond the corner, its layered edge interlocked with new concrete walls. The point at which this outer wall originally connected to the bridge wall is clearly marked by the vertical line where the Scaligeri brick masonry steps back to reveal the Commune wall's rounded stones.

7.18 CASTELVECCHIO MUSEUM RENOVATIONS; THE SCULPTURE GALLERIES' FOURTH ROOM WITH TOMBA'S *CRUCIFIXION* AND *SAINTS*, ILLUMINATED BY SOUTHERN LIGHT

7.19 CASTELVECCHIO MUSEUM RENOVATIONS; THE SCULPTURE GALLERIES' FIFTH ROOM, THE ARCHED DOORWAY OPENS TO THE OPEN-AIR, COVERED SPACE BETWEEN THE NAPOLEONIC BARRACKS AND THE BRIDGE WALL

7.20 CASTELVECCHIO MUSEUM RENOVATIONS; AERIAL VIEW OF THE OPEN-AIR, COVERED SPACE BETWEEN THE NAPOLEONIC BARRACKS AND THE BRIDGE WALL

7.21 CASTELVECCHIO MUSEUM RENOVATIONS; VIEW FROM THE BRIDGE WALL TO THE CANGRANDE AND SCULPTURE GALLERIES

7.21

To the left of the archway through which we exited, the Cangrande's tower-like concrete pedestal rises from the shadowed space beneath the pavement, set back from the wall of the pedestal. This L-shaped pedestal lifts the Cangrande statue 6 metres (19 ft 8 in) above the terrace on which we stand, projecting it into the covered space between the gallery walls and bridge. The pedestal's two legs are U-shaped sections of *in situ* concrete, the vertical leg opening towards the wall behind and the horizontal leg at the top opening to below. The wood-board formwork is oriented horizontally up to the midpoint, after which it rotates to be vertically oriented. The midpoint is marked by an inset steel channel terminating at a small, inverted T-shaped opening. The vertical leg's two outer corners have steel angles cast into the concrete, forming re-entrant corners. The pedestal's top has a notched end, while a slot opened where the horizontal floor meets the vertical wall allows light to wash down the shadowed vertical wall. This is reminiscent of the light produced by the Sacello's rooflight, and here it imparts a measure of independence to the Cangrande, which appears to float forward into the space. **(7.21)**

From this position, we are looking up at the Cangrande from approximately the same angle and distance as its original position above Santa Maria Antica's door, as recorded in John Ruskin's sketches of the Cangrande.[16] The statue and his horse also look down at us, something indiscernible when we first saw the statue from the courtyard. Oriented to the east, the statue matches its original position above the church; this final orientation came quite late in Scarpa's design process. In the position next to the Torre del Mastio where Avena had the statue placed in 1924,[17] it was oriented in the opposite direction, and in both Scarpa's initial studies for the northeast corner location and the final northwest corner location, the statue was also oriented to the west, towards the bridge and the Reggia. In its final position, the concrete pedestal aligns with the building's walls and projects to the west, yet the Cangrande himself faces east, looking into the galleries' upper level, with the statue rotated off the axis of its pedestal. Scarpa said, **'I decided to turn it slightly, to emphasize its independence from the structure supporting it; it is part of the whole, yet it still lives its own separate life.'**[18]

The castellated masonry Adige Bridge wall stands in the reopened Scaligeri moat, and, at the far corner, beneath the clock tower, the new bridge spans across the moat from a small opening in the wall to the gravel parking court. This thin bridge is made of two U-shaped steel beams between which span irregularly sized, black steel-framed concrete floor panels, with double-steel bar handrails above, and vertical double-steel compression struts, set off-centre towards the wall, and tension cables below. The courtyard side of the bridge is above the ground level, so a series of wide concrete landing-like stairs step down, near where a small church's ruined foundations are preserved.

Descending the stone stairs we enter the Porta del Morbio, the city's original Commune wall gate at the river's edge, closed by the Scaligeri when the Adige Bridge was built, but discovered and reopened by Scarpa during the renovation. A narrow suspended walkway passes through this space, its *in situ* concrete floor cast into steel frames. On the other side of the Commune wall, a new concrete ramp carries the pedestrian street above to the bridge. Scarpa pulled the edge of this ramped street away from the Commune wall's western face, allowing light to wash down the wall, clearly differentiating ancient from modern and articulating the historical boundary represented by the city wall.

Descending several deep, landing-like Prun stone steps we exit the deep shadows into the Reggia courtyard, which, until 1825, was the termination of the Scaligeri Bridge. To the left, a black steel and *in situ* concrete staircase, used by the museum's resident caretaker, runs up the masonry wall beneath the ramped street. Above the roadway, we can see the castle's crenellated western walls. The massive Torre del Mastio, which was the castle's keep, rises to the right, at the courtyard's northern end. We enter the tower, passing through the 2.5 metre (8 ft 2 in) thick masonry walls to the square room at its centre. The floor is made up of differently dimensioned, white Prun stone slabs, while the wall's lower portion is faced with massive, rough, quarry-faced pink Prun stone slabs secured by brass bolts. The walls above the stone panels, and the ceiling's barrel vault, are faced in rough stucco plaster, while a staircase, U-shaped in plan, winds its way around three of the walls, disappearing behind the vaulted ceiling. The projecting, polished white Prun stone treads are set on a wall made of brick pavers, recycled from the Reggia's floors, its thickness revealed by narrow vertical slots opened randomly on its faces and by the corbelled slots at its inside corners. The large Prun stone landing, forming the staircase's first step, turns towards where we stand inside the doorway, while the staircase's first run is set away from the outer wall, its first landing, in the room's left corner, is set at the top of the stone wall panels. The staircase's handrail at the inner edge is supported by two black double-steel bar posts, the first standing on the floor, the second mounted to the brick wall beneath the staircase and rising past the edge of the ceiling to the first floor above. The handrail is made of a steel bar structural beam set below and to the staircase's outer edge, supporting the cylindrical wood handrail, set above and to the inside edge, where it is easily grasped.

At the top of the staircase, we pass through a doorway and walk across an open-sided, steel-framed, ash wood-floored bridge to reach the Reggia's door. The main hall is a long space that bends to the right, following the river's edge. Its polished, white Clauzetto marble floor joints are almost invisible, while the walls are finished in rough, light grey-coloured plaster, tinted with India ink and Prussian blue. Bearing on projecting stone impost blocks, the original ceiling's massive wood beams run from wall to wall. At the corner, between the wall and floor, a raised, soft-white Vicenza stone curb runs the room's perimeter, with the floor set below it – the reverse of the ground floor galleries' curb detail. To our left is a freestanding switchback staircase, with a shorter first run, a broad landing at eye level and a longer second run rising through an opening in the ceiling. The staircase, opening towards the main room in front of us, has walnut treads and landings set in a black steel frame, the whole supported on a single, black double-steel post beneath the landing, joined with pairs of brass pins. **(7.22)**

Paintings are mounted on this room's wall in pivoting steel frames adjustable to changing lighting conditions. In the room's centre, sculptures and crosses stand on stone and steel pedestals, including Michele Giambono's *Dormitio Virginis*, a wide fresco depicting the sleeping Virgin. **(7.23)** Set in a walnut frame, it is supported by a black steel beam resting on two steel brackets that emerge from a large, rectangular block of pitted-faced, Alpine green marble set directly below the Virgin's bed in the painting above. At the main room's far end, a tall, steel-edged doorway steps in towards the top, giving views into the museum's westernmost room. **(7.24)** Two walnut steps bring us to the walnut-board floor of this room, which is brightly lit by large south-facing windows. Paintings are displayed on the white rough-plaster walls and on the rosewood easels joined with brass fittings, which Scarpa first employed in the Correr Museum. The four rooms along the Reggia's southern side have walnut floors with wide boards that creak as we pass over, as Scarpa intended. Some walls carry partial frescos of varying dates, the rest are finished in smooth white plaster above Vicenza stone curbing. At the ceilings the original wood beams, boards and corbel blocks are exposed, many of which are intricately painted.

7.22

7.23

7.24

In the Reggia rooms, Scarpa mounted paintings and frescos on the walls, in easels and in steel frames supported by suspended, floor-to-ceiling steel rods. Each artefact is treated as an individual, positioned to receive the most appropriate light from the south-facing windows, set high in the wall. As an example, the *Madonna col bambino* by Bonsignori, of which only a fragment survives, is mounted in a frame sized to the original painting, allowing us to imagine the outline of the complete painting. The Reggia's second-level floors are all made of walnut boards with Vicenza stone curbing. In the main room, the large panel holding the *Trionfo della Castita* and *Trionfo dell'Amore*, by Liberale di Verona, is suspended from the ceiling by steel rods on either side and pinned off the wall to one side by a steel bar, this floating effect emphasizes the painting's missing column bases. In a southern, smaller room, a three-part painting, of which the bottom of the original frame is missing, is set into a Scarpa-designed U-shaped frame. Its finger-jointed corners are connected by cylindrical steel pins, while its stepping base, rising to replace the original frame, is supported by a steel bracket and two steel bars projecting from the wall behind.

7.22 CASTELVECCHIO MUSEUM RENOVATIONS; REGGIA (MAIN HALL), SWITCHBACK STAIRCASE WITH BLACK STEEL-FRAMED WALNUT TREADS AND LANDINGS
7.23 CASTELVECCHIO MUSEUM RENOVATIONS; REGGIA (MAIN HALL)
7.24 CASTELVECCHIO MUSEUM RENOVATIONS; STEPPED-PROFILE DOORWAY FROM THE REGGIA TO THE MUSEUM'S WESTERNMOST ROOM

7.25

We exit the Reggia at the upper level through a concrete walled, floored and roofed bridge, with high pivoting, city-facing windows, and a rooflight at the Reggia end of the complexly folded, board-formed concrete ceiling; after Scarpa's death Arrigo Rudi designed the displays for this bridge and the Torre del Mastio's upper room beyond. Walking outside at the top of the crenellated castle wall and down a narrow, concrete-walled staircase, passing through an opening in the Commune wall, we arrive at a landing overlooking the Cangrande space from above. To the left a set of triangular alternating stairs, only climbed by placing the left foot on the first tread, accesses the rampart at the top of the wall along the river. To the right, an angled bridge crosses to the gallery's upper floor. The bridge is supported by two steel I-beams, into which an irregularly sized, rectangular steel-edged concrete panel floor is set; black steel handrails stand above the pinewood sidewalls set in black steel frames secured to the vertical steel posts that support the handrails. **(7.25)** Both the pinewood bridge sidewalls and gallery facade across the way have been burnt with an oil lamp flame, a traditional method of preserving wood against decay and insect damage. This process burns out the wood's soft pulp, later removed with a steel brush, leaving the wood almost black with dark red streaks.

Overhead, the complex structure of the projecting, irregularly edged roof is revealed. A massive, timber double-ridged beam emerges from the gallery facade, spanning across to the Commune wall to bear on a double L-shaped steel anchor. Two-thirds of the way across the beam emerges from beneath the roof; a copper sheath covers the exposed portion's top and sides. At the gallery facade's edge, and partway across this span, the beam is supported by double L-shaped steel posts, which in turn bear on double steel I-beam crossbeams running across the space from the masonry wall's edge along the river to a double steel I-beam cantilevered from the top of the gallery wall. Large timber rafters, set in a stepping pattern and trussed with steel compression struts and double-steel tensioning rods, span from the beam to the walls on either side. Above these, wood purlins support the roof's wood decking. **(7.26 a/b)**

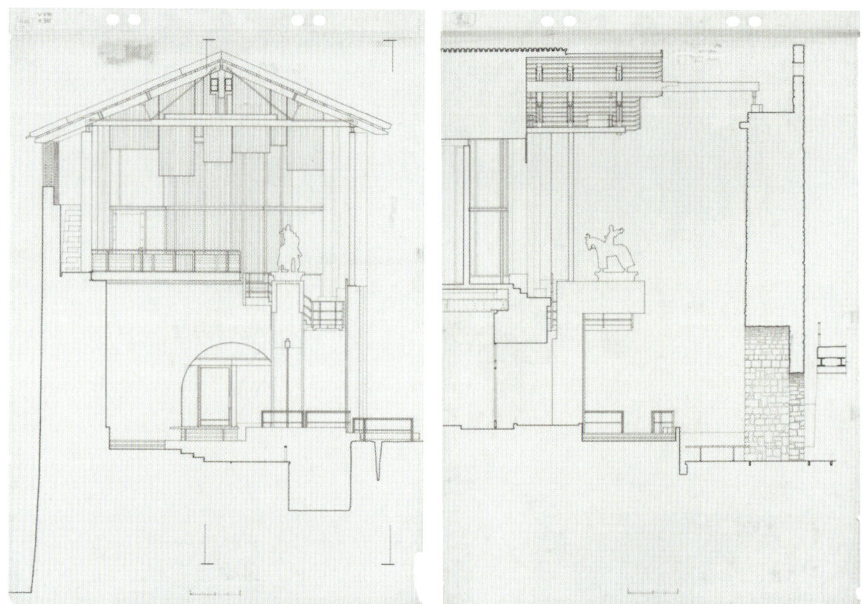

7.26 a/b

7.25 CASTELVECCHIO MUSEUM RENOVATIONS; VIEW BACK TO THE COMMUNE WALL ACROSS THE ANGLED BRIDGE THAT CROSSES THE CANGRANDE SPACE

7.26a CASTELVECCHIO MUSEUM RENOVATIONS; SECTION THROUGH THE CANGRANDE SPACE, LOOKING EAST (REDRAWN BY RICHARD MURPHY)

7.26b CASTELVECCHIO MUSEUM RENOVATIONS; RICHARD MURPHY, SECTION THROUGH THE CANGRANDE SPACE, LOOKING SOUTH

7.27 CASTELVECCHIO MUSEUM RENOVATIONS; FIRST FLOOR GALLERY, VIEW ALONG NORTHERN RIVERFRONT WALL

7.28 CASTELVECCHIO MUSEUM RENOVATIONS; FIRST FLOOR GALLERY, BEVEL-WALLED WINDOW NICHE IN RIVERFRONT WALL

7.27

7.28

Walking across the angled bridge we see the Cangrande statue for a third time, now at eye level. At the end of the bridge we can walk along the gallery facade's edge, down a set of stairs on to a north-facing, cantilevered balcony, offering closer views of the statue. Beneath the projecting roof, the gallery's upper facade is faced with a series of steel-framed, burnt wood hanging panels of different lengths, forming a serrated pattern at the bottom, while the lower facade is a densely layered composition of burnt wood panels and glazing framed by black steel. To the left of the bridge, we step down on to a white Prun stone floor and enter the gallery's first floor through the glass and steel door.

Directly ahead, the white, rough-plastered riverfront wall runs the length of the first floor gallery wing, gently bending in, then out again. The five, light-grey plastered walls running across this space, dividing it into six rooms, are set a short distance from the riverfront wall, forming a full-height passageway along the galleries' left-hand side, open from the Prun-stone floor to the grey polished-plaster ceiling. **(7.27)** To the left, bevel-walled window niches open at irregular intervals in the riverfront wall. **(7.28)** To the right a terracotta floor made of tiles of irregular depth and matching width are set in a seemingly random, but carefully designed pattern, with aligned joints running from the river to the courtyard sides. This slightly raised floor is surrounded by a continuous stepped white Prun stone curb, separating the floor from the walls.

The cross walls intersect with the right side's outer wall, opened with a series of trefoil-arched windows. At the lower-right corner, a narrow doorway is opened in each of the cross walls, allowing us to see along the edge of the outer, courtyard wall. The terracotta tile flooring and Prun stone curbing wrap into the cross walls' openings; the joint between the rooms is marked by a thin double Prun stone band at the cross wall's centre. Black steel bands run up the edges of the rough plastered doorways' inner faces, turning before the top to form L-shapes with the joint at the wall's centre, matching the tile floor below; small metal discs, with holes centrally drilled, are inserted into the inside corners of the L-shaped steel profile. By lowering these room's floors, Scarpa was able to position the existing windows higher on the wall, allowing light to penetrate deeper into the rooms and resulting in the exterior balconies in two of the rooms being 60 centimetres (2 ft) above the new floor. Access to the balcony doors is provided by narrow, cantilevered, steel-edged concrete staircases running along the bottom of the outer walls, below which radiators are placed, and on which people can sit.[19] **(7.29)**

7.29

7.30

7.31

The first floor galleries' ceilings are made of black steel-framed, polished-plaster panels; set into the centre of each to provide ventilation, is a rectangular, double-layered, gridded wood screen, made of yellow framire below and red padauk above. The ceilings are incrementally lowered from west to east, subtly changing the rooms' proportions as we move from one to the next, as is the colour of the ceilings' polished-plaster surfaces, with subtly different shades of olive-grey in the first five rooms, black in the sixth room and cobalt blue in the Avena room.[20]

7.29 CASTELVECCHIO MUSEUM RENOVATIONS; FIRST-FLOOR GALLERY, VIEW ALONG SOUTHERN WALL, CONCRETE STEPS LEAD TO WINDOW BALCONIES

7.30 CASTELVECCHIO MUSEUM RENOVATIONS; FIRST-FLOOR GALLERY

7.31 CASTELVECCHIO MUSEUM RENOVATIONS; FIRST-FLOOR GALLERY, FIRST ROOM, CANGRANDE STATUE VISIBLE THROUGH THE WESTERN END'S FULL HEIGHT WINDOW

7.32 CASTELVECCHIO MUSEUM RENOVATIONS; FIRST-FLOOR GALLERIES, AVENA ROOM, INTENSE COBALT-BLUE, POLISHED-PLASTER CEILING WITH YELLOW GRIDDED WOOD VENTILATION SCREEN

The upper galleries' circulation down either edge complements the sculpture galleries' circulation on the ground floor below, where we moved along the central axis. Walking through these rooms, we can look back through the small doorways along the south wall to see the Cangrande statue through the western end's full-height window. **(7.31)** The large paintings are hung against the wall on wires secured at the ceiling, while smaller canvases are displayed in wooden easels, mounted on the freestanding steel-framed, polished plaster-faced walls set between the galleries and the pathway along the riverside wall, or at eye level on the walls near the small doorways between the galleries, attracting our attention as we pass. In the fifth room, four steel display stands with double feet and legs, and double-layered steel plate tilted tops, house small reproductions or 'paragons' for the paintings displayed on the surrounding walls. Artificial highlighting is provided by steel-framed, three- and four-tube fluorescent fixtures hanging from the ceiling and mounted on the wall. **(7.30)**

In the final, Avena room, the last space constructed to Scarpa's earlier designs, the intense cobalt-blue, polished-plaster ceiling brings out the blues in the large, eighteenth-century paintings. **(7.32)** This is enhanced by the absence of the warm southern light and the abundance of cool bluish northern light entering through the large clerestory windows, giving views of the north-eastern castle tower. The eastern wall's bevel-walled window niche, with two stone window seats placed above radiators, provides a view to the Arco di Gavi.

The exit staircase, which begins in the large, bevel-walled window niche off the sixth room, descends in two runs, with a woven steel grate covering the large window at the large, half-landing. The outer wall is faced in rough white stucco plaster, while the polished-plaster inner wall is set in a steel-edged frame that steps down in large, irregular sections. The stairs have terracotta tile treads and Prun stone risers, their front faces rough and quarry-faced, while their top edges, aligning with and edging the tile treads, are polished and bush-hammered. This detail of the riser overhanging the tread inverts the normative stair design; as a result our movement downwards seems subtly accelerated. We exit under the three concrete planes set above a steel beam that we saw upon entering. But from the other side the T-shape is upright with members of equal thickness, rather than being inverted with a thick bottom, as it appears when seen from the entrance hall. The exit floor is one step above the entrance hall, and an asymmetrical step, made of polished Veronese red marble, with eased corners is inset into its edge.

Castelvecchio, which many believe is Scarpa's greatest work, is a densely layered **'spatio-temporal'** experience,[21] filled with innumerable details revealing the laminations of the history of human occupation of this place, allowing the building to be experienced as a series of spatial joints, simultaneously new and old, thereby weaving history into the present moment.

7.32

As Magagnato noted:

'In implementing the surgical renewal within which he works to restore unity and life (and what else than this kind of probing can be the basis for true "historicist" restoration?), Scarpa not only reveals the essential coordinates of the complex but also the materials that constitute its corporeal essence. This is the story of what happened at the Castelvecchio, both directly, in the excavation and rediscovery of old stonework, marble, and brickwork, and also in Scarpa's familiarity with the city, enabling him to absorb the local colour of its walls, streets, pavements, and stone cladding. In this way, not the form but the corporeal essence of medieval Verona comes to life in the restoration ...'[22]

CHAPTER 08
CELEBRATION OF THE JOINT

The Fondazione Querini Stampalia is an important library and art collection donated to the public in 1869 by Count Giovanni Querini Stampalia. The sixteenth-century Querini Stampalia palazzo, in which the Fondazione is housed, has its primary double archway water entry facing on to a narrow canal, the Rio S. Maria Formosa, running along the edge of the Campiello S. Maria Formosa, a small plaza on the south side of, and slightly behind the church. The four-storey building is made up of a ground-floor entrance and garden, first-floor library and second-floor art gallery. Scarpa was first asked to make studies for the building in 1948 by the director Manlio Dazzi, but work was not able to proceed due to lack of funding. In 1958 Scarpa's university classmate, fellow IUAV faculty member and close friend, the architectural historian Giuseppe Mazzariol, became director of the Querini Stampalia, and he re-engaged Scarpa, who began designing the extensive ground-floor renovation in 1959, with construction commencing in 1961.

When Scarpa began work the Querini Stampalia ground floor was regularly unusable due to periodic flooding. Scarpa removed the partitions and columns, added in the nineteenth century, exposing the doorways' original stonework, reinforced the walls and clad all the surfaces, floors, walls and ceilings with new materials. The original land entryway was through the service doorway that opened off the extremely narrow, southwestern passageway, slightly over 1 metre (3 ft 3 in) wide, connected to the Campiello by a small stone bridge. This cramped and dark doorway was not an appropriate primary public entrance, so Scarpa proposed a new entrance bridge to come directly from the Campiello to an existing ground-floor window on the right side of the palazzo's front facade, next to the arched water entrance. Scarpa said the transformation of this ancient window into a contemporary doorway made it **'a living window'**.

While the idea for the new bridge and entrance came quite early in the project, and was felt to be essential by both Scarpa and Mazzariol, it was refused permission by the city's building Soprintendente on the grounds that its did not match the building's historical style, and that it was a violation of the window. Due to this opposition, the new bridge and entrance were among the last elements to be completed, installed in 1963 after the Soprintendente was over-ruled by the Mayor of Venice. [1] In this project, as in others, Scarpa found himself increasingly in conflict with the official definition of 'restoration', which required formal mimicry, rather than the living, evolving quality of architecture for which Scarpa argued. This is reflected in Scarpa's conception of building renovation as a process of learning from what others before us have made, related to Vico's aphorism *Verum Ipsum Factum*, which put special emphasis on the way buildings and their constituent elements are put together in different historical periods. As Scarpa said, the joints and connections between elements **'are points every builder takes an interest in and always has, but the solutions are different in different periods. I think this is the drawback of eclecticism: the important point of the past is not so much the final solutions but the themes that have to be dealt with in the building.'** [2]

We approach the Fondazione Querini Stampalia by crossing the grey stone-paved Campiello, separated from the buildings along its southern edge by the small canal. **(8.1, 8.2)** Other than the new entry bridge, Scarpa's interventions on the front facade are minimal. The reddish-tan coloured stucco extends from the roof cornice down to the top of the ground-floor windows, where it stops in an erratic line, revealing the brick masonry structure beneath. The finish coat of stucco on Venetian facades is constantly being renewed, and just as constantly peeling off, eroded by the moisture wicking up the brick walls from the canals. Tall windows, inset into the thick wall's inner face, have white Istrian stone frames; the first and second floor windows have round arches at the top and circular dark red stone tondos in each upper corner. Scarpa replaced the upper three floors' windows with symmetrical, wood-framed casements, while, on the ground floor, Scarpa's renovation is subtly revealed by the new wood-framed windows' asymmetry, each has a wide hinged section on the left and a narrow fixed pane on the right. As is typical for Venetian palazzi, each floor has a large central room running from the canal at the front to the back garden, opened at both ends by continuous sets of windows.

At the canal edge, below the four arched windows of the palazzo's central rooms, are two new gates Scarpa inserted into the double archway of the gondola entrance. **(8.3)** In these arches vertical brass rods, held in black steel brackets in which a three-quarter hole has been drilled, hang from the curved black steel outer frame above to the tops of the three grilled doors below. In each archway a taller, thinner door is set between two lower, wider doors; all three hinged grilled doors can be opened. The doors are framed in black steel, with flat steel bars running horizontally between the vertical stiles. Between the flat steel bars, pairs of short, horizontal brass rods are held at each end by rectangular steel elements, hanging on the outer edge and projecting up at the centre to form T-shaped central voids with L-shaped voids to either side. The door grilles' brass rods are inserted into a three-quarter cylinder holes drilled in the steel elements' top or bottom edges; the rods project slightly beyond the end, exposing their reflective golden-coloured surfaces on all sides. While these cylinder-in-a-cylindrical-hole joints do not actually move, they imply that the gates' entire metal fabric is hinged, and thus is capable of rippling in the same way as their reflections in the canal surface.

8.1 CARLO SCARPA, FONDAZIONE QUERINI STAMPALIA RENOVATIONS, VENICE, 1961–3; VIEW OF THE FONDAZIONE AND NEW BRIDGE FROM THE CAMPIELLO

FONDAZIONE QUERINI STAMPALIA RENOVATIONS
VENICE, 1961–1963

8.2 FONDAZIONE QUERINI STAMPALIA

RENOVATIONS; GROUND-FLOOR PLAN (REDRAWN)

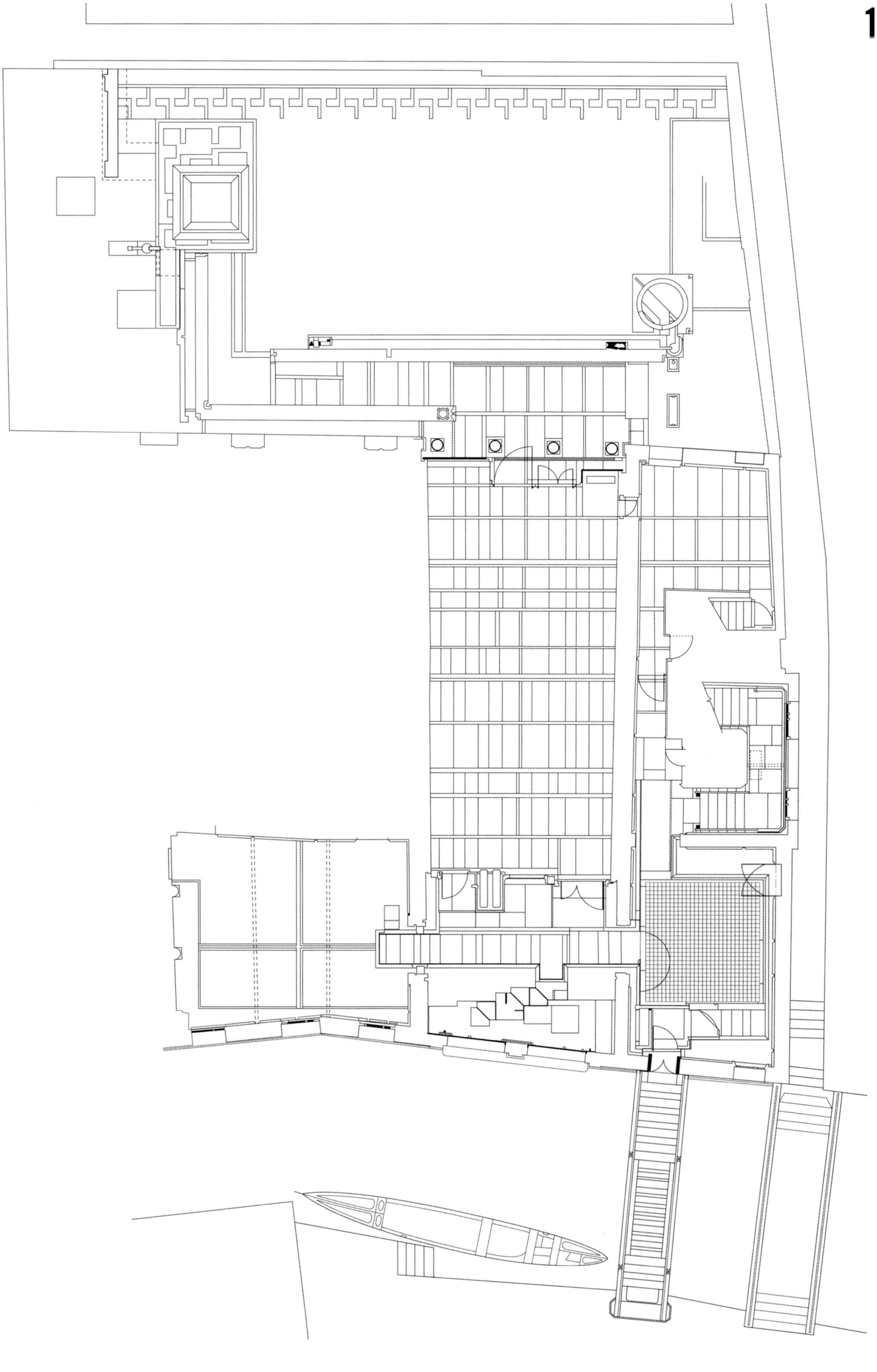

8.2

8.3

8.3 FONDAZIONE QUERINI STAMPALIA RENOVATIONS; NORTHERN, CANAL FACADE WITH NEW STEEL DOUBLE GATES

8.4 FONDAZIONE QUERINI STAMPALIA RENOVATIONS; NEW BRIDGE, WITH ISTRIAN STONE TREADS ON THE CAMPIELLO, LEADING TO THE FONDAZIONE ENTRANCE

8.5 FONDAZIONE QUERINI STAMPALIA RENOVATIONS; BRIDGE HANDRAILS SUPPORTED ON DOUBLE, VERTICAL BLACK STEEL POSTS

8.4

The new bridge, made of stone, steel and wood, sits close beside the similarly sized, typical Venetian stone bridge leading to the narrow passageway along the building's southwest side. Because of their proximity, the bridges' differences are highlighted in our experience, whether crossing the new bridge or looking at it from the old bridge. Among this project's few remaining sketches are a series of bridge studies, indicating that Scarpa originally considered making the new bridge horizontal. The final design follows the logic of typical Venetian bridges, with an arched bottom allowing boats to pass, stairs at both ends and a landing at the top, in the middle of the span. Almost everything else about how the new bridge is made forms a counterpoint to the neighbouring bridge, particularly in the way its wood deck and steel structure complements the massive, masonry of the Querini Stampalia's interior. As Frampton noted, the interior is **'a stereotomic earthwork, laid into the undercroft of a sixteenth century palace, [which] is accessed by a lightweight bridge that acts as a kind of fixed hinge between the terra firma of the campo and the transformed shell of the palazzo.'** [3] One of few new bridges in Venice, it celebrates our passage to the building, its stone steps emerging from the Campiello floor, its wooden steps descending to the new window-doorway's stone threshold.

A wide landing-like tread of white Istrian stone with three-sided ends stands on the grey-stoned Campiello. A smaller Istrian stone tread, down-turned L-shape in section and canted forward to shed water, sits upon the first tread. Beneath this second tread, a large Istrian stone block is set into the canal wall, forming the bridge's buttress. Above the second tread, two slightly inclined wood treads are made of two full-width solid oak boards separated by an open joint, joined by steel edge-bands at their ends, set in S-shaped steel brackets that interlock the treads together with those above and below each. [4] **(8.4)** The front tread board is secured to the top of the steel brackets beneath by double bolts running through small recessed steel plates at both ends. The second tread and its mirror image on the opposite side are set flush with the bridge's slightly curving central deck, distinguished from the treads by the continuous edge boards and the narrower boards between them, each separated by an open joint. Five oak treads descend towards the palazzo entrance, the bottom tread set flush with the top of the Istrian stone curbs on either side. Below this, a concave curve-faced Istrian stone block buttress cantilevers out of the palazzo wall. Springing from above the Campiello floor and well below the palazzo window, the asymmetrical arched bridge structure, hinged at the centre and both ends, is formed by two curved, steel plate planes, one above the other, joined by square steel spacers welded to both plates at 50 centimetre (1 ft 7 in) intervals. The two primary hinged arches are divided by a wide joint on the bridge's centreline, visible through the joints between the tread and deck boards.

The bridge's handrail is supported on double, vertical black steel posts, four on each side, bearing into the Istrian stone landing's upper face at the Campiello, the Istrian stone abutment's side at the palazzo facade and the bridge's steel structure on both ends of the central deck. A vertical, L-shaped black steel bar, mounted between the double steel posts, is welded to the horizontal black steel tube forming the handrail's structural rail. The horizontal steel tubes are bent to form three straight sections of unequal lengths, following the bridge's asymmetrical rise and fall; their ends are given hemispherical brass caps. Small upward curving steel brackets, in pairs except at the ends, are welded to the steel tube, supporting the teak handrail from beneath. Frampton noted, **'In this combination, a lower structural rail in tubular steel and an upper handrail in teak, we find that synthesis of structural economy and ergonomic form that is so characteristic of Scarpa's work.'** [5] Both the two interlocked joints at the bends and the teak handrails' ends are capped in brass plate. The handrail is a horizontal, oval shape in section, with its inner face cut off flat, so we grasp its largest curve. Unlike Scarpa's other staircases, the wood handrail is set outside of the steel structural tube, and is tilted up towards the outside, inviting us to lean on the handrail, against the tube at the landing, and view the canal. **(8.5)**

8.5

Passing through the window-doorway, framed by glass and steel doors that fold flat against the jambs, we access the small, raised, Istrian stone-floored entry vestibule, enclosed by frameless glass. Here we turn right, parallel to the canal, open the glass door and step down on to an Istrian stone landing, its 45-degree angled outer face acts to turn us again, through two steps and onto the entrance hall's 4 metre (13 ft 1 in) square, mosaic floor. This vibrant floor is made of a complex, nonrepeating pattern of L-shaped, three-quarter square, white and pink-orange marble stone pieces, with inset dark-green and dark-red marble square pieces fitting into the one-quarter square void of the L-shaped pieces, all surrounded by a white marble border and polished to a highly reflective finish.[6] The colours of the stones are reminiscent of ancient church floors, such as Santa Maria dei Miracoli, yet its seemingly random pattern is only to be found in Scarpa's own work, as in the Sacello at the Castelvecchio, completed at the same time. One drawing by Scarpa, showing this floor's final design, confirms that, like the Sacello, Scarpa gave exact instructions on each stone's colour and position. **(8.6)** Descriptions of this room to date have stated that, initially at least, the mosaic pattern was directly inspired by a painting by Josef Albers. However, like the Sacello's, this mosaic's random pattern seems much closer to gridded watercolours by Klee, or Mondrian's early paintings, than to any work by Albers.

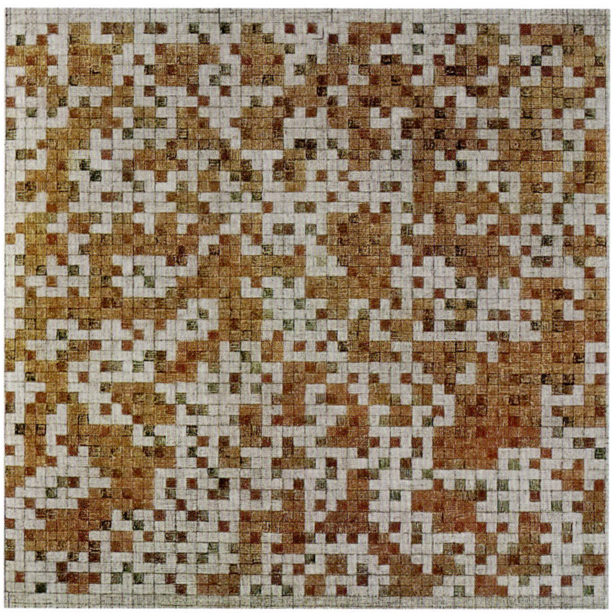

8.6

8.7

Yet, in a floor plan from late in the Querini Stampalia design process, Scarpa has drawn, in the square entrance hall floor, an exact copy of Albers' *Bundled* of 1925, a square, flashed glass artwork.[7] The figure's orientation in the floor is the same as the artwork, the top of the artwork at the back of the room and its bottom at the room's edge nearest the canal, where we enter. **(8.7, 8.8)** Albers' flashed glass pieces, such as *Bundled*, were all made during his time at the Bauhaus and were brought with him to America in 1933. Until recently, Albers' early flashed glassworks received far less attention and publicity than his later paintings, such as the *Homage to the Square* series, and thus we ask: how did Scarpa know about this work at the time he was working on the Querini Stampalia floor design? *Bundled* is part of the Josef Albers Foundation's collection, and, according to Albers' own records, this piece was first published in 1958, in an article on Albers' glassworks in the German glass publication *Glaswelt*, and shown in London in 1962 as part of the 'Painters of the Bauhaus' exhibition.[8] Given Scarpa's lifelong interest and involvement with glass design, including his 1962 appointment as a member of the committee for Form and Design of the International Glass Commission in Paris, as well as his extensive use of glass elements in his works, Albers' early flashed glassworks, discovered at some point during or just prior to his Querini Stampalia design, would have held special meaning for him.[9] Although the drawing indicates that Scarpa used Albers' *Bundled* as the starting point for the entrance hall floor pattern, he later abandoned it to develop his own pattern.

It is important to point out that the basic form underlying this entrance hall floor pattern and the Castelvecchio Sacello facade mosaic is directly related to Scarpa's own detailing language. The L-shape, made of a square from which a quarter square has been removed, with its two equal legs, is yet another double figure. When we look at the Scarpa-designed floor pattern, we also find multiple double figures in the matching of small squares, set adjacent or at a 45-degree angle to one another, and in the matching of the L-shapes, producing T-shapes, U-shapes, H-shapes and so on. Of equal importance is the fact that the incomplete, three-quarter square, as well as the three-quarter circle, were now firmly established as Scarpa's standard detail for metal and stone pieces' inside corners. This detail is a celebration of the process of making, involving drilling a small hole at the point at which the saw cuts will meet; it also is a way of joining one metal to another, as seen in his museum easels' brass connections and the Querini Stampalia water gates' brass cylinders and square brackets. Scarpa employed the three-quarter square as a way of forming the inside corners of both the entrance opening in the concrete facade and the mural on the Gavina Showroom's back wall; he also used this detail in the Querini Stampalia stone radiator enclosure.

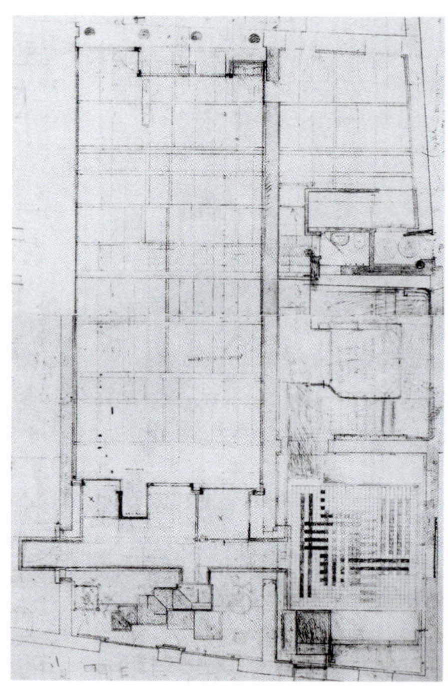

8.8

The entrance hall's mosaic floor is edged by a tall, Istrian stone-faced curb with a bevelled Istrian stone cap. A moat-like, exposed-aggregate concrete trench between the curb and the irregularly angled walls contains the *acqua alta*, allowing the below flood-level floor to be used in all seasons. The trench, running across all the canal front rooms, is connected by pipes penetrating the exterior wall to the canal, draining water as the flooding recedes, but also allowing water to enter as the *acqua alta* rises. The stone curb and concrete trench is an all-seasonal reminder of Venice's intimate relationship to the water, while simultaneously reinforcing the sense that the new square marble floor has been set within the irregular existing walls. Visiting the Querini Stampalia during the *acqua alta*, surrounded by the water-filled, moat-like trench, the sunlight's flickering reflections play off the surface of the water and across the walls and ceilings, mingling with the mosaic floor's shimmering surface, while the reverberant echoes of our footsteps, people's voices in the Campiello and passing canal boats, are all magnified and extended. **(8.9)**

The entrance hall walls are clad in black steel-edged, light-grey plaster panels spaced in irregular widths, which fold around the corners so that all vertical joints are on the flat wall faces. The panels' tops rise past the ceiling's edge and their bottoms stop at the top of the trench. They are held forward of the wall, allowing air to circulate so as to control the rising damp from the saturated ground. On the right-hand wall, the rectangular electrical cabinet is accessed by two interlocking, L-shaped polished brass-faced doors, with three-quarter circle brass rings set into their inner corners. The entrance hall ceiling, made of dark-red polished plaster, is composed of a three-quarter square L-shape, running along the canal wall and the left wall, above the room's three doorways; a square panel is set in the L-shape. Between the two ceiling panels is a wide steel-plate joint, parallel to the canal, and a narrow steel-plate joint, perpendicular to the canal, subtly indicating our next destination lies through one of the two doorways on the room's left side. The formally simple, large-scaled reflective ceiling complements the small-scale, multicoloured complexity of the marble mosaic floor beneath.

8.9

8.6 FONDAZIONE QUERINI STAMPALIA RENOVATIONS; CARLO SCARPA, DRAWING FOR ENTRANCE HALL MOSAIC FLOORING, GRAPHITE ON PAPER

8.7 JOSEF ALBERS, *GEBUNDELT [BUNDLED]*, C.1925; FLASHED GLASS, 30.16 X 31.12 CM (12 X 12.25 IN)

8.8 FONDAZIONE QUERINI STAMPALIA RENOVATIONS; GROUND FLOOR PLAN DRAWING WITH A REPRODUCTION OF JOSEF ALBERS'S *GEBUNDELT [BUNDLED]* IN THE BOTTOM LEFT, GRAPHITE ON PAPER

8.9 FONDAZIONE QUERINI STAMPALIA RENOVATIONS; ENTRANCE HALL WITH THE MOSAIC FLOOR

8.10

To access the library, we enter the passageway opening off the entrance hall across from the door, passing through one of the oval-shaped stone archways Scarpa uncovered, walking across a brush mat set into the floor and turning right into the U-shaped staircase. A lift was placed into what was once the original, central open space, around which the staircase climbs, now framed by solid walls. The staircase walls are lined with steel-edged white polished-plaster panels, the bottoms of which step in an irregular serrated pattern, exposing the original plaster walls. Matching the entrance hall, the ceiling, a continuous plane of dark red polished plaster, inclining upwards, curving back on itself where it meets the flat ceiling of the landing, then inclining upwards again to the first floor. Above the library doors, a second plane of black steel-framed, red polished plaster is set below the upper ceiling, forming a canopy-like soffit. At either side of the door, linear lights are recessed into the ceiling behind frosted glass; at the centre, a steel-edged, intersecting double circle aperture has been opened in the soffit through which light shines from the upper ceiling's circular fixture. **(8.10)**

Again it is the floor that attracts our attention. The original, well-worn Istrian stone stair treads, risers and landings, the surfaces of which are matte and flaked, have new sharp-edged, polished white marble slabs placed on top of them. The new marble is kept well away from the walls, revealing the old stone stairs' outer portions, while also creating a shallow trench between the new flooring and walls. A new marble riser is inset from the edge of the new marble tread to form a T-shape when seen from the front, and at the riser's centre, a small vertical slot reveals the

8.10 FONDAZIONE QUERINI STAMPALIA RENOVATIONS; NEW MARBLE STAIRCASE, SET ON TOP OF AND CUT INTO THE EXISTING STONE STAIR, LEADING TO THE FIRST-FLOOR LIBRARY

8.11 FONDAZIONE QUERINI STAMPALIA RENOVATIONS; VIEW ACROSS WATER ENTRY ROOM FROM ENTRANCE HALL, WITH THE WATER GATES (L) AND RADIATOR ENCLOSURE AND GLASS WALL (R)

8.11

8.12

As typically defined, 'restoration' would require the old Istrian stone staircase to be destroyed, removed and replaced with one of the same material made to look like the old staircase. Scarpa proposed an entirely different approach, one that allows the old worn staircase to be preserved beneath and to either side of the new marble staircase, allowing the new and old to coexist simultaneously in our everyday use. However, architects, critics and historians have taken Scarpa too literally, stating that the new treads and risers are simply set on the old staircase, which, presumably, could be uncovered at any time, as suggested by the axonometric drawings showing the new marble lifted off the old treads, shown as still intact.[12] But closer inspection reveals that Scarpa in fact cut out the old staircase's nosing and moulding to accept the new risers, meaning that his 'restoration' permanently joins the old, now scarred Istrian stone stairs and floors to the new ones – literally fusing the old and new, locking them together.

Walking parallel to the canal from the entrance hall, we open the glass door of the frameless glass screen set on the top of the curb, step on to the polished Istrian stone floor and pass through an oval-shaped stone arched doorway. On the entrance hall side of this archway, a thick layer of concrete with limestone aggregate reinforces the wall; small notches, revealing the concrete layer's thickness, mark the arch's spring points and centre. The Istrian stone-faced curb turns and passes through the doorway, carrying the moat-like trenches on both sides into the next room. The Istrian stone floor continues to the other side of the water entry room, passing through a matching arched opening into the shadowed space beyond. We are standing in the original water entry, opening to the canal through the double gateway on the left, which we saw from outside; light from the sky above the Campiello reflects off the gates' vertical brass rods, while light bouncing off the surface of the canal is reflected by the horizontal rods. **(8.11)** The water entry sidewalls are made of a layer of new brick masonry, and brick has been used to reinforce the canal wall. The ceiling is a single large plane of steel-edged polished plaster, originally green in colour, with stepping edges at the inside and outside. Above the water gates the polished plaster steps back to reveal a rough wood-board ceiling, into which a frosted glass-faced light is recessed.

The space's floor steps down to either side of the central, causeway-like walkway. Towards the water gates, the high curb turns close to the entrance hall doorway, connecting to a square tread, set level with the top of the curb. Set on a tall concrete riser, the thick Istrian stone tread's corner towards the water gates is cut off at a 45-degree angle, forming a three-quarter square variant. From this upper tread, a series of similarly 45-degree angle-cornered Istrian stone treads lead downwards in a meandering path until reaching a larger landing, elevated above the original water entry floor on a concrete plinth. **(8.12)** This lower Istrian stone slab landing has long slots cut at the points where its dimensions match the smaller stairs above. Beyond the water gates, the building's original Istrian stone stairs, now perenially underwater, descend into the canal. Turning to climb the stairs, we notice the elevated walkway is deeply undercut, allowing water to move under the walkway, thus enabling us to quite literally walk on the *acqua alta*.

The walkway, and its curbs, passes through the arched doorway at the water entry's far end, projecting 1 metre (3 ft 3 in) into the next room where the curbs return to form a small, walled platform. Intended for exhibitions, this room has a new, exposed-pebble aggregate concrete floor, framed at two of its edges and across the middle by Istrian stone bands, set just above the original floor. Three of the walls are covered with steel-edged plaster panels, while two pairs of steel beams cross the red, polished-plaster ceiling. Three windows open into this room from the canal, and two original stone columns are embedded in the far wall, where the original brick masonry is exposed. **(8.13)** Because this floor is not elevated, this room is inundated with every *acqua alta*; two Istrian stone steps, set level with, and slightly away from, the top of the curb, access the lower floor. **(see c.1)**

original stair's rounded nosing and moulding. At the bottom of the staircase, a new marble floor slab projects forward, its upward-curved, curb-like edges aligning with the new marble riser's outer edges. At the landing at the staircase's midpoint, a new marble surface is placed on top of the original flooring, with an upturned curb-like edge around the outer three walls; next to the inner wall the marble slab is unedged, and a three-quarter circle has been drilled into the inner corners, where the floor turns to meet the staircase. The black steel handrails, forming intersecting double ovals in section, with brass capped ends, are supported by a series of steel rods anchored into the old treads, then bent inwards around two, 90-degree corners aligning with the new treads' edges.[10] Above the landing is a double lamp, with two rectangular frosted glass panes, into which intersecting circles have been etched, held in a Brazilian rosewood frame; the whole carried on a steel horizontal arm, a double polygon in section, running from wall to wall. Regarding this staircase, Scarpa said:

> 'Do you remember how I dealt with the restoration of the staircase leading to the upper floors in the Querini Stampalia [by placing new slabs of marble over the old steps]? In this way I renewed the staircase without destroying it, preserving its identity and its history, increasing the tension between the new and the old. I was very concerned to articulate the points of junction so as to explain the visual logic of the union of the different members.'[11]

8.13

8.14

We step down into the ground floor's main room, intended for exhibitions and lectures; it is a double square in plan measuring 6 metres (19 ft 8 in) wide by just over 12 metres (39 ft 4 in) long. **(8.14)** The white polished-plaster ceiling, set at the same height as those in the water entry and entrance hall, lacks jointing and detailing, originally carrying only small wall-washer lights, so that our attention, again, is drawn to the floor. Its woven composition of precast concrete paving slabs run from side to side in 11 irregularly sized bands, both separated and joined by single, and occasionally double, polished Istrian stone strips. In each band the concrete floor paving panels are of varying widths and matching depths, and are set in an irregular, occasionally repeating pattern. These exposed-pebble aggregate concrete slabs have a rough, nonreflective finish, while the polished bands reflect the strong southwestern light filtered through the full-height glass wall at the room's garden end. Running down the floor's centre are staggered Istrian stone strips whose reflections mark a meandering line leading towards the garden.

Opposite the water gates, the water entry's ephemeral inner surface is set between the moat-like trenches, and is formed by a largely frameless glass wall that folds in and out between six irregularly spaced, narrow, Istrian stone posts, which are L-shaped in plan. A frameless glass door is set against the left curb, a frameless glass double door is set against the right curb and Istrian stone paving slabs step down in front of both doors. Between the two doorways, to the left of wall's centre, is a massive three-sided enclosure for a pair of radiators. The floor-to-ceiling walls of this hollow, pier-like volume are made of Istrian stone; solid at the bottom and slowly eroded by rectangular cuts as they rise, their voids filled with frameless glass set back from the stone's face. Three-quarter square openings are cut into the voids' inner corners, and the stone walls also are inscribed with a series a series of recessed grooves and bands, whose inner surfaces are pressed with gold leaf. **(see pp. 160–1)** This detail is repeated in grooves running the full height of the Istrian stone posts, and long thin inset lights, set behind frosted glass panels, are positioned at the posts' tops. Before stepping down into the larger of the two doorways, we notice a steel plate projecting from the floor, into which a nonrepeating pattern of conical holes has been drilled, from which light emerges. After dark, this light fixture creates a star-like pattern on the polished-plaster ceiling, as if the stars are being reflected off the canal's surface. The Istrian stone posts, which during the day appear as dark lines against the light coming from the garden and canal, are reversed at night, when their linear lights and reflective, gold-leafed grooves appear as bright lines against the darkness.

8.12 FONDAZIONE QUERINI STAMPALIA RENOVATIONS; WATER ENTRY ROOM, ISTRIAN STONE-SLAB TREADS DESCENDING TO THE RISING CANAL WATER

8.13 FONDAZIONE QUERINI STAMPALIA RENOVATIONS; SMALL EXHIBITION ROOM, VIEW BACK THROUGH THE WATER ENTRY ROOM TO THE ENTRANCE HALL

8.14 FONDAZIONE QUERINI STAMPALIA RENOVATIONS; MAIN EXHIBITION ROOM

8.15

8.16a

8.16b

At the room's sides, the concrete slabs and the stone bands turn up the walls, the concrete ending exactly at the height of the Istrian stone-faced moat curb in the rooms along the canal. While there is no evidence that the *acqua alta* enters this room, the concrete curb running around the room's three sides, together with the garden's similar, curb-like wall, form a shallow, tub-like floor pushed below the *acqua alta* level. A thin, polished Roman travertine band sits above the concrete curb; above this, large, unframed, polished travertine slabs are set in two equal-depth bands, separated at eye level by a polished, slotted brass plate providing anchorage for exhibition panels. The travertine, a white-coloured, porous stone full of small voids running in veins, revealed by the crosscut, is set with its pronounced grain horizontal in the larger slabs and vertical in smaller slabs. As on the entrance hall walls, the travertine is a cladding, held away from the ceiling and forward of the ancient masonry walls so as not to trap moisture. Vertical lighting fixtures are recessed into the wall between the travertine slabs, with florescent tubes behind frameless, flush-set frosted glass. The lights are arranged as single; double side-by-side with a brass vertical between; or stacked one above the other and staggered so the right edge of one aligns with left edge of the other. Where these light fixtures meet the travertine band above the floor, a thin brass plate is inserted to separate the glass edge from the stone. **(8.15)**

At the right-hand wall's far end the slotted brass band is interrupted by an L-shaped, vertical travertine slab. **(8.16a)** This unique slab, standing above a step-like opening carved from the concrete curb, is surrounded by open joints and has a Z-shaped hole opened at its upper-left corner, through which light emanates. Pushing on this stone panel, it swings open accessing a small annex off the main exhibition space. **(8.16b)** Scarpa said, **'Do you remember the marble door [in the Querini Stampalia]? Well, the material is the same as on the wall, but you realize it is a door because this is shown by the joints between door and wall. It is a door that invites you to reach out and open it. It is a different way of dealing with the ancient problem.'** [13] In a way similar to the stone door at Olivetti Showroom, this door causes us to reconsider the walls' stone cladding and the way it is hung, separated at its midpoint by the reflective brass band. As Frampton noted, **'Stone thus appears in two aspects; in the first simply as cladding and in the**

8.17

second as a kind of "wood," where it is incised, inlaid, and hinged as though it were petrified cabinet-work ... Throughout, brass is the key for this metonymic transposition between stone and wood, since the inlaid picture rail, running around the gallery, recalls a similar use of brass connectors in the bridge handrail.'[14]

Four ancient stone columns, supporting the palazzo's back wall, stand outside the frameless glass wall at the room's garden edge. In the right corner a horizontal radiator is lifted off the floor on a double-steel bar stand. (8.17) At the centre, the glass wall steps in to meet three narrow Istrian stone posts, rotated with respect to each other. Between the two inner Istrian posts, which have gold-leafed grooves and inset light fixtures, are two unequal frameless glass doors opening to the garden. These glass doors, secured to metal hinge plates at floor and ceiling, have vertical frosted glass safety strips rising to the base of the posts' inset light fixtures. In the outer corners, the concrete curb is met by an Istrian stone curb of equal height standing beneath the glass wall, while the travertine panelling stops at the glass line, beyond which is the new brick masonry and the original stone pilaster. At the ceiling the polished plaster stops at the folding glass line, beyond which is a rough-wood ceiling, similar to the water entry's outer edge. While material changes in the wall and ceiling subtly demarcate the line between interior and exterior, the pebble-faced concrete and Istrian stone banded floor carries through the glass wall, past the four original columns, terminating in the garden wall, almost seamlessly joining the inside and outside.

8.15 FONDAZIONE QUERINI STAMPALIA RENOVATIONS; MAIN ROOM WITH CONCRETE FLOOR, TRAVERTINE STONE WALLS AND VERTICAL LIGHTING FIXTURES

8.16a FONDAZIONE QUERINI STAMPALIA RENOVATIONS; MAIN ROOM, CLOSED L-SHAPED TRAVERTINE DOOR TO ANNEX

8.16b FONDAZIONE QUERINI STAMPALIA RENOVATIONS; MAIN ROOM, OPEN DOOR

8.17 FONDAZIONE QUERINI STAMPALIA RENOVATIONS; MAIN ROOM, FRAMELESS GLASS BACK WALL LEADING TO GARDEN

8.18

Entering the garden at its lowest level, a concrete retaining wall directly ahead separates the lower, pebble-faced concrete and Istrian stone paved terrace from the main grass lawn, lifted 61 centimetres (2 ft) above. At the bottom of the retaining wall, a narrow Istrian stone gutter separates the terrace paving from the wall and drains off rainwater. At the top of the retaining wall, a narrow watercourse flows parallel to the canal at the entry; occasional flashes of light are reflected off fish swimming in its depths. The water flow's source, towards the wall's east end, is a double horizontal brass spout feeding multiple small water streams into a small rectangle of Apuan marble, pale yellow with purple-black veins, carved to produce a rectangular spiralling, maze-like outflow that trickles into the watercourse. A slot cast into the wall's top, partway down, reveals that the wall is not as thick as it first appears, and that the watercourse extends back up under the retaining wall's cantilevered top, similar to the water entry's walkway. **(8.18)** Towards the end of the retaining wall, at the garden's western end, the watercourse passes under a small marble lion, facing back towards the source. Found by Scarpa during the garden renovation, the sculpture is part of the Querini family's coat of arms. [15] At the watercourse's western end, a hinged brass spout pours water into a spiral channel, carved into an Istrian stone slab. The channel carries the water to the drain beneath the garden's original cylindrical marble wellhead, set on a square concrete plinth broken open by several 45-degree angled fissures. The water's east to west flow, and the stone lion, also the symbol of Venice, serve to subtly remind us of Scarpa's lifelong interest in the flow of cultural influence from the East to Venice.

The garden is surrounded on all sides by tall brick walls, with the palazzo's upper windows opening above. To the right, next to the original pilaster in the palazzo's outer wall, the risers of two steps are formed of interlocking L-shaped Istrian stone blocks, while the treads are two square brass plates. Stepping sideways rather than forwards to use the stairs, they reverberate as feet strike them, producing musical sounds as if the stair was an instrument. In the brick wall at the garden's right edge, a new gate, giving access from the narrow passageway, is made with vertical larch wood boards, pivoting open from an off-centre steel hinge. Next to the brick wall at the back of the garden, now heavily overgrown with ivy, runs a series of L-shaped stepping stones, their longer, thinner legs alternating from left to right while their shorter, wider legs align to form the path, suggesting that, like the Japanese gardens Scarpa so admired, the garden's land and the water must both be crossed by stepping stone. **(8.19)**

At the sunken garden terrace's left side, a series of broad, Istrian stone-edged concrete steps are set between the concrete retaining wall and the slightly higher concrete wall running parallel to it, near the palazzo's brick wall. The low garden walls and the plinth beneath the old wellhead are made of concrete with exposed white Istrian stone aggregate. Istrian stone blocks, each carved into a different form, have been cast into the corners and ends of the concrete planes, forming three-quarter square inside corners, re-entrant outer corners, recessed stepping ends and interlocked ends; together they impart to the concrete masses the honorific status of stonework. At the garden's eastern edge, the right-side's low wall stops shortly after the watercourse source, while the left-side's low wall turns and runs across the garden, terminating next to a large rectangular pool. **(8.20)**

Behind this low wall, two taller concrete walls are set in a staggered pattern, overlapping in the middle to produce two interlocked L-shaped forms, off of which roof-like planes cantilever at the front and back. The walls' horizontal casting layers have been finished to produce different surface textures, from exposed Istrian stone aggregate to smooth, grey cement. In the nearest wall's centre, a single vertical recessed band runs from the ground up to a slot at the top of the wall, where a cruciform lamp, made of twelve intricately interlocked bent and cut sheets of brass, is mounted. At eye level, a band of reflective Murano glass tiles, silver, gold and black, are set flush with the concrete walls' surface, with a single row of tiles on the front wall and a double on the back wall. This tile mosaic, made by De Luigi, forms the garden's internal horizon line, similar to the main room's eye-level, horizontal slotted brass band. **(8.21)**

8.18 FONDAZIONE QUERINI STAMPALIA RENOVATIONS; GARDEN, VIEW ALONG RETAINING WALL AND WATERCOURSE SEPARATING THE TERRACE FROM THE MAIN LAWN

8.19 FONDAZIONE QUERINI STAMPALIA RENOVATIONS; L-SHAPED STEPPING STONES ALONG THE GARDEN'S BACK WALL

8.20 FONDAZIONE QUERINI STAMPALIA RENOVATIONS; GARDEN, VIEW FROM THE WESTERN END OF THE RETAINING WALL WITH A MARBLE LION, A BRASS SPOUT POURS WATER INTO A SPIRAL CHANNEL, WHICH DIRECTS IT TO THE ORIGINAL CYLINDRICAL WELLHEAD AND A CARVED STONE BLOCK CAN BE SEEN CAST INTO THE CONCRETE CORNER

8.21 OVERLEAF > FONDAZIONE QUERINI STAMPALIA RENOVATIONS; GARDEN, EASTERN SIDE WITH STAGGERED PRECAST CONCRETE WALLS, BANDS OF MURANO GLASS TILES AND AN L-SHAPED POOL WITH SQUARE BRASS BASIN

8.20

8.19

8.22

A large, shallow, L-shaped pool, diagonally across from the sunken terrace, anchors the formal garden's eastern corner. The pool's narrower leg slides between the two concrete walls, under the small horizontal plane that spans between them, and into the service court behind. There, a small Istrian stone scupper spills water into a shallow circular pool, carved from a block of Istrian stone set flush with the paving stones, out of which a narrow channel carries water to a square drain. The pool's larger, rectangular leg fills to the brim a shallow, concrete-walled tray-like basin, the bottom and inner sides of which are lined with a mosaic of square Murano glass tiles set in a stepping pattern on a white concrete background, clearly visible through the thin plane of water. Into this pool a brass tray-like basin is set, formed of an outer and inner square separated by a narrow channel of water. The central square's inner edge is lined with small projecting brass discs, mirrored in the water's surface, and its black depths, in which a water lily grows, contrasts with the larger pool's transparent shallowness. In fact, the brass double-square basin, reused from the 1961 Turin exhibition, is mounted above a pool whose bottom is set at the main room's floor level. Of this pool Richard Murphy noted, **'The complete composition is of a watery world floating in the middle of a shallow sea; a final reference perhaps to his city of Venice.'** [16]

The Querini Stampalia interior is never far from the lagoon water, which, in reality and by implication, appears beneath and beside us at every point in our perambulations. The main room spans between the canal and garden, connecting both, and it is interesting to note that the distance from the edge of the Campiello to the edge of the water entry's walkway, a space filled with water, matches the distance from the garden's brick back wall to the front retaining wall, a space filled with elevated earth. [17] In Venice, gardens have traditionally been elevated above the building's ground-floor levels, allowing trees roots to avoid briny groundwater. Here, Scarpa reasserted the water's dominance by using a wall of water – the retaining wall and watercourse basin – to define the garden, so that even the elevated earth is only allowed to rise to the water level. As Michael Cadwell noted in his perceptive essay on the Querini Stampalia, **'Scarpa's was an aquatic sensibility, saturated by Venice.'** [18]

In the Querini Stampalia, Scarpa achieved a complete fusion of past and present, his design giving equal weight to both the reality of the historical building spatial fabric and the demands of contemporary use. The entire design's jointed spatial fabric is constructed of sensuous materials of complementary textures and colours, formed in quiet planes with active edges, and joined by articulately detailed gaps and frames. The whole, a highly crafted celebration of joints, simultaneously feels as if it could be taken apart into its constituent elements. It is such buildings that have led to the debate regarding whether Scarpa, never formally trained or licensed as an architect, should be considered a craftsman, an artist or an architect. Of course he would say he was all three. In 1964, while in Venice to work on his ultimately unrealized project for a new municipal hospital, Le Corbusier, whose early *Vers une architecture* had inspired Scarpa and many others to embrace modern architecture, visited the recently completed Querini Stampalia, after which he asked, **'Qui est ce beau artisan?'** [19] This is usually translated as **'Who is this fine craftsman?'**, but the connection to art in the word 'artisan' is likely more appropriate for Scarpa. **(8.22)**

In 1962, while constructing the Querini Stampalia, Scarpa and his family moved from Venice to Asolo, a small, picturesque hillside town in the Treviso province, home to many famous writers and artists. Scarpa would live in Asolo for ten years, until he moved for the last time, in 1972, to Vicenza.

Among this period's related designs, the exhibition, 'The sense of colour and the control of water', housed in the Veneto Pavilion at the Italia 1961 Exposition in Torino, is perhaps the most closely related to the Querini Stampalia's water themes. The exhibition intended to present the almost entirely water-defined world of Venice and its close connection to colour. Scarpa wrapped the Pavilion's outer walls with gridded wooden screens, display panels and a series of vertical, coloured glass panels from Murano, demonstrative of the varied glass-making techniques, through which light streamed in from outside. At the large, square floor's centre, Scarpa inserted a new topography, more liquid than solid, placing a series of layered planes of platforms and shallow brass trays overflowing with water, their bottoms covered with Murano glass tile mosaics. The highest layer of this topographic composition, rising just above the floor, was the brass tray-like basin formed of nested squares that he would reuse in the Querini Stampalia garden. Hanging beneath a rooflight in the room's centre, above the largest pool, was a massive cascading crystal chandelier, designed by Scarpa and made by Venini. Running across the room, and framing the pools, was a steel-edged plaster wall, eroded in an irregular serrated pattern and carrying Murano glass tile murals by De Luigi, which hung like a curtain from the structure above, its inner corners emphasized by three-quarter square notches. All of these layers, of varied orientations, geometries and colours, were reflected and fused in the pools' rippling surfaces, anchoring the composition. **(8.23)**

8.22 FONDAZIONE QUERINI STAMPALIA RENOVATIONS; SCULPTED RADIATOR ENCLOSURE SEEN FROM THE EASTERN EXHIBITION ROOM

8.23 CARLO SCARPA, 'THE SENSE OF COLOUR AND THE CONTROL OF WATER' EXHIBITION, VENITO PAVILION, ITALIA '61, TORINO

8.23

The lawyer Ettore Gallo, who successfully defended Scarpa against the charges of practising architecture without license, commissioned Scarpa to renovate the early nineteenth-century Palazzo Brusarosco in Vicenza; the project was built from 1962–5. In the ground-floor portico, Scarpa reinforced the existing wooden beam ceilings to accept bookshelf loads by running new steel beams, set on steel brackets projecting from the walls, beneath the existing wooden beams, with double struts rising to support the old beams. On the first floor, the new ceiling structure takes the form of two pairs of beams crossing at the room's centre, similar to the Castelvecchio gallery rooms. Here, a double laminated wood beam carries the old ceiling beams, and is in turn carried by a double steel beam, bearing on steel brackets cantilevered from the plaster-faced masonry wall. **(8.24)** At the centre, where the double beams cross, the wood beams are hollowed out to form a pair of down-turned C-shapes, and the load is transferred from the wood to the steel beams by two pairs of upturned C-shaped steel channels. As a result, the most intense structural moment is paradoxically voided. On the second floor, added after the building sustained Second World War bomb damage, the apartment is detailed similarly to the Gipsoteca, including white Clauzetto marble floors, their joints almost invisible, separated from the polished plaster walls by black steel bands, polished-plaster ceilings running into the recess at the top of the walls and corner windows pushed up against the tallest room's ceiling. **(8.25)** Throughout the apartment, the plaster walls' corners are rounded, which, when combined with their black steel band bases and the recessed reveals at their tops, imparts an independence from the floor, ceiling and even from the other walls, as if the walls could slide from one position to another.

Like the Gallo residence, the Venice apartment and studio for Luigi Scatturin of 1962–3 has a series of visual axes cutting through the large plan, connecting the various rooms together and giving city views, even from deep within the interior. The floor is made of tight-set, polished terracotta tiles, and the floor is separated from the polished-plaster, curved-edged walls by a small stone gutter, similar to the Castelvecchio upper-level galleries. In a unique detail, the low, multicoloured textured-plaster ceiling, which appears to be gold, red or grey depending on the daylight angle, is set away from the walls, window and door heads by curving bands of polished plaster, carried up from the walls below. A black leather-clad door leads from the living room to the low-ceilinged, wood veneer-walled office with Scarpa-designed furniture; a plaster-sided and wood-topped wardrobe is stepped to form a series of Z-shaped risers and offset treads accessing the roof terrace. **(8.26)**

8.24

8.25

8.26

8.27

Finally, though it was built at the very end of his life, the pavement Scarpa designed in 1978 for the Torresino Church in Padova is directly related to his Querini Stampalia design. Set on an elevated octagonal central platform defined by eight columns, Scarpa made a slightly raised marble mosaic floor with bevelled edges and three-quarter squared corners. The marble mosaic is made of L-shaped, three-quarter square pieces, coloured light pink and white, within which smaller square tiles are set, coloured dark red and putty grey. **(8.27)** Unlike the apparently similar non-repeating patterns in the Querini Stampalia entrance hall and Castelvecchio Sacello walls, this floor pattern does repeat: after every six rows left to right, and after every two rows up and down. This fact has not been commented on before, and the likely reason is that the repeating pattern is not immediately evident. Scarpa limited himself to only four orientations for the four mosaic pieces when set into a square grid formation, allowing three different ways of pairing the two small grey and red square pieces, two diagonally and one side-by-side, and four different ways of pairing the pink and white L-shaped pieces, two T-shapes and two U-shapes. Unlike in Scarpa's other uses of mosaic elements, these L-shaped pieces are always separated by an L-shape of another colour, never touching like-coloured pieces. Seen from the sanctuary, the elevated, polished mosaic floor pattern shifts in and out of alignment, recalling the isometric geometries of Romanesque and Renaissance church floors, the Palladian villas' interwoven wood inlay floors, the syncopated rhythms of the Bauhaus' tapestries and fabrics, and Albers' flashed glass works, all of which are strongly suggestive of spatial depth compressed within a perfectly flat surface. This floor's highly reflective surface, and its complex suggestion of hidden depths, is an example of the way Scarpa transposed the characteristics of glass, which combines the qualities of surface and depth into his architecture. As Cadwell noted, 'Scarpa knew glass first, and its lessons stayed with him.'[20]

8.24 CARLO SCARPA, GALLO HOUSE, VICENZA, 1962–5; FIRST FLOOR, NEW STRUCTURE OF TWO CROSSING PAIRS OF BEAMS SUPPORT THE EXISTING WOODEN CEILING

8.25 GALLO HOUSE; SECOND FLOOR WITH CLAUZETTO MARBLE FLOORS AND POLISHED PLASTER WALLS WITH ROUNDED CORNERS

8.26 CARLO SCARPA, SCATTURIN HOUSE, VENICE, 1962–3; OFFICE WITH WOOD-VENEER WALLS AND WOOD-TOPPED WARDROBE, STEPPED TO FORM A STAIRCASE TO THE ROOF TERRACE

8.27 CARLO SCARPA, TORRESINO CHURCH PAVING, PADOVA, 1978; RAISED, MARBLE MOSAIC FLOOR AND ALTAR

CHAPTER 09
THE WHOLENESS OF INSEPARABLE ELEMENTS

ZENTNER HOUSE
ZURICH, SWITZERLAND, 1964–1968

9.1

In 1967, after receiving the President of the Republic's award in Rome, Scarpa travelled to the United States, where he visited the works of Frank Lloyd Wright for the first time. There he also met the American architect Louis Kahn, with whom he began a close friendship and association. Kahn had designed the Olivetti-Underwood factory in Harrisburg, Pennsylvania, in 1966 and the sign he placed in front of the building displayed the lettering Scarpa had designed for the company's Venice showroom. In early 1968, with Scarpa's support, Mazzariol offered Kahn the commission to design a Palazzo dei Congressi for Venice.[1] Between 1968 and 1974, Kahn came to Venice repeatedly to present designs for the congress hall, initially proposed to be built in the Biennale gardens and later in the Arsenale, the city's ancient and massive shipbuilding complex. In the end it was never realized. In 1969, during a trip to present the first design, Kahn was inspired by the curved lead-clad roofs of San Marco, and later used similarly sized and detailed sheets of lead-coated zinc to clad the barrel-vaulted roofs of his most famous building, the Kimbell Art Museum in Fort Worth, Texas.

Kahn was Scarpa's guest on each of his Venice trips; photographs from 1969 show Kahn and Scarpa avidly discussing Scarpa's copy of Wright's 1925 Wendingen publication, signed by Wright. Intriguingly, the book was opened to the drawings of the circle-filled murals Wright designed for Midway Garden's walls (Chicago, 1913). Scarpa and Kahn shared not only an interest in Wright's work, but, more importantly, a profound respect for ancient architecture and the generative power of historical spaces. They also shared the fundamental belief that the joint, the detail and the expression of how a building was made were both a moral imperative and the only appropriate source for ornament in modern construction. The last thing that Kahn wrote for publication before his death in 1974 was a foreword in the form of a poem for a book on Scarpa's work, in which he alluded to many concepts dear to his heart, including **'the wholeness of inseparable elements'** where **'the joint inspires ornament, its celebration.'**[2] **(9.1)**

Designed for his close friend Savina Zentner, the widow of Scarpa's frequent early associate Angelo Masieri, the Zentner House was Scarpa's only built work outside Italy. During Scarpa's time working on the house, it was frequented by key figures from Zurich's vibrant cultural scene. These included the architect and artist Max Bill;[3] one of the founders, as well as the architect, of the Ulm School of Design, which had been modelled after the Bauhaus, and which included the former Bauhaus faculty members Josef Albers and Johannes Itten among its guest teachers in the 1950s.[4]

The municipal building regulations required that the overall volume of this pre-1914 house not be changed in its renovation, and that the three publically-visible facades maintain a similar appearance. Scarpa reconstructed the facades on the three public sides, and on the street-facing facade he gave the lower floor a concrete base beneath continuous windows. Above the windows hovered a white stucco brass-edged plane, similar to the Palais Stoclet built by Josef Hoffmann (Brussels, 1910), into which square windows with mitered corners were opened, and varnished, vertical wood board fascias rising above to cover the upper, bedroom floor. The new lift was housed in a *vesica piscis* plan-shaped concrete tower embedded in the building's street facade. At its centre a Murano glass tile mosaic ran up a recessed slot. **(9.3)** On the southern, garden side, Scarpa was free to make an entirely new facade, constructing a horizontally layered composition with a board-formed concrete wall at the ground, carrying an eye-level linear Murano glass tile mosaic; and above this a glass-walled living room was set beneath an overhanging horizontal roof. **(9.2)**

We enter the house beside the lift tower's curving, vertical board-formed concrete wall, stepping down on to the entry halls' white Clauzetto marble floor. The ceiling is a cream-coloured, polished plaster and stops just short of the white, polished-plastered walls. **(9.4)** Set into the ceiling are Z-shaped, recessed light fixtures formed by two offset, square mottled, clear-glass panels edged with thin, polished brass bands. To our left, a beautiful wood floor, in contrasting yellow Tanzanian wood and brown wenge, extends into the entry hall from the living room, inviting us to move in that direction. We walk around a pair of parallel, steel-edged, white plaster walls between which a white Clauzetto marble stretched-circle-shaped landing cantilevers outwards, hovering over the wood floor. **(9.5)** The Clauzetto marble treads of this staircase lead up to the bedroom floor; and the stair can be closed at the bottom by a wood and glass door, which, when open, sits against the steel-edged screen wall. The top of the door's wooden panel is carved out in a stretched-circle shape with one straight edge, a form Scarpa used repeatedly in this house.

9.2

9.3

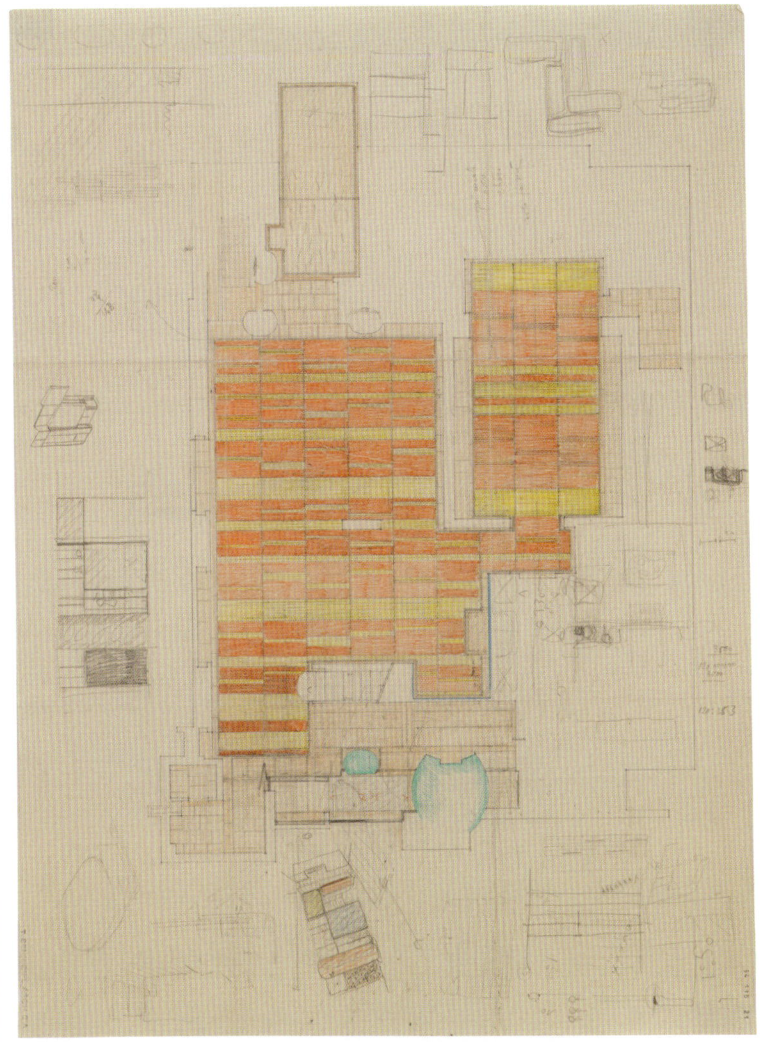

9.1 PERIOD PHOTOGRAPH, VENICE, 1969; CARLO SCARPA (L), LOUIS KAHN (C) AND KAHN'S ASSISTANT, CARLOS VALLHONRAT (R), LOOKING AT FRANK LLOYD WRIGHT'S *WENDINGEN PORTFOLIO* (1925)

9.2 CARLO SCARPA, ZENTNER HOUSE, ZURICH, 1964–8; SOUTHERN, GARDEN FACADE

9.3 ZENTNER HOUSE; VIEW FROM THE STREET OF THE NORTHERN AND WESTERN FACADES

9.4 ZENTNER HOUSE; GROUND-FLOOR PLAN SHOWING COLOURED FLOORING, GRAPHITE AND COLOURED PENCIL ON PAPER

9.5 ZENTNER HOUSE; CANTILEVERED MARBLE LANDING, WOOD AND GLASS DOOR WITH THE MARBLE STAIRCASE BEHIND

9.4

9.5

9.6

9.7

9.8

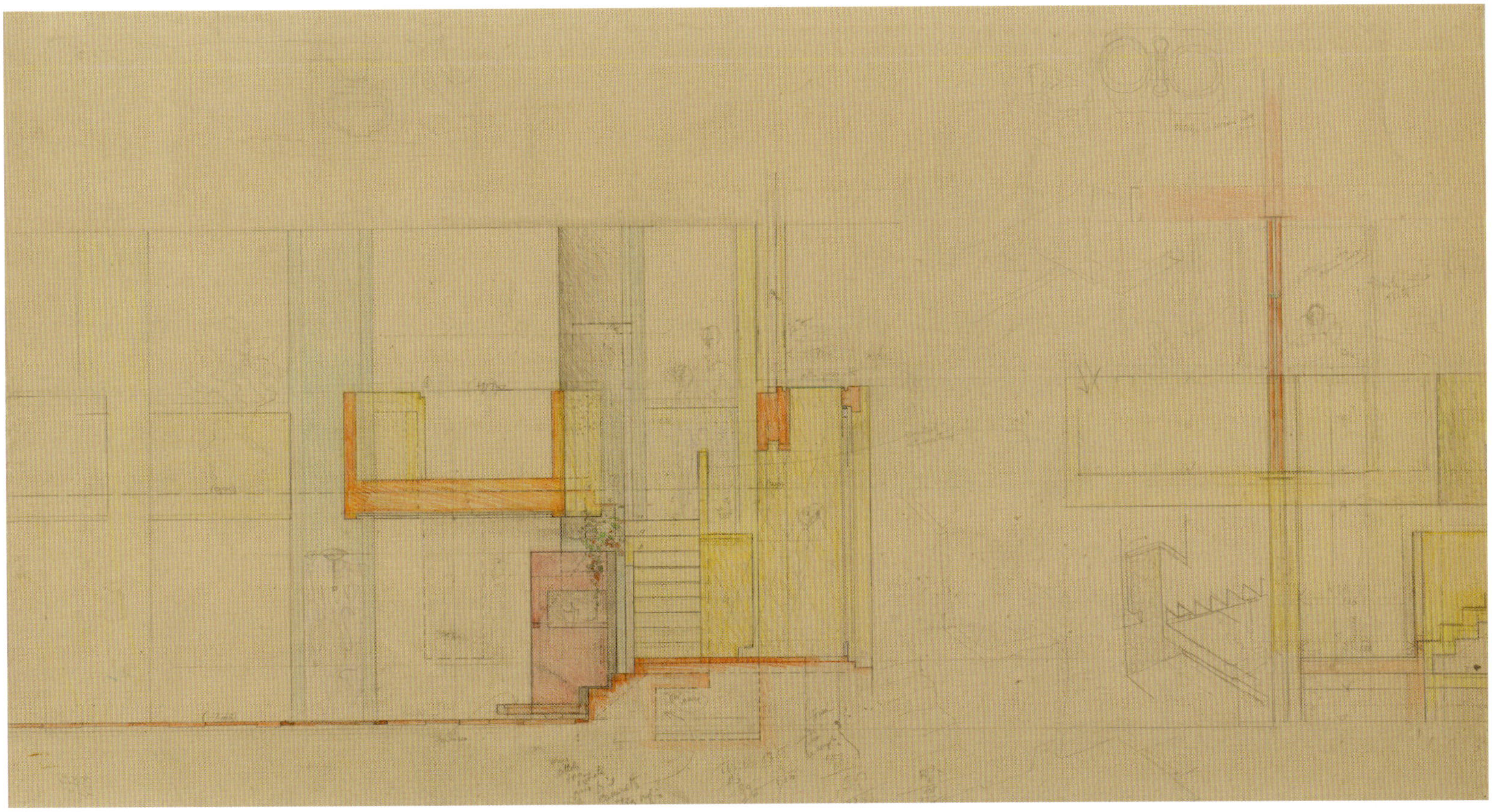

The large living room, extending from the northern, street-side facade to the southern, garden facade, opens out before us. This room is grounded by the syncopated pattern of the bicoloured wood floor, made of boards of equal length and differing widths with aligned joints running from north to south. The wood floor is separated from the walls on either side by a band of white Clauzetto marble – its joints almost invisible. The reflective, cream-coloured, polished plaster ceiling is set slightly back from the walls that run up behind its outer edge. Spotlights, housed in asymmetrical, conical-shaped projections, join to the ceiling with smoothly curved edges. **(9.6)** At the southern end of the living room, three large columns, D-shaped in plan, are finished in polished plaster – two in white and one in black. Two large, full-height windows open to the left, pouring light into the fireplace niche, set back into the wall on the right, and the main sitting area at the southern end overlooking the garden. **(9.7)** On the right, just past the fireplace, the two-tone wood floor continues into the dining room, where the wood floor is again edged by marble. The wall separating the dining room and living room is opened with a stretched-circle-shaped window, which is set against the ceiling, with the polished plaster of the ceiling passing right through the frameless glass to join the two rooms and allow a view of the shared ceiling's continuous reflective surface.

A low, white polished-plaster-faced wall, with a curved stone cap, stops the wood floor at the southern ends of the living and dining rooms. The ceiling continues across, covering the double-height space below that opens on to the garden. A balcony off the dining room cantilevers into this space, its outer face made of horizontal board-formed concrete. **(9.9)** Off the living room, a stone staircase descends to the left, and at the centre, a stone-floored, concrete-walled balcony projects through the glass wall and over the garden. The living room's double-height section is paved in bands of Vipiteno quartzite stone of differing widths, extending through the glass wall to form a garden terrace beneath a projecting canopy. **(9.8)** In the Zentner House, as in the Querini Stampalia, the floors are the most active elements, while the walls and ceilings serve to reflect the floor's patterns, the elegantly detailed fittings and furniture, changing light and the figures of the inhabitants.

9.9

9.6 ZENTNER HOUSE; LIVING ROOM WITH BICOLOURED WOOD FLOOR, LOOKING NORTH ALONG EASTERN GARDEN WALL

9.7 ZENTNER HOUSE; LIVING ROOM, LOOKING THROUGH TO D-SHAPED COLUMN

9.8 ZENTNER HOUSE; SECTION THROUGH THE DOUBLE-HEIGHT SPACE AND STAIRCASE, GRAPHITE AND COLOURED PENCIL ON PAPER

9.9 ZENTNER HOUSE; VIEW OF THE DOUBLE-HEIGHT, GLAZED GARDEN WALL FROM THE PROJECTING BALCONY OFF THE DINING ROOM

9.10

9.11

9.12

The apartment for Loredana Balboni in Venice, constructed to Scarpa's designs from 1964–74, is located on the ground and first floors of a building whose eastern facade sits directly on the Grand Canal. We access the apartment through a garden and, in front of the existing building's red-coloured stucco wall, Scarpa has projected a rectangular, asymmetrical, grey stucco-faced volume with a shallow balcony above. At the centre of this modern projection is the recessed and covered entrance to this apartment opening directly into a long hallway, with cream-coloured, polished-plaster walls and ceiling, and a floor made of staggered slabs of red Veronese marble and bands of white Lasa marble, their edges accentuated by inscribed lines. Along the left wall of the hallway, the ceiling is opened by two large curving voids. **(9.10)**

At the hallway's far end a freestanding spiral staircase rises from a white Lasa marble circular disc standing in the centre of a rectangular alcove. The monolithic treads and risers of the staircase are slightly concave, appearing to unfurl like waves from the central, polished-plaster cylindrical column. **(see pp. 182–3)** This impression is reinforced by the shallow, step-like set of marble planes rising beneath the staircase, reminiscent of the canal boat's rippling backwash on the water's surface. [5] A series of staggered, vertical windows are set in the wall behind the staircase, while the central column terminates at the top of the staircase, forming a pedestal for a stepped wooden sculpture. On the upper level, curved stairs, like ripples from the spiral staircase, are set at both ends of the hallway, accessing the east and west bedroom suites. The low, polished-plaster ceiling reflects the shimmering sunlight bouncing off the Grand Canal, while the handrails around the two curved voids are cupped as if to channel water along them. **(9.11)**

The living room, where a pair of thin, cylindrical steel columns stand off-centre, opens on to the Grand Canal through five large glass doors leading to a wide, Istrian stone paved terrace. **(9.12)** The room is surfaced entirely in shades of white, with the exception of the pale red marble floor slabs interwoven in both directions with irregular bands of Lasa marble. Reflecting the flickering light of the adjacent canal, the room's white polished plaster walls are held back from the ceiling and separated from the floor by a narrow marble gutter. The strong connection to the nearby Grand Canal is carried in a different way into the marble-floored dining room, which opens immediately to the right upon entry. The western wall, overlooking the garden, is opened in a prow-like, half-octagon bay window forming a T-shape with two high, multi-paneled windows framing a tall, thin central window, evocative of a boat's front windows.

9.10 CARLO SCARPA, BALBONI HOUSE, VENICE, 1964–74; ENTRANCE HALLWAY WITH VIEW TO FREESTANDING SPIRAL STAIRCASE (L)

9.11 BALBONI HOUSE; FIRST-FLOOR HALLWAY WITH CURVED VOIDS TO THE GROUND FLOOR AND POLISHED-PLASTER CEILING

9.12 BALBONI HOUSE; LIVING ROOM, PAIR OF STEEL COLUMNS AND GLASS DOORS TO THE GRAND CANAL

The original commission for the Masieri residence was given to Frank Lloyd Wright after his 1951 tour of Italy. The project site, just off the Grand Canal, led to one of the greatest controversies over whether any modern structures should be built in Venice's historic centre. Angelo Masieri, the 30-year-old architect and former student and associate of Scarpa on the Bank in Tarvisio, the Veritti Tomb, and the Romanelli House, asked Wright to design a replacement for his house on Volta de Canal, at the corner of the Grand Canal and Rio Foscari, neighbour to Palazzo Balbi and facing the side of Ca' Foscari. In 1952, Masieri and his wife Savina went to the United States to visit Wright's works and meet with Wright about the project, but during the trip Masieri was tragically killed in an automobile accident. Savina Masieri and the IUAV, with Scarpa as their representative, then commissioned Wright to design a residence and study centre for architecture students on the Masieri house site, to be called the Masieri Memorial Foundation. Wright's design, despite being an elegant and uncharacteristically restrained abstraction of the typical Venetian palazzo, nevertheless ignited a fierce international debate between those who maintained that Venice should remain a museum, untouched by modern building, and those who insisted that, in order to survive, Venice must be a living, evolving city. **(9.13)** Bernard Berenson, the Italian Renaissance art historian and long-time resident of Florence, opposed the project, as did Wright's fellow Oak Park resident Ernest Hemmingway, who said that if Wright's design was built, Venice deserved to be burnt to the ground; to which Wright retorted, **'A voice from the jungle.'** [6] The international outcry, as well as pressure from the Venetian Tourist Commission, eventually forced the city to reject Wright's design in 1954.

For years, Scarpa kept Wright's drawings in hopes that the decision might be reversed. In the last year of his life, while he was overseeing construction of his design for the Masieri Foundation, Scarpa commented both on the increasing conservative definitions of architectural preservation and on Wright's design:

> **'Do you recall the house Wright proposed to build in Venice? Wright did not copy the windows next door. He proposed a work for his time, without forgetting that the essential feature in Venice was and is water. As I said, I have had nothing but trouble from planning rules in Venice and the bureaucrats who interpret them. They order you to imitate the style of the ancient windows, forgetting that those windows were produced in different times, by a different way of life, with "windows" made of other materials, in other styles, and with a different way of making windows. Anyway, stupid imitations of that sort always look wretched. Buildings that imitate look like impostors, and that is just what they are. No one is fooled. Of course, I have been free in designing interiors.'** [7]

In the years after Wright's design was rejected, the Masieri Foundation commissioned Valeriano Pastor to design a renovation, but this too was rejected by the city. In 1968, fourteen years after the decision regarding Wright's design, Scarpa was given the commission, with the city now requiring that the main facade, which can be seen from the Grand Canal, be kept exactly as it was, while making the necessary structural reconstruction of the decaying floors and walls on the building's interiors. Despite this requirement, Scarpa's initial designs endeavored to make subtle modifications of the main facade, as he had done on all his other buildings, in order to reveal the modern intervention within. When these were rejected, he proposed adding a floor, from three to four stories, during the necessary gutting and rebuilding of the interior; this too was rejected. In 1969, Scarpa, with the assistance of Franca Semi and the engineer Maschietto, made the final design, which was approved four years later in 1973. [8] Part of all Scarpa's designs for the Masieri Foundation was his proposal to reconstruct the second ancient chimney, to the left of the facade, to match the still-existing chimney that projected forward on the right side. This was also initially rejected, but when Scarpa found a drawing by Canaletto showing the two chimneys as they originally existed, he was finally given permission. [9] Construction was underway when Scarpa died in 1978 and Semi and Maschietto oversaw the final work on the Masieri Foundation, which was completed in 1983.

FONDAZIONE MASIERI RENOVATIONS
VENICE, 1968–1978

9.13

9.14

9.15

9.13 FRANK LLOYD WRIGHT, FONDAZIONE MASIERI DESIGN, 1952; PERSPECTIVE, VIEW FROM THE GRAND CANAL, GRAPHITE AND COLOURED PENCIL ON PAPER

9.14 CARLO SCARPA, FONDAZIONE MASIERI RENOVATIONS, VENICE, 1968–78; VIEW OF THE FONDAZIONE FROM THE GRAND CANAL, WITH THE CA' FOSCARI (L) BEHIND SCAFFOLDING SCREENS AND THE PALAZZO BALDI (R)

9.15 FONDAZIONE MASIERI RENOVATIONS; MAIN GROUND FLOOR ROOM WITH DOUBLE STEEL COLUMNS, FRAMELESS GLASS WALL AND CEILING VOID

The modest, brick-faced facade of the Masieri Foundation can be seen from the Grand Canal, with the massive, white stone-faced Ca' Foscari, where Scarpa executed some of his earliest work, set perpendicular on the left, across the Rio Foscari, and the equally massive, white stone-faced Palazzo Baldi, with its facade bent in the middle to follow the edge of the canal, on the right. **(9.14)** These neighbouring buildings are twice the height of the three-storey Masieri Foundation. Furthermore, the facade reveals little of the new interior's character, with the only hint of Scarpa's intervention visible in the new water entry gates, a three-part construction of steel similar to those at the Querini Stampalia. The arched water entry is flanked by two brick chimneys, rising from arched bases set just above a white stone base. Slightly protruding from the building's surface, the chimneys rise above the clay tile roof, where they are topped by large, traditional terracotta chimney caps.

Approaching the Masieri Foundation, we walk down a narrow, high-walled street that leads to the building's entrance, located in the back corner of its triangular-shaped plan. The street continues to the end of the building, offering a view across the canal to the side of the Ca' Foscari. To the left of the entrance, a narrow, dead-end passage separates the Masieri building from its eastern neighbour, the Palazzo Baldi. Two broad, Istrian stone-faced steps set parallel to the street edge lead up to the steel-framed, concrete entry door. Inside, three steps lead to the terrazzo ground floor, which is raised above the level of the *acqua alta*. We then enter a narrow hallway with a rising staircase immediately on our left, and guided by the strong light ahead, we reach the main ground-floor room.

9.16

This large, open room runs along the Grand Canal facade. The floor is made of light-grey, polished terrazzo with metal joints, while the ceiling is made of board-formed, grey concrete framed by imbedded, reddish-black, H-shaped steel beams, their bottom flanges set flush with the ceiling. Double-steel tube columns run to the floor from the points where these beams intersect in the ceiling. The double columns' bases are set into dark brass sleeves and stand in recessed, reverse brass bases that, instead of rising up to receive the columns' weight, step down into the floor in three concentric cylindrical rings. This highly unusual detail would appear to be intended to reference the soft, sinking ground beneath Venice's buildings. Framed between a ground-level black steel band and a narrow recess below the ceiling, this room's inner walls are made of polished plaster. In the far corner of the room, a large, cylindrical chimney flue, faced in grey plaster and standing on an outward-stepping brass ring base, is projected off the wall by a massive, double L-shaped steel bracket and rises up to the roof through openings in the floors above.

At the outer wall, overlooking the canal, the floor is edged by an Istrian stone curb, on the outside of which is a lower, concrete moat-like trench. Clipped to the floor and ceiling, a frameless glass wall encloses the arched water gate we saw from the outside, and its two L-shaped doors are made of interlaced, thick steel bars and thin steel rods. Either side of the water gate are new wood-framed casement windows. Low radiators, set in front of the Istrian stone curb, are fed by pairs of bright red pipes that run up the wall and out of sight. Stepping closer to the outer wall, we realize that the steel-edged concrete floor stops well short of the wall, and a void, less than 1 metre wide (3ft 3in), runs from the ground level to the roof. At the ends of the ceiling's steel beams, L-shaped I-beams are welded to the C-shaped steel channel at the edge of the concrete floor, connecting to the new structure embedded in the masonry outer wall by bolted steel plates set forwards of the polished plaster. **(9.15)** This disengagement of the new interior floors and the Grand Canal's historical masonry facade makes clear the relationship between the old and new, as well as creating a modern spatial connection between all of the levels.

Rising next to the polished-plaster back wall, the stairs to the upper floors are made of wood board treads and steel-plate risers and are partially enclosed by steel-edged, flame-blackened wood panels. The ground-floor landing has windows that open on to the street with apertures covered by stone panels pierced by a grid of circular holes, while an irregularly shaped rooflight above the first floor's inner landing provides a view up to the sky. **(9.16)** The two upper floors have board-formed cast concrete ceilings and red-leather coloured, smooth concrete floors, both exposing the steel beams, imparting a strong, almost cage-like, spatial structure to the rooms. The vertical void at the front of the first floor's main space is edged by a balustrade made of horizontal radiator pipes set between steel posts. On the second floor, a full-height corner window opens above the first floor rooflight, and three freestanding, slightly oval-plan shaped bathrooms are set along the right-hand side of the room, perpendicular to the main facade. Behind these glossy *marmorino* polished-plaster walls, one in cobalt blue and the other two in white, are small bedrooms. **(9.17)** On all levels, the full height, vertical void invites the sounds, both outside and inside, to reverberate throughout the space, as well as allowing the sunlight, both direct and reflected off the canal surface, to play through this spatial joint between the old and new, constantly reminding us of our proximity to the water.

9.16 FONDAZIONE MASIERI RENOVATIONS; FIRST FLOOR LANDING WITH IRREGULARLY SHAPED ROOFLIGHT AND FLAME-BLACKENED PANELS BORDERING THE STAIRCASE

9.17 FONDAZIONE MASIERI RENOVATIONS; SECOND FLOOR, CURVED, *MARMORINO* POLISHED-PLASTER WALLS ENCLOSE THREE BATHROOMS, BEHIND WHICH ARE THREE SMALL BEDROOMS

9.17

9.18

9.19

9.20

In 1968, Scarpa was commissioned to make permanent changes to the Venice Biennale's central pavilion. By inserting new mezzanine levels into the taller rooms he effectively doubled the old building's floor area. The new floors were separated from the original walls and floors by narrow slots of space illuminated from above, while the stairs and walkways were set away from the original building surfaces to allow views through the new section. **(see c.3)** The new construction was executed in light-weight, thin, planar materials with open joints, in contrast to the massive, monolithic plastered masonry structure of the existing building – all of which helped clearly differentiate the new interventions from the original building fabric, in a similar way to the Masieri Foundation. **(9.18)** At the front entrance, Scarpa made a temporary facade for the 34th Biennale composed of a series of five white-washed, concrete block walls. Four of of these walls stepped back one-half block in each course to form a 45-degree angle with respect to the facade of the original pavilion. The patterned wall edges were formed by alternating the smooth faces and ribbed ends of the blocks. **(9.19)**

For the 34th Biennale 1968, Scarpa also designed the exhibition 'Lines of Research: From the Formless to the New Structure', which included paintings, sculptures, and the works of four architects: Franco Albini, Paul Rudolph, Kahn and Scarpa. The work of the first three architects was placed in separate, uniformly white-surfaced rooms, each tailored to the character and scale of the elements presented. This included Kahn's drawings, which were displayed horizontally on long low plinths, Rudolph's tall models of cantilevering housing towers and large photographs presented on inclined planes, and Albini's furniture and full scale segment, in steel and marble, of the La Rinascente department store facade in Rome of 1957–61.

Located in the larger painting and sculpture room, Scarpa's own exhibit presented three of his pieces: a travertine sculpture entitled *Erme*, composed of three L-shaped pieces; a 6 metre (19 ft 8 in) long, 6 centimetre (2 in) square, wood pole, inlaid with bronze and copper strips, entitled *Asta* – its ends carved into blade-like shapes, with a gilded egg-shaped piece of wood attached to the upper portion, all mounted on a brass pivot at the centre point; and a textile fabric. Scarpa also included three sculptures by Alberto Carolo, including the diamond shaped *Crescita*, comprising metal cubes, displayed for many years at the Olivetti Showroom's staircase base.[10] Scarpa literally embedded his own exhibit, entitled 'Ambiente' (Room), in the floor of the larger hall, constructing a small, rectangular interior courtyard in the now two-level central exhibition hall. From the upper level, one looked down into the small, darker courtyard below, surrounded by a double, square steel tube structural frame – forming the upper storey railings and the support for the lower space's freestanding stretched fabric panels. **(9.20)** The sculpture *Asta*, mounted on a brass pivot joint at the centre of one of the long sides of the steel railing, hung down into the small court as well as rising up into the large hall's upper space. Visitors could set this pole into motion from both above or below, resulting in sudden, mysterious movements, similar to a pendulum or metronome, signalling inhabitation while at the same time evoking images of the similar wood pole used to propel and steer gondolas.

9.18 CARLO SCARPA, ITALIAN PAVILION, 34TH BIENNALE, VENICE, 1968; PERIOD PHOTOGRAPH, 1968, NEW INTERIOR WITH MEZZANINE

9.19 ITALIAN PAVILION; PERIOD PHOTOGRAPH, 1968, TEMPORARY FACADE OF FIVE WHITE-WASHED, CONCRETE BLOCK WALLS

9.20 CARLO SCARPA, 'AMBIENTE' EXHIBITION, 34TH BIENNALE, VENICE, 1968; PERIOD PHOTOGRAPH, 1968, SCARPA'S CONSTRUCTED INTERNAL COURTYARD SEEN FROM THE UPPER LEVEL

9.21 'AMBIENTE' EXHIBITION; PERIOD PHOTOGRAPH, 1968, SCARPA'S COURTYARD SEEN FROM THE LOWER LEVEL, WITH ITS STEEL FRAME ACTING AS A CLERESTORY, BRINGING LIGHT DOWN TO SURROUNDING SPACES

9.22 CARLO SCARPA AND SERGIO LOS, IUAV ENTRANCE, 1972; SALVAGED CHURCH DOOR FRAME AND PEDIMENT WITH CONCRETE POOL

9.23 IUAV ENTRANCE; ENTRY PORTAL WITH BUTTERFLY-ROOFED, CONCRETE CANOPY

When approached from the lower level, the characteristics of the space were reversed from those it had when seen from above, as it now served as a strong light source for the more dimly lit spaces beneath the closely spaced wood joists of the ceiling above. The ceiling's hanging steel frame formed an open clerestory through which light poured into the surrounding spaces. The steel-framed, fabric wall panels, which Scarpa called veils, were set in a rotating, pinwheel pattern, secured to the frame above and held up off the floor by a single pin. The panels' white translucent fabric transmitted light, allowing views when seen perpendicularly and appearing solid when viewed from an acute angle. The sole exception was the panel surfaced in an opaque, bright green fabric, giving a sudden infusion of colour to the otherwise largely black and white composition. **(9.21)** Standing outside this space, one saw ghostly images of the people and sculptures within, while, standing within the space, one was surrounded by overlapping cloud-like planes.

While Scarpa had no relationship with Rudolph, who had been invited to exhibit by Mazzariol, he did have relationships with Kahn, as we have seen, and Albini, a colleague of Scarpa's on the IUAV faculty. Albini's renovation work in museums, such as the Palazzo Bianco, 1950–1, and the Palazzo Rosso, 1952–61, both in Genoa, had significant parallels with Scarpa's work, including the use of pivoting and projecting painting frames and individually designed steel sculpture stands, and indicates that Scarpa was hardly alone in his interest in positioning art in a more dynamic relation with the observer.[11]

In 1966, Scarpa was commissioned to design a new entry for the IUAV, which was located in the former Tolentini monastery. He made two designs, the second, in 1972, was used to execute the project after Scarpa's death by his assistant, Sergio Los, in a somewhat modified form. Scarpa proposed employing a massive Istrian stone door frame and pediment salvaged from the Tolentini church renovation. This was not used as the actual entry portal; instead he placed it on the ground in the back corner of the small entry court above a concrete pool, the sides and bottom of which were made of right-angled steps forming a diagonal wall, as in a ziggurat. The path from the entry portal to the school's door is recessed below a slightly raised stone-lined grass plane to the left and a higher, concrete-edged, brick-paved plane on the right. At the outer edge of the entry court, both of these planes terminate in inclined brick-paved surfaces, tilting the ground plane upwards and erasing the horizon line. **(9.22)**

The outer wall, separating the entry court from the Campiello and backing up to the tilted ground planes, is formed of two sections of concrete wall, to the left and right, the stepped surfaces of which incline outwards. At the centre, a butterfly-roofed, concrete canopy covers the entry portal on both sides of the wall, its outer section matching the angle of the tilted ground planes. The left-hand-side concrete wall is fronted by a black, steel-framed gate, carrying a large pane of glass on the right, and a large, inscribed Istrian stone slab on the left. Steel wheels at the top and bottom allow the steel gate to be rolled to the right, the glass pane closing the entry portal. The Istrian stone slab, a square with its upper right corner cut off at a 45-degree angle, is inscribed with the school's initials and Vico's aphorism, *Verum Ipsum Factum*. **(9.23)** While Scarpa's gate and outer wall designs were realized fairly faithfully, Scarpa's early drawings show a much more dynamic entrance court: a folded and tilted space creating a steeply inclined, polygonally faceted topography – a contrast to the horizontal city of Venice.

9.21

9.22

9.23

9.24

In 1972, the year of the second, eventually executed design for the school entrance, Scarpa was appointed rector (dean) of the IUAV. In one of his first official acts as dean, Scarpa had Vico's aphoristic phrase, *Verum Ipsum Factum*, imprinted on the students' graduation diplomas. This phrase, which can be translated as 'we only know what we make' or 'truth through making,' implies that thought is embodied in construction and that architects can only learn by making. This precisely defined Scarpa's understanding of an architect's training and practice, where thinking and making, construing and constructing are joined irrevocably in the realization and enactment of a work of architecture. Scarpa's deanship at the IUAV came during a tumultuous time for universities around the world, when student uprisings were quite common, but Scarpa emphasized learning by making and had no tolerance for imprecise work. Scarpa's obsessive focus on craft led to a number of incidents, as when, during a university student protest demonstration, he tore down his students' signs, stating their lettering was atrocious and that he would not abide such careless work.

Also in 1972, Scarpa and his family moved their home for the last time, to Vicenza, Scarpa's hometown. Choosing not to locate his architectural office and studio in the historic centre, Scarpa placed them in the renovated stables of the Villa Valmarana, called the Villa 'dei Nani' after the dwarf figures on top of the east wall of the villa's formal gardens. Located south of Vicenza, 1 kilometre (0.6 miles) from the city walls, Villa Valmarana is set along a steep-sided ridge, parallel to the Bacchiglione River to the east, and a verdant valley to the west. Dating from 1668, the villa comprises three primary buildings arranged linearly along the north-south walled garden, which runs along the top of the ridge. The main villa, standing in the centre of the long rectangular, elevated garden, is a three-storey rectangle that runs east-west from one garden wall to the other, dividing the garden in two. The villa has large terraces opening off the elevated first floor, or *piano nobile*, to the gardens. This floor's rectangular main room runs north-south, and thus connects the gardens on either side. The walled garden, villa and main room form three nesting rectangles, rotated 90 degrees in respect to one another. Entered from a small plaza at the garden's southern end, the columned entry portico and *foresteria* (or guest rooms) wrap around the garden's southwest corner. The *foresteria* has a long, double-height room with a vaulted ceiling, housing the library and opening on to the garden, behind which are four smaller rooms, opening on to the western hillside. Both the villa and *foresteria* have a series of celebrated frescos painted by the Tiepolo family.

Scarpa's studio is accessed by a winding ramp south of the portico. The studio is housed in the ground floor of the small, cubic stables, with a pedimented front, pale yellow plastered walls and hipped clay tile roof – similar to the main villa. Entered through a vaulted three-bay portico, with narrow bays to either side of the larger central bay, the stables' interior is a single, tall room, a square in plan. The studio's central arched door and two tall windows open in the opposite wall, matching the portico's inner wall. The solid east wall indicates that the stables are embedded into the hillside, while the west wall is opened with three high windows. Four large columns, matching those in the portico, stand in the space and support the vaulted ceiling's arches. To the east and west, three smaller, freestanding columns stand between the two larger columns, marking the original division of the horse stalls. Carrying no beams, these smaller columns are tied to the larger columns and the front and back walls by black steel bars. Given the same architectural details as the *foresteria* and the villa, the stables have carved stone frames, sills and cornices around the doors and windows, wall brackets at the arches' spring points and column capitals and bases. Working in this space for the last six years of his life, Scarpa centred his large drawing tables in the stable's square space, beneath the vaulted ceiling. From the stables and the *foresteria* library, where Scarpa held meetings beneath the Tiepolo frescos, views open to the west across the valley to the Basilica of Monte Berico. **(9.24)**

A five-minute walk down the road from the stables of the Villa Valmarana is Palladio's Villa Rotonda and, intriguingly they both share the cruciform-in-square shaped plan. Scarpa visited the Rotonda, Palladio's greatest domestic work, at every hour of the day and in every season, enabling him to see how it responded to the changing daylight. He would have seen that the white walls of the Villa Rotonda are tinted blue in the early morning, ochre in the evening light of sunset and iron grey when it rains. This remarkable range of colours resulted from Palladio's mixing of quartz sand into the stucco plaster used on the building's exterior walls,[12] reminding us of the long Venetian tradition, of which Scarpa was a part, of manipulating the effects of reflected sunlight through glass-making materials.

9.24 PERIOD PHOTOGRAPH, C. 1975; CARLO SCARPA IN HIS VILLA VALMARANA STUDIO, VICENZA

9.25 CARLO SCARPA, VILLA ZOPPAS, CONEGLIANO, 1952–3; GROUND-FLOOR PLAN, GRAPHITE AND COLOURED PENCIL ON PAPER

9.26 CARLO SCARPA, VILLA IL PALAZZETTO, MONSELICE, 1971–8; VIEWED FROM ABOVE, FOLDED POLYGONAL PLANES OF BRICK-PAVED COURTYARD

9.27 OVERLEAF > VILLA IL PALAZZETTO; CONCRETE PERGOLA WITH FREESTANDING FIREPLACE IN THE NORTHWEST CORNER

With the exceptions of the early Veritti House and the late Ottolenghi House, Scarpa's designs for freestanding residential structures remain unrealized. The 1952–3 design for the Villa Zoppas, in Conegliano, is notable for both the way the house is anchored, not by its walls but by the massive, hollow cylindrical columns clustered in an incomplete grid at the joint of the T-shaped plan, and the large, circular windows, similar to Chinese gardens' moon gates, in the street facade's long wall.[13] **(9.25)** The first scheme for the Casa Cassina at Ronco di Carimate in 1963 had rooms unfurling from a curving retaining wall set against the steep hillside, while the final design terraced the structure down the hillside to accommodate the 10 metre (37 ft 9 in) difference in elevation. The 1965–72 annex to the De Benedetti-Bonaiuto House in Rome, while not freestanding, was realized. Oval-shaped in plan with one face cut off, the structure's curving walls are plastered concrete and the flat wall is wood-framed glass. Inside, the first floor rooms are raised above an open garden room at ground level.

The 1971 project for the Roth House in Asolo also involved an incomplete grid of large cylindrical columns, and the master bedroom's bathroom was enclosed in a large cylindrical volume, acting as a pivot at the joint of the irregular L-shaped plan. The 1972 floor plan for the Lupi House, in the outskirts of Vicenza, was composed of a series of polygonal spaces opening off a bending hallway that ran the length of the house. The 1975–6 project for three vacation houses for the Faccinetto family in Quero proposed a colonnade of large, cylindrical columns running along the hillside, linking them into a continuous volumetric composition. Finally, the 1975–6 Urbinati House renovation in Pesaro, incorporating the existing villa's cubic volume, was ordered around a central L-shaped line of massive cylindrical columns.

Commissioned by his friend, Aldo Businaro, Scarpa worked on the Villa Il Palazzetto renovation in Monselice from 1971–8, with the major work accomplished from 1973–5. Located between the side of the main house and the two barns (one of which Scarpa renovated as a dark spruce clad garage), the courtyard and threshing floor became a constructed topography: a subtly folded surface formed of brick-paved polygonal planes, edged by concrete curb walls at its perimeter and by concrete ribs at the planes' joints. **(9.26)** The flat tops of two cylindrical Nanto stone blocks, located at the polygons' intersections, rise just above the folded brick surfaces' highpoints to define the centre of the elevated planes; Scarpa called these 'sun' and 'moon.'[14] The courtyard's plan is centred on a stretched diamond shape, crossing the rectangular surface at a diagonal. The diamond shape's narrow points terminate in the lower left and upper right corners; its two widest points intersect the other polygons at the circular stone discs. This shape also appears on the cover of Scarpa's copy of a book on the Fibonacci number series, making it clear that Scarpa intended to engage this ancient proportional geometry in this site-specific design.[15]

Cutting through the elevated courtyard, a recessed walkway leads to the new entry terrace and the house's larch door, which is surrounded by low concrete walls. Scarpa placed a concrete pergola and a walled outdoor room on the garden's eastern wall. Paved in the same brick as the courtyard, the pergola is made from horizontal, board-formed concrete with inset panels of polished plaster in pale yellow, dark grey and deep red-brown. Two of the walls form an L-shape in plan, leaving an open side facing the house; the southwest corner has a freestanding, stone-walled fireplace. **(9.27)** The room is defined at its top by a concrete edge beam that runs the full perimeter and by a single and a double concrete beam that cross at the centre. A slab of concrete, its top faced with white stone, is cantilevered through a horizontal opening in the garden wall. This is closed by a metal screen, opened by a series of pulleys on the outside wall, similar to what Scarpa would do at the Brion Cemetery. The hearth and floor of the fireplace are elevated, cantilevered concrete slabs, the latter of which hovers inches above the brick floor. Above the hearth rises a vertical board-formed concrete mantle and chimney block whose face carries a single vertical line of multicoloured Murano glass tiles.

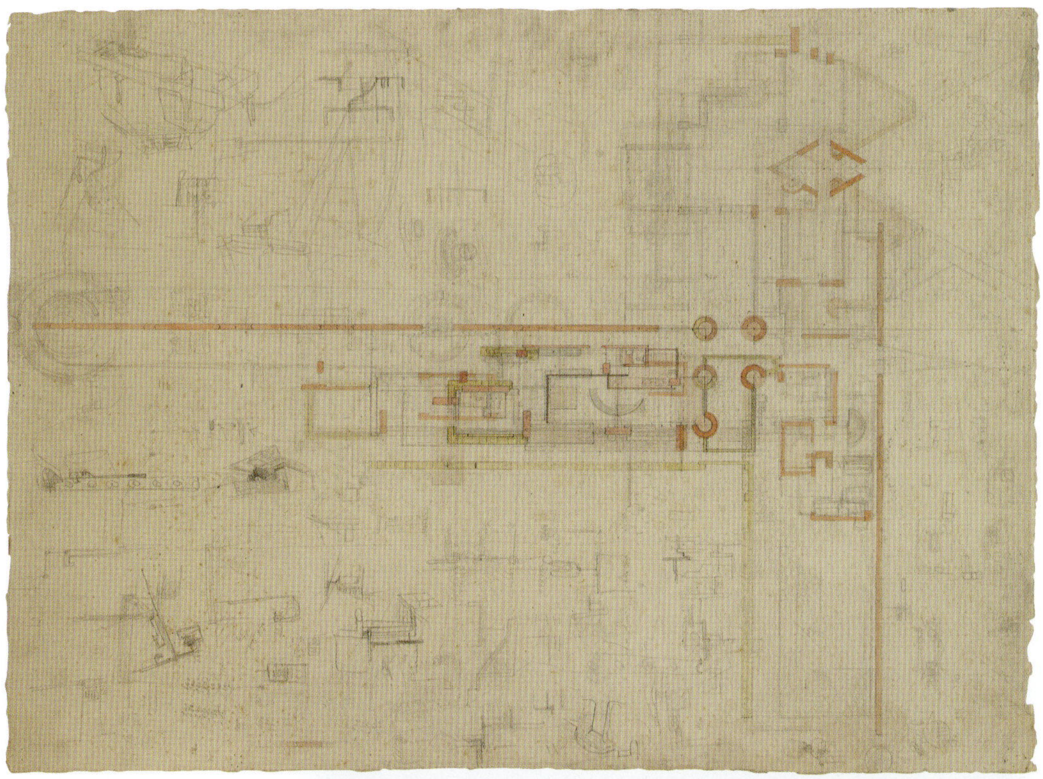

9.25

9.26

Despite going through six iterations during the design and construction phase, the basic plan form for the Villa Ottolenghi was set from the start.[16] Commissioned by the Venetian lawyer Carlo Ottolenghi for his son Alberto, this house was substantially completed at the time of Scarpa's death. The final aspects of its construction were supervised by two of Scarpa's former students: his assistant Giuseppe Tommasi, assisted by Guido Pietropoli. The site, occupied by an old farmhouse and vineyards, was on a south-facing hillside offering views over Lake Garda. Local planning codes limited any new building to one floor above ground level and required substantial setbacks from the property boundaries. There were no pre-existing architectural or historical conditions, beyond the sloping topography, to serve as boundaries and limitations for Scarpa's design and, in the absence of contextual restrictions, as Forster has noted, Scarpa created his own 'obstacles' to be overcome and resolved in the Villa Ottolenghi.[17] **(9.28)**

Entered from a street to the north of the site, a gridded wooden gate leads to a small terrace, which opens to the house's brick-paved roof that spreads out before us at the same level; the house itself is embedded in the hillside below. Doubling as a roof and a terrace this space offers panoramic views of the surrounding landscape and Lake Garda. **(9.29)** The roof is composed of a series of gently folded, polygonal brick-paved planes with concrete curb beams at their folded joints, low concrete curbs at its outer edges, and low concrete cylinders at the intersections, similar to Il Palazzetto's 'sun' and 'moon'. The roof reminds us of both an ancient place, the gently sloping medieval Campo in Sienna, its polygonal sections of brick paving edged in stone, as well as a modern place, the Casa Malaparte in Capri, 1938–40, designed by the writer Curzio Malaparte based on Adalberto Libera's plan, set on a rock promontory over the ocean, which is fronted not by a facade, but by a polygonal-plan stone stair leading to a paved roof terrace. At the Villa Ottolenghi, the elevated, plinth-like topography of the roof terrace's folded polygonal planes serves, at the very start, to anchor and embed the house into the landform.

Between staggered concrete walls, we enter the house by descending the narrow, twisting staircase, made of concrete treads and risers with steel nosing plates. Our eye level soon passes beneath the roof terrace's ground line as we descend. At the bottom, the staircase bends around to the left and we find ourselves in what appears to be a narrow *calle*, a typical Venetian passageway, running west to east, with the wall of the house on the right and a massive retaining wall on the left. Both walls are finished in extremely rough 'thrown' stucco plaster, which, as its name implies, involves throwing wet stucco against the walls. **(9.30)** Windows are opened in the wall of the house, while, at two places along the *calle*, the retaining wall curves into the hillside producing shallow light wells. At the second, larger light well, a recessed entrance to the house leads past the kitchen into the living room. Entry may also be made by continuing down the *calle*, turning into the tunnel-like *sottoportico* leading out into the garden, from which broad steps lead up into the living room.

OTTOLENGHI HOUSE
BARDOLINO, 1974–1978

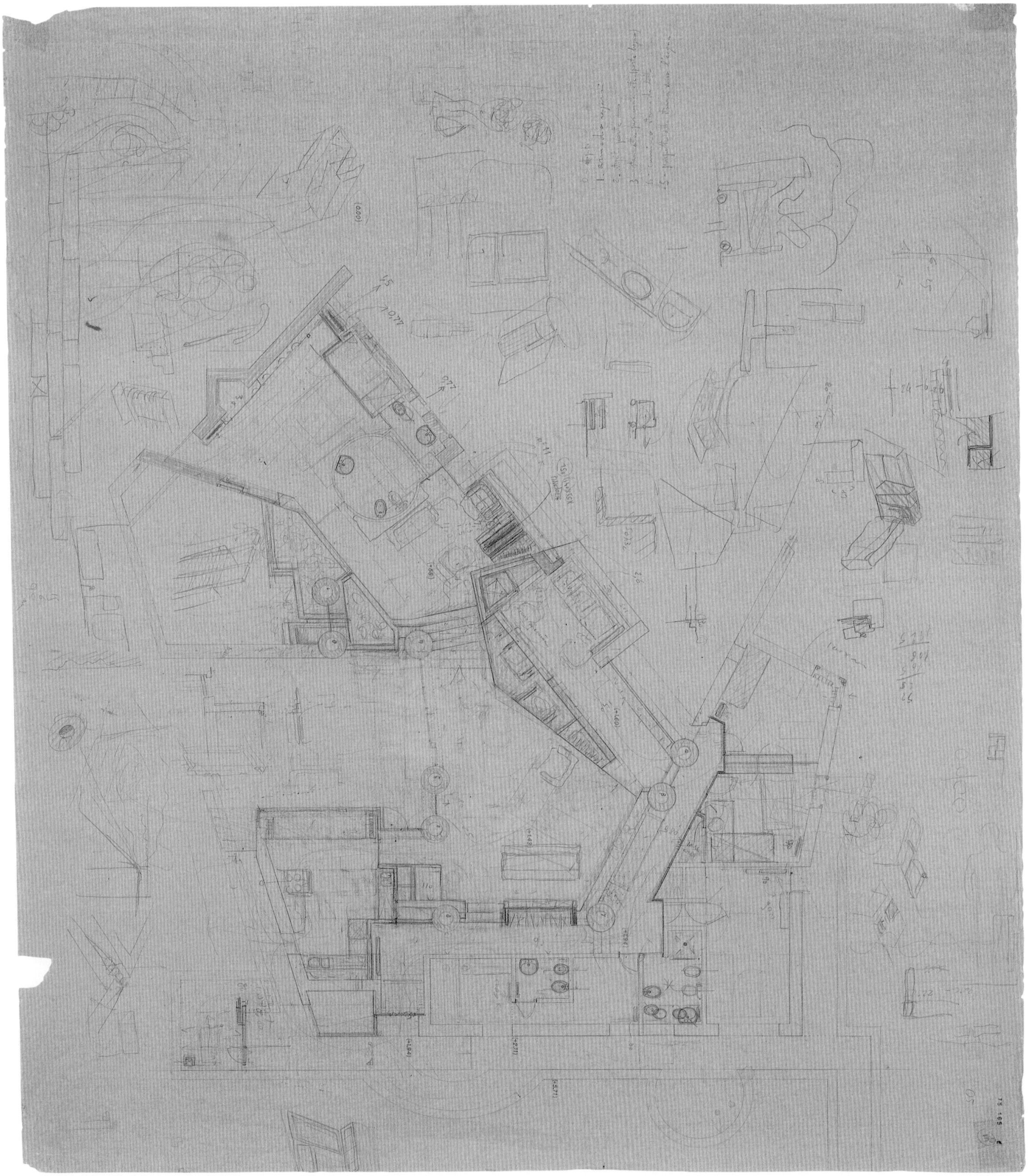

9.28 CARLO SCARPA, OTTOLENGHI HOUSE, BARDOLINO, 1974–8; PLAN, 1:50, GRAPHITE AND COLOURED PENCIL ON PAPER, 64.5 X 75.5 CM (25.25 X 29.75 IN)

The entrance door leads to a walkway, three steps above the main level, which runs along the main space's north and west edges, giving access to a series of small rooms. The large dining room, library and living space at the centre of the house open to the south in an irregular fan shape, stepping down the slope in four levels and wrapping around the eastern garden. This internally oriented, labyrinthine space is anchored by, and pivots around, a series of nine massive cylindrical columns constructed of large rings of smooth-faced, grey concrete interspersed with pink Prun stone and white Trani stone rings, finished by being chipped with chisels. **(9.31)** These columns and their sedimentary layers are reminiscent of the 'rusticated' columns on Palladio's Villa Sarego, and their method of construction, by stacking a series of masonry discs, parallels the way the Greek temples' columns were built out of drum-like sections. The columns are 88 centimetres (2 ft 10 in) in diameter, and it is hardly coincidental that this is a multiple of 11.[18] As the plan of the house has no perceivable right angles, the columns serve as landmarks, helping us to navigate throughout the house.

The striated cylindrical columns also stand out because of the irregular and recessive background formed by the stepping and folding of the fractured outer walls of the house. The outer walls are faced in white polished plaster while a black steel band separates the walls from the floor. Various sized and shaped rectangular windows allow light to enter the space from every direction. The columns are disengaged from the outer walls, standing within the large space, connecting the ceiling to the floor. The ceiling is a continuous, unjointed, gently folded plane, its polygonal facets mirroring those of the roof above, originally finished in white polished plaster, allowing the outer walls and ceiling to appear to fold into one another. At Tommasi's suggestion the ceiling was refinished in glossy, black polished plaster, making for both a stronger demarcation between the ceiling and walls and a clearer relationship between the horizontal polished planes of the floor and ceiling. The glossy black ceiling reflects the sunlight bouncing upwards off the pool surface and the electric uplights mounted on low walls, forming a permanent night sky.

Standing directly on the floor, the columns stop short of the ceiling, where the polished plaster curves down to meet their tops. The ground and polished floor is made of tan-grey terrazzo with black and white marble aggregate, into which broken terracotta tiles, alternating between a mustard and a deep red-brown colour, were placed. Scarpa carefully designed the curving, meandering pattern formed by the lines of terracotta, dividing the floor into irregularly shaped sections, similar to large flagstones. The natural and inevitable cracks in the terrazzo floor follow the lines of the softer terracotta. Given the lack of recognizable geometric order, the floor's monolithic cast planes, stepping down in four large sections along the southern slope, form a topography anchored to the earth. Lacking beams and structural elements the ceiling's continuously folding, tent-like fabric complements the floor's heavy, layered and embedded grounding.

9.30

9.29 OTTOLENGHI HOUSE; VIEW ACROSS THE BRICK-PAVED ROOF TERRACE TO LAKE GARDA BEYOND

9.30 OTTOLENGHI HOUSE; VIEW THROUGH THE NARROW *CALLE* BACK TOWARDS THE EASTERN STAIRCASE LEADING FROM THE ROOF TERRACE

9.31 OVERLEAF > OTTOLENGHI HOUSE; SOUTHEASTERN VIEW ACROSS THE DINING ROOM IN THE OPEN PLAN, CENTRAL AREA, COLUMNS WITH ALTERNATING RINGS OF CONCRETE AND PINK PRUN STONE ANCHOR THE SPACE

9.29

9.32

The large living room is divided into four spaces by the stepped floor and by the long, low folding wall that crosses the room's centre. While its top and bottom are edged with black steel bands, the wall's outer face is finished in a light blue-coloured polished plaster and its inner face a yellow-ochre-coloured polished plaster. Penetrating the wall, a two-sided fireplace opens both to the upper living room, where to the fireplace's right are bright red-coloured polished plaster recesses, and to the smaller, southwest library, elevated one step above the living room. The only part of the wall to touch the ceiling is the fireplace's L-shaped, rectangular chimney, finished to match the rest of the wall.

Leading down to the lower sitting area along the low wall, six broad terrazzo steps, in two sets of three, form a spatial joint between the living room's three main levels. As we descend the stairs, a small pool to the left is set between three columns, beyond which we see a much larger pool in the garden outside. **(9.32)** The two planes of water, the windows' minimal frames and the columns' rustic quality (two of which are outside and the other inside), together act to blur the boundary between interior and exterior. The house's largely glazed southwest wall opens to lake views, while the house's eastern side wraps around and opens to the garden and pool.

In the centre of the lower sitting area the master bath is housed in a large cylindrical volume; its glossy, white polished-plaster wall separated from the floor by a black steel band, while its top stops short of the ceiling. **(9.33)** Moving around the volume, we enter the master bedroom, where a steel-framed, T-shaped fireplace is recessed into the far wall. This is reflected in a rectangular, two-way mirror set into the flat inner face of the cylindrical bathroom, allowing one to see into the marble-clad bathroom when its lights are turned on. One notable detail is the black steel pipes rising from the floor near the walls, their tops carrying electrical sockets and light switches, leaving the walls untouched. **(9.34)** Throughout the house, the interior space's continuity is constantly reinforced by the unbroken, faceted planar surfaces of the floor, ceiling and walls, punctuated by the massive cylindrical columns.

9.33

Despite the absence of his accustomed contextual limitations, Scarpa composed the Ottolenghi House from fragments, elements and ordering principles derived from the city of Venice, which, when experienced, serve to remind the inhabitants that they remain in the Veneto. Beginning with the entry through the narrow *calle* and *sottoportico* and continuing with the floor's inlaid terrazzo (reminiscent of the terraced levels of the typical *campi*), the spaces' lack of regular rhythm or right-angle grid may be understood as relating to Venice. While in Venice, it is the walls that shape the passages that lead us through the labyrinth of the city, here the walls are broken and recessive, the massive anchoring columns acting like Venice's *campanili* (church bell towers), providing directional landmarks. The house's enclosure of the sunken garden and pool serves as another reminder of Venice, particularly in the way the water's reflective surface appears both outside and inside. Finally, while the roof terrace references Sienna's Campo and Capri's Villa Malaparte, for residents of the Veneto the roof's elevated brick-paved plane is most reminiscent of places much closer to home – the slightly folded brick surfaces of the Venetian *campi*, which were paved and organized into inclined planes in order to collect rainwater in the cisterns buried beneath. **(9.35)**

9.34

9.32 OTTOLENGHI HOUSE; LOWER SITTING AREA, LOOKING UP TO THE MAIN SPACE, THE SMALL POOL AND EASTERN GARDEN (R) AND A LOW, FOLDING WALL (L)

9.33 OTTOLENGHI HOUSE; LOWER SITTING AREA WITH THE LARGE CYLINDRICAL VOLUME, HOUSING THE MASTER BATH, AND DOOR TO THE MASTER BEDROOM

9.34 OTTOLENGHI HOUSE; MASTER BEDROOM, THE T-SHAPED FIREPLACE IS REFLECTED IN THE TWO-WAY MIRROR SET INTO THE FLAT INNER FACE OF THE CYLINDRICAL BATHROOM

9.35 OTTOLENGHI HOUSE; FOLDING BRICK PLANES OF THE ROOF TERRACE, THE INTERIOR COLUMNS PROJECT THROUGH THE SURFACE IN THE FOREGROUND WHILE THE SUNKEN GARDEN DROPS AWAY TO OUR LEFT

CHAPTER 10

THE DETAIL AS THE ADORATION OF NATURE

BANCA POPOLARE
VERONA, 1973–8

In 1973 the Banca Popolare di Verona commissioned Scarpa to expand and reorganize their company headquarters located in an eighteenth-century building in Verona's historic centre on Via Conventino, the southeast side of Piazza Nogara. Located nearby to the southwest is the Roman Arena, one of the major surviving examples of this building type, while the Porta dei Borsari, one of Verona's Roman city gates, is situated to the northwest. Retaining its ancient facade on one side, the gate is notable in particular for the upper-level windows housed in the aedicule supported by small columns, their fluting spiralling clockwise and counter-clockwise from one column to the next.

Verona's great, late Renaissance architect Michele Sanmicheli, employed the columns' unusual treatment in his Palazzo Bevilacqua, located on the same street that passes through the Porta. Scarpa was well aware that Sanmicheli was as important an architect for Verona as Palladio was for Vicenza, having built Verona's Renaissance city gates, two churches and several palazzi.[1] Perhaps the most intriguing of these in relation to the facade of Scarpa's Banca Popolare is the Palazzo Canossa, its facade made of multiple thin layers with gradated rustication in the lower half and double pilasters interweaving with the smooth plaster bands and walls behind in the upper half. Scarpa was also aware of Sanmicheli's Venetian works, including the Palazzo Grimani, with its deeply layered facade and three levels of double columns, and the Palazzo Cornaro, its facade composed of a complex set of overlapping, interweaving and syncopated rhythms.

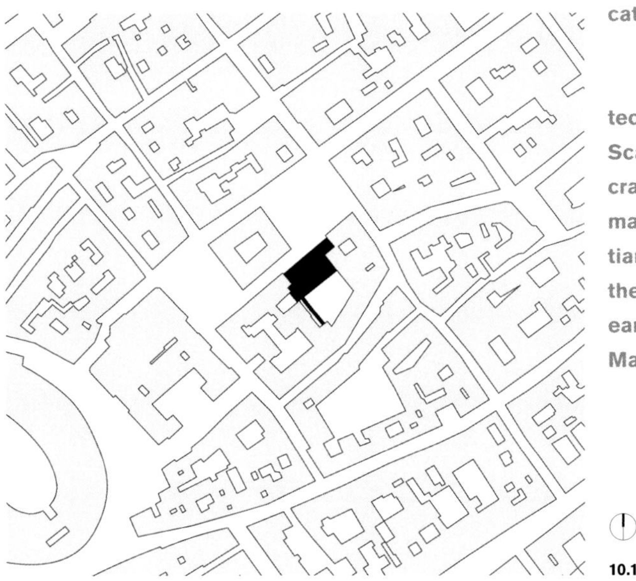

10.1

When Scarpa began work on the Banca Popolare, the city had already approved the bank management plan to expand into the southwest site by removing the adjacent building. Scarpa's initial insight related to the project's urban context:

> **'Behind the Verona Arena, there are two piazzi; you don't realize it's a single space divided in two. In one piazza is a run-of-the-mill church, in the middle there is a building dividing up the two piazzi, and on the corner a bank, an 18th century building. When I was given the commission to design the new bank, the adjoining lot had been bought to enlarge the premises. The first thing I said was that more land had to be purchased, because that was the only way the bank facade could extend beyond the building dividing the two piazzi.'[2]**

The bank acquired the two southwestern, adjacent buildings, both of which were neo-classical structures built in the years between the world wars, and had them demolished. **(10.1)**

Scarpa's new addition, which by planning regulation was not allowed to exceed the demolished buildings' volume, is a narrow building that meets the right edge of the bank's eighteenth-century structure, extending behind the building that divides the piazzi. In plan Scarpa's northwest-facing facade aligns with the edge of Piazza Nogara while the southeast-facing facade forms the edge of the courtyard behind; the internal crosswalls and structure are slightly skewed to align with the walls of the existing buildings on either side. The new building is organized over four main floors; a floor set a half-level below the piazza, the main public floor set a half-level above the piazza, and the first and second floors, where the executive offices are located. A service basement sits beneath while the paved roof serves as a terrace. The new building overlaps with and connects to the existing bank building and is adjoined to the bank offices located across the courtyard by a new bridge. **(10.2 a/b/c/d, 10.3)**

In his work on the Banca Popolare, Scarpa was associated with the Verona architect Arrigo Rudi and assisted by Scarpa's former student, the Verona architect Valter Rossetto. **(10.5)** The Banca Popolare is rightly considered the highpoint in Scarpa's joining of modern construction methods to traditional Venetian crafts. The craftsmen who worked on the bank, and other projects, included: the Venetian stucco mason Eugenio De Luigi, the Venetian metal craftsman Francesco Zanon and the Venetian master carpenter Saverio Anfodillo. The rich, deep and saturated colours used on the Banca Popolare's *marmorino* polished plaster walls differ from those of Scarpa's earlier projects, as Scarpa had directed De Luigi to precisely match the colours in late Mark Rothko paintings.

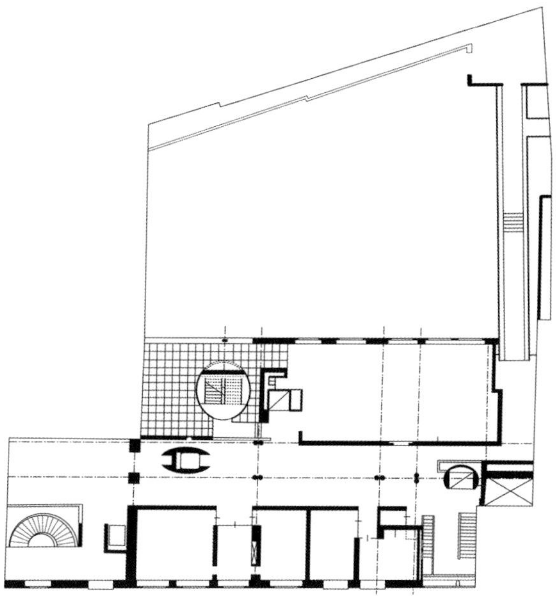

10.2c

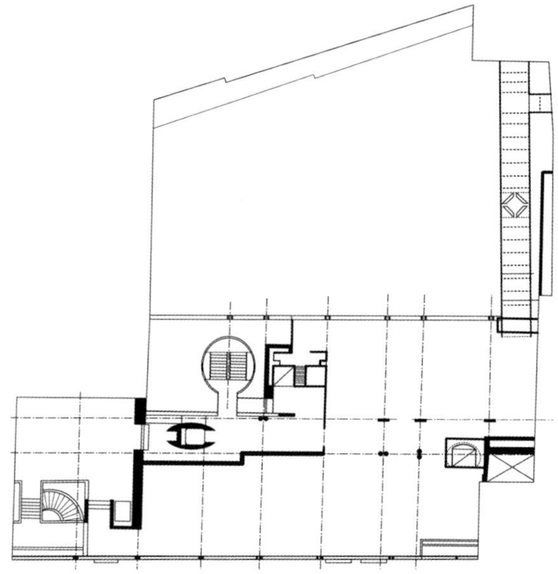

10.2d

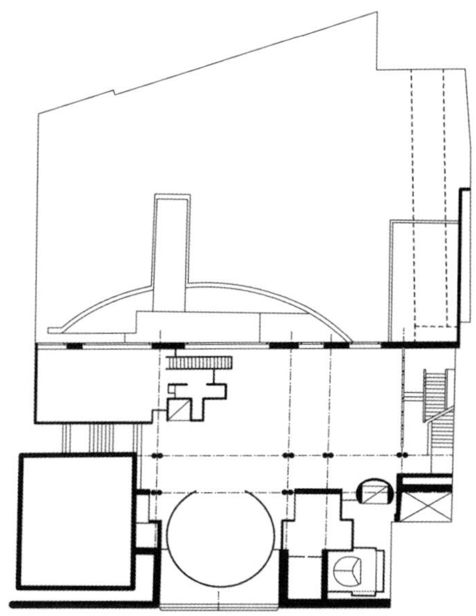

10.2a

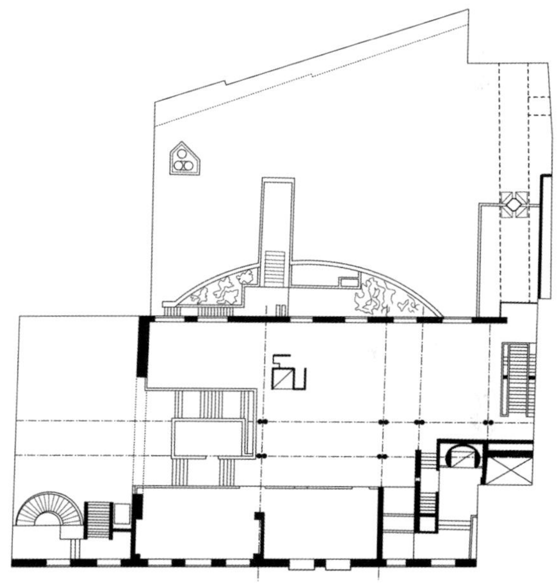

10.2b

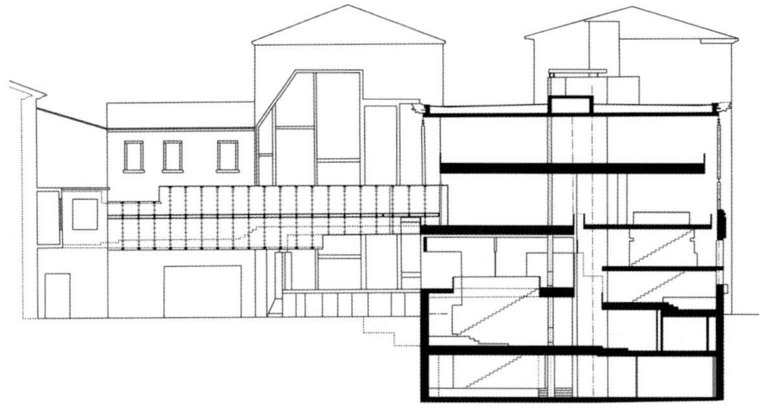

10.3

10.1 CARLO SCARPA, BANCA POPOLARE, VERONA, 1973–8; SITE PLAN (REDRAWN)

10.2a BANCA POPOLARE; LOWER GROUND-FLOOR PLAN (REDRAWN)

10.2b BANCA POPOLARE; ELEVATED GROUND-FLOOR PLAN (REDRAWN)

10.2c BANCA POPOLARE; FIRST-FLOOR PLAN (REDRAWN)

10.2d BANCA POPOLARE; SECOND-FLOOR PLAN (REDRAWN)

10.3 BANCA POPOLARE; NORTHWEST-SOUTHEAST SECTION THROUGH SCARPA'S ADDITION AND REAR COURTYARD (REDRAWN)

10.4

Rudi notes that Scarpa was 'a daily and constant presence on the building site', this being 'necessary due to the peculiarity and complexity of the project'. When Scarpa died in late 1978, Rudi stated:

> 'The project was complete in all its parts, the two facades had been completed … and most of material for finishing the interior had long been ordered. During the following period, until the project was finished construction in spring 1981, I completed the job with the assistance of the architect Rossetto, availing myself of the detailed drawings, instructions on construction, material indications, and proposed methods of execution previously discussed with Scarpa, which as a whole were quite exhaustive.' [3]

While the interior spatial experience was always of primary importance to Scarpa, his comments regarding the role of the Banca Popolare's facade indicated that this also extended to the urban 'interior' spaces of streets, canals and plazas, and the facades that enclose and shape them. By extending beyond the edge of the building that divided the two piazzi, Scarpa said, 'the new facade would help unify the two spaces, establishing and embodying the continuity. It was neither necessary nor possible to knock down the building between the two squares – it was enough to show the space was continuous. This is the facade's role.' [4] (10.4)

Because of the portion of its facade that runs down Via Conventino behind the building dividing the piazzi, the entirety of the Banca Popolare's new facade can never be seen when viewed from Piazza Nogara. Most visitors view the new building diagonally across Piazza Nogara, as the main banking hall entrance is through the eighteenth-century building on the corner. Scarpa closed the existing building's arched portal on the left side of the facade, shifting the central axis of the combined buildings towards the addition to the right, and assuring that people would be close to the surface of the new facade as they entered. Scarpa described the facade's design as a dialogue between new and old:

> 'The new building is an extension of the old one, but the additions are bigger than the existing building. You couldn't just copy the original architecture, but you have to understand it. The old builder knew there were critical points, which have to be worked on more than others … The cornice, window, plinth, steps (a dominant element of the interior): the same places as always concerned builders in the past. The problems involved are the same as ever; only the answer changes.' [5]

10.5

10.6

When seen as a whole, the Banca Popolare's new facade **'appears to be articulated according to [Gottfried] Semper's four elements, so that we are presented with an earthwork in stone, a screen wall in plaster, and a steel framed loggia at the top of the building'**, as Frampton noted. [6] Yet, the longer the facade is examined the more this initial reading proves the beginning of a more complex story. While the facade has a clear base, middle and top, the regular rhythm of the upper loggia's steel columns does not correspond to the projecting, flush and receding windows and their irregular spacing below. Despite a few localized moments of symmetry, the facade's composition as a whole is asymmetrical and constantly changing.

The unravelling that happens at the facade's ends complements the dynamic tension created by the centrally located windows' syncopated patterns. A vertical slot at the top-left edge cuts the plaster wall away from the existing bank building, while at the right edge a large, two-storey, recessed glass, shadowed void, corresponding to the main stair behind, is carved into the plaster wall and framed by the steel floor beam and final pair of steel columns. In the densely layered facade's 'figure-ground' composition, the plaster wall constitutes the consistent, ground-like plane, behind which is the skeletal steel frame that emerges at the top floor, while the stone and glass surfaces appear as figures, projecting and receding with respect to the ground-like plaster plane. **(10.6)**

For Scarpa, a **'critical point was the contact with the ground. Here I used more finished stonework, to stress the plinth.'** [7] The facade's base is a solid wall of large, tightly jointed slabs of smooth-faced, white Botticino marble rising to just under 4 metres (13 ft 1 in) above the piazza floor. Adjacent to the existing bank building, the wall is almost solid and is topped by a light-pink coloured, red Veronese marble moulding carved into a receding, stepped ziggurat profile; each step is parallel to the building's face, measuring 5.5 centimetres (2.25 in), and those perpendicular to its face measuring 3.5 centimetres (1.5 in). The number 11, and its multiples and subdivisions, regularly recurs in the Banca Popolare's fabric (5.5 is one half of 11 and 3.5 is nearly one-third of 11). At regular intervals the ziggurat moulding returns to the front face, presenting its V-over-inverted-V-shaped profile. Corresponding to the joint between the two demolished buildings, the moulding bends down to half the base wall's height then bends again to resume its horizontal course. Continuing at the same height above the moulding, the stone base is recessed, sitting flush with the plaster wall behind. Beneath the moulding, a series of operable, brass-faced, folding doors allow light into the lower level conference room.

10.4 BANCA POPOLARE; NORTHWESTERN FACADE AS SEEN FROM ACROSS THE PIAZZA NOGARA, SHOWING THE BANK'S ORIGINAL EIGHTEENTH-CENTURY BUILDING (L) AND SCARPA'S ADDITION (R)

10.5 BANCA POPOLARE; PERIOD PHOTOGRAPH, 1978, ARRIGO RUDI (L), CARLO SCARPA (C) AND RENATO SCARAZZAI (R), THE PROJECT ENGINEER, AT THE BANCA POPOLARE HEADQUARTERS

10.6 BANCA POPOLARE; NORTHWESTERN FACADE OF SCARPA'S ADDITION, SHOWING THE MARBLE BASE, *COCCIOPESTO* STUCCO MIDDLE WITH IRREGULARLY SPACED, RECESSED AND PROJECTING WINDOWS AND THE RECESSED, GLAZED LOGGIA

Interrupting the stone base and moulding to the right of this long, low aperture is a deeply recessed door faced in horizontal brass sheets, serving as the building's public entrance. Massive blocks of red Veronese stone form the door's lintel and jambs, with recessed, concentric semicircular lines incised on either side of the door. Where the ziggurat moulding meets the door, the stone jambs part, revealing the ziggurat sectional form. Standing on the red Veronese marble threshold, surrounded by the layered stonework, we are able to see the ziggurat profile carving of the inner faces of the door's upper jambs and lintel. A vertical slot window with a bevel-edged Botticino stone frame is opened in the plaster wall above the door; measuring 22 x 143 centimetres (8.75 in x 4 ft 8 in), the larger dimension being a multiple of 11 (13 x 11 = 143). To the right of the doorway, a grille is opened in the monolithic, Botticino stone slab, formed by a series of small rectangular openings measuring 5.5 x 16.5 centimetres (2.25 x 6.5 in), constituting a 1:3 ratio. Creating a pattern of six vertical rows, possibly relating to Romanesque Italian and Japanese precedents, the grille forms a pair of larger figures, defined by horizontal openings, each containing another pair of figures, defined by vertical openings. Above the grille, and separated from it by narrow horizontal slots, a pair of stone-trimmed, vertical slot windows stand on U-shaped stone sills, illuminating the staircase behind. **(10.7)**

Above the stone base and moulding, the wall is a solid, unjointed plane of smooth-faced *cocciopesto* stucco, made of lime plaster mixed with ground terracotta to give it a pale reddish tint. Running along the plaster wall's top edge is a thin Botticino stone moulding, made of a rectangular horizontal cap, which casts a shadowline into its concave, deeply recessed inner face beneath. At the plaster wall's ends the moulding terminates into cubic blocks of Botticino stone, with the same stone used to trim the vertical wall edges. All of the stone edge trim is set flush with the face of the plaster wall. At the second floor a continuous line of oak-framed windows is set above the plaster wall and behind the loggia's steel structure beneath the cornice.

A variety of windows are opened in the plaster wall's surface. Sitting flush on the facade's left side on top of the moulding are five rectangular, brass-framed windows opening into the elevated main floor. The first floor has a series of five stretched circular openings, each a circle divided into two semicircles pulled 11 centimetres (4.25 in) apart; as Rudi described it, two circles with centres 11 centimetres (4.25 in) apart, relating it to a *vesica piscis*. Behind these three large and two smaller openings; located in the same plane as the line of second floor windows above, are rectangular, oak-framed windows divided into three primary panes of glass, two wide verticals above a narrow horizontal. The circular openings have an outer edge band of convex Botticino stone, set flush with the plaster, whereas five pieces of Botticino stone are joined to form the interior surfaces. Extending vertically from the bottoms of the stretched circle openings on the external wall are recessed bands of red Veronese stone 11 centimetres (4.25 in) wide. These bands channel rainwater down the pair of grooves that are carved into their surfaces, and small projecting copper scuppers project at the bottom to drain rainwater caught behind the plaster wall at the window opening above. As Frampton noted, **'These lines not only accommodate the weathering of the facade but also emphasize the watermark from the very beginning, thereby anticipating the inevitable transformation of the building over time.'** [8]

10.7

The windows that attract the most attention, especially when seen from an acute angle, are the five cubic, vitrine-like windows with glazed fronts, sides and tops projecting outwards 16.5 centimetres (6.5 in). The three located on the first floor, two to the right and one on the left, stand on red Veronese stone sills, cantilevering from the plaster wall and undercut with the ziggurat pattern. 16.5 centimetres (6.5 in)above each of these three windows is a rectangular Botticino stone block sitting upon a cantilevered, ziggurat-carved red Veronese stone sill, its face flush with the window's below, its top edge aligning with the top of the plaster wall's cornice. Located on the elevated main floor, the remaining two projecting windows are positioned at the same height as the five flush rectangular windows. These two windows stand on T-shaped, red Veronese stone sills undercut with the ziggurat pattern, which project from the recessed Botticino building base. **(10.8)** The projecting windows meet the stone sills at the line where the stone base meets the plaster wall. Seen at an acute angle from both building ends, we can look through these vitrine-like windows to see the plaster facade on the other side. From other angles, these windows become mirors, reflecting the sky and surrounding buildings, such as the medieval Torre dei Lamberti in Piazza dei Signori, the main plaza of the city. The most dramatic effects come in the afternoon, when these windows cast faint, light-filled greenish-coloured shadows across the plaster wall as the sunlight passes through one glass face and out another.

10.7 BANCA POPOLARE; NORTHWESTERN FACADE, PUBLIC ENTRANCE, DEEPLY RECESSED BRASS DOORS SURROUNDED BY A VERONESE STONE LINTEL AND CARVED ZIGGURAT MOULDING

10.8 BANCA POPOLARE; NORTHWESTERN FACADE, A PAIR OF PROJECTING MAIN-LEVEL WINDOWS SIT ON RED VERONESE STONE SILLS, UNDERCUT WITH THE ZIGGURAT PATTERN

10.9

Excluding the second floor's continuous line of windows, all other windows are openings carved into the wall, with the glass set inside, outside or flush. When asked about the prevalence of curtain walls in contemporary architecture and its relation to the Banca Popolare, Scarpa said:

> 'Mies was a great architect. The Seagram building in New York is a wonderful building. But when you go up to it and have a good look, all you see are reflections of the buildings around it. Too much plate glass: you lose sight of the structure. There never was a period in history when so much glass was used as now. Builders formerly used solid materials. The problem was how to make the openings. In making them the craftsman could show his mastery, so marking one of the critical points in any building. The window is a very important item in the bank in Verona.' [9]

Bringing this densely layered planar composition to life are the reflections off the the facade's three very modern layers of glass: the deeply recessed, oak-framed layer of glass behind each of the stretched circular openings, and running continuously behind the upper level's steel columns; the layer of brass-framed glass set flush with the plaster wall; and the layer of frameless glass that projects outwards to form vitrine-like cubic windows.

At the top of the plaster wall, a series of small, double cylindrical steel columns stand on the Botticino moulding and support an architrave composed of two steel I-beams 60 centimetres (2 ft) deep above and 18 centimetres (7.13 in) deep below, which are joined to those to either side by riveted H-shaped steel plates. A mosaic of small, square multicolored tiles is recessed into the horizontal slot between the upper and lower architrave beam. Above each double column, a brass block incised with two interlocked spheres interrupts the tiles' pattern. **(10.9)** The columns have brass collars at their tops and brass bases set into square recesses milled into the 22 millimetre (0.9 in) thick steel base plates bolted to the masonry below. Structurally locking the pairs of columns together at their tops and bottoms are small brass connectors, their underside carved in the ziggurat pattern. **(10.10)**

10.10

10.11

Scarpa's intention to engage, shape and reinforce Verona's urban space is indicated by the bank's flat roof terrace providing views across Verona's historic centre, and the only place where we can see the top of the stone cornice's deeply-inset, ziggurat carving. The roof is paved with square, precast concrete pavers measuring 60 centimetres (1 ft 11 in) square, with small sections paved in quarry-faced, red Prun stone. Scarpa noted:

'The coping is another important element. I treated it as a kind of overhead piazza. The "floor" of the roofing is made the same way as the piazza below and I suggested putting some tubs there that will fill up with rainwater. The birds will come and splash about in them and when we go up there it will remind us of a piazza, an extension of the urban space to the top of the building.' [12] (10.11)

The steel architrave carries a cornice made of two layers of close-set Botticino blocks, its upper layer projecting forward. The lower layer's bottom and the upper layer's top have a carved ziggurat pattern, on a module of 5.5 x 3.5 centimetres (2.25 x 1.5 in). Scarpa made the cornice by literally turning the existing building's classical dentil moulding upside down:

'The cornice and plinth called for work, they are the points of contact with sky and earth. On the eaves I inverted the pattern of the existing building. In this way the eaves stand out in an interesting pattern against the sky: a line with a geometrical shape produced by industrial techniques, which lighten the building through its coping.' [10]

Scarpa often talked about the importance of the Venetian buildings' cornices and how they capture the light, create shadow patterns on the walls and form the building's profile against a blue sky. It has been noted that the cornice of the bank **'continues the Venetian tradition of crowning ancient palaces: in particular, the projecting surfaces, suggestive of a *trapezium* trapping the strong light, are inspired by the crowning of the Fondaco dei Turchi in Venice.'** [11]

10.9 BANCA POPOLARE; NORTHWESTERN FACADE, THIRD-FLOOR LOGGIA WITH DOUBLE-STEEL COLUMNS IN FRONT OF A CONTINUOUS LINE OF GLAZING

10.10 BANCA POPOLARE; PLAN AND ELEVATION DETAIL OF THE LOGGIA' S DOUBLE COLUMNS, GRAPHITE, PEN AND COLOURED PENCIL ON PAPER, 66.2 X 25.7 CM (24.5 X 10 IN)

10.11 BANCA POPOLARE; PAVED ROOF TERRACE AND CARVED ZIGGURAT CORNICE

10.12

Double steel columns march across the top of the wall, carrying a steel beam architrave and marble cornice. The cornice stops to the right of the facade's centre, near the cylindrical staircase, while the architrave and columns continue across to the existing bank building. In front of the staircase, two steel columns rise from the lower plaster wall, supporting the free-spanning architrave. At its midpoint, the columns are attached to a stone panel extending from the plaster wall's end. This panel carries, in red Veronese stone, the bank's insignia designed by Scarpa, consisting of a single, lower-case letter form which is rotated and inverted to form the bank's initials, 'b p v'. **(10.13)** The tall double column bears upon a ziggurat-cut, red Veronese stone block set into the top of the plaster wall. The double column is also given a unique, brass base that transforms from a four-sided square to an octagon, to a sixteen-sided shape and finally to a cylinder. **(10.14)** This base, its faceted surface visible from the staircase, has parallels in both Indian and Romanesque architecture.

In the brick-paved courtyard, the new southeast-facing facade is made of the same materials and details as the piazza-facing facade. At the ground, a curved retaining wall forms a sunken garden to which large, glazed windows are opened, bringing light into the lower below-grade floor. The red Veronese ziggurat moulding runs across the top of the fragmented Botticino stone plinth, turning before reaching the edge of the plaster wall above to run down a Botticino stone wall, screening the mechanical plant. Above the stone moulding, the plaster wall is opened on the elevated main floor by rectangular, flush-set windows, while the first floor has five of the stretched circular openings with recessed windows behind. The plaster wall stops short of the courtyard's left corner where a copper-clad bridge, a stretched circle in section, emerges to connect to the bank offices in the building on the back street. On the courtyard's right side, the plaster wall cuts down in a Z-shape to reveal a cylindrical steel-framed, glass-walled staircase standing on the terrace behind. **(10.12)**

Entry to the bank is through the marble-framed, brass-faced door off the Piazza Nogara, which opens into a white Clauzetto stone-paved vestibule, set halfway between the lower level and the elevated level above, both of which are visible as we enter, as are the layered vertical voids surrounding the staircase. To the right, we step up on to a broad, stone-paved landing illuminated by the Botticino stone grille. On the inner face, the grille's small apertures are chamfered, maximizing light infiltration, and reveal the same pattern we saw outside, now formed by white light rather than black shadow. The wall ahead is made of wide, white Clauzetto marble slabs alternating with thin, Alpine-green marble bands. Set slightly in front of this wall is a narrow opening to below, framed by a low, white polished plaster wall with a white marble rail cap. Overhead, the angled surface beneath the staircase is clad in wide green marble slabs and thin white marble bands.

10.13

10.14

Three broad marble steps lead up to the lift and staircase landing, where a full-height slab of Calacatta (a type of onyx) stone is set into the right-hand wall, lit from behind to reveal the stone's yellow colour and dark veining. Directly ahead, the lift, with its black, leather-clad doors, is housed in a vertical enclosure, the plan of which is a stretched circle with one straight edge. The enclosure's curved surface is finished in highly polished, deep blue *marmorino* plaster and it stands in a narrow void, opening to the lower level and upper floors. To our left, one step leads to the staircase's landing, while to either side white marble-framed walls have sideway-V-shaped, ziggurat-patterned indentations at their tops. Across the landing, the white polished-plaster wall's vertical opening, with a ziggurat-carved marble frame, gives a view across the main space. **(10.15)**

The five steps to the right lead to a large open room on the elevated main floor, the building's most public space. This floor, and all the floors of the bank's public and circulation spaces, is made of polished, white Clauzetto marble slabs with almost invisible joints, shifted so as not to align. Where the white polished-plaster walls meet the floor, a low curb, made of the same marble, with a continuous horizontal groove at its centre, sits flush with the wall's face. Defining the central circulation space, two lines of double columns run parallel to the exterior facades, with two wider spaces running along the outer edges. **(10.16)** Each of the double columns are made of concrete, the upper two-thirds cast into faceted, wood board formwork that aligns with the facets of the lower third's 1 metre (3 ft 3 in) tall, steel base-sheath. At the floor, the pairs of cylindrical steel bases are set into rectangular steel plates, and marking the joint between columns and floor plate are three tiny, recessed rings, making the columns appear to sink slightly into the floor (as in the Masieri Foundation). Near their tops, incised gold-leafed bands encircle the columns. Above these bands the columns are joined by a steel connector, into the bottom face of which is inset a brass block incised with two interlocking spheres: a small three-dimensional *vesica piscis* sparkles from the shadows between the double columns. Separated by a thin, shadowed reveal, the concrete columns stop just below the exposed board-formed concrete structural beams. **(10.17)** Set flush with the concrete beams' soffits, steel-edged panels of light grey-coloured polished plaster form the space's suspended ceiling and carry recessed rectangular air vents and pairs of circular lights. Thus the ceiling, while forming a continuous flush horizontal plane, also clearly exposes the concrete structure, with its matte finish, and allows it to be distinguished from the nonstructural suspended ceiling, with its reflective polished finish.

10.15

10.16

10.17

10.12 BANCA POPOLARE; SOUTHEASTERN FACADE FROM THE REAR COURTYARD

10.13 BANCA POPOLARE; SOUTHEASTERN FACADE, DOUBLE COLUMNS RISING FROM THE PLASTER WALL, SUPPORT THE STEEL ARCHITRAVE IN FRONT OF THE CYLINDRICAL, GLASS-WALLED STAIRCASE

10.14 BANCA POPOLARE; SOUTHEASTERN FACADE, DETAIL OF THE DOUBLE COLUMNS' BRASS BASE, BEARING UPON A ZIGGURAT-CUT, RED VERONESE STONE BLOCK

10.15 BANCA POPOLARE; STAIRCASE LANDING BETWEEN THE LOWER AND ELEVATED GROUND FLOOR

10.16 BANCA POPOLARE; ELEVATED GROUND FLOOR, VIEW EAST ACROSS THE MAIN PUBLIC SPACE WITH THE GLOWING ONYX PANELS AND PROJECTING VOLUME OF THE STAIRCASE AND LANDINGS (R) AND THE SKY BLUE *MARMORINO*, T-SHAPED SCREEN WALL (L)

10.17 BANCA POPOLARE; ELEVATED GROUND FLOOR, DETAIL OF THE CONCRETE COLUMNS' TOPS, STOPPING SHORT OF THE CEILING'S EXPOSED BEAMS

10.18

At the connection to the original building on the room's northeast side, a wide staircase descends from the first floor above, while an equally wide staircase rises from the lower level; between them is a small landing where we can stand on the top of the bank vault. The staircase's landings and treads are made of polished, white Clauzetto marble, like the floor, while the low walls are made of white polished plaster with curved marble rail and end caps. At the room's other end, the staircase's plaster-walled volume projects into the space and is opened at its centre by a marble-framed slot, which allows us to see the lower and upper landing's glowing onyx panels. Beyond the staircase, at the room's far end, a highly polished, pale sky blue *marmorino*, T-shaped screen wall is set forward of the rear wall. Formed of two inverted L-shaped, brass-edged panels connected by a pair of brass cylinders, this T-shaped screen wall stands above a low, brass-edged wall lifted by H-shaped brass bases that are recessed into a notch in the wall. Interlocking T- and C-shaped brass connectors attach the T-shaped screen wall's two arms to the adjacent walls, leaving a space between the edge of the screen wall and the room's outer walls.

Passing beneath the T-shaped screen wall's right arm we find a white marble staircase descending to the lower floor. On its inner face, the T-shaped screen wall is finished in white *marmorino*; brass cylinders anchor two black rods which run across the staircase overhead, suspended from that are a pair of rectangular, onyx faced, brass-framed lights. At the outer wall, a low brass-edged wall opens to a narrow slot of space, giving a view of a second staircase below. At the lower floor, the second staircase descends to the basement, where staff services are located. The upper staircase and lower staircase are offset from one another and their serrated walls are interlocked, allowing the upper staircase to bear on the lower staircase's wall. The upper staircase's wall has a violet-coloured *marmorino* finish, edged in brass, while the lower staircase's wall has a deep green-coloured *marmorino* finish, edged in white marble. **(10.18)** Set into an inner corner of the violet-coloured upper wall, around which we walk to reach the last three steps down to the lower level, is a three-quarter square brass section, celebrating the joint. **(10.19)**

Along the piazza edge of this lower space is a freestanding conference room, its stretched cylindrical volume formed by thin, curved, steel-edged walls finished in leather-coloured *marmorino*. Lit from a long horizontal window adjacent to the entry door, this room can be darkened by closing a curtain hung on the curved perimeter rail or by raising the outer wall's brass-clad, shutter door. At this level, the double columns are cast in floor-to-ceiling, cylindrical steel sleeves. Across the space from the employee's double staircase is a wide marble staircase that rises up to the original bank building's ground level, its lowest tread running across to form the vault's base; the face of which is lit by a narrow opening in the ceiling.

10.19

Returning to the staircase we first entered, we climb the stairs to reach the upper floors, passing the main elevated level to arrive to the landing over the entry door, where light enters through two vertical slot windows, their inner surfaces carved in the ziggurat pattern, so that each edge catches the light. At the stair's inner turn, we pass the second backlit onyx stone slab at the mezzanine level, across from which the wall's marble frame has a carved, V-shaped ziggurat pattern, projecting further out at the top than at the bottom. These carved details at the tops of the staircase walls, with 5.5 centimetre horizontals and 3.5 centimetre verticals (2.25 x 1.5 in), are repeated from the lower level to the mezzanine landing below the first floor. At the first floor, where the executive offices are located, the stair ends at a landing opening on to the Via Conventino through a two-storey, steel-framed glass wall, rising up through the ceiling's slot-like opening. This landing is separated from the glass wall and the white plaster wall to the right, by low marble-capped plaster walls, behind which narrow slots of space open to the stairs below.

On the right-hand side of the landing, a variation of the intersecting double circle is carved into the white polished-plaster wall and edged in brass plate, revealing a second plaster wall behind. **(10.20)** The figure's upper half is composed of a stretched circle, with two semicircles separated by a narrow, vertical slot extending to the ceiling, while the bottom half is formed of two curved lobes, turning up to form a central, square-topped rib. Unlike the geometrically generated double circle forms, the unique variation's morphology is more closely related to human anatomy. During the day this form is illuminated by sunlight coming from the glass wall, casting a shadow on the plaster wall behind; at night, inset lighting illuminates the plaster wall, transforming the aperture into a light source.

10.18 BANCA POPOLARE; INTERLOCKED, SERRATED WALLS OF THE EASTERN CORNER'S UPPER AND LOWER STAIRCASES

10.19 BANCA POPOLARE; DETAIL OF THE THREE-QUARTER SQUARE BRASS JOINT IN THE INNER CORNER OF THE VIOLET-COLOURED UPPER WALL

10.20 BANCA POPOLARE: FIRST-FLOOR LANDING OF THE WESTERN STAIRCASE, A DOUBLE CIRCLE CARVED INTO THE POLISHED-PLASTER WALL LIT BY THE NORTHWESTERN TWO-STOREY, STEEL-FRAMED GLASS WALL

10.21

10.22

10.23

Walking back towards the leather-clad, deep blue *stucco lucido*-faced lift, the white Clauzetto marble paving continues from the staircase into the wide central hallway, running the length of the first floor. The steel-framed, cream-coloured polished-plaster ceiling panels carry pairs of circular recessed downlights. The double columns, in faceted concrete and steel, are similarly detailed to those on the main floor below, but at the ceiling only the concrete beam's downturn is exposed. Set flush with the suspended ceiling, the faces of the capital-like beam downturns are smoothly finished and divided into two squares by a central reveal. To the left of the lift, the first set of double columns are set perpendicular to the long, outer walls, while the other three are set parallel to the outer walls, indicating the primary direction of movement is towards the old bank building. **(10.21)**

The wide hallway's walls, made of white polished plaster with white marble curbs, run up behind the polished plaster ceiling's steel frames. Recessed into the walls near the floor are pairs of circular emergency lights, occuring on all levels. The office's inner wall towards the courtyard has a large doorway at its centre: an inverted, T-shaped opening filled with brass-framed, frosted glass. Light from the courtyard windows enters the hall through the doorway and through the clerestory windows made of recessed, frameless clear glass running along the top of the wall and wrapping around the corner. The executive offices' inner wall is solid, with tall wooden doors set into recessed foyers. The executive offices have carpeted floors, light grey-coloured polished plaster walls and steel-framed, leather-coloured polished plaster ceiling panels divided by slotted brass bands from which lights are suspended. The stretched circle, Botticino stone-framed apertures, set outside the rectangular, oak-framed windows, create three layers of illumination: the shadowed walls surrounding the window, the marble frame's indirectly illuminated back surface and the actual opening. **(10.22)** Due to their curved stone edges, the stretched circles of bright light appear to float in the more dimly lit wood-framed window.

Behind the deep blue lift enclosure, a corridor leads to the copper-clad bridge connecting the new building to the bank offices across the courtyard. The end of the bridge extends a short distance inwards through the outer wall, at the top of which is a continuous clerestory window. The edge of the arched tube-like volume is framed in steel while its inner walls and curved ceiling are lined with wood veneer-faced panels. The new building's marble floor extends a short way into the bridge after which a narrower section of white carpet continues. The horizontal line of narrow, brass-framed windows is set low in the wall, allowing views of the courtyard and the sunken garden. Halfway across the bridge, six steps bring the floor down to meet the other building's level, so that the windows are now at eye level, offering views of the new facade and three zinc-plate chimney stacks, two cylinders joined by straight walls and an octagon. **(10.23)**

10.21 BANCA POPOLARE; FIRST FLOOR, SOUTHEASTERN VIEW ACROSS THE WIDE HALLWAY TOWARDS THE STAIRCASE AND BLUE STUCCO LIFT SHAFT WITH THE OFFICE'S INVERTED, T-SHAPED OPENING ON THE LEFT

10.22 BANCA POPOLARE; FIRST-FLOOR EXECUTIVE OFFICE

10.23 BANCA POPOLARE; VIEW THROUGH THE WOOD-VENEER PANELLED BRIDGE SPANNING THE EASTERN SIDE OF THE REAR COURTYARD, FROM EXISTING BANK BUILDING TO SCARPA'S ADDITION

At the other end of the wide hallway stands the leather-faced, executive lift, running from the first to the second floors. *Vesica piscis*-shaped in plan, the lift is housed in a freestanding enclosure, its two outer curved walls finished in deep red-coloured highly polished *marmorino*. The curved walls have a floor-level, slotted marble curb; ends that are cut away from the ceiling; and a white marble-clad recessed entry with ziggurat-carved edges and inner faces. A full-height, vertical slot window, framed in ziggurat-stepping marble, pours light on to the lift enclosure's sidewall, bouncing red-tinted light on to the hallway's white walls. **(10.24)** On the same side of the hallway, a low wall and three stairs lead up to the lower landing of the glass-walled staircase enclosure, which stands in the paved terrace overlooking the courtyard.

A stretched circle in plan, the staircase is enclosed in a faceted curving skin made by tall, narrow panes of glass set between steel mullion posts, running from the first landing to the flat roof. Inside, the square plan-shaped stair, with two flights of nine steps, is suspended away from the curving wall in a cage-like structure of vertical tubular steel. The steel tubes have a green-grey-coloured, varnish finish and fixed 90-degree brass joints. The stair treads are made of latticed plate steel with the rectangular cells filled with impact-resistant concrete and are supported on double, horizontal steel tubes. Supported by brass brackets, the wood handrail also has brass end caps. When we step out from the office floor's dimly lit, thick-walled, marble-floored enclosure into this brightly lit, glass-walled structure, the contrast could not be greater; the staircase acts as a spatial hinge, taking us out of the building, into the courtyard and back again. **(10.25)**

At the top of the staircase, we arrive in a glass-walled hallway, where the executive lift's curved, red sidewall rises through an opening in the floor. Behind the lift, three stairs lead up to the top floor of the space overlapping between the new and old buildings. A half-flight of stairs leads down to a landing, running along the outer wall next to the piazza, illuminated by the continuous wood-framed windows beneath the cornice.

From here we look down to see the semi-cylindrical staircase spiralling down to the ground floor, which was completed by Rudi after Scarpa's death. The complexly curving walls and bottom are finished in a thin coat of deep red *marmorino*, highly polished to shine like lacquer, contrasting with the white marble stairs. At each floor, the curving staircase passes through a rectangular opening framed by low, polished white plaster walls with curved marble caps, differing from the red staircase's wooden handrail cap. The suspended, steel-framed, polished plaster ceilings of the spaces into which the stair opens are leather-coloured. The stair's landing on the first floor is illuminated by a contrasting pair of windows: a stretched-circle aperture, rectangular wood-framed window and a frameless glass, vitrine-like window. We can see the spiralling red staircase from the central circulation spaces on each of the upper three floors it serves, forming a visual and acoustic connection between the old building's ground floor to the new building's top floor. **(10.26)** In a complementary way, the two lifts anchor the two ends of the central circulation zone. The red-walled, *vesica piscis*-plan executive lift opens along the building's long axis, while the blue-walled, stretched circle-plan public lift opens along the building's short, cross axis, forming an asymmetrical pair.

10.24 BANCA POPOLARE; FIRST FLOOR, THE EASTERN END OF THE WIDE HALLWAY, THE FREESTANDING EXECUTIVE LIFT SHAFT RUNS UP TO THE SECOND FLOOR

10.25 BANCA POPOLARE; GLASS-WALLED STAIRCASE WITH STEEL MULLION POSTS

10.26 BANCA POPOLARE; DETAIL OF THE SEMI-CYLINDRICAL, SPIRALLING STAIRCASE, FINISHED IN A HIGHLY POLISHED, DEEP RED *MARMORINO*

10.26

Scarpa believed that throughout history builders had always articulated stairs, and they were one of the 'points' of construction that revealed something of the time in which they were made. Regarding the four stairs in the Banca Popolare, he said, **'I tried to make the steps a kind of "walk in space".'** [13] Scarpa's staircases created a series of complementary spatial hinges, connecting the building's spaces. The entry staircase, a dimly lit, marble-clad, vertical labyrinth, sits diagonally across the plan from the courtyard terrace staircase, a brightly lit, suspended glass and steel cage. In a similar way, the employee's staircase, made of stairs and multicoloured walls that shear and slide past and over one another, creating a powerful sense of compression and rupture, sits diagonally opposite in plan from the smoothly curving spiral staircase, its red colour flowing through the building, its space unfurling to create an undeniable sense of release. Upon further examination, more complementary relationships emerge: the glass-enclosed staircase's exposed skeletal structure, which is the inverse of the red-walled spiral staircase's smooth-skinned structure; and the entry staircase's massive, monolithic carved space, which is the inverse of the light, floating planar composition of the employee's staircase.

In the Banca Popolare's interior and exterior spaces, details and functional elements enrich our tactile and sensuous experience. The densely layered planes both outside and inside, combined with the reflections off various surfaces of marble, glass, metal and polished plaster, makes the definition of the space ambiguous, encouraging our exploration of its edges and boundaries. In these spaces, Scarpa creates a labyrinthine quality that is paradoxically achieved through light and colour, making an interior that seems infinite in experience. Taken altogether, the Banca Popolare indicates the degree to which an admirably functioning contemporary office interior can be made a place of both spiritual mystery and sensory enrichment.

The 36th Biennale of 1972 was Scarpa's last as an exhibit designer. In addition to 'Aspects of Contemporary Italian Sculpture' and 'Masterworks of Painting in the 20th Century (1900–1945)', Scarpa curated and designed the exhibit, 'Four Projects for Venice'. This exhibit presented architectural projects by the masters of modern architecture proposed for Venice between 1953 and 1972: Wright's Masieri Memorial, Le Corbusier's Venice Hospital, Kahn's Palazzo dei Congressi and a park between the sea and lagoon at Jesolo by Isamu Noguchi. At the time there was still reason to hope that all of these, except Wright's design, would be realized, and part of Scarpa's intent with this exhibit was to emphasize the importance of building modern works in Venice. The year before, in a television interview, Scarpa said, **'Venice, more than any other Italian city, can accept modern architectural designs [because of its characteristics of] asymmetry, varying heights, buildings tall and short, streets narrow and wide, with beautiful internal spaces.'** [14] This was the period in which, in his own work, Scarpa was encountering increasing resistance from those he called **'the bureaucrats'** in the Venice planning office, and in the end, none of the 'Four Projects' were realized. Particularly regrettable was the failure to build Le Corbusier's Venice Hospital, one of the twentieth century's foremost architect's greatest and most innovative designs, influencing generations of later designers. Owing to its remarkable synthesis of modern spatial concepts and Venice's medieval urban form, it is still a subject of study and emulation today. [15]

10.27

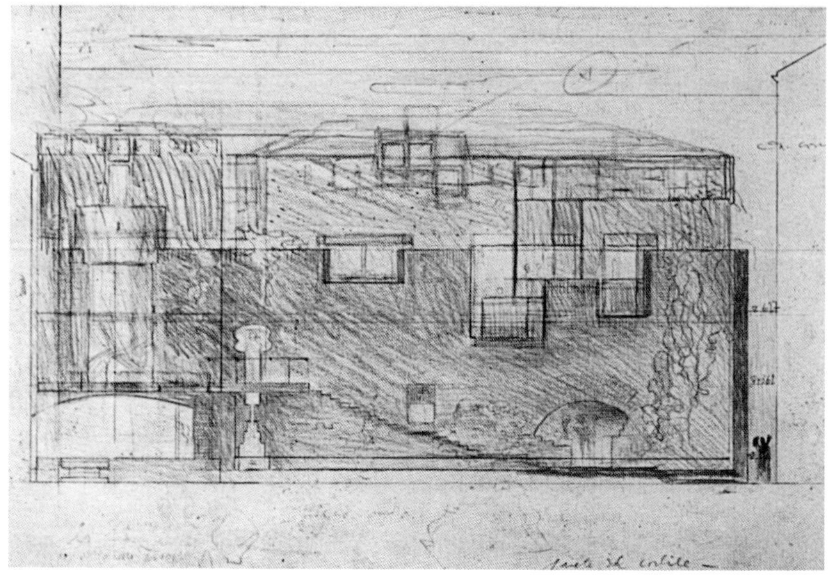

In 1973, across the garden from the palazzo, Scarpa was commissioned to design an addition to the Querini Stampalia to house book storage, scholars' guest rooms and a director's apartment. In his design for the new building, which remained unrealized, Scarpa incorporated the narrow passage running behind the garden wall, placing in it a long staircase connecting to the first floor, double-height entry hall, lifted on four cylindrical columns above a new *sottoportico*, which allowed access to the service garden. The double-height, elevated entry hall was separated by a narrow space from the four-storey main block, housing book stacks and scholars' rooms. The design also created a director's apartment, spanning across both blocks at the roof, and an elevated corridor connecting to the main building's first floor. Scarpa maintained the brick garden wall, but carved large notches into the top through which windows, balconies and stairs projected. Seen from the garden, the new building would have appeared to be composed in two layers, the old brick garden wall through which new elements projected, and the new stucco-faced wall rising just behind. **(10.27)**

Scarpa's 1974 design for Giacomo Borgo's Apartment House in Vicenza was his only realized multifamily structure, and one of his very few designs for this building type. As seen from the south, this building presents itself as a thin slab lifted off the ground by a concrete plinth and column structure, and we cannot perceive the large portion of the T-shaped plan extending to the rear until we enter the eastern courtyard. The right half of the south-facing, four-storey slab volume is lifted off the ground, creating a loggia beneath. **(10.28)** Single and double columns, alternating perpendicular and parallel to the building's front face, comprise rectangular or square concrete shafts, respectively. The columns have chamfered corners and steel capitals at their tops. Deep, steel I-beams, with notched ends forming an L-shape, bear on the column capitals; all of the steel is painted a deep red. The three floors of apartments have tall, full-height windows, and exposed concrete floor slabs form a stringcourse. The building's nonrepeating window layout creates a changing composition of darker voids and lighter plaster wall surfaces, originally pink, now white. A U-shaped Vicenza stone sill with ziggurat patterning supports the deeply recessed windows. The recessed sills alternate with occasional projecting Vicenza stone balconies, also carrying the ziggurat pattern. At the top, the plaster wall is given a repeating pattern of recesses: smaller cylindrical indentions alternating with larger, conical-shaped recesses. Resting on a lifted concrete base, the building's rear has four apartment floors and no loggia, the whole mass hovering 30 centimetres (1 ft) off the ground to provide light to the garage below. The entry terrace, covered by a wood board-formed concrete trellis and the loggia, is paved in simple concrete bricks, set with their sides up, their cylindrical holes plugged with white concrete.

10.28

10.27 CARLO SCARPA, FONDAZIONE QUERINI STAMPALIA ADDITION, 1973; ELEVATION, GRAPHITE, PEN AND COLOURED PENCIL ON PAPER

10.28 CARLO SCARPA, GIACOMO BORGO APARTMENT HOUSE, VICENZA, 1974; SOUTHEASTERN CORNER OF THE STREET FACADE. CONCRETE COLUMNS CREATE A LOGGIA BENEATH THE FOUR-STOREY STRUCTURE

In 1974, Scarpa was commissioned to renovate and extend the former San Sebastiano convent to house the Faculty of Literature and Philosophy of the University of Venice, then directed by Scarpa's friend, the historian Mazzariol. Scarpa made extensive proposals, including small new buildings to be placed both within the convent's courtyards and outside in the campo, but the planning authorities did not approve his plans and only a conservative restoration was permitted. In 1976, he was commissioned to redesign an entrance in the old church's side facade. Scarpa added a new Istrian stone layer, with small circular penetrations forming grilles, a three-quarter circle opening framing an existing bas-relief and a ziggurat-patterned frame surrounding the door, to which interlocking marble steps lead. His assistant Guido Pietropoli completed the entrance in 1979, after Scarpa's death. **(10.29)**

Scarpa designed the 1967 Arturo Martini sculpture exhibit in the former convent of Santa Caterina in Treviso in which he placed sculptures both in the church, positioning them beneath a folded fabric ceiling, and in the cloister courtyard. In the cloister, where his structures for this exhibit still remain today, Scarpa set a new reflecting pool with a ziggurat-patterned bottom and linear planes of steel-framed concrete paving slabs, either set into the courtyard's open centre or appearing to slide out from under the arcade. **(10.30)** Beneath the arched ceiling of the arcade, Scarpa placed parallel sets of large, rectangular, steel-edged concrete paving slabs of constantly varying and nonrepeating dimensions. These concrete slabs were aligned along a central joint, stepping to create a serrated edge along the outside at the wall and colonnade. Scarpa put rounded pebbles into the spaces not occupied by the concrete, creating the same ambiguous relationship between the slabs and gravel in the arcade as occurred in the courtyard with the slabs and grass. **(10.31)**

10.29

10.30

10.31

10.29 CARLO SCARPA AND GUIDO PIETROPOLI, FACULTY OF LITERATURE AND PHILOSOPHY, UNIVERSITY OF VENICE, CONVENTO DI SAN SEBASTIANO ENTRANCE, VENICE, 1976–9

10.30 CARLO SCARPA, ARTURO MARTINI EXHIBITION, SANTA CATERINA CONVENT, TREVISO, 1967; CLOISTER COURTYARD WITH ZIGGURAT-PATTERNED REFLECTING POOL

10.31 ARTURO MARTINI EXHIBITION; COVERED ARCADE WITH CONCRETE SLAB AND ROUNDED-PEBBLE FLOOR

10.32 CARLO SCARPA, SANTA CATERINA MUSEUM DESIGN, TREVISO, 1974; ELEVATION, GRAPHITE, PEN AND COLOURED PENCIL ON PAPER

10.33 CARLO SCARPA, FELTRE RUINS PIAZZA, FELTRE, 1973–8; PLAN, GRAPHITE, PEN AND COLOURED PENCIL ON PAPER

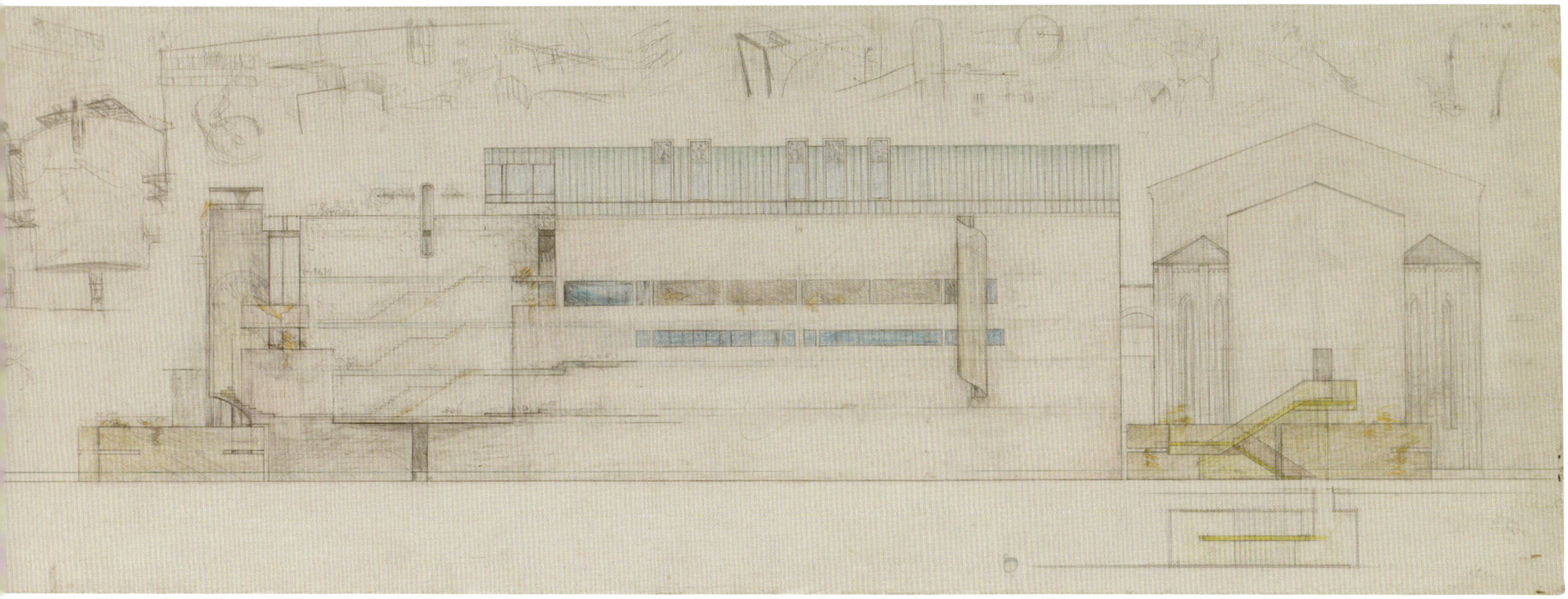

10.32

In 1974, Scarpa was commissioned to design a comprehensive renovation and addition for the Santa Caterina convent, converting it into the municipal art museum.[16] One year later, Scarpa presented his design to the city officials, who, despite their enthusiasm for the design, were ultimately unable to realize it. Beyond renovating the existing church and the large and small cloisters, Scarpa proposed to make a substantial addition. This comprised an L-shaped plan to include a library, an elevated cubic gallery with a loggia beneath, a set of ramps for public circulation and long, parallel galleries set beneath semi-barrel-vaulted roofs. Scarpa carefully proportioned the new exterior facade, making a symmetrical, curving, apse-like projection, housing a stair, to correspond with the symmetrical apse of the church. It is intriguing to note that based on Scarpa's final drawings he did not intend to preserve his own earlier works in the cloister. **(10.32)**

From 1973–8, Scarpa worked on the unrealized elevated piazza above the archaeological ruins discovered in front of the Cathedral of Feltre. Scarpa proposed a skeletal plane, opened to provide views into the ruins below, to be elevated several feet above the city streets and supported by a series of parallel, bridge-like beams, using the piazza's upper surface as the compression member and steel cables beneath as the tension members. **(10.33)** Scarpa's section of the piazza-bridge indicates his intention to both conceal and extend the moment of bearing by pulling the edge of the steel-framed, stone-paved piazza away from the wall of the excavations below, projecting the concrete buttresses out over the excavations; and recessing the steel beams that actually effected the load transfer deep into the shadow of the piazza, placing them on the ends of the projecting buttresses. **(10.34)** As Frampton noted, the Feltre project is exemplary of Scarpa's **'hieratic elaboration of his joints ... Rather than simply juxtapose the support and the load, Scarpa would "postpone" the final moment of support.'**[17]

10.33

10.34

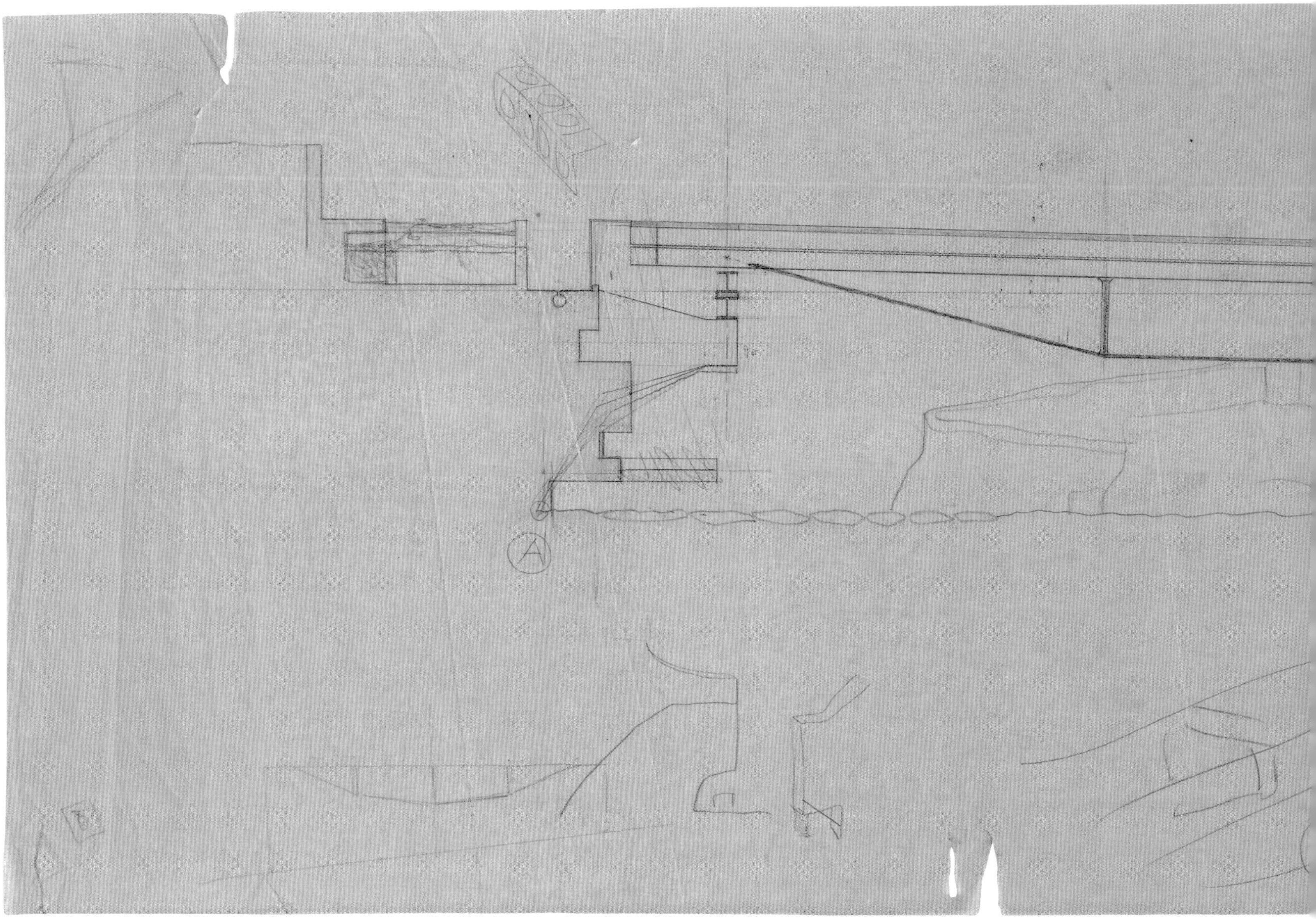

10.35

In 1968, Scarpa designed the base for the ***Monument to the Female Resistance Fighter***, a reclining figure designed by Augusto Murer. Scarpa placed the sculpture in the lagoon, at the edge of the *fondamenta*, a water-fronting street to the south of the Biennale gardens. At the edge of the lagoon Scarpa placed a dense series of cubic freestanding, island-like stepping stones, made of concrete with Istrian stone pavers. The sculpture is placed at the outer edge of the steps, on a floating, rectangular, copper-clad caisson that rises and falls with the tides. **(10.35)** The water enters between the square stone blocks, and the transition from the solid paving of the *fondamenta* to the island-like outer blocks gives the appearance that the ground beneath our feet is breaking apart. After many years of being inaccessible, a recent restoration allows visitors to walk out into the lagoon to be with the fallen figure, as Scarpa intended.

10.34 FELTRE RUINS PIAZZA; SECTION, GRAPHITE, PEN AND COLOURED PENCIL ON PAPER

10.35 CARLO SCARPA, BASE FOR THE *MONUMENT TO THE FEMALE RESISTANCE FIGHTER*, VENICE, 1968; AUGUSTO MURER SCULPTURE ON A DENSE BASE OF CUBIC STEPPING STONES IN THE VENETIAN LAGOON

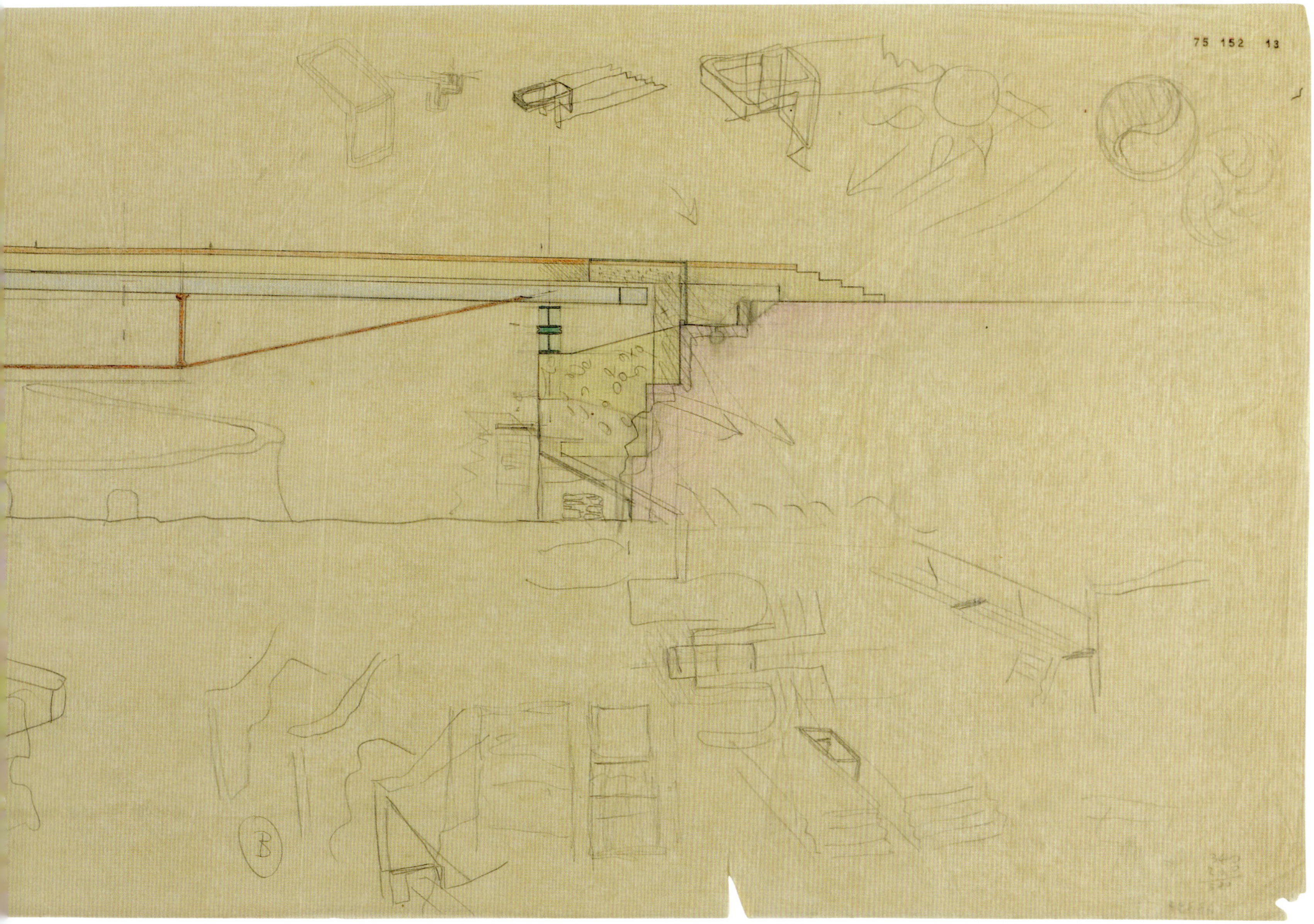
75 152 13

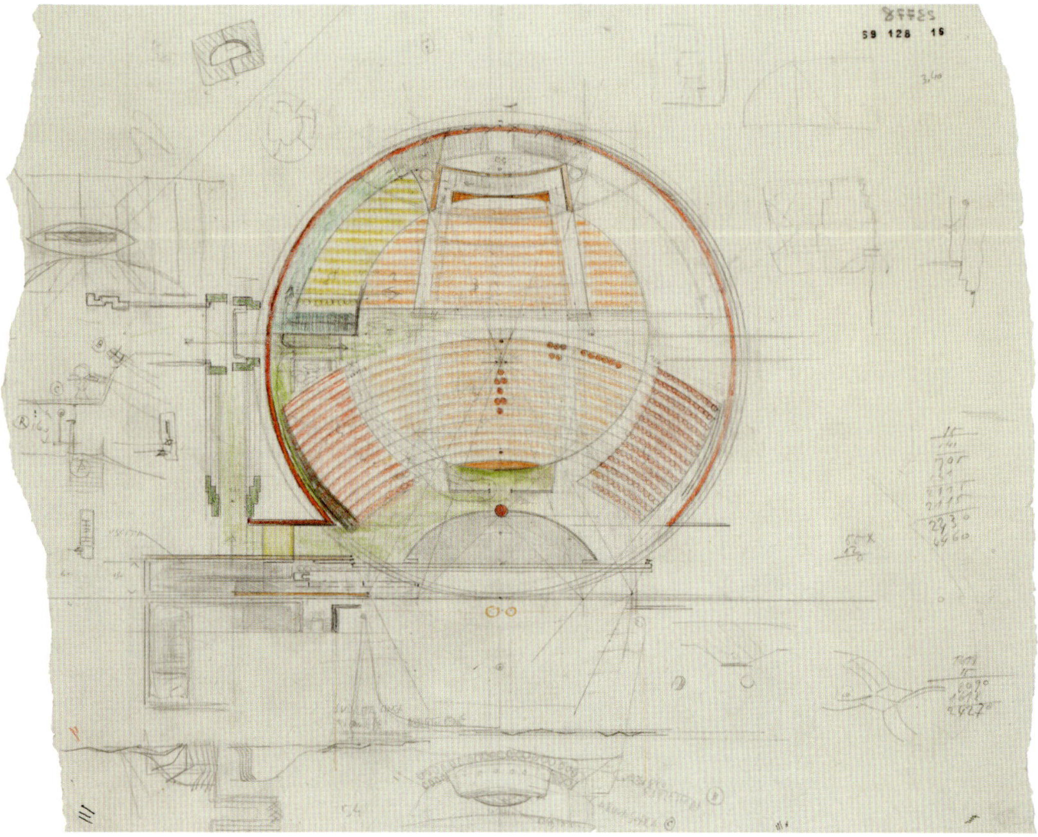

10.36

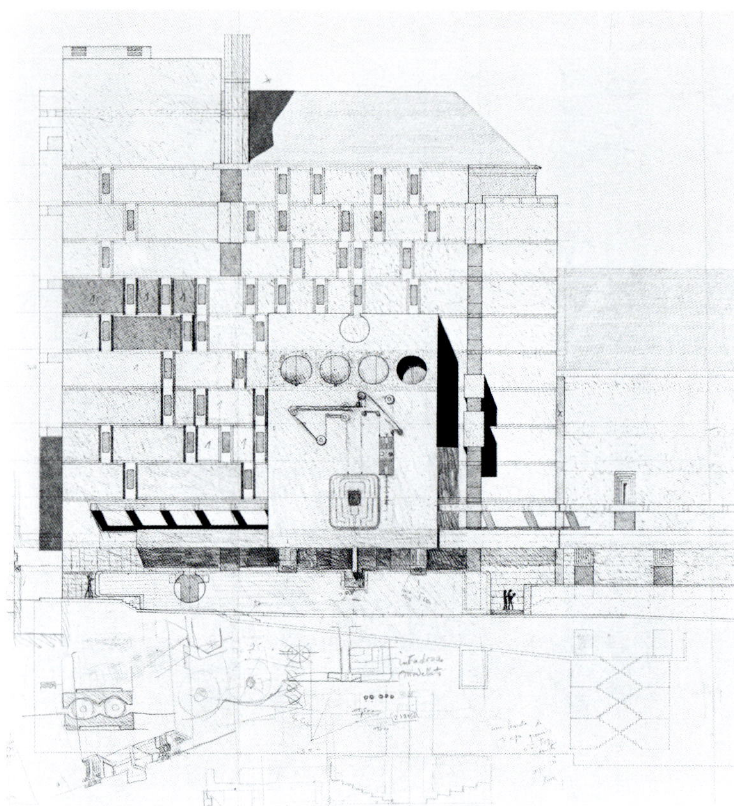

10.37

Scarpa worked from 1963 until 1976 on the unrealized reconstruction of the war-damaged Carlo Felice Theatre in Genoa. Among this project's many drawings are a number relating to his own work. One of these shows an elevation with a series of vertical windows in a nonaligning and nonrepeating pattern, (as in the Vicenza apartment building), below which is a series of pulleys and cables operating an aperture in the facade, (similar to the Brion Cemetery's door mechanism). **(10.37)** Another elevation shows a low, arched window running across the masonry facade, beneath which is a small rectangular central opening, the whole remarkably similar to several designs by Scarpa's friend Kahn, especially the 1966–73 Fort Wayne Performing Arts Centre's facade.

Scarpa entered the competition for the 1968–9 new Teatro Comunale in Vicenza; the other competitors were his IUAV colleagues Gardella and Albini. Scarpa's design for the site at the northeast corner of the Campo Marzo park involved a cylindrical seating volume opening to a large rectangular backstage and fly volume: the stage itself was a *vesica piscis* in plan. **(10.36)** The seating volume's shallow-sloping, conical roof, opened at its centre by a rooflight, reminiscent of the Pantheon in Rome, was supported by cables running from two pairs of massive concrete piers, similar to Le Corbusier's celebrated design for the 1931 Palace of the Soviets competition. One of Scarpa's very few completely symmetrical designs, the pure geometries of the Vicenza theatre design and their diagonal arrangement with respect to the corner site, were reminiscent of Kahn's early designs for the Fort Wayne buildings, and, like Kahn's work, Scarpa's project also engaged architecture's ancient and modern traditions.

10.38

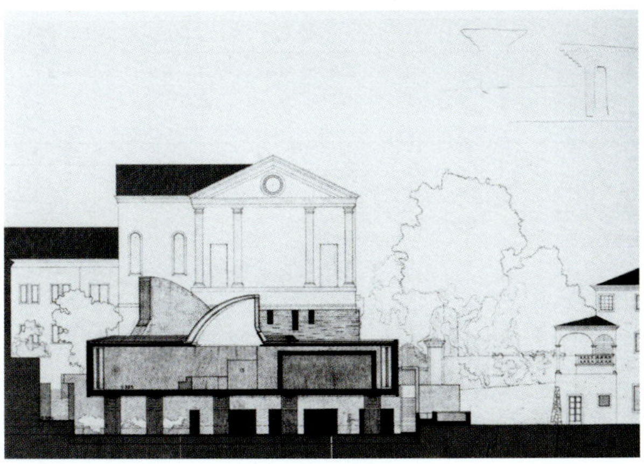

10.39

In 1974, Scarpa was commissioned to design a new building to house the Gallerie Nazionale d'Arte of Messina. Located on a large, irregularly shaped site containing fragments of buildings and sculptures salvaged from the 1908 earthquake that levelled the city's historic centre, Scarpa's plan proposed a series of densely interlocked rectangular volumes, connected by a series of linear passages. **(10.38)** Three small, medium and large curved galleries, arranged along the eastern side, were intriguingly similar to a number of Alvar Aalto's designs. Scarpa's notes on this project indicate his intentions, as Francesca Fenaroli has related:

> **'He wished to create the sensation of spatial continuity found in the medieval and Renaissance squares of ancient cities, and through this sequence of informal perspectives within a context of continuous movement, to provide an antithesis to the destruction of the historic center of Messina.'** [18]

Sited in the town's historic centre, Scarpa's unrealized design for the 1976–7 Banca Antoniana in Monselice proposed housing the bank in a rectangular box with corners chamfered and cut open. This volume was to be elevated on double piers, creating a street-level, covered public loggia. Large quarter-circle clerestory vaults rose above the bank's roof, facing east and west, their vertical apertures folded to create an angled opening in the ceiling overhead, again recalling Aalto's work. **(10.39)** Similar vaults also appeared in Scarpa's preliminary designs for the 1978 Banca Popolare in Gemona. Scarpa's last sketches for this project, in November 1978, were on the New Otani hotel's stationary in Sendai, Japan, where he died. In Scarpa's initial proposal, the nine curved vaults, of differing widths, were set along the outer walls of the main banking hall, rising out of the flat ceiling to frame sky views. The architect Luciano Gemin used Scarpa's sketches and preliminary plans to develop the design and execute the building, which though filled with Scarpa-inspired elements, is rightly credited to Gemin. [19]

10.36 CARLO SCARPA, TEATRO COMMUNALE, VICENZA, 1968–9; PLAN, GRAPHITE, PEN AND COLOURED PENCIL ON PAPER

10.37 CARLO SCARPA, CARLO FELICE THEATRE, GENOA, 1963–76; ELEVATION, GRAPHITE AND PEN ON PAPER

10.38 CARLO SCARPA, GALLERIE NAZIONALE D'ARTE, MESSINA, 1974; PLAN, GRAPHITE, PEN AND COLOURED PENCIL ON PAPER

10.39 CARLO SCARPA, BANCA ANTONIANA, MONSELICE, 1976–7; SECTION, GRAPHITE AND PEN ON PAPER

CHAPTER 11
MAKING THE SPIRIT EXPLICIT

BRION CEMETERY
SAN VITO D'ALTIVOLE, 1969–1977

The addition to the municipal cemetery of San Vito d'Altivole, a small village within sight of the Dolomite Mountains and the foothills of Asolo, has proved to be Scarpa's most visited, studied and famous work. San Vito d'Altivole was the birthplace of Giuseppe Brion, founder of the internationally recognized Brionvega electronics company, whose radios, televisions and other products received numerous awards for their design quality, and examples of which are held in various museum collections, including New York's Museum of Modern Art. When Brion, described by Scarpa as someone who **'had come up from the people, who had started at the bottom and risen to become an important figure through his work',**[1] died in 1968, his wife Onorina commissioned Scarpa to design a memorial to him. The family owned the mausoleum spaces at the eastern end of the northern most of three sections of the existing, typical small Veneto village cemetery; a square walled space south of town with tombs in the ground at the centre and family mausoleums along the northern and eastern sides. But the Brion family decided to provide more space for the tomb setting, purchasing 2,200 square metres (23,681 sq ft) of land: a very large L-shaped site wrapping completely around the existing cemetery's northern and eastern sides. Constructed from 1970–7, this was the last project Scarpa saw completed, and nearly all his design drawings have survived, now conserved in his archives.[2]

Scarpa's earliest studies, which exclude the chapel, already contain the arched tomb for the husband and wife, originally located at the L-shaped plan's southern end, with a tower-like, wooden meditation space at the joint between the L-shape's two arms. Scarpa said, **'This piece of land was so large it became a lawn ... and to rationalize this expanse of space we thought it useful to add a small temple for funeral purposes.'**[3] In Scarpa's initial designs, the funeral chapel is shown as a pair of overlapping cylinders, a *vesica piscis* in plan, with a hemi-cylinder as the entrance. The March 1970 plan, submitted for approval to the San Vito d'Altivole town council, shows the arched tomb moved to the plan's hinge, or pivot point, in the northeast corner at the intersection of the L-shaped's two arms, where it was placed in a sunken circular niche and rotated 45 degrees from the cemetery walls. This plan also shows the eventual positioning, at the two ends of the L-shaped space, and plan forms of the rotated square chapel and the small meditation pavilion, both surrounded by water. While the shelter for the relatives' tombs is shown in the position along the northern wall where it would eventually be built, the approach to the meditation pavilion to the south is shown as a serrated, stepping stone bridge extending from the edge of the lawn and on axis with the arched tomb. **(11.1)** The cypress bosque (a stand of trees planted in a grid formation) at the western end came after the village priest saw the first model, as Scarpa recalled, **'Then he said: "And what about us poor priests?" I said I had not thought about this problem. I thought that in the country, in Italy, priests were buried inside the church ... So I divided off a section ... had the ground lowered 10 cm [3.75 in] and immediately had planted eleven, 9.5 m [31 ft 2 in] high, cypresses ... That is how we devise the space for the death of the priests.'**[4] **(11.2)**

More than in any other of Scarpa's works, the Brion Cemetery employs the ziggurat stepping articulation, which, here, is not limited to mouldings but used to give form to the edges and openings of nearly every surface. All concrete surfaces, the cemetery's dominant material, are given the ziggurat stepping articulation, often resulting in pyramidal, V-shaped forms that produce different readings depending on whether they are solid or void, oriented vertically or horizontally. It is important to note that this ziggurat stepping pattern is directly related to, and derived from, Scarpa's floor and wall patterns involving the L-shaped, three-quarter square, which is the ziggurat pattern's basic 'building block'. Scarpa explained the use of the 5.5 centimetre (2.25 in) module to proportion the ziggurat stepping pattern, **'I needed a certain kind of light and I worked out everything on a grid of 5.5 cm. This motif, which seems nothing special, is actually rich in expressive scope and movement ... I measured everything with the numbers 11 and 5.5.'**[5] Scarpa's reason for connecting light to the module of the ziggurat pattern becomes clear when we experience the incessant bands of light and shadow that characterize so many of the cemetery's surfaces. **(11.3)**

In a lecture given during the last year of his life, after the cemetery was completed, Scarpa begins with a typically ironic, yet revealing comment regarding his design:

> **'For the Brion tomb, I could have suggested planting a thousand cypresses – a thousand cypresses are a large, natural park, and a natural event, in the years ahead, would have produced a better effect than my architecture. But as always happens at the end of any piece of work, I have been thinking: "Dear me, I have done it all wrong!" Yet probably whoever built the pyramids did not have a mind that worked like that ... We lack certainties – everything is debatable, architecture is a shambles, while in the past, to take an example, the architecture of Catalonia was similar to that of France, of Provence, of Italy, of Sicily. That world spoke a language which varied little.'**[6]

11.1

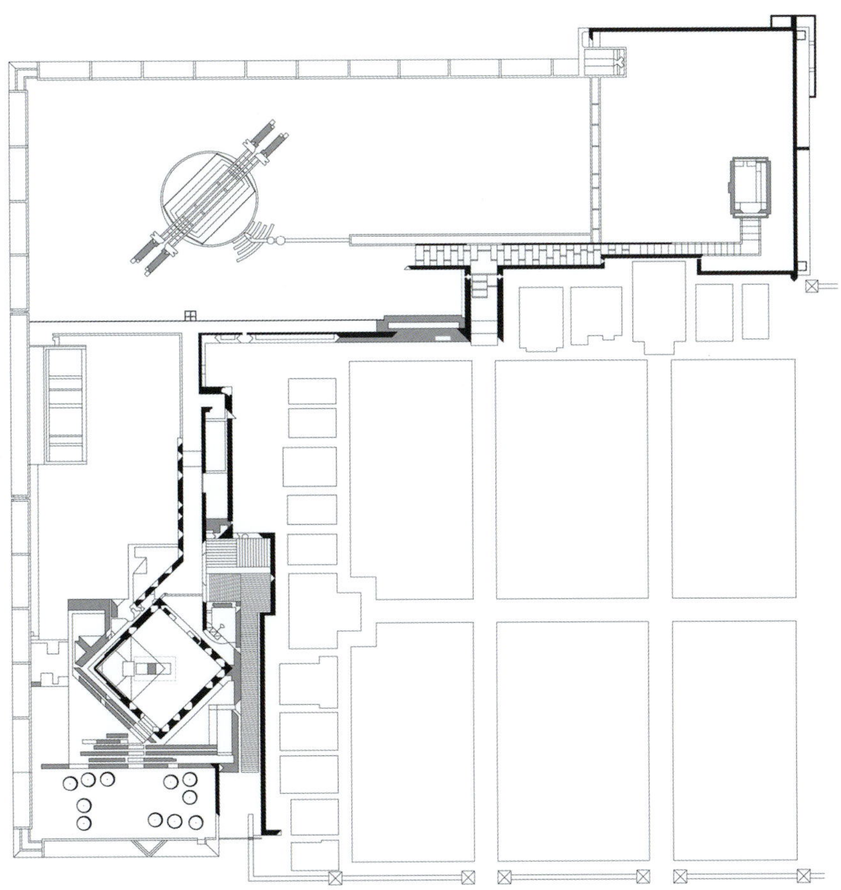

11.2

11.1 CARLO SCARPA, BRION CEMETERY, SAN VITO D'ALTIVOLE, 1969–77; PLAN, GRAPHITE, PEN AND COLOURED PENCIL ON PAPER, 1970

11.2 BRION CEMETERY; PLAN (REDRAWN)

11.3

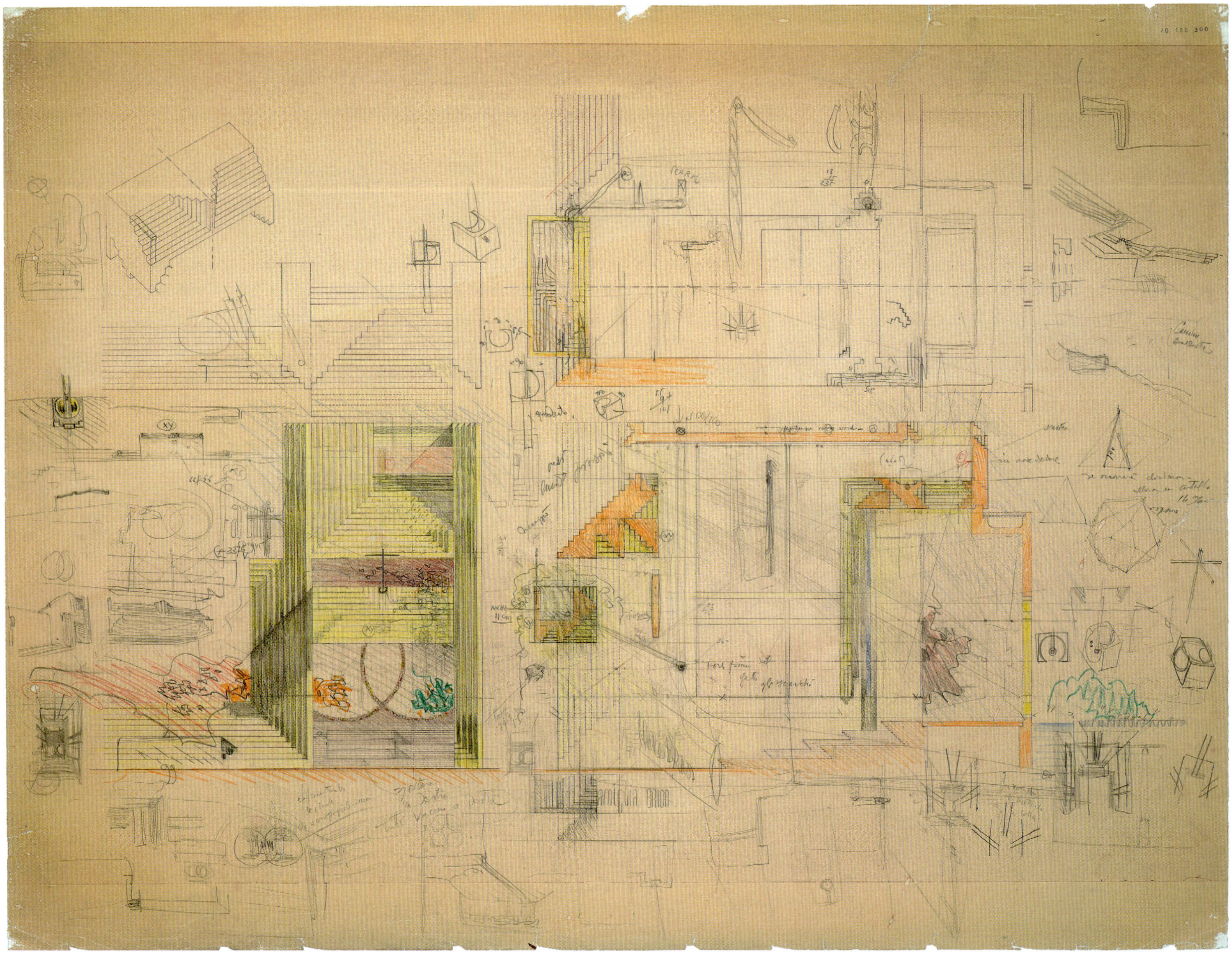

The Brion Cemetery is approached, as Scarpa said, **'along the traditional, cypress-lined avenue you find in all Italian cemeteries,'**[7] a small road leading from the village's main piazza, in front of the west-facing church, directly south through agricultural fields to the existing cemetery's western edge. A massive concrete wall, seen as we approach, surrounds the Brion complex's northern and eastern sides; made of an inwardly inclined plane of horizontal board-formed concrete, angled 60 degrees from the horizontal, 30 degrees from the vertical, and measuring, from the outside, 240 centimetres tall (7 ft 10 in); well above eye level. Vertical, blade-like concrete buttress walls periodically brace the bounding wall. **(11.4)** At the wall's pyramid-shaped northwest corner, between two buttresses, its upper portion is opened as a concrete lattice window, through which we glimpse sunlight playing off the grass. A series of horizontal slots forming the Chinese ideogram for 'double happiness,' often used at weddings, are cast into the concrete corner window, hovering above the solid base below. **(11.5)** An ideogram is presented on each face, and the horizontal slots and bands of concrete that wrap around the corner bind the pair together. Rising behind the wall are eleven tightly planted cypress trees, further in, two concrete-walled volumes rise above the wall; the nearer one, behind the cypress bosque, is rotated 45 degrees with respect to the wall, the further one, near the wall's edge, is tilted to align with the 60-degree angled wall. Open to the villagers, the nearer, taller volume is the funeral chapel and has a separate entrance closed by a concrete sliding door. The concrete wall on the new burial complex's western side is set back from the piers of the existing village cemetery wall, the new subtly deferring to the old.

Entry to the existing cemetery is, like the village church, from the west through two gateways opened in the stucco-faced masonry wall. A stone-paved walkway runs across the cemetery from the western entrance gate, to the east, where the entry portal to the Brion tombs sits on axis with the walkway. Scarpa called this portal the *propylaeum*, a reference to the similarly narrow, T-shaped entry structure at the Acropolis, Athens. **(11.7)** Family mausoleums line the old cemetery's northern and eastern sides, and the *propylaeum* fills the space of one mausoleum, while to its left, an opening in the tall, outer wall gives a limited view, over a low, ziggurat stepped concrete wall, into the Brion tomb complex behind, where we can see the top of the low-arched, shell-like tomb cover. The concrete *propylaeum's* entire surface is densely stepped in 5.5 centimetre (2.25 in) bands, vertically and horizontally, receding at a 45-degree angle from the wall's front face. The only exception to this incessant stepping is the low, projecting lintel, which is flat-faced, carrying a small, cubic brass piece centrally cast into its top edge, into which is carved a sphere that pierces the top, forming an inverted Ω shape. At the *propylaeum's* base, the ziggurat stepping turns to the left on both sidewalls, while at the top, the canopy's stepping moves to the right.

11.4

11.5

11.6

11.7

11.3 BRION CEMETERY; PLAN, 1:20, SECTION AND ELEVATION OF THE *PROPYLAEUM*, GRAPHITE AND COLOURED PENCIL ON PAPER, 60 X 7 CM (23.5 X 2.75 IN)

11.4 BRION CEMETERY; INCLINED CONCRETE WALL BORDERING THE NORTH SIDE OF THE BRION COMPLEX

11.5 BRION CEMETERY; DETAIL OF THE BOUNDARY WALL'S PYRAMID-SHAPED NORTHWESTERN CORNER, THE CONCRETE LATTICE FORMS THE CHINESE SYMBOL FOR 'DOUBLE HAPPINESS'

11.6 BRION CEMETERY; *PROPYLAEUM*, ENTRY PORTAL STAIRS WITH VIEW TO DOUBLE CIRCLE APERTURE

11.7 BRION CEMETERY; *PROPYLAEUM*, ENTRY PORTAL TO THE BRION TOMBS, ITS SURFACE DENSELY STEPPED IN CONCRETE BANDS

11.8

The cemetery walkway's stone paving is carried into the *propylaeum*, where it meets the first of three landing-like steps running across its width, upon which are set three narrower steps. While all six concrete steps are faced in grooved stone with a thin steel band cast into the concrete tread's edge, the rhythm of the two layers of steps do not match; the smaller set of three steps closer to the left wall also has a small brass piece centrally inset into the top of the riser. After passing beneath the low lintel, the ceiling lifts above our heads and light enters from both in front and behind through high clerestory openings. The *propylaeum's* concrete ceiling is faced in rectangular sections of white polished plaster, with concrete bands exposed between; round brass discs are positioned at the plaster section's outer corners. Starting at the first step, the concrete sidewalls are also faced in white plaster sections; their polished surfaces reflect the light coming in through the large, double-circle aperture, wider than the entry passage, opened in the concrete wall ahead. **(11.6)**

But is this opening a window or a door? **'The first impression you get from the cemetery is by looking through these two "eyes"'** as Scarpa called them.[8] The aperture, on the *propylaeum* passage's centreline, is formed by two large circles intersecting to form a *vesica piscis*, its outer ring-like edges are brass channels carrying rectangular Murano glass mosaic tiles, set flush with the concrete wall's inside and outside faces. The rings of tiles, pink on the left and blue on the right, signify the wife and husband, female and male, who rest in the tomb. The aperture's top is below head height, while the bottom is just above the floor. Through the opening, we see that the *vesica piscis* portal hovers above the surface of a narrow, deep watercourse on the other side of the wall. Closing our view on the far side is the inclined perimeter wall, its inner face finished with white polished plaster edged in narrow concrete bands; and between the two is a broad, elevated grass plane, set at the same level as that on which we stand. The cemetery's ground surface is raised 75 centimetres (2 ft 5 in) above the level of the surrounding countryside. As Frampton noted, for Scarpa, **'the raising of the general datum is the principal device by which the space is guaranteed its remoteness, its sense of being apart ... from a mid-axial approach, people in the garden are perceived as elevated figures who are at once remote and paradoxically accessible.'**[9]

11.9

Standing on the raised ground plane, the inclined perimeter wall's top is now at eye level, 165 (11 x 15) centimetres (5 ft 5 in), forming a perfectly flat horizon line. Our passage through the *propylaeum* has erased the larger world's horizon line, replacing it with the cemetery's new, elevated datum. At the top of the staircase we enter a narrow corridor running north-south; an opening in the ceiling illuminates the landing. In the morning, the sun casts an intersecting double-circle shadow on the corridor floor, which is made of steel-edged, precast concrete paving slabs spanning across the corridor; cast into the surface of each is a steel band, running parallel to the walls. In front of the double circle-opening, two brass pieces frame narrow, track-like slots in the floor, the bottoms of which slope downwards and then back up in an arcing curve. **(11.8)** These slots open to below at their centres, allowing us to perceive the reflective surface of a pool of water beneath us, running parallel to the watercourse outside the wall. The concrete ceiling's surface is formed of equal-width strips of grey concrete and darker, black bands of embedded Cor-Ten steel, a special formulation protected by a layer of rust, that run parallel to the corridor's long walls. The surface of the rusted steel bands is matte, reflecting no light, while the concrete is slightly reflective.

This corridor opens to left and right, and one must now choose to turn with the pink ring to the left, towards the tomb, seen at the end of the northern corridor, or right, with the blue ring, where the southern corridor's longer length is darker, becomes narrower and its destination less clearly visible in the bright lines of light at the end. While the ceilings are the same, the floors differ left and right: the concrete floor panels' slightly reflective steel bands step back and forth regularly to the left, appearing as dark lines in the concrete; while, in the darker corridor to the right, the steel bands reflect the slices of bright southern light, shining in the floor's dark surface as they ratchet from right to left until they align along the centre of the narrowed corridor. The left side's shorter, brightly lit corridor opens to the lawn and tombs, contrasting with the right side's longer shadowed corridor cut open with vertical slices of sunlight, clearly indicating the public nature of the former route and the private nature of the latter, which is reserved for family members. **(11.9)**

11.8 BRION CEMETERY; *PROPYLAEUM* CORRIDOR, LOOKING NORTH, AN INTERSECTING DOUBLE-CIRCLE WALL OPENING (R) AND CEILING VOID CAST LIGHT INTO THE NARROW SPACE

11.9 BRION CEMETERY; *PROPYLAEUM* CORRIDOR, LOOKING SOUTH AT THE PASSAGEWAY WHERE IT NARROWS AND DARKENS

Turning to the right, the narrow concrete passage resounds hollowly with our footsteps, reminding us of the water beneath. Frampton has pointed out **'the ambiguous role played by water in the Brion Cemetery: on the surface, as slow-moving water [of the watercourse], it symbolizes life, as opposed to its containment in a long sump or channel covered by precast paving slabs. In this morbid form, as it were, it leads us from the threshold of the Brion cemetery toward the meditation pool.'** [10] The corridor narrows to half its width at the point where the large pool begins outside, and we must move left, towards the water, following the floor's steel bands and passing by a vertical slot in the wall to the right, its sides stepping inwards in the ziggurat pattern. A few steps down this narrow corridor, we approach a strangely ephemeral gate, made of a thick glass sheet held by clips from brass tubes at the sides and top, set just below eye level at half the height of the corridor. To be opened, this glass gate must be pushed down into a slot in the concrete floor, requiring us to crouch down. Stepping across this threshold, we walk to the end of the corridor, and hearing the gate sliding back up, we turn to see water running off the glass, and realize that when pushed down into the floor, the glass was submerged in water. Seen as we approached, the glass door appeared completely transparent; seen from outside, the door is a mirror, reflecting our image within the shadowed corridor.

Walking out of the corridor into the bright sunlight, the floor changes to simple, unedged concrete slabs with a double-step ziggurat curb. The corridor walls' white polished-plaster sections stop, and the left wall is carved open, revealing the large pool at the L-shaped site's southern end. The inner wall's edges are lined with Murano glass tiles set in a brass channel frame, yellow-gold on the inside and blue-green outside, while the right wall is set back and our narrow path now has water on both sides. **(11.10)** The right side's tall, board-formed concrete wall surrounds three sides of the large square pool, and a band of inset white, black, green, gold and silver glass tiles is set just below eye level, matching the height of the inclined perimeter wall, and together forming the cemetery's internal horizon line. The concrete causeway leads to a small, wood-walled, box-like pavilion hovering over a small, concrete island, set towards the large pool's southwest corner. The bottom of the elevated pavilion wall sits just above the horizon line of the coloured glass tiles behind. **(11.11)** Now, if the glass door is opened again, we can see the brass and stainless steel cables, wheels and paired counterweights moving on the other side of the wall. This is perhaps the most dramatic example of Scarpa's interest in allowing people's movements in one space to be registered in another, signalling that others inhabit the place with us.

11.10

11.10 BRION CEMETERY; *PROPYLAEUM* CORRIDOR, SOUTHERN EXIT LEADING TO THE LARGE, SQUARE POOL, THE BRASS AND STAINLESS STEEL GATE MECHANISM CAN BE SEEN ON THE OUTSIDE OF THE *PROPYLAEUM*'S EASTERN WALL

11.11 OVERLEAF > BRION CEMETERY; 'MEDITATION PAVILION', SET IN A LARGE SQUARE POOL SURROUNDED BY A BOARD-FORMED CONCRETE WALL WITH A BAND OF COLOURED TILES JUST BELOW EYE LEVEL

11.12

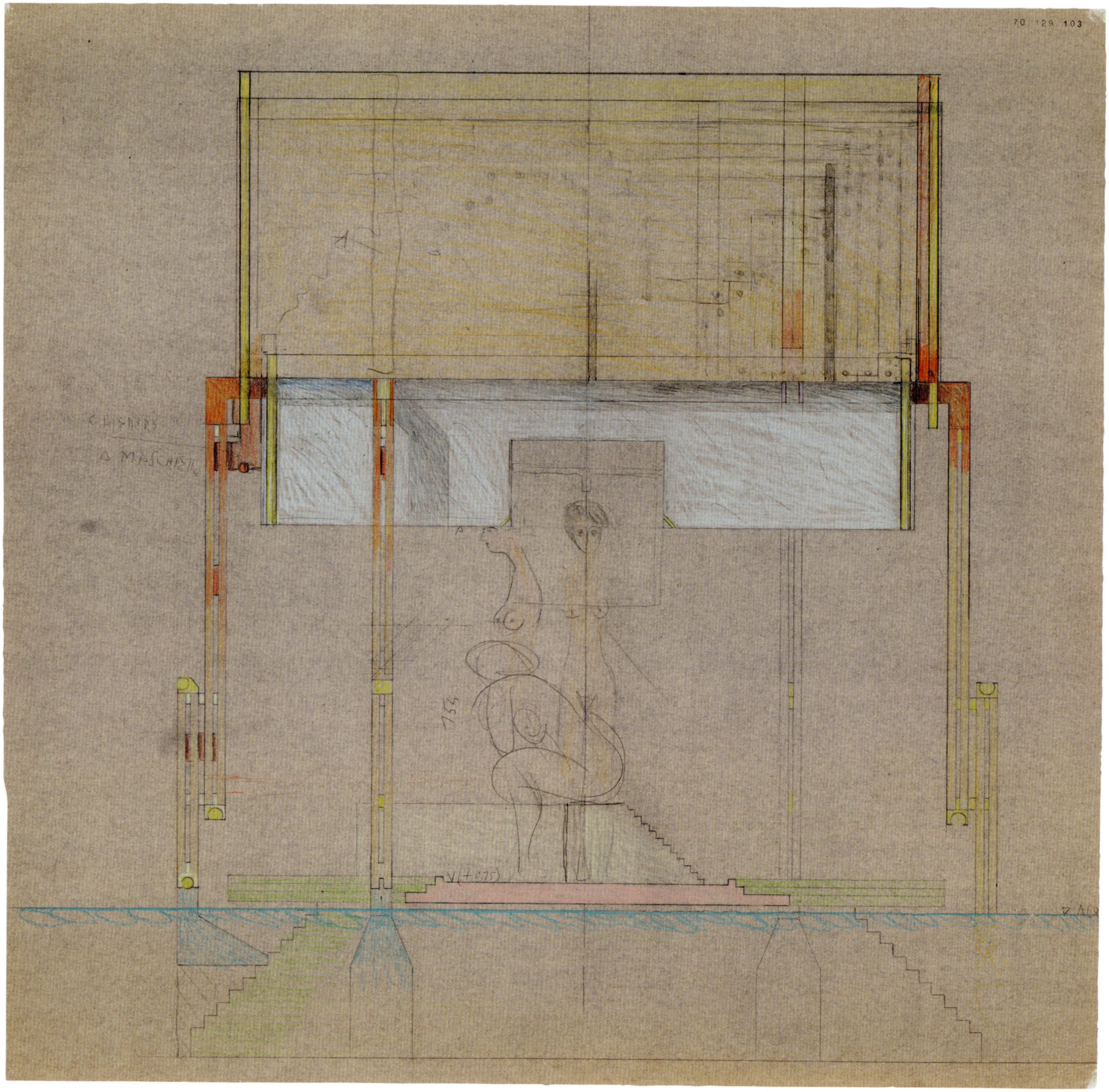

11.12 BRION CEMETERY; MEDITATION PAVILION ELEVATION, GRAPHITE AND COLOURED PENCIL ON PAPER, 42.2 X 60 CM

11.13 BRION CEMETERY; DETAIL STUDY FOR MEDITATION PAVILION'S EXTERNAL POSTS, GRAPHITE AND COLOURED PENCIL ON PAPER

11.14 BRION CEMETERY; MEDITATION PAVILION

11.13

The elevated canopy of the **'meditation pavilion'**, as Scarpa called it, has an outer steel-edged shell of thin, larch wood boards inlaid with ebony; the larch board revetment is set in a flat version of the ziggurat pattern, similar to the labyrinth-like line patterns in some Klee paintings. An inner sheath of brass-edged, dark green lacquered panels, with tiny ziggurat stepped corners pieces, drops down to eye level, aligning with the glass tile inner horizon line, while an opening at the causeway allows us to enter. **(11.12)** The pavilion is supported by four external posts, set at one-quarter points in from each side, forming a pinwheel in plan, which are an exercise in elaboration of the structural joints and postponing support. The first segment, anchored by a large brass pin to a concrete footing in the water, is a square in plan, formed of four square Cor-Ten steel bars bound together by brass connectors with a brass cap carved with a tiny, U-shaped ziggurat pattern. A second segment of the post, also a square cluster of four steel bars, is set towards the pavilion, to the inside of the base segment, from which it is separated by a slice of light, and to which it is connected by two recessed steel brackets, secured by two pairs of fasteners. At the bottom of this upper segment is a brass cap into which a sphere has been carved out to form a Ω figure. At the top of the post's upper segment, just beneath the larch wood revetment's lower edge, a pair of steel L-shaped plates, bound together by a brass corner bracket carved with a tiny U-shaped set of ziggurat steps, connect the vertical post to the double horizontal steel bars spanning across inside the pavilion, forming the pinwheel plan-shaped structural frame that supports the suspended wood walls. **(11.13, 11.14)**

The pavilion floor is separated from the causeway by a small gap, just enough to make us pause and look down into the water. The thin edges of the concrete island-like platform hover above the surface of the water, which runs up underneath. Submerged concrete ziggurat planes can be seen disappearing into the depths below the water's surface. While the pool's two sidewalls rise from beneath the water, the long back wall, at the cemetery's southern end, and thus usually in shadow, is formed of three shallow concrete layers that recede inwards, becoming thinner as its descends; the massive wall stops just above the surface of the water, which disappears into the shadow beneath the wall.

11.14

11.15

The outer sections of the meditation pavilion's elevated canopy, at the sides and back, are open to the sky, with larch board revetment cladding the inner surfaces. The small roofed section of the pavilion keeps the interior surfaces in shadow, making us aware of the way our view is edited by the lacquered lower wall. Our restricted view below the horizon line focuses our attention on the water and its submerged, stepped concrete constructions, reminiscent of Venice in the *acqua alta*. In the front and back walls, vertical, brass-edged slots are opened in the lacquered inner wall, and at the bottom of the one facing the cemetery's northern side is a brass connector carved with an incomplete intersecting double circle, forming another, much smaller pair of eye-like openings, through which to survey the cemetery. Yet this eyepiece is set too low for most men, and in one of Scarpa's pavilion elevation drawings, he drew correctly sized figures of himself, his son Tobia and his wife Nini, and only her eyes align with the aperture. The majority of the pavilion drawings, as for all of Scarpa's projects, are populated by female figures, often naked, and these drawings often included his female clients. In this instance, Scarpa designed the double-circle aperture to be used for viewing by a standing woman, most likely his client, Onorina Brion, while most men have to bend down to obtain the same view.

Looking through this double-circle aperture, our eyes meet the intersection of two lines – the inclined boundary wall's horizon line and the vertical line of the arched double tomb's central axis. Rising above the perimeter wall in the distance, between the tomb and *propylaeum* corridor wall, is the bell tower and parish church of San Vito d'Altivole, with the Dolomite Mountains beyond. As Scarpa said, **'I decided all at once that over the pond there had to be a perspective element to break up the view. I am fond of water, perhaps because I am a Venetian … I designed the watercourse, which wells up at a certain point, and in the sunlight I laid out two sarcophagi to contain the bodies of Brion and his wife.'** [11] From where we stand at the cemetery's southern end, the sun brilliantly illuminates the cemetery that lies before us to the north. In the pool, an octagonal concrete bamboo planter appears to float to the right, while a square, mosaic tile-lined fountain, with arms extending to left and right, appears to float in the foreground. Cantilevering over the pool's right corner, the inclined concrete perimeter wall terminates in a V-shaped form, with recessed ziggurat patterning. To the left, the entrance corridor wall carries the Klee-like steel cable, black wheel and counterweight assembly above the pool. The narrow watercourse runs from the large pool along the wall's edge and beneath the double-circle opening at the entrance. **(11.15)**

11.15 BRION CEMETERY; WATER PAVILION, VIEW NORTH ACROSS THE POOL TO THE ARCHED BRION TOMB, WITH BRASS DOUBLE-CIRCLE EYE-LEVEL OPENING ABOVE

11.16

Walking back through the concrete passage, past the double-circle opening, we step out from under the ceiling on to the grass, with the double tomb ahead. As at the corridor's other end, the white polished-plaster wall sections stop and the board-formed concrete continues out into the sunlight. The left concrete wall, towards the existing cemetery, terminates in a ziggurat stepping edge, while the wall to the right is notched and edged in glass tiles set in brass channels, blue-green on the inside and yellow-gold outside, the reverse of the tile colours at the corridor's other end. Stepping over the concrete walled watercourse and on to the grass lawn, we look back south towards the meditation pavilion in the water, where the faces of the pavilion and the wall behind are in shadow. On the outside face of the right corridor wall we see that in the intersecting double-circle opening both pink and blue tile rings keep the same orientation we saw on the wall's inner face upon entering (pink to left, blue to right), and we realize that each ring contains both colours on its two sides. Near the double intersecting circle window, a low steel post rises from the inside of the watercourse wall and carries a stainless steel cylinder, with a hexagonal end cap, anchoring six stainless steel cables – three cables doubled by being wrapped around three set pins – that are stretched across the lawn to the inclined bounding wall. These cables, intended to discourage children approaching the pond's edge, are set at a height that, when we step over them, our toe inevitably hits the cables and they strike against one another to make a twanging sound. **(see pp. 238–9)**

11.16 BRION CEMETERY; PLAN AND ELEVATION FOR THE FAMILY TOMB, GRAPHITE AND COLOURED PENCIL ON PAPER

11.17 BRION CEMETERY; DOUBLE FAMILY TOMB, BENEATH A LOW VAULT, WITH A NARROW CONCRETE WATER COURSE LEADING BACK TO THE LARGE POOL

11.18 BRION CEMETERY; DOUBLE FAMILY TOMB

Standing next to the double tomb, although we can see out over the bounding wall to the surrounding countryside, agricultural fields and village, people outside the wall cannot see in, offering a sense of seclusion. **(see i.2)** Here, the watercourse's source is found in a pair of small cylindrical concrete vessels, out of which the water flows in a narrow channel, similar to the keyhole-shaped source in the Court of the Myrtles, Alhambra, connecting to the wider watercourse that flows back towards the large pool. We also become aware of the pool surrounding the chapel to the west, as well as the sunken, moat-like, ziggurat-patterned, concrete walled trench running beneath the inclined bounding wall at the cemetery's outer edge, reinforcing the impression that we are on an island, separated from the everyday world. Frampton has noted, 'Once again we are confronted with a Venetian metaphor, not only because the elevated earthwork is inseparable from an equally extensive water-work, but also because the hermeticism of the whole is sufficient to recall the necropolis of the island of San Michele, in the midst of the Venetian lagoon.'[12] **(11.17, 11.18)**

The arched double tomb's location in the northeast corner is constantly in sunlight, as Scarpa noted, 'The tomb of the Brion couple is the sunniest place. And it offers the most beautiful view. The deceased had asked to be close to the earth since he was born in this village – so I decided to build a small arch, which I call the *arcosolium*, a Latin word from the time of the early Christians; in the catacombs, important persons or martyrs were buried in them … it is nothing more than a simple arch from the Catholic tradition.'[13] In fact, the low vault that covers the tombs is closer in form to a bridge than an arch. Made of concrete, with four central rib-like beams, it spans from one ziggurat-carved buttress to another, and two thin, curving, visor-like roof planes cantilever off the outer rib-beams to the front and back. The rectangular buttresses are deeply carved at their centre, with each half receiving one pair of the rib-beams, while beam-like extensions, ziggurat-carved on all four faces, cantilever out from the buttresses, counter-balancing and extending the vault's bridging leap. These cantilevered counterweights were more visible before the cemetery became overgrown, as were the small brass pivot-hinge and pin-bearing posts that rise from the top of buried foundations to support the massive concrete vault. At the top of the curving rib-beams, a recessed flat section, marked at its edges by brass hinge-like brackets, stands directly above the double tomb below. **(11.16)**

11.17

11.18

11.19

11.19 BRION CEMETERY; HINGE POINT OF THE CEMETERY COMPLEX, THE INTERNAL BOUNDARY WALL SET IN A SUNKEN WALKWAY RUNNING NORTH TO THE 'RELATION'S SHRINE'

11.20 BRION CEMETERY; DOUBLE FAMILY TOMB, GREEN AND BLUE MURANO GLASS TILES DECORATE THE CEILING AND THE NAMES OF THE DECEASED ARE INSET IN IVORY LETTERS INTO THE SARCOPHAGI'S OUTER FACES

11.21 BRION CEMETERY; DOUBLE FAMILY TOMB, PAIR OF GRANITE AND MARBLE SARCOPHAGI INCLINED TOWARDS EACH OTHER WITH LIDS OF HORIZONTAL EBONY WOOD BOARDS

11.20

11.21

The tombs stand in a circular space beneath the vault, recessed into the earth and surrounded by a low concrete wall, its pebble-faced concrete floor inlaid with marble bands. This space sits at the bottom of a gently sloped, conical-shaped, grass valley. Although the tombs appear to be sunken, the concrete floor on which they stand is at the same level as the landscape surrounding the cemetery. On the valley-like depression's southwest side, nearest the entrance corridor, arcing concrete steps lead down to the tombs, forming a small rustic amphitheatre. The lowest step, an extension of the top of the circular floor's outer wall, terminates at either end in stone blocks facing inwards to the tombs. A variation of the Greek and Celtic equal-armed cross is carved into their inner faces, formed of four recessed *vesica piscis* shapes filled with gold leaf. The watercourse source extends a narrow dry channel that turns at a 45-degree angle to align with the arched double tomb's centre, terminating in a cylindrical basin for flowers and a ziggurat-stepped, cruciform plan-shaped concrete pier standing at the edge of the tomb space's curb wall. Bending down to enter beneath the low, curving concrete roof, centrally split in two by a slot between the rib-beams above, we see that Murano glass tiles, in alternating bands of green and blue with gold highlight bands, are embedded into the ceiling over the tombs. **(11.20)** These tiles reflect a faint blue-green, shimmering, watery light from the sun striking the grass, giving the compressed space beneath the vault a surprising sense of lightness, which acts to deny the heaviness of the concrete cover so close overhead.

The two tombs stand on white marble bases, their bottoms slightly curved, and have trapezoidal-shaped granite end walls, all of which are intricately carved with 3.5 centimetre (1.5 in) ziggurat-stepped pyramidal patterns. A wide band of darkly veined, pale yellow marble is inset into the floor between the two tombs, and a narrower band of black and white marble squares, set in an alternating, chequerboard pattern, runs across the circular floor beneath both tombs, paralleling the slot in the ceiling. The rectangular sarcophagi are enclosed at the bottom and both narrow ends by granite slabs, while the lids' top, front and back are made of horizontal ebony wood boards, secured with brass fittings. The names of the deceased are inset in Scarpa-designed ivory letters on the sarcophagi's inclined outer faces, beneath an ebony handle and small, intersecting double-circle brass plaque. The tombs' ebony tops align to form a horizontal line, while their curved marble bottoms appear to touch the earth lightly. The tombs of the husband and wife incline towards each other, surely one of the most touching architectural gestures imaginable. Scarpa said, **'It is wonderful that two people who had loved each other during their lives on earth should bend one toward the other so as to be able to greet one another, after death.'**[14] **(11.21)**

The tall concrete wall separating the Brion tomb from the existing cemetery is faced with wide, white polished-plaster bands, with brass discs set at the outer corners, repeating the entry *propylaeum* and corridor interior wall surface treatments. Across from the steps down into the double tomb, a full-height vertical slot is opened in this wall, its outer face serrated with vertical ziggurat stepping bands, and the white plaster panels terminate to either side. The wall with the 'internal' finish carries around the corner and into the portico leading to the chapel, and the polished plaster bands, stained and weathered by rain, give an ambiguous reading as to interior and exterior at the hinge point of the cemetery's L-shaped space. This plaster-clad wall stands in a concrete-walled sunken walkway, paved in small square stones, that cuts across the elevated lawn, dividing it into two sections, a larger section running north-south from the pool to the north bounding wall, and a smaller section running east-west from the sunken walkway to the chapel pool. **(11.19)** Close to the vaulted tombs, four alternating steel-edged concrete steps are set into a notch in the sunken walkway wall, which, when we strike them with our feet, make sounds of differing pitches.

11.22

Rising along the north bounding wall, the **'relation's shrine'**, as Scarpa called it, is a massive concrete enclosure, slightly lifted off the ground, its roof tilted to form a 60-30-degree angle, aligning with the inclined outer wall. This rectangular mass hovers around 1 metre (3 ft 3 in) above the grass, and the sloping roof is drained through a pair of thick, tube-like brass scuppers that appear to have been cut and pried open, with circular holes drilled at the cut's inner joint. This shrine can only be entered along the sunken walkway, bounded right and left by a straight and a ziggurat-stepped wall, which turns and merges with the moat-like trench running beneath the inclined bounding wall. We must bend down slightly to enter this shadowed space, where the graves of the Brions' relatives are marked by marble tombstones placed in a nonrepeating pattern on the elevated ground. The tall space overhead is crossed at its centre by deep concrete wall-beams, their bottoms carved with ziggurat stepping bands. The ceiling's and wall-beams' upper surfaces are faced with black polished plaster sections, their corners anchored by brass discs. At the roof's peak, a south-facing slot is opened between the inclined planes, pouring a bright line of light into the dark, almost cave-like space. **(11.22)**

Returning to the sounding steps, the sunken walkway turns west, widening and ramping upwards, following the cemetery's tall, concrete outer wall on the left. A second, thicker concrete wall, its edges serrated with vertical stepping bands, rises along the right side of the sunken walkway, and a roof covers the entrance to the corridor-like **'portico'**, as Scarpa called it, which leads to the chapel. We climb several broad steps and walk past a series of full-height, slot-like apertures, their outer faces bevelled by vertical stepping bands, opening in the right wall at irregular but closely spaced intervals, providing views to the lawn. To the left, a door made of a complex, symmetrically composed steel framework infilled with white concrete, resembling both Japanese and Egyptian doors, leads to the sacristy and treasury. **(11.24)** This small room, illuminated by windows to the chapel entrance court to the west and modelled on the sacristy treasuries of churches, houses ingenious cabinets containing two layers of secret compartments, the second for real treasures, protected by complex locks, hidden hinges and spring-loaded latches. [15] At the end of the portico, light pours into the chapel's triangular plan-shaped vestibule from the wide horizontal portal to the left, opening to the public, processional entrance path. The narrow vertical slot apertures to the right open on to the chapel pool, allowing us to see that the water's surface is at the same level as the stone-paved floor on which we stand.

The **'temple'**, as Scarpa called the chapel, was donated to the villagers by the Brion family and is completely integrated into the Brion tomb complex. Used for funerals, the chapel's public entrance begins on the cypress-lined village road, at the end of the inclined bounding wall, next to the small cypress bosque. A massive, steel-framed concrete door, lifted slightly off the ground, is set at the inclined bounding wall's inside edge, matching its height. A square steel arm projects to the front and back from a steel-edged opening at the bottom of the door, and the brass wheels at its outer edges run along steel rails embedded in the concrete paving. Horizontal steel channels, into which fit the guide pins, are cast into both faces of the door, separating the horizontal board-formed concrete below from the vertical board-formed concrete above. A steel frame infilled with white concrete in the form of a cross, open at its centre and lower edges, is set within a square, steel-edged notch in the top centre of the concrete door, allowing views into the space beyond. The L-shaped, solid, stainless steel cylinder door handle fits in the end of the horizontal channel, not allowing the door to completely close, and thereby protecting our fingers. **(11.25)** Considerable effort is required to open the heavy door, emphasizing the ritualized nature of its operation.

11.23

Walking into the chapel's entryway, our left and right view is blocked by high concrete walls, while directly ahead the chapel's diagonal wall, a rotated square in plan, rises from a pool set behind a low concrete wall. The side of the chapel is opened by a series of five narrow vertical apertures, their inner faces ribbed with vertical ziggurat stepping bands, with sheets of glass inset, stopping just above the water's surface. Towards the centre, a ziggurat stepped positive projection and matching negative indention are cast into the surface, and the plane they share carries a cross formed by four gold-leafed *vesica piscis* shapes. **(11.23)** The entryway's upward ramping surface is paved with long, thin rectangular concrete slabs, with grass growing in their joints, set perpendicular to the sidewalls, crossing our direction of movement and measuring our paces. Walking up the ramp, the chapel's left back corner comes into view, surrounded by water, beneath the surface of which can be seen a complex series of ziggurat stepped concrete rib-beams, appearing as submerged ruins.

11.22 BRION CEMETERY; 'RELATION'S SHRINE', A SOUTH-FACING SLOT IN THE TOP OF THE INCLINED ROOF PROVIDES A LINE OF LIGHT INTO THE DARK, COVERED SPACE

11.23 BRION CEMETERY; CHAPEL ENTRYWAY, SOUTHEASTERN FACADE, RISING FROM A POOL CONTAINED BY A LOW CONCRETE WALL

11.24

11.24 BRION CEMETERY; 'PORTICO', VIEW EAST THROUGH THIS COVERED, CORRIDOR-LIKE SPACE TOWARDS THE FAMILY TOMB, WITH THE ENTRANCE DOOR TO THE SACRISTY ON THE RIGHT

11.25 BRION CEMETERY; CHAPEL ENTRYWAY, PUBLIC ENTRANCE IN THE WESTERN SIDE OF THE COMPLEX'S INCLINED BOUNDARY WALL

11.25

11.26 11.27

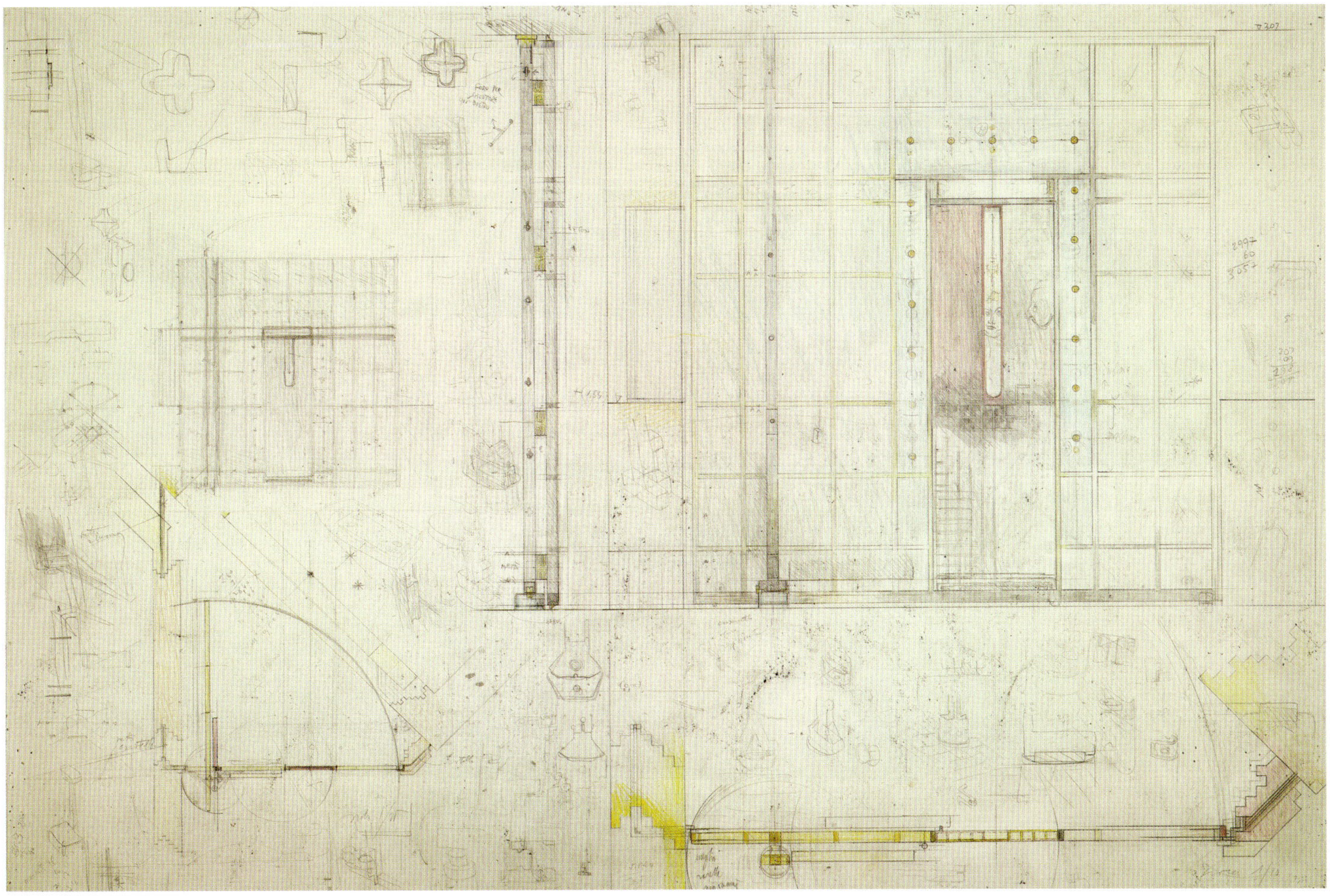

At the top of the ramped entryway, the right wall steps back and we enter a small forecourt, its concrete slab floor set in a pinwheel pattern. Opening in the northern concrete wall, the portal to the chapel vestibule is a very wide, rectangular gateway with two cantilevered arms projecting from either side, and a steel-edged slot cut in the massive lintel above. To the left, the pool's subterranean pump room is beneath a massive concrete lid into which is cast a small steel-edged opening in the form of a rotated square and slot. To the right, the sacristy facade, made of a steel frame infilled with white concrete into which slot-like windows have been opened, is recessed into a protective niche. **(11.26)** Passing beneath the lintel, we enter the shadowed triangular plan-shaped chapel vestibule, paved with small rectangular stones set in an overlapping running bond pattern, while the ceiling is finished with wide, white polished-plaster bands. At the end of the portico to the right, we see the edge of the double tomb's vaulted roof, while ahead we look out through the vertical slot apertures to the pool surrounding the chapel.

The chapel entrance is through a double door, one nested inside the other. Used for funerals, the massive wall-door, a steel frame and lattice infilled with white concrete, hovers just above the floor and beneath the ceiling. The door opens by turning on a square steel pivot hinge that runs from ceiling to floor, where it rotates on ball bearings recessed into the floor, its pivot joint contained in a faceted brass cylinder. Because of its distinctive pattern of black lines framing white rectangles, Scarpa called this pivoting concrete wall **'the Mondrian-style door'**. **(11.28)** A smaller door is opened at the pivoting wall's centre, made of solid boards above and square grating below, both of ebony, with a vertical central window. The concrete and steel door pivots open with surprising ease, standing against the left wall when fully opened; the outer triangular plan-shaped vestibule then merges with the similarly sized and shaped interior space. **(11.27)** The floor steps down, an angled brass threshold plate transitioning the levels, smoothing the ride of the wheeled casket cart, and the lower floor is paved in square stones set in a grid aligning with the outer cemetery's walls, thus at a 45-degree angle to the chapel's rotated walls.

11.28

11.26 BRION CEMETERY; CHAPEL ENTRYWAY, POOL AND SUBTERRANEAN PUMP ROOM TO THE LEFT OF THE CHAPEL VESTIBULE'S PORTAL

11.27 BRION CEMETERY; CHAPEL DOOR DETAIL, GRAPHITE AND COLOURED PENCIL ON PAPER

11.28 BRION CEMETERY; CHAPEL ENTRYWAY, STEEL AND CONCRETE OUTER 'MONDRIAN-STYLE' DOOR, WITH A SMALLER DOOR AT ITS CENTRE

11.29

11.30

11.31

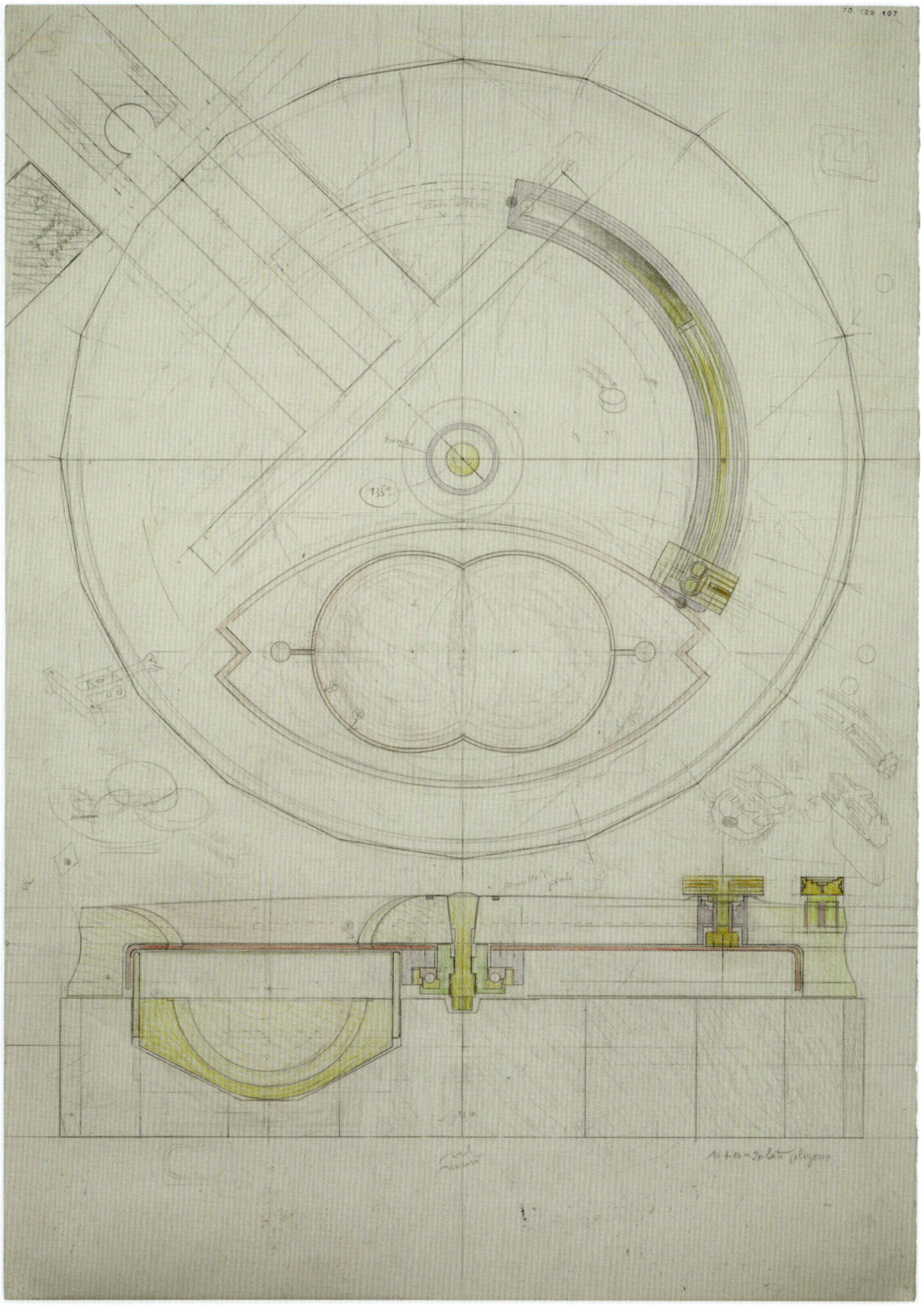

To the left of the narthex, cantilevered off the wall and illuminated by the vertical window's light, is a small white Carrara marble font of holy water, cylindrical in shape with faceted outer faces and curved edges. The font's lid has an intersecting double-circle opening, which can be closed by a brass sliding cover plate mounted on the lid's inner surface, the handle of which has inscribed stepped banding. **(11.30, 11.31)** Ahead, a full-height, freestanding, circular horizontal board-formed concrete gateway, an Ω shape in elevation, set away from the concrete walls and ceiling, opens into the chapel. The gateway's last segments are lifted off the floor and edged in steel; the inner faces of the circular opening to left and right are recessed, painted a deep blue, with gold-leafed ziggurat-stepped edging at top and bottom. A small square brass plate, with a raised cross dividing it into four squares and an inscribed cross dividing it diagonally, is set into the stone floor at the exact centre of the gateway's circular opening, marking the transition from the rectangular to rotated square geometries, like a tiny hinge point. **(11.29)**

11.29 BRION CEMETERY; CIRCULAR GATEWAY TO THE CHAPEL

11.30 BRION CEMETERY; CHAPEL NARTHEX, CARRARA MARBLE FONT

11.31 BRION CEMETERY; PLAN AND SECTION OF THE MARBLE FONT, GRAPHITE AND COLOURED PENCIL ON PAPER, 70.5 X 51 CM (27.75 X 20 IN)

11.34

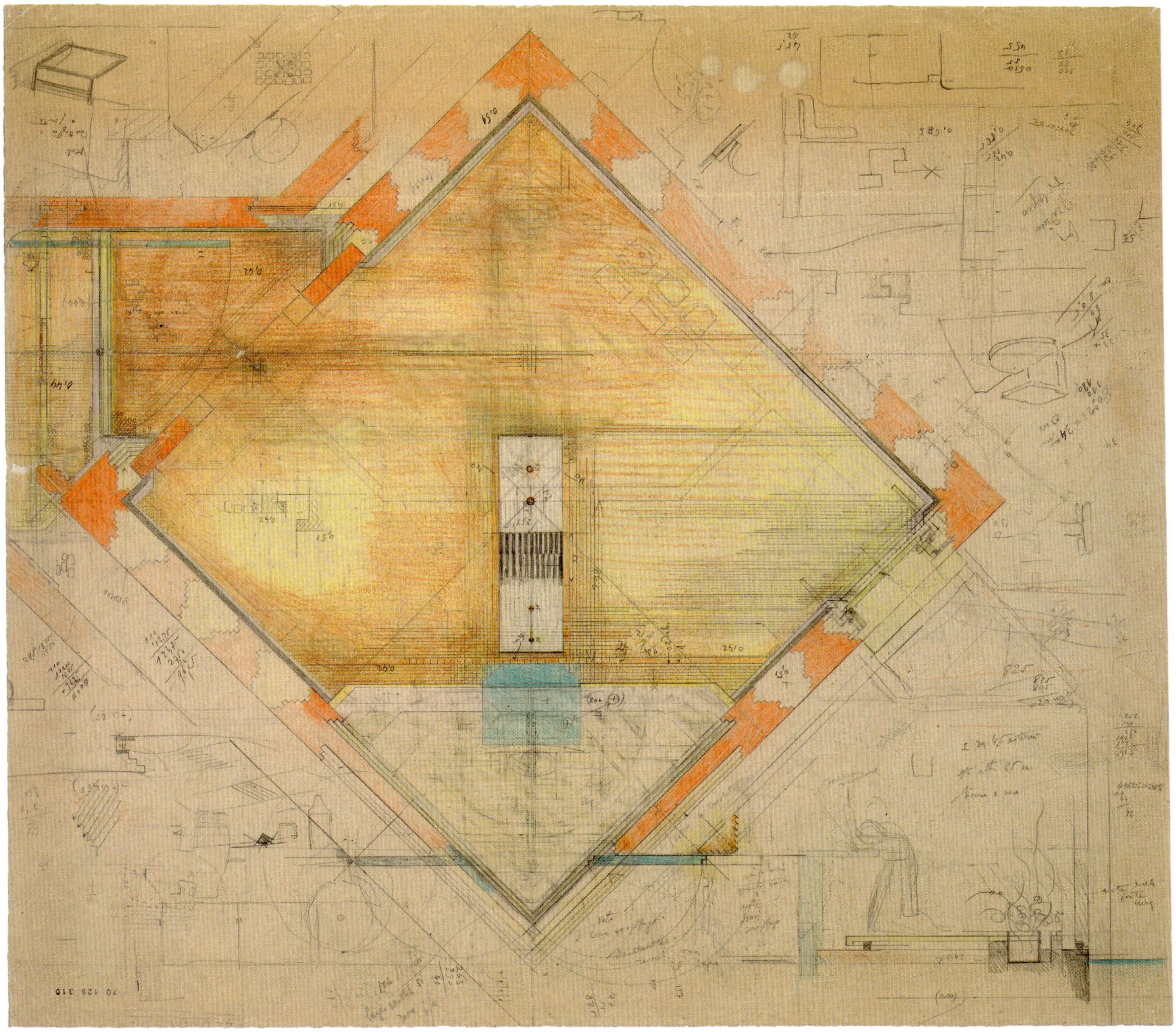

11.32

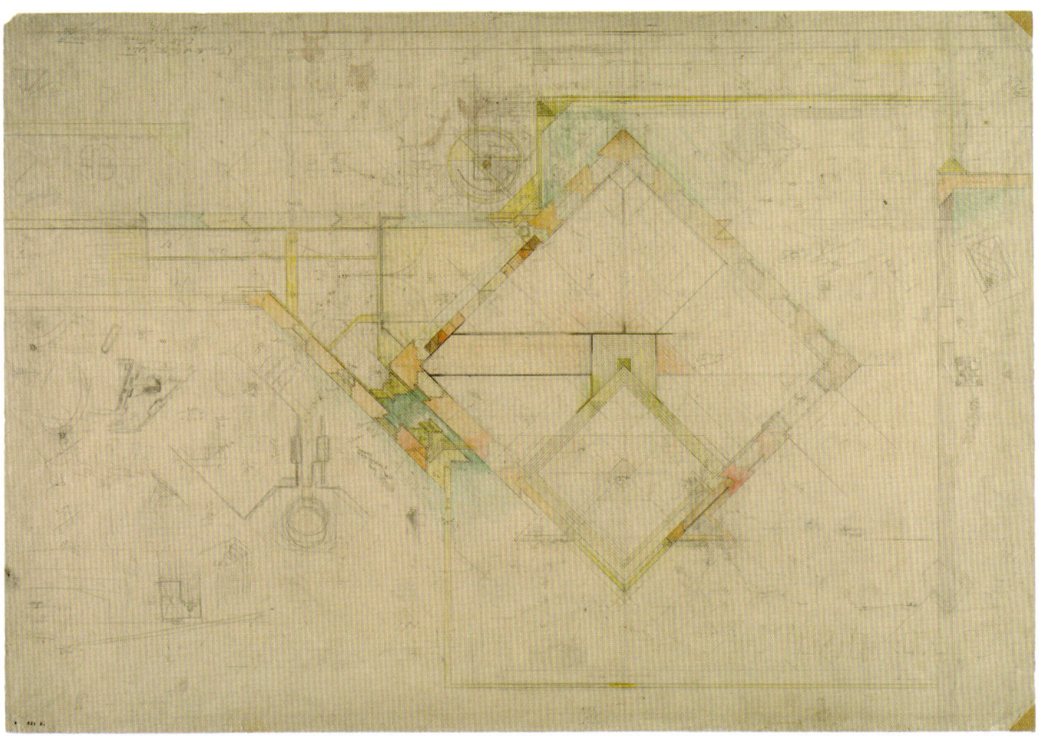

11.33

The small chapel is at once focused and calm, yet also highly dynamic and polycentric: despite its multiple symmetries and pure geometries, no formal axis or static composition can be found, and the longer one looks, the more complex and layered the design is revealed to be. Square in plan, the chapel is rotated to a 45-degree angle with respect to the cemetery's outer walls, and placed within a pool. The chapel walls are opened with ten tall vertical windows, their inner faces stepped in vertical bands, giving views of the water surrounding the chapel's perimeter; the water is set at the same level as the floor on which we stand, so that the sunlight bounces off the water's surface on to the walls and ceiling. The chapel ceiling is made of steel-edged, dark grey polished-plaster panels set in an L-shaped, three-quarter square, into which a one-quarter square ziggurat-stepped concrete and wood pyramidal dome is opened at the northern corner, above the altar. **(11.35)** The square stone paved floor is pulled away from the outer walls and edged by a flush set concrete curb, behind which is a small, deeply shadowed trench, slightly overhung by the concrete outer wall. At the floor's centre, aligned with the altar, the casket's position during funerals is marked by a smooth-faced, marble rectangle inlay formed of two white marble slabs separated by a series of narrow black and white marble bands. Its position is also marked on the ceiling by a section of the ziggurat-stepped concrete surrounding the dome that rotates on to the altar's 45-degree angle axis and frames the floor's marble rectangle. **(11.32, 11.33, 11.34)**

11.35

11.32 BRION CEMETERY; CHAPEL FLOOR PLAN, GRAPHITE AND COLOURED PENCIL ON PAPER

11.33 BRION CEMETERY; CHAPEL REFLECTED CEILING PLAN, GRAPHITE AND COLOURED PENCIL ON PAPER

11.34 BRION CEMETERY; CHAPEL ELEVATION AND SECTION, GRAPHITE AND COLOURED PENCIL ON PAPER

11.35 BRION CEMETERY; CHAPEL, VIEW UP INTO CONCRETE AND WOOD PYRAMIDAL DOME CUPOLA

11.36

11.37

11.38

The altar is set directly below the square oculus of the pyramidal-stepped wood dome. Scarpa had originally intended to make the altar of exposed concrete, using an additive that produces a smooth, shiny surface. However, this proved unsuccessful, and the same form was fabricated in sheet bronze, which was then 'filled with reinforced concrete to stop it from rattling.'[16] (11.36) The altar's front face, standing on the chapel floor, is T-shaped, with recessing ziggurat stepping in the lower corners, the joints between the four bronze sheets, their edges secured by small paired fasteners, forms a cross shape. A notch at the altar's top centre holds a crucifix, while a delicate candelabra, made of three pear wood rods, 22 millimetres (1 in) in diameter with brass end caps, curved single and double brass brackets and silver-plated, brass rod candleholders, hangs from within the wooden dome above.

11.36 BRION CEMETERY; CHAPEL, MARBLE FLOOR INLAY AND BRONZE ALTAR BENEATH THE STEPPED WOODEN DOME'S SQUARE CUPOLA

11.37 BRION CEMETERY; CHAPEL, BRONZE ALTAR IN FRONT OF STEPPED FLOOR AND FOUR, SQUARE WINDOWS INSET WITH BRASS-FRAMED TRANSLUCENT MARBLE

11.38 BRION CEMETERY; CHAPEL, LOW PIVOTING WALL PANELS BEHIND THE ALTAR IN THE CHAPEL'S NORTHERN CORNER, AS SEEN FROM THE EXTERIOR

Four small square windows, set in a stepping pattern, are opened in each of the two concrete walls behind the altar. In each window, coloured light shines through a brass-framed, translucent pink Portuguese marble panel. The windows' inner edges are cast in a pyramidal ziggurat pattern, on to which gold leaf is applied, increasing the amount of bounced light. Behind the altar, the chancel floor steps up in two planes, a large, stone-paved triangle and a smaller, brass-edged, hardwood-floored rotated square, respectively, with wide brass bands at the edge of each step, deeply undercut with the ziggurat pattern. (11.37) At the elevated chancel's back corner, the concrete outer wall runs down behind a tall concrete curb, and at the corner, two low solid panels pivot open from their hinged outer edges, their bottoms just above the pool's surface, rotating 120 degrees to create an open corner through which shimmering light bounces up into the chapel. Both steel-framed panels hold two slabs of marble, black granite on the outside, with an inscribed small square and cruciform, and white Clauzetto marble on the inside, inlaid with discs of green Stella serpentine stone and deep red porphyry to form intersecting double circles. When opened, we see the ziggurat-stepped concrete beams submerged beneath the pool outside the chapel. (11.38)

A glass-framed doorway set in the chapel's western corner, together with the ten vertical windows, forms the space's eleventh aperture. Alternatively, we can read the door as being set between and interrupting two additional vertical windows, giving the chapel a total of twelve apertures, a number with appropriate religious significance. The door literally stands in light, with tall narrow apertures on both sides, where the doorframe would normally be, and two 56 x 65 centimetre (1 ft 10 x 2 ft 2 in) rectangular clerestory windows above, on either side of the inverted T-shaped concrete lintel.[17] Each leaf of the double door is L-shaped in plan, made from a steel frame infilled with white concrete, and pivots on cylindrical ziggurat step-inscribed brass hinges set in the floor and lintel. A double vertical window is opened at the door's centre, and when the door is opened, the leafs rotate 90 degrees outwards, so that the L-shape's shorter leg blocks the light slots on either side, while the centre is open. A small brass drain channel, inscribed with a miniature version of the three circular watercourse sources, is inset into the centre of the door's brass-edged stone and concrete threshold, and we exit beneath a cantilevered concrete canopy.

Wide concrete stepping stones rise out of the water from their anchorage to seven ziggurat-stepped 'ribs', as Scarpa called them, submerged in the pool on both sides, reminiscent of both ruins and foundations. As Stokes has written, 'So deeply laid are the imaginative foundations of Venice, to such an extent has stone abrogated the meaning of soil in our minds, that decay, as we have seen, takes the form of metamorphosis, and even of renewal. Weight is below: foundations are visible ... but these projections, like the roots of trees, suggest a rising sap and strong grip captured for growth.'[18] (11.42) We walk across these stepping stones to the sunken cypress bosque, its grass plane set at the same level as the water's surface, with six cypress trees clustered to the left and five to the right, set in an erratic and incomplete grid, as if unfinished, or as if time had taken its toll. Summarizing his intentions, Scarpa said 'At San Vito I wanted to express the natural meaning of water and fields, of water and earth: water is the source of life.'[19] Surrounded by water filled with dimly seen ruins, with the Italian cypress garden of memory filling the view ahead of us, everything is at once so close yet so far, and in this carefully constructed experience Scarpa has left for us, the fusion of architectural space and human action, of ancient and modern, light and water – all so typical of Venice and the Veneto region – is complete. (11.39) The Viennese philosopher Ludwig Wittgenstein wrote, 'It is a great temptation to make the spirit explicit',[20] and here, in the Brion Cemetery, Scarpa succeeded in making the spirit explicit to a degree unmatched by any of his contemporaries.

11.39

11.40

11.41

While not Scarpa's last project, chronologically, the Brion Cemetery admirably serves as a conclusion to our narrative by the simple fact that Scarpa himself, at his request, is buried here. It is therefore with no small amount of pathos that we today visit Scarpa's grave, remembering his words regarding the Brion Cemetery from 1978, the year of his death, **'This is the only work I go to look at with pleasure, because I feel I have captured the sense of the countryside, in the way the Brions wanted. Everyone is very happy to go there – the children play, the dogs run around – all cemeteries should be like this.'**[21] Scarpa's grave is located in the inner corner of the Brion Cemetery wall lining the edge of the old cemetery, so he is at once in both the old and new cemeteries. From the small forecourt to the chapel, we can look over a low concrete gate, into which is cast a four gold-leafed *vesica piscis* cross, into a long narrow space between the sacristy's concrete back wall and the rear walls of the family mausoleums facing into the old cemetery to the right. Opening this heavy concrete gate, we walk to the corner where Scarpa chose to be buried. His marble headstone was designed by his son Tobia, and he was buried standing up, an ancient custom. Paul Klee, so close to Scarpa in so many ways, especially with respect to their shared sensitivity to the passage of time, summarized the tragedy and triumph of human kind in a way that comes close to capturing the qualities of the Brion Cemetery, **'Man's ability to measure the spiritual, earthbound and cosmic, set against his physical helplessness; this is his fundamental tragedy. The tragedy of spirituality. The consequence of this simultaneous helplessness of the body and mobility of the spirit is the dichotomy of human existence.'**[22] **(11.40, 11.41)**

On 28 November 1978, during one of his visits to Japan, where he wore traditional Japanese clothing, participated in the tea ceremony and visited Japanese buildings both ancient and modern, Scarpa died after falling down a roof stair in Sendai; according to some, while trying to obtain a better view of a nearby building. In the last numerical coincidence of his life, Scarpa lived for exactly 11 days after the fall, but was unable to speak, and during that time he made a series of drawings; these were given to his family and friends following his death, which occurred in the eleventh month of the year. Two aspects of this event are characteristic of Scarpa's life: his abiding love for architecture, both ancient and modern, and the cultures that are inextricably intertwined with it, and his constant need to draw in order to see the world, to see what he had made – because he could only know what he had made.

'I want to see things, I don't trust anything else.
I place things in front of me, on the paper, so I can see them.
I want to see, therefore I draw.
I can see an image only if I draw it.'[23]

11.39 BRION CEMETERY; CHAPEL, SEEN FROM THE CYPRESS BOSQUE

11.40 BRION CEMETERY; PERIOD PHOTOGRAPH (1978), CARLO SCARPA ON THE STEPPING STONES OUTSIDE THE CHAPEL

11.41 BRION CEMETERY; SCARPA'S TOMB, THE MARBLE HEADSTONE DESIGNED BY HIS SON, TOBIA SCARPA

11.42 BRION CEMETERY; CHAPEL, VIEW ACROSS THE POOL WITH THE ZIGGURAT-STEPPED 'RIBS' IN THE FOREGROUND AND, IN THE BACKGROUND, THE WIDE CONCRETE SLABS ACTING AS STEPPING STONES FROM THE CHAPEL TO THE SUNKEN CYPRESS BOSQUE

11.42

c.1

In a moving tribute to their profound friendship, deep respect and shared values, the last thing that Louis Kahn wrote before his death in 1974 was the following foreword to the book *Carlo Scarpa Architetto Poeta*:

In the work of Carlo Scarpa
'Beauty'
the first sense
Art
the first word
then Wonder
Then the inner realization of 'Form'
the sense of the wholeness of inseparable elements.
Design consults Nature
to give presence to the elements.
A work of art makes manifest the wholeness of the 'Form'
a symphony of the selected shapes of the elements.
In the elements
the joint inspires ornament, its celebration.
The detail is the adoration of Nature.[1]

Kahn's deep architectural understanding of Scarpa's work, drawing on his experience both of Scarpa's buildings and the man himself, is complemented by the 1987 comments of the Italian philosopher Gianni Vattimo on the relation between philosophy and architecture, which, as Frampton noted, are of particular relevance to Scarpa's work:

> 'Edification has two principle meanings – to build and to be morally uplifting ... That is, edification must be ethical, entailing communication of value choices. In the present situation ... the only possibility of edifying in the sense of building is to edify in the sense of "rendering ethical", that is, to encourage an ethical life: to work with recollections of traditions, with the traces of the past, with the expectations of meaning for the future ... There follows then edification as a fostering of emotions, of ethical present-ability, which can probably serve as the basis for an architecture which is determined not by the whole but by the part.'[2]

Related to both of these very different ways of reading Scarpa's work is his act, during his deanship of the IUAV, of having Vico's aphorism, *Verum Ipsum Factum*, inscribed on the graduating students' diplomas, as well as above the school's portal he designed. Scarpa's use of Vico's insight that we can only find 'truth through making' – or more revealingly, that 'we only know that which we and our kind have made' – to summarize the task of the architect, and twentieth-century architectural education, brings full circle his integration of the most ancient and most Modern elements of his world.

In 1961, the French philosopher Paul Ricœur wrote an essay entitled 'Universal Civilization and National Cultures', which is of particular pertinence to Scarpa's work. Ricœur warned of the growing split between an emerging modern universal civilization, desired by all around the world, and pre-existing ancient local cultures, grounded in a particular place, arguing for the need to be at once ancient and modern, 'There is the paradox: how to become modern and return to sources; how to revive an old, dormant civilization and take part in universal civilization.' Ricœur held that the only local cultures that would be able to survive this confrontation were those that could transform themselves through the engagement of universal civilization, while simultaneously transforming the universal civilization through grounding it in the unique qualities of the local place, 'The problem is not simply to repeat the past, but rather to take root in it in order to ceaselessly invent.'[3]

In a lecture in Madrid in the summer of 1978, shortly before his death, Scarpa said:

> 'I want to make a confession: I would like some critic to discover in my works certain intentions I have always had. I mean an immense desire to belong to tradition, but without having capitals and columns, because you just cannot do them anymore. Not even a god could design an Attic base nowadays. That's the only decent one – all the rest are junk; even Palladio's, in this respect, are just trash. In handling the columns and trabeations, only Greece has reached the heights of splendour, it is only in the Parthenon that shapes live like music ...'[4]

CONCLUSION
WE ONLY KNOW WHAT WE MAKE

c.2

c.3

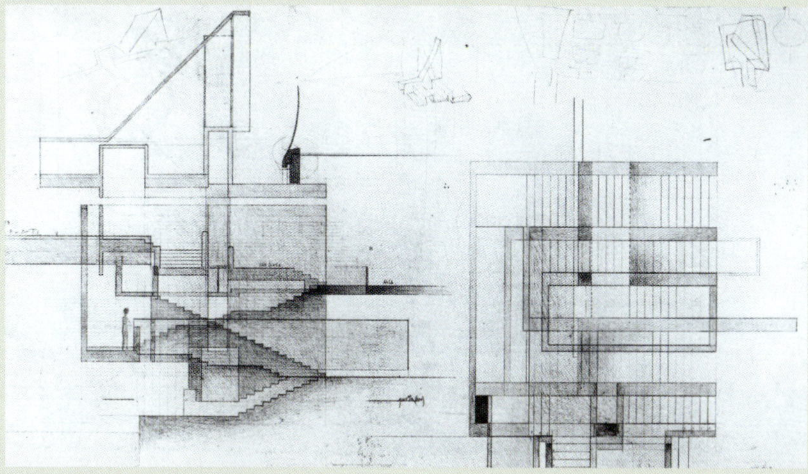

Scarpa, who described himself as **'a man of Byzantium who came to Venice by way of Greece'**, belonged to the tradition of Venetian architects going back to the Roman times. A remarkable number of the elements appearing in his works, seeming to contemporary observers to be unique formal inventions, can in fact also be traced to sources within the Venetian lagoon. **(c.1)** On the island of Torcello can be found pivoting stone shutters on the Basilica Santa Maria Assunta, like the stone doors of the Olivetti Showroom and Querini Stampalia; ziggurat-stepped moulding around the windows of Santa Fosca, like the concrete mouldings of Scarpa's Brion cemetery; and a stretched circular masonry aperture set in front of a rectangular wood-framed window, like the windows of the Banco Popolare di Verona;[5] while in Venice itself can be found endless parallels for almost every one of Scarpa's 'unique' details and forms.

'Venetian architecture after the Byzantine period is always concerned with the wall,' [6] as Stokes has pointed out. In 1964, Scarpa gave an inauguration lecture to the assembled student body and faculty of the IUAV in which he indicated the depth of his anchorage in the Venetian building culture described by Stokes, as well as Scarpa's fundamental criticism of mid-century mainstream Modern architecture:

> **'It is said that perspective opens up space, but I beg to disagree. One need only visit Maser or the villa Valmarana to see that the impression of the wall is always there. What I want to say is that the sense of space is not communicated by a pictorial order but always by physical phenomena, that is, by matter, by the sense of mass, the weight of the wall. This is why I assert that it is apertures, openings and orifices that create spatial relationships. Modern architecture, abstractly stereometric, destroys all sensitivity to framework and surface composition.We have created a void around things. What can we offer when we decide to participate with our works in the creation of a more meaningful life for people? We no longer have thick walls, we tend towards extreme thinness, we have even abolished the wall ... As men of our time we have redeemed many things, both morally and socially. But as architects we have not yet redeemed the form of humble, everyday things.'** [7]

Like his contemporaries Alvar Aalto and Louis Kahn, Scarpa's work falls outside the dominant ideological schools of thought for his day, being disengaged from the debates on style and politics in Italian architecture, as well as from the parallel international discourses in the middle half of the twentieth century. In this, Scarpa could be said to be a true outsider regarding these aspects of his contemporary world. Yet while Scarpa's thought and work were certainly informed by his understanding of the history of his place, and the rich intellectual confluence that formed Venetian culture, he remained essentially engaged in his own time. His approach to architecture, grounded as it was in his deep sense of culture, allowed Scarpa to see beyond the transitory and superficial conceptualizations of his time to that which was essential, that which connects past, present and future, and that which only lives in our experience of place. **(c.2)**

As Frampton has so perceptively pointed out:

> **'It is difficult to write about Scarpa's work in a systematic manner, for in the last analysis his achievement can only be comprehended as a continuum ... in his case there is never the intention of an ideal whole in either a humanist or an organic sense. There is only the "nearness of things" and their unfolding progression from part to part and joint to joint. Spatial interpenetration is largely absent in his work. Place is there, but only as a momentary location that is constantly modified by movement and the fluctuation of light. It is above all a disquisition on time, on the paradoxical durability and fragility of things.'** [8]

To a greater degree than those of any other Modern architect, the works of Carlo Scarpa must be experienced 'in the flesh' to be understood – engaging his architecture requires our *being there*. From a distance, outside the uniquely layered historical, material and spatial context of Venice and the Veneto, Scarpa's architecture is easily misinterpreted, misunderstood and even dismissed as a local phenomenon, due to its seemingly obsessive density of detail. **(c.3)** Yet, in our increasingly 'globalized' world, where every place is filled with the same 'mediocre civilization', so scathingly described by Ricœur, it is exactly this grounding of the liberative spatial and social conceptions of modernism in the archaic, anachronistic and emphatically local phenomena of Venice that makes Scarpa's architecture worthy of closer study. Visiting Scarpa's buildings is a transformative experience, one that makes us acutely aware of the laminated nature of place, which reveals human history as it is inscribed into things – things we can know only because people like us made them.

c.1 FONDAZIONE QUERINI STAMPALIA IN *AQUA ALTA*

c.2 CASTELVECCHIO MUSEUM; *MADDONNA INCORONATA* SCULPTURE

c.3 ITALIAN PAVILION, 34TH BIENNALE, STAIRCASE PLAN AND SECTION

c.4

Unlike the majority of his contemporaries, Scarpa believed that a deep understanding of the history and culture of a place were necessary to the making of an architecture appropriate to that place. Commenting on the Castelvecchio late in life, and his efforts to integrate the Gothic windows that had been placed on the facades in the 1920s, Scarpa said:

> 'This called for something more, but then I got tired ... yes, because I never finish my works. If there are any original parts, they have to be preserved. Any other intervention has to be designed and thought out in a new way. You cannot say: "I am modern – I am going to use metal and plate glass." Wood might be more suitable, or something more modest. How can one make certain statements if one is not educated? – educated, as Foscolo says, "to histories", i.e. with a broad knowledge? – if there is no education in the things of the past?' [9]

In retrospect, it seems clear that some ancient Venetian building crafts would likely have vanished had Scarpa not employed the craftsmen and their materials in his projects, in this way reviving what is today a thriving construction and fabrication industry. As a direct result of their redeployment by Scarpa, Venetian polished plaster and other crafts are now employed all over the world. [10] Scarpa employed the same group of craftspeople on each project, at their wood, metal or stone workshops, and on the construction site, and their suggestions as to the best way to realize the design were invited, respected and honoured by Scarpa. (c.4) In his thoughtful study, Giuseppe Zambonini noted that Scarpa's work, as an extension of artisan craft, **'is first concerned with the embodiment of an idea through a unique materiality ... [which] deals simultaneously with preservation and innovation ... Scarpa has shown that invention is tied to a process where one must interpret and extrapolate from established tradition.'** Zambonini held that Scarpa's work is defined primarily by *continuity*, which **'speaks of relationships in time'**, where **'history will inevitably be felt as an active component of the work'**, and *integration*, which **'is fundamentally opposed to the perceived necessity for standardization and specialization'**. He also points out that Scarpa's architecture should not be interpreted as intentionally fragmented, but, as Scarpa himself said so often, as something that is never finished, **'I believe Scarpa's work should be regarded as an expression of a design and building process rather than a fully realized form; it is "incomplete" rather than "fragmented".'** [11] (c.5)

It is a pity that Adrian Stokes (1902–72), the greatest art and architecture critic of ancient Venice, never turned his attention to the work of his near contemporary, Scarpa, for rarely has there been a critic better suited to assess the strengths of a subject. Stokes' writings on Venice and other Italian cities are filled with characterizations that apply precisely to Scarpa's works, as well as Scarpa's choice of materials and his continuation of craft traditions. Stokes noted, **'Every Venetian generation handles the Istrian stone of which Venice is made.'** [12] In addition, Scarpa's way of making was almost entirely defined by *carving*, by subtracting material, which, according to Stokes, distinguished great spatial artworks from the rest, which began additively, through *modelling*. [13] Scarpa's way of making was also entirely about materials, particularly stone, glass and water, which Stokes felt were the very essence of Venice. While Stokes was close friends with the British painter Ben Nicholson and sculptor Barbara Hepworth, Stokes was also somewhat distanced from his own modern period. In this, Stokes was like Scarpa, who knew his fellow modern artists and architects, but who practised an entirely different form of architecture, one connected to a specific place and its laminated history, and to the materials and traditions that went into its making.

Recalling the influence of modern masters such as Hoffmann and Le Corbusier, Scarpa said:

> 'It is highly unlikely that we have any masters at present at all: they are all dead. A master is someone who expresses something new and which others listen to and understand if they can ... I do not consider myself a master; our poor heads are full of modern elements of the men I have just now claimed – for all of us, sad to say – are all dead. Not one of the great modern architects is still living. The last one, Louis Kahn, passed away in the saddest of ways. And these are grave losses, because, in my opinion, they cannot be replaced.' [14]

While Scarpa did not consider himself to be a modern master, from our perspective today, 35 years since his death, we can say that he has had the influence of a master, though perhaps it has not taken the typical form. In his relation to history, culture and place, his deployment of local building traditions, his celebration of the joint and detail, and his engagement of materials in the enrichment of human experience, Scarpa influenced his contemporaries, and continues to inspire many contemporary architects, such as Steven Holl, Fumihiko Maki, Tod Williams and Billie Tsien, John and Patricia Patkau, Shin Takematsu, Bridget Shim and Howard Sutcliffe, Thom Mayne, Richard Murphy, Kathryn Dean and Charles Wolf, Mario Botta, and the late Sverre Fehn, to name only a few.

In addition, the overall quality of Scarpa's works can be said to have increased in the last years of his life, a rare characteristic among modern architects. Regarding Le Corbusier, Frampton noted, **'Except for Louis Kahn, there is perhaps no other architect of the twentieth century whose creative capacity increased rather than diminished during the final period of his activity.'** [15] It is clear that the same can also be said of Scarpa.

c.5

c.6

As a person, Scarpa was, and remains, essentially inscrutable at the deepest levels. **(c.6)** Yet his architectural works are fundamentally engaged in the life-world and all its present and absent realities. History lives in our time within his works, as in precious few other places in the world today. This is why it is surprising to discover that, were he to propose them today, Scarpa would not be allowed to build a single one of his masterpieces of enlightened 'restoration' in his beloved Veneto.[16] This is due to the fact that the city of Venice, the nation of Italy, the European Union and the whole of the increasingly 'globalized' world have come to accept a highly delimited and reductive definition of 'restoration', a definition requiring strict distinctions between the constructions of different periods, and selection of a single time period for use in making 'restorations' involving formal imitations, rather than the acceptance of the actual layers of history resulting from human making and inhabitation of a particular place – thus precluding exactly the kind of integrated renovations and laminations of place and time Scarpa has left to us. For Scarpa, restoration was not simply preservation, but a fundamentally transformative process, **'By "restoration" is not meant only repair work on old buildings; our duty is rather to give them a new lease on life so that they may be able to live today and tomorrow ... In my architecture, all the existing buildings form a part of the *métier*.'**[17]

Scarpa noted that the purely formal definition of preservation, based on imitation of historical elements, which excluded what he defined as the true 'restoration' of historic buildings so that they live again in contemporary use, was already in place during his lifetime. **'The problem of historical materials, which we can never ignore but cannot imitate directly either, is an issue that has always concerned me. The stupid imitations imposed now, for instance by the Fine Arts Superintendent in Venice, lead in the wrong direction. They don't solve anything. You cannot imagine how hard I have had to struggle against these bureaucratic follies ...'**[18] Despite the bureaucratic opposition Scarpa received in all his works, Ellen Soroka noted, **'Against a reactionary preservationist culture, Scarpa generated a critical stance weaving an oppositional path between architectural languages, functional programmes and different materials, achieving, especially in his restorations, an acute understanding of history and, paradoxically, a Bergsonian sense of timelessness at the same time.'**[19]

And, perhaps predictably, these same planning authorities have largely failed to protect Scarpa's works from inappropriate and insensitive change in the years since he passed away. One of the greatest ironies of the modern era, which has redefined architectural preservation and restoration in the narrowest possible way, based entirely on chronological and formal issues of style, rather than historical issues of how buildings were *made* and *inhabited* (following Vico's conception of history as our knowledge of what others before us have made), is that works of Modern architecture have generally not been considered worthy of preservation and protection, much less restoration and renewal.

A more appropriate way of dwelling with and in our historical places may be found in Scarpa's experientially based and culturally grounded understanding of what it is to live simultaneously in historical and contemporary worlds; to live through celebrating architecture's profound capacities to engage our senses; to live through our embodied experience *taking place* in the rich reality composed of both the present moment and the presence of the past; and to live through inhabiting an architecture that we know because it speaks to us about how we and our kind have made it.

c.4 PERIOD PHOTOGRAPH, 1978; CARLO SCARPA (C) WITH MICHELE 'LINO' CONTIN (L), DURING THE CONSTRUCTION OF SCARPA'S *VALMARANA* TABLE, IN CONTIN SRL, THE WOODWORKING SHOP WHERE MANY OF HIS FURNITURE PIECES WERE FABRICATED

c.5 PERIOD PHOTOGRAPH, 1970; PROTOTYPES OF DETAILS USED IN THE BRION CEMETERY

c.6 PERIOD PHOTOGRAPH; CARLO SCARPA IN THE CASTELVECCHIO MUSEUM, IN FRONT OF *QUATTRO SANTI CAMALDOLESI*, C. 1760–70, BY GIANDOMENICO TIEPOLO

CARLO SCARPA NOTES

INTRODUCTION

VERUM IPSUM FACTUM

1 / This was made particularly clear to the author during one of many visits with Kenneth Frampton to Scarpa's Querini Stampalia garden, where Frampton insisted that the brass disks that line the inside face of the brass basin that floats above the large pool had not been there on his previous visit; he had no memory of them at all

CHAPTER 1

A MAN OF BYZANTIUM WHO CAME TO VENICE BY WAY OF GREECE

1 / Maria Antonietta Crippa, *Carlo Scarpa: Theory, Design, Projects* (Cambridge: MIT, 1986), 216
2 / Giuseppe Mazzariol, Giuseppe Barbieri, 'The Life of Carlo Scarpa,' *Carlo Scarpa: The Complete Works*, Francesco Dal Co, Giuseppe Mazzariol, ed. (New York: Rizzoli, 1985), 10
3 / Caroline Constant, *The Palladio Guide* (New York: Princeton Architectural Press, 1985), 138–9
4 / 'Un architetto a regola d'arte,' Scarpa, in conversation with Barbara Radice, *Moda* (January–February 1979), 19–21; translated by Crippa, 13
5 / 'Interview with Carlo Scarpa,' Martin Dominguez, 1978, in Dal Co and Mazzariol, op. cit., 297
6 / Ibid.
7 / 'Un architetto a regola d'arte,' Crippa, 14
8 / Dal Co and Mazzariol, op. cit., 9
9 / William H. McNeill, *Venice: The Hinge of Europe, 1081–1797* (Chicago: University of Chicago Press, 1974), passim
10 / John Larner, *Marco Polo and the Discovery of the World* (New Haven: Yale University Press, 1999), 1
11 / John Premble, *Venice Rediscovered* (Oxford: Oxford University Press, 1995), 75
12 / Henry James, *Italian Hours* (Boston: Houghton Mifflin, 1909), 69
13 / Joseph Brodsky, *Watermark* (New York: Farrar, Straus and Giroux, 1992)
14 / Adrian Stokes, Venice: *An Aspect of Art* (1945) in *Critical Writings of Adrian Stokes, Volume II* (London: Thames and Hudson, 1978), 96; *The Stones of Rimini* (1934), in *Critical Writings of Adrian Stokes, Volume I* (London: Thames and Hudson, 1978), 184–5
15 / Premble, op. cit., 114
16 / Constant quoted in Roland Mortier, *La Poetique des ruines en France* (Geneva, 1974); Premble, 127
17 / Giacomo Boni, 'Venezia imbellata,' cited in Alvise Zorzi, *Venezia scomparsa*, 140; Premble, op cit., 137
18 / Camillo Boito, *Gite di un artista* (Milan, 1884), 35; as paraphrased by Ellen Soroka in 'Restauro in Venezia,' *Journal of Architectural Education* (May 1994), 226
19 / *Builder*, 26 July and 30 August 1902; Premble, op. cit., 157–8
20 / Colin Rowe, 'Preservation, Reproduction, and Simulation: Meditations on Places Old and New,' *From the Past, For the Future: Redefining Architectural Preservation for the 21st Century*, Robert McCarter, editor (unpublished manuscript), 118, 123. This was Rowe's contribution to the book based on the symposium of the same name, which took place on February 15 and 16, 1996, honoring the establishment of the Beinecke-Reeves Distinguished Chair in Architectural Preservation at the University of Florida, of which Rowe was one of the original six appointees, teaching at the University of Florida in 1997
21 / Stokes, *The Stones of Rimini* (1935), *Critical Writings, Volume I*, op. cit., 185
22 / Gigi Scarpa, 'Four Glass Pieces by Carlo Scarpa,' in Marino Barovier, Carlo Scarpa: *Glass of an Architect* (Milan: Skira, 1998), 21
23 / Carla Sonego, 'Carlo Scarpa at Maestri Vetrai Muranesi Cappellin & C. 1925–1931,' in Barovier, op. cit., 33
24 / Marina Barovier, 'Carlo Scarpa at Venini & C. 1932–1947,' in Barovier, op cit., 40
25 / Ibid., 41
26 / Dal Co and Mazzariol, op. cit., 20
27 / Stokes, *Venice: An Aspect of Art* (1945), *Critical Writings, Volume II*, op. cit., 96
28 / Eugenio Montale, *Mediterraneo*, in *Ossi di Seppia* (1927), *Eugenio Montale: Collected Poems 1920–1954*, trans. Jonathan Galassi (New York: Farrar, Straus and Giroux, 1998), 75
29 / From a 1981 interview of Businaro, quoted in Giuseppe Zambonini, 'Process and Theme in the Work of Carlo Scarpa,' *Perspecta 20* (Cambridge: MIT Press, 1983), 22

CHAPTER 2

NOTHING COMES FROM NOTHING

1 / Wright's lamps for Midway Gardens of 1913 take the form of a single vertical post off of which are cantilevered alternating stepped rectangles; Wright designed a similar zigzag lamp, in wood, in 1932. In Klee's Bauhaus teaching notes from 1923–4, he called similar alternating projections 'zigzag construction', 'vertebral structures', and 'oscillating balance'; Paul Klee, *Notebooks, Volume 1: The Thinking Eye* (Basel: Schwabe and Co. Verlag, 1956), 211, 389
2 / This are documented in Nancy Troy, *The De Stijl Environment* (Cambridge: MIT, 1983)
3 / Scarpa, 'Can Architecture Be Poetry?,' lecture given in 1976 at the Akademie der bildenden kunst in Vienna, *Space Design: The Drawings of Carlo Scarpa* (Tokyo, January 1992, No. 328), 129
4 / Sandro Giordano, 'Biographical Profile,' in Dal Co and Mazzariol, op. cit., 305–6
5 / Sergio Cortesini, Bice Lazzari: *l'arte come misura* (Rome: Gangemi, 2002), passim
6 / Giordano, 'Biographical Profile,' in Dal Co and Mazzariol, op. cit., 305–6
7 / Mazzariol and Barbieri, op. cit., 11
8 / Raffaella Vendramin, 'Carlo Scarpa's Library,' Dal Co and Mazzariol, op. cit., 307
9 / Ibid.
10 / Quoted in Zambonini, op. cit., 28. I am indeed indebted to my late friend Beppe Zambonini for pointing out to all of us the significance of this passage for understanding Scarpa's life and work
11 / Bruce Brooks Pfeiffer, introduction, 'Sixty Years of Living Architecture,' Pfeiffer, ed., *Frank Lloyd Wright: Collected Writings*, Vol. V (New York: Rizzoli, 1995), 31
12 / Bruno Zevi, 'Wright and Italy: A Recollection,' Anthony Alofsin, ed., *Frank Lloyd Wright: Europe and Beyond* (Berkeley: University of California Press, 1999), 66–70
13 / Alan Irvine, 'Memories of Carlo,' Barovier, op. cit., 25
14 / Mazzariol and Barbieri, op. cit., 14
15 / Zevi, in Alofsin, op. cit., 72–73
16 / Guido Beltramini and Italo Zannier, *Carlo Scarpa: Architecture and Design* (New York: Rizzoli, 2007), 78
17 / Scarpa's exhibition and building designs for the Venice Biennale are comprehensively documented in Orietta Lanzarini, *Carlo Scarpa: L'architetto e le arti* (Venice: Marsilio/Regione del Veneto, 2003)
18 / The book pavilion was destroyed by fire just before the opening of the 1984 Biennale, and was replaced a few years later by a book pavilion designed by the British architect James Stirling

CHAPTER 3

BEAUTY, ART, WONDER

1 / Carlo Scarpa in 'Incontri a cura di Gastone Favero: Un'ora can Carlo Scarpa,' Radiotelevisione Italiana documentary, 1970
2 / Eugenio De Luigi described Venetian polished plaster as follows; 'To make *stucco alla veneziana*, technically speaking, an *intonaco* is first applied to the wall. This layer is properly called the *sottofondo* and the best one, developed through long tradition, is made only of *grassello di calce* (hydrated lime and sand). This technique has either been forgotten by many craftsmen or is avoided by them, because of the intense labor involved in pressing the *calce* by hand onto the wall surface. Another *sottofondo* is made with a finely crushed *cotto*, derived from discarded or broken clay bricks and roof tiles. *Cotto* is excellent for us in Venice because it absorbs the humidity from the air and so no condensed water runs down the *stucco*. Coarser sand is used for the *sottofondo* and a finer sand for the finish coat. However, *calce* must be in the *sottofondo* to aid in the absorption of moisture. The *calce* that goes on the finish coat is as pure as possible, although it may contain some added colour. This technique of mixture and application dates back to the Romans, as fragments of similar stucco have been found in Ercolano and Pompeii. The Romans were mixing *calce* with ground dirt and clay, but the technique eventually evolved into the conception of the beautiful *marmorino*. *Marmorino* is obtained by mixing a marble powder with the *calce* and applied only to an intonaco of cotto. With its marble-like hardness, a result of the intense pressure of hand application, and its shine, imparted with a hot iron, *marmorino* is both extremely resistant to moisture and exceptionally beautiful.' De Luigi also noted that Scarpa always wanted to use the local sands in the plasterwork of his buildings; from an interview with Giuseppe Zambonini, December 1985; quoted in Zambonini, 'Notes for a Theory of Making in a Time of Necessity,' *Perspecta* 24 (New York: Rizzoli, 1988), 9, 8
3 / Frampton, *Studies in Tectonic Culture*, op. cit., 311
4 / Beltramini and Zannier, op. cit., 52
5 / In 1963, Le Corbusier was given a tour of Venice by Scarpa's friend, colleague, and client, Giuseppe Mazzariol, and during his visit to the Accademia Le Corbusier made a sketch of Saint Ursula on the raised litter, which he shared with Guillermo Jullian de la Fuente, the project designer for the hospital; Pablo Allard, 'Bridge over Venice,' *Le Corbusier's Venice Hospital*, Hashim Sarkis, ed. (Munich: Prestel, 2001), 22–23
6 / Presented in Lazzarini, op. cit., 32–40
7 / Paul Klee, *Notebooks, Volume 1: The Thinking Eye* (London: Lund Humphries, 1961), 360
8 / Marisa Dalai Emiliani, *Carlo Scarpa*, Guido Beltramini, Kurt Forster, Paola Marini, ed. (Milano: Electa, 2000), 104–5
9 / Giuseppe Mazzariol, 'Opere dell'architetto Carlo Scarpa,' L'architettura. *Cronache e storia*, 3, 1955, 347.
10 / Francesca Fenaroli, in Dal Co and Mazzariol, op. cit., 110.
11 / Peter Noever, 'Reminiscences,' in *The Other City, Carlo Scarpa, Die Andere Stadt* (Berlin: Ernst & Sohn, 1989), 8
12 / This building and the process of renovation are meticulously documented in Paolo Morello, *Palazzo Abatellis* (Treviso: Vianello, 1989)

CHAPTER 4

ARCHITECTURE DETERMINED NOT BY THE WHOLE BUT BY THE PART

1 / Scarpa, quoted in Sergio Los, *Carlo Scarpa, Architetto Poeta* (Venice: Cluva, 1967), 17
2 / Marco Frascari, 'The Tell-the-Tale Detail,' VIA 7: *The Building of Architecture* (1984), 24
3 / Kenneth Frampton, *Studies in Tectonic Culture* (Cambridge: MIT, 1995), 307
4 / Klee, 1923–4, *The Thinking Eye*, op. cit., 5, 340, 361, 49, 291, 292, 311, 76, 383, 463, 449
5 / Manfredo Tafuri, 'Carlo Scarpa and Italian Architecture,' Dal Co and Mazzariol, op. cit., 86–95
6 / Frampton, *Studies in Tectonic Culture*, op. cit., 314, 333.
7 / What Orietta Lanzarini calls the 'tormented' story of this project is documented in Lanzarini, op. cit., 136–154
8 / Ibid., 156
9 / I am describing the Venezuelan Pavilion as it originally was experienced. Over the years, the building has been allowed to deteriorate badly, and was subjected to an inappropriate renovation in the 1960s. It is currently undergoing a complete restoration under the supervision of Francesco Rovetta, documented in 'Progetto di restauro e ripristino del Padiglione de Venezuela ai Giardini della Biennale di Venezia,' in Forster and Marini, op. cit., 371–391
10 / These handrails, which do not appear in the photographs of the house that were taken when it had just been completed and occupied, were added at a later date. While the rails may not have been necessary at the entry bridge, the cantilevered balcony at the first floor would hardly be safe to use without them. Of course, there are precedents for Scarpa not providing handrails and guardrails where they are normally expected to be, and, by building code, often required to be – most notably, in the new stair he constructed in the Palazzo Abatellis
11 / This project, which, due to its remote location, is far less well-known than most of Scarpa's other built works, is documented in Paolo Biadene, *Edoardo Gellner e Carlo Scarpa: La Chiesa di Corte di Cadore* (Venice: IUAV Archivio Progetti, 2000)

CHAPTER 5

EDIFICATION AS THE FOSTERING OF EMOTIONS

1 / There appears to be some controversy over this, as some sources credit Giuseppe Segusini as the architect of the first Canova museum of 1836 (Dal Co and Mazzariol, op. cit., 117), but the majority of the sources credit Lazzari. The two most comprehensive publications of Scarpa's work are Judith Carmel-Arthur, *Carlo Scarpa: Museo Canoviana, Possagno* (Stuttgart: Axel Menges, 2002) and Gianna Ghizzoni, ed., *Carlo Scarpa a Possagno* (Possagno: Fondazione Canova, no date)
2 / This is the third project, along with the Venezuelan Biennale Pavilion and the Church at Corte di Cadore, where Scarpa employed rotated columns composed of double cylinders or H-shaped steel. All of these rotated configurations are very likely related to Pierre Chareau's Dalsace Residence in Paris, known as the 'Maison de Verre' (House of Glass) of 1927–32, one of the most famous first generation Modern houses. As in Scarpa's buildings, at the Maison de Verre the rotation of the H-shaped steel columns is employed to articulate intersecting paths of spatial movement
3 / Carmel-Arthur, op. cit., 14
4 / Scarpa, quoted in 'Volevo ritagliare l'azzurro del cielo,' *Rassegna* (July 1981), 82–84; translated in Crippa, op. cit., 130
5 / 'Incontri a cura di Gastone Favero: Un'ora con Carlo Scarpa,' op. cit.
6 / Scarpa, from 'Volevo ritagliare l'azzurro del cielo,' op. cit. After Scarpa's addition was complete, his intuition regarding the best colour for the walls was proven correct, and the dark grey interior walls of the original gallery were repainted in white and light cream colours
7 / Ibid.

CHAPTER 6

GIVING PRESENCE TO THE ELEMENTS

1 / Scarpa, in Dal Co and Mazzariol, op. cit., 287
2 / Ibid.
3 / Stefania Potinari, 'Negozio Olivetti a Venezia,' in *Carlo Scarpa e la scultura del '900*, ed, Guido Beltramini (Venice: Marsilio/Regione del Veneto, 2008), 187
4 / Ranalli, in *Carlo Scarpa Architect: Intervening with History*, op. cit., 98
5 / Sergio Los, *Carlo Scarpa* (Koln: Benedikt Taschen, 1993), 96
6 / It is important to note that I have been describing the Olivetti Showroom as it existed up until 1998, when the company moved out of the showroom. The space, from which the teak display tables and other details were removed, has until recently housed a commercial tourist shop, and the plaster walls were almost entirely covered, and the windows filled, with cluttered displays, rendering Scarpa's design almost unrecognizable. However, in July 2009, the owner of the showroom, an insurance company, announced it was granting the Fondo Ambiente Italiano (the National Trust for Italy) use of the former Olivetti showroom on Piazza San Marco as a public venue for cultural events and visitor information. At the time of this writing, the showroom was being renovated back to its original condition, and this was completed in 2012
7 / Valter Rossetto, in an interview with Giuseppe Zambonini, 'Process and Theme in the Work of Carlo Scarpa,' *Perspecta* 20 (Cambridge: MIT, 1983), 40
8 / Forster, in a lecture given at the Vicenza Institute of Architecture, 5 September 2000.
9 / Frampton, *Studies in Tectonic Culture*, op. cit., 312.
10 / Guido Pietropoli, 'L'invitation au voyage,' *Spazio e Societa*, June 1990, 90–98.
11 / Marco Frascari, 'A Deciphering of a Wonderful Cipher: Eleven in the Architecture of Carlo Scarpa,' Oz 13 (1991)
12 / Beltramini and Zannier, op. cit., 110

APPENDIX

CHAPTER 7

WORKING WITH TRACES OF THE PAST AND EXPECTATIONS OF FUTURE MEANING

1 / Licisco Magagnato, 'The Castelvecchio Museum,' in Dal Co and Mazzariol, op. cit., 159
2 / Richard Murphy, *Carlo Scarpa and the Castelvecchio* (London: Butterworth, 1990), 4–7. This exemplary study, including new measured drawings, remains one of the best books on Scarpa
3 / Magagnato, in Dal Co and Mazzariol, op. cit., 159
4 / The drawings, held in the collection of the Castelvecchio, are cataloged and published in Alba Di Lieto, *I disegni di Carlo Scarpa per Castelvecchio* (Venezia: Marsilio/Regione del Veneto)
5 / 'Interview with Carlo Scarpa,' in Dal Co and Mazzariol, op. cit., 298
6 / Arrigo Rudi, 'An Eyewitness Account,' in Murphy, op. cit., 167
7 / Frascari, 'The Tell the Tale Detail,' op. cit. The *Piranesi* story comes from Henri Focillon, Piranesi (Bologna, 1962), 166
8 / Scarpa's intentions for the hedge were described to me by Arrigo Rudi during a visit to the Castelvecchio, September 1997
9 / 'Interview with Carlo Scarpa,' in Dal Co and Mazzariol, op. cit., 298.
10 / In this description of the Castelvecchio, my source in citing the specific materials is the meticulous and exhaustive research undertaken by Richard Murphy, in Murphy, *Carlo Scarpa and the Castelvecchio*, op. cit.
11 / 'Interview with Carlo Scarpa,' in Dal Co and Mazzariol, op. cit., 298
12 / Ibid.
13 / Ibid.
14 / The photograph by Ugo Mulas has been published many times, and is included in *Carlo Scarpa nella fotographia*, CISA (Venice: Marsilio/Regione del Veneto, 2004), where it is on page 61
15 / Murphy, *Carlo Scarpa and the Castelvecchio*, op. cit., 87
16 / Two of Ruskin's sketches are published in Licisco Magagnato, 'Cangrande della Scala at Castelvecchio,' Murphy, *Carlo Scarpa and the Castelvecchio*, op. cit., 190
17 / There are historic photographs showing the Cangrande facing both west and south in the Reggia courtyard, but in any event, never east
18 / 'Interview with Carlo Scarpa,' in Dal Co and Mazzariol, op. cit., 298
19 / Murphy, *Carlo Scarpa and the Castelvecchio*, op. cit., 145
20 / As shown in Scarpa's drawing of the reflected ceiling plan and section of the first floor galleries, published in Alba Di Lieto, op. cit., 238, drawing inventory number 31950; also mentioned in Murphy, *Carlo Scarpa and the Castelvecchio*, op. cit., 145
21 / The 'spatio-temporal' is a key concept for Paul Klee, as is repeatedly noted in his *The Thinking Eye*, op. cit.
22 / Magagnato, 'The Castelvecchio Museum,' in Dal Co and Mazzariol, op. cit., 159

CHAPTER 8

CELEBRATION OF THE JOINT

1 / Richard Murphy, *Querini Stampalia Foundation: Carlo Scarpa* (London: Phaidon, 1993), 13; the 'living window' quote from Scarpa is on the same page
2 / Scarpa, 'Interview with Carlo Scarpa,' in Dal Co and Mazzariol, op. cit., 297
3 / Frampton, *Studies in Tectonic Culture*, op. cit., 299.
4 / The majority of sources agree that the bridge treads and deck are made of oak, though they are listed as larch, which is an excellent wood for exterior conditions, in the generally accurate Bianca Albertini and Sandro Bagnoli, Carlo Scarpa: *Architecture in Details* (Cambridge: MIT, 1988), 204.
5 / Frampton, *Studies in Tectonic Culture*, op. cit., 304
6 / The exact genus of these four stones is not given in Scarpa's few surviving drawings, but the dark red stone is most likely porphyry, as are many of the disk-like ornaments on Venetian palazzo facades, and the pink-orange stone is likely either Prun stone or red Veronese marble
7 / We can discern that the floor plan came later rather than earlier in the design process because it shows all the details as they would appear in the final built work; Tadashi Yokoyama, Hiroyuki Toyota, 'Carlo Scarpa: A Special Celebration,' *Space Design*, Tokyo (1977), 96
8 / *Bundled* is numbered 'GL-5' in the Josef Albers Foundation, and was first published by Eugen Gomringer, 'Abstakte Kompositionen auf opakem Glas: Die Glasbilder von Josef Albers,' *Glaswelt* (Stuttgart), 17 (November 1958), 14–5; and first exhibited in 'Painters of the Bauhaus,' Marborough Fine Art Ltd., London, March-April 1962; *Josef Albers: Glass, Color, and Light* (New York: Guggenheim Museum, 1994), plate 11; this correspondence to the Albers glass work was noted by Marta Mazza, *Carlo Scarpa alla Querini Stampalia: Desegni inediti* (Venezia: Il Cardo, 1996), 38–9
9 / The International Glass Commission citation is from Dal Co and Mazzariol, op. cit., 306. In a striking parallel, Louis Kahn, whose father had been a stained glass artist, was also fascinated with Albers' flashed glass artworks, which Albers first showed to Kahn sometime in the late 1940s, and which were exhibited at Yale, where they were both teaching, in 1956. See McCarter, *Louis I. Kahn* (London: Phaidon, 2005), 49
10 / The Scarpa drawings in Peter Noever, *Carlo Scarpa: The Craft of Architecture* (Ostfeldern-Ruit, Germany: Hatje Cantz/MAK, 2003), 44–45, have been mislabeled as being for the bridge handrail, not the stair handrail
11 / Scarpa, 'Interview with Carlo Scarpa,' in Dal Co and Mazzariol, op. cit., 297–98
12 / See the 'exploded' isometric drawing in Murphy, *Querini Stampalia Foundation*, op. cit., unpaginated; and the different but equally inaccurate 'exploded' isometric drawing in Anna-Catrin Schultz, *Carlo Scarpa: Layers*, op. cit., 108
13 / Scarpa, 'Interview with Carlo Scarpa,' in Dal Co and Mazzariol, op. cit., 298
14 / Frampton, *Studies in Tectonic Culture*, op. cit., 301–2
15 / Murphy, *Querini Stampalia Foundation*, op. cit., unpaginated
16 / Ibid.
17 / This matching dimension was pointed out in a lecture by Ilaria Abbondandolo, given at the Vicenza Institute of Architecture on 5 September 2000
18 / Michael Cadwell, 'Swimming at the Querini Stampalia,' *Strange Bodies* (Cambridge: MIT Press, 2007), 12
19 / Murphy, *Querini Stampalia Foundation*, op. cit., unpaginated
20 / Cadwell, op. cit., 10

CHAPTER 9

THE WHOLENESS OF INSEPARABLE ELEMENTS

1 / Giuseppe Mazzariol, 'Un progetto per Venezia,' *Lotus* 6 (1969), 17
2 / Kahn, 'Foreword' (1974), in Alessandra Latour, *Louis I. Kahn: Writings, Lectures, Interviews* (New York: Rizzoli, 1991), 332. This poem is included in its entirety in the Conclusion of this book. Kahn and Scarpa's relationship is documented in McCarter, *Louis I. Kahn* (London: Phaidon, 2005), 424–430
3 / Kurt Forster, 'Alla ricerca *dell'architectus absconditus*,' *Studi su Carlo Scarpa*, Forster and Marini, op. cit., 16
4 / Also on the Ulm faculty was Eugen Gomringer, author of the article in *Glaswelt* on Albers' flashed glass pieces; as noted earlier, the likely source for Scarpa's use of one of Albers' glass pieces in the initial design for the floor of the entry hall of the Querini Stampalia
5 / Beltramini and Zannier, op. cit., 214
6 / Bruce Brooks Pfeiffer, 'A Biographical Sketch,' *Frank Lloyd Wright: Complete Writings, Vol. 5*, Pfeiffer, ed. (New York: Rizzoli, 1995), 16
7 / 'Interview with Carlo Scarpa,' in Dal Co and Mazzariol, op. cit., 297
8 / Paolo Ceccarelli, *Fondazione Angelo Masieri* (Venice: Masieri Foundation, no date)
9 / Sergio Los, *Carlo Scarpa: An Architectural Guide* (Venice: Arsenale, 1995), 98
10 / 'XXXIV Esposizione Internationale d'Arte di Venezia,' Stefania Portinari, *Carlo Scarpa e la scultura del' 900*, Beltramini, ed., op. cit., 244–92; the exhibition is also presented in Lanzarini, op. cit., 211–223
11 / See the excellent Stephen Leet, *Franco Albini: Architecture and Design 1934–1977* (New York: Princeton Architectural Press, 1990)
12 / The colours of the walls of the Villa Rotonda, and Palladio's quartz plaster mixture, discovered during a recent renovation, were pointed out by the historian Wilma Barbieri during a tour of historical works forming the context for Scarpa's work, organized by the author and Franca Stocco and held at the Vicenza Institute of Architecture on 3 September 2004
13 / It is interesting to note that both hollow columns and circular openings would be common features of the later work of Louis Kahn
14 / Beltramini and Zannier, op. cit., 246
15 / The book is *I Numeri di Fibonacci*, by N. N. Vorobyov, part of the series Argomenti di Matematica from Progesso Technico Editoriale of Milan. The same figure is also seen on page 26. The cover and page 26 are published, with the clear intent of revealing this relationship to the plan of the villa courtyard, by Kurt Forster, 'Alla ricerca dell'*architectus absconditus*,' op. cit., 18
16 / The house and its design are comprehensively documented in Francesco Dal Co, *Villa Ottolenghi: Carlo Scarpa* (New York: Monacelli, 1998).
17 / Forster, lecture at Vicenza Institute of Architecture, 5 September 2000
18 / Giuseppe Tommasi, 'Note su casa Ottolenghi,' in *Carlo Scarpa*, Beltramini, Forster, Marini, ed., op. cit., 404

CHAPTER 10

THE DETAIL AS THE ADORATION OF NATURE

1 / The best book on this important Renaissance architect is Lionello Puppi, *Michele Sanmicheli: architetto di Verona* (Padova: Marsilio, 1971)
2 / 'Interview with Carlo Scarpa,' in Dal Co and Mazzariol, op. cit., 299
3 / Arrigo Rudi, 'Notes on the design and construction,' *La Sede Centrale della Banca Popolare*, Arrigo Rudi and Valter Rossetto, ed. (Verona: Banca Popolare di Verona, 1983), 5
4 / 'Interview with Carlo Scarpa,' in Dal Co and Mazzariol, op. cit., 299
5 / Ibid.
6 / Frampton, *Studies in Tectonic Culture*, op. cit., 329
7 / 'Interview with Carlo Scarpa,' in Dal Co and Mazzariol, op. cit., 299
8 / Frampton, *Studies in Tectonic Culture*, op. cit., 329
9 / 'Interview with Carlo Scarpa,' in Dal Co and Mazzariol, op. cit., 299
10 / Ibid.
11 / Albertini and Bagnoli, op. cit., 216
12 / 'Interview with Carlo Scarpa,' in Dal Co and Mazzariol, op. cit., 299
13 / Ibid.
14 / 'Un'ora con Carlo Scarpa, a cura di G. Favero,' op. cit.
15 / See, for example, Hashim Sarkis, ed., *Le Corbusier's Venice Hospital and the Mat Building Revival* (Munich: Prestel, 2001)
16 / Scarpa's design is comprehensively documented in *Carlo Scarpa: il progetto per Santa Caterina a Treviso*, Boccato, Dupre, Guariglia, Val, Viscuso, eds. (Treviso: Vianello, 1984)
17 / Frampton, *Studies in Tectonic Culture*, op. cit., 309
18 / Dal Co and Mazzariol, op. cit., 140
19 / The building is documented in *Banca Popolare di Gemona, Luciano Gemin Architetto* (Treviso: Vianello, 1986); included are copies of Scarpa's final sketches made in Sendai

CHAPTER 11

MAKING THE SPIRIT EXPLICIT

1 / Scarpa, 'Can Architecture Be Poetry?,' lecture given at the Akademie der Bildenden Kunst Vienna, 1976, *The Other City: Carlo Scarpa: Die Andere Stadt*, Peter Noever, ed. (Berlin: Ernst & Sohn, 1989), 17. This lecture is given three rather different translations in Noever, in Philippe Duboy, 'Scarpa/Matisse: Crosswords,' in Dal Co and Mazzariol, op. cit., 170–171, and in Sergio Los, *Carlo Scarpa: An Architectural Guide* (Venice: Arsenale, 1995), 90–94
2 / The drawings, a gift of the Scarpa family, are part of the collection of the Direzione generale per l'architettura e l'arte contemporanee (DARC) of the Ministero per la Cultura, and are housed in the Centro Carlo Scarpa in the Archivio di Stato di Treviso. Scarpa's drawings for the Brion Cemetery have been published far more than any of his other drawings, and are comprehensively published in two books, Noever, *The Other City: Carlo Scarpa: Die Andere Stadt*, op. cit., and *Carlo Scarpa: I disegni per la Tomba Brion, Inventario*, Erilde Terenzoni, ed. (Milan: Electa/OperaDARC, 2006)
3 / Scarpa, 'Can Architecture Be Poetry?,' op. cit., 18
4 / Ibid., 20
5 / Scarpa, 'A thousand cypresses,' lecture given in Madrid in 1978, in Dal Co and Mazzariol, op. cit., 286
6 / Ibid.
7 / Ibid.
8 / Scarpa, 'Can Architecture Be Poetry?,' op. cit., 18
9 / Frampton, *Studies in Tectonic Culture*, op. cit., 319–320
10 / Ibid., 314–15
11 / Scarpa, 'A thousand cypresses,' op. cit., 286
12 / Frampton, 'Notes on the Fragmentary Architecture of Carlo Scarpa,' *Fragments, Architecture and the Unfinished*, Barry Bergdoll and Werner Oechslin, eds. (London: Thames & Hudson, 2006), 378
13 / Scarpa, 'Can Architecture Be Poetry?,' op. cit., 18
14 / Ibid., author's translation from the Italian. Brion's wife, Onorina, lived a number of years after her husband's death, and at a certain point the family lost the instructions for opening the cleverly hidden locks of the sarcophagi. A Brion cousin, Mr. Marcolin, who has acted as a caretaker for the Brion Cemetery since it was vandalized in the later 1980s, told the author that he and the other members of the family labored long and hard before finally deciphering the complex locking mechanism for Onorina's sarcophagus; from author's conversation with Mr. Marcolin on 2 September 1999
15 / The author was shown the sacristy treasury and its secret compartments by employees of Brionvega in 1981 and 1983, and again by the Brion family member/caretaker for the cemetery, Mr. Marcolin, in 1999
16 / Scarpa, 'A thousand cypresses,' op. cit., 286
17 / Measured by the author and Kenneth Frampton on 3 September 1998; this is one of the few measurements of the Brion Cemetery that is not a multiple or fraction of 11 centimetres, and indicates that Scarpa employed the 5 and 6 letter breakdown of his own name's 11 letters as an ordering device; 56 and 65
18 / Stokes, *The Image in Form: Selected Writings of Adrian Stokes*, ed. Richard Wollheim (New York: Harper and Row, 1972), 277, 272
19 / Duboy, 'Scarpa/Matisse: Crosswords,' in Dal Co and Mazzariol, op. cit., 171
20 / Ludwig Wittgenstein, *Culture and Value* (Chicago: University of Chicago Press, 1980), 8
21 / Scarpa, 'A thousand cypresses,' op. cit., 286
22 / Klee, *The Thinking Eye*, op. cit., 407
23 / Scarpa, quoted in Sergio Los, *Carlo Scarpa, Architetto Poeta* (Venice: Cluva, 1967), 17

CONCLUSION

WE ONLY KNOW WHAT WE MAKE

1 / Kahn, 'Foreword' to 1974 RIBA publication, *Carlo Scarpa: Architetto Poeta*, reprinted in *Louis I. Kahn: Writings, Lectures, Interviews*, ed. Alessandra Latour (New York: Rizzoli, 1991), 332
2 / Vattimo, quoted in Frampton, *Studies in Tectonic Culture*, op. cit., 299
3 / Paul Ricœur, 'Universal Civilization and National Cultures' (1961), *History and Truth* (Evanston: Northwestern University Press, 1965), 277, 282
4 / Scarpa, 'A thousand cypresses,' lecture given in Madrid, 1978, in Dal Co and Mazzariol, op. cit., 287
5 / These and others are documented in Schultz, op. cit., 74; Richard Murphy has also pointed out many similar parallel details to be found in Venice in his two books on Scarpa, op. cit.
6 / Stokes, *The Image in Form: Selected Writings of Adrian Stokes*, ed. Richard Wollheim (New York: Harper and Row, 1972), 275
7 / Scarpa, 'Furnishings,' in Dal Co and Mazzariol, op. cit., 282
8 / Frampton, *Studies in Tectonic Culture*, op. cit., 332
9 / Scarpa, 'A thousand cypresses,' in Dal Co and Mazzariol, op. cit., 287
10 / An example from the 1980s would be Steven Holl's use of a Venetian plasterer, retired to Florida from Venice, for polished plasterwork on his Seaside, Florida building, and then bringing the plasterer to New York to work on other Holl buildings
11 / Giuseppe Zambonini, 'Notes for a Theory of Making in a Time of Necessity,' *Perspecta* 24 (New York: Rizzoli, 1988), 4, 5, 8, 10, 13, 14
12 / Stokes, *The Image in Form: Selected Writings of Adrian Stokes*, op. cit., 265
13 / Ibid., 47–66
14 / Scarpa, 'Can Architecture Be Poetry?,' *The Other City: Carlo Scarpa: Die Andere Stadt*, op. cit., 16
15 / Frampton, Le Corbusier (London: Thames & Hudson, 2001), 224
16 / See the excellent essay on Scarpa and preservation by Ellen Soroka, 'Restauro in Venezia,' *Journal of Architectural Education* (May 1994), 224–41
17 / Scarpa, quoted in Toyoda, Hiroyuki and Tadashi Yokoyama, eds. 'Carlo Scarpa: A Special Celebration,' 153 (June 1977), 4
18 / 'Interview with Carlo Scarpa,' in Dal Co and Mazzariol, op. cit., 297
19 / Soroka, op. cit., 224

CARLO SCARPA LIST OF WORKS 1922–1978

Compiled with the assistance of the Carlo Scarpa Archive, Centro Archivi Architettura, MAXXI, Rome

Key: Projects are listed in chronological order based on the Project Record number provided by the Centro Archivi Architettura, MAXXI, followed by project description, location and client (where applicable). All dates given in the list of works correspond to the records held by the Carlo Scarpa Archive

PRJ: project
COM: competition project
EXE: executed
PAR EXE: partially executed
DMD: demolished
PAR DMD: partially demolished

–
PRO/1/001
1922–4 / Lazzari House (EXE) / w. Vincenzo Rinaldo / Venice, Italy / (for Bice Lazzari)
–
PRO/1/002
1923–4 / Management of the construction of religious buildings: the church of Travettore (Vicenza), bell Pradipozzo (Venice), the church of S. Maria di Sala (Venice); bell tower of Aviano (Pordenone) (EXE) / w. Vincenzo Rinaldo / Italy
–
PRO/1/003
1924–5 / Extension of the Velluti House (EXE) / Sambruson di Dolo, Venice, Italy
–
PRO/1/004
1925–6 / Direction of the restoration of Palazzo da Mula and construction of new industrial buildings (EXE) / Murano, Venice, Italy / (for Cappellin & C.)
–
PRO/1/005
1926 / Industrial building, Velo company (EXE) / Fontaniva, Padova, Italy / (for the Velo company)
–
PRO/1/006
1926 / Giovanni Campagnolo House (EXE) / Fontaniva, Padova, Italy / (for Giovanni Campagnolo, through the Velo company)
–
PRO/1/007
1926–7 / Industrial building with living quarters (EXE) / Fontaniva, Padova, Italy / (for R. Gabborin, through the Velo company)
–
PRO/1/008
1926–7 / Restoration of the Velo House (EXE) / Fontaniva, Padova, Italy / (for Angelo Velo)
–
PRO/1/009
1926–7 / Martinati House (EXE) / Padova, Italy / (for Aldo Martinati through the A. Cellante company)
–
PRO/1/010
1927 / Capellin & C. Showroom, III International Exhibition of Decorative Arts (EXE) / Monza, Milan, Italy / (for Capellin & C.)
–
PRO/1/011
1927 / Casa del Fascio (PRJ) / w. Angelo Velo / Fontaniva, Padova, Italy
–
PRO/1/012
1927 / Shop interior and window displays, Cappellin & C. (EXE) / Florence, Italy / (for Cappellin & C.)
–
PRO/1/013
1927 / Sociale Theatre (PRJ)
–
PRO/1/014
1929 / Dining room and Bedroom of the Dona House (EXE) / Murano, Venice, Italy / (for Vittorio Dona)
–
PRO/1/015
1929–32 / Mosaic, *Il Bagno* [The Bathroom], XVIII Biennale di Venezia (EXE) / w. Mario de Luigi / Venice, Italy
–
PRO/1/016
1930 / Cappellin & C. Showroom, IV International Triennial of Modern Decorative and Industrial Arts (EXE) / Monza, Milan, Italy / (for Cappellin & C.)
–
PRO/1/017
1930 / Cappellin & C. mosaic artists' studio (PRJ) / Paris, France / (for Cappellin & C.)
–
PRO/1/018
c. 1930 / Living room, dining room and bedroom of the Venier House (PRJ) / Venice, Italy
–
PRO/1/019
c. 1930 / Living room of the Ferro House (PRJ) / Venice, Italy
–
PRO/1/020
c. 1930 / Furniture of the Majoli House (PRJ) / Ravenna, Emilia-Romagna, Italy
–
PRO/1/021
c. 1930 / Games room of the Royal Automobile Club of Italy (PRJ) / Ravenna, Emilia-Romagna, Italy
–
PRO/1/022
c. 1930 / Kiosk (PRJ) / Venice, Italy
–
PRO/1/023
c. 1930 / Renovation and furnishings of the Officers' Club of Venice (PRJ) / Venice, Italy / (for the Italian Navy)
–
PRO/1/024
c. 1930 / Renovation and furnishings for the Polato shoe store (EXE) / Venice, Italy / (for Polato)
–
PRO/1/025
c. 1930 / Renovation and furnishings of the American Bar (PRJ) / Venice, Italy
–
PRO/1/026
c. 1930 / Detached House (PRJ)
–
PRO/1/027
1931 / Furnishings for the living room of the Pelzel House (EXE) / Venice, Italy / (for Franz Pelzel)
–
PRO/1/028
1931 / Furnishings for the living room/bar and children's bedroom of the Asta House (DMD) / w. Mario de Luigi / Venice, Italy / (for Ferruccio Asta)
–
PRO/1/029
1931 / Interior and furnishings of the Café Lavena (DMD) / Venice, Italy
–
PRO/1/030
c. 1931 / Elementary School (COM) / Vaprio d'Adda, Milan, Italy
–
PRO/1/031
1932 / Interiors for the atrium, living room and terrace of the Riviera Hotel (EXE) / Lido, Venice, Italy
–
PRO/1/032
1932 / Furnishings for the De Luigi House (DMD) / Venice, Italy / (for Mario de Luigi)
–
PRO/1/033
1932 / Accademia Bridge (COM) / w. Angelo and Benedict Piamonte / Venice, Italy
–
PRO/1/034
1932 / Renovation and furnishings for the Sfriso silverware store (DMD) / w. Mario de Luigi / Venice, Italy / (for Mario Sfriso)
–
PRO/1/035
c. 1932 / Monument to the Fascist Martyrs (PRJ) / Venice, Italy
–
PRO/1/036
1934 / Exhibition design, XIX Biennale di Venezia (EXE) / Venice, Italy / (for La Biennale di Venezia)
–
PRO/1/037
1934 / Bassani House with two apartments (PRJ) / Cortina d'Ampezzo, Belluno, Italy / (for G. Bassani)
–
PRO/1/038
1934 / Departures building of the Nicelli Airport (COM) / w. Benedict Piamonte and G. Pellizzari / Lido, Venice, Italy
–
PRO/1/039
1934 / Masterplan for the town of Mestre (COM) / w. Mario de Luigi and Angelo and Benedict Piamonte / Venice, Italy / (for the Comune di Venezia)
–
PRO/1/040
1935 / Furnishings for the Nicelli Airport (PRJ) / Lido, Venice, Italy
–
PRO/1/041
1935 / Interior of the atrium and library of the Confederation of Professionals and Artists (COM) / Rome, Italy / (for the Society of Decorative Arts)
–
PRO/1/042
1935 / Interior design and furnishings for the Asta yacht (PRJ) / (for Ferruccio Asta)
–
PRO/1/043
1935–7 / Ca' Foscari renovations for the University of Venice's School of Economics and Commerce (EXE) / w. Angelo Piamonte / Venice, Italy / (for the University of Venice)
–
PRO/1/044
1935–7 / Furnishings of the students' accommodation, University of Venice (PRJ) / Venice, Italy / (for the University of Venice)
–
PRO/1/045
1936 / Venini & C. showroom, VI Triennale di Milano (EXE) / Milan, Italy / (for Venini & C.)
–
PRO/1/046
1936 / Exhibition design, XX Biennale di Venezia (EXE) / Venice, Italy / (for La Biennale di Venezia)
–
PRO/1/047
1936–7 / Renovation of the Teatro Rossini movie theatre (EXE) / Venice, Italy
–
PRO/1/048
1936–7 / Interior and furnishings for the private room at the Venice Casino (PAR EXE) / Lido, Venice, Italy
–
PRO/1/049
1937 / Exhibition 'Oreficeria Veneziana,' Loggia of Sansovino (EXE) / Venice, Italy
–
PRO/1/050
1937 / Renovation and furnishings for the Sacerdoti House (EXE) / Dorsoduro, Venice, Italy / (for Gino Cesare Sacerdoti)
–
PRO/1/051
1937 / Design and furnishings for veranda of the M. House (PRJ) / Lido, Venice, Italy
–
PRO/1/052
1937 / Station project for the ACNIL (PRJ) / w. Mario de Luigi / Lido, Venice, Italy
–
PRO/1/053
1938 / Exhibition design, XXI Biennale di Venezia (PRJ) / Venice, Italy / (for La Biennale di Venezia)
–
PRO/1/054
1938 / Interior and furnishings for the first floor of the Colomba restaurant (EXE) / Venice, Italy
–
PRO/1/055
1939 / Flavio perfumery and hairdresser (EXE) / Lido, Venice, Italy
–
PRO/1/056
1940 / Exhibition design, XXII Biennale di Venezia (EXE) / Venice, Italy / (for La Biennale di Venezia)
–
PRO/1/057
1940 / Venini & C. showroom, VII Triennale di Milan (EXE) / Milan, Italy
–
PRO/1/058
1940 / Furniture for the Ufficio Passeggeri dell'Ala Littoria (EXE) / Venice, Italy
–
PRO/1/059
1940 / Renovation of an apartment in the Palazzo Mocenigo (PRJ) / Venice, Italy / (for Ferruccio Alta)
–
PRO/1/060
c. 1940 / Expansion of the Gironcoli Hospital (PRJ) / Conegliano, Treviso, Italy
–
PRO/1/061
c. 1940 / Apartments in the Sarfatti House (PRJ) / Venice, Italy / (for Sarfatti)
–
PRO/1/062
c. 1940 / Villa Amor (PRJ)
–
PRO/1/063
1940–1 / Renovation of the first and second floor of the Sacerdoti House (EXE) / Venice, Italy / (for Gino Cesare Sacerdoti)
–
PRO/1/064
1940–1 / Vettore Rizzo Tomb, cemetery of San Michele (EXE) / San Michele in Isola, Venice, Italy
–
PRO/1/065
1940–3 / Renovation and alteration to the Sacerdoti House (EXE) and apartments (PRJ) / Venice, Italy / (for Gino Cesare Sacerdoti)
–
PRO/1/066
1941 / Furnishings for the bedroom, dining room and kitchen of the Scarpa (Gigi) House (EXE) / Venice, Italy / (for Gigi Scarpa)

–
PRO/1/067
1941 / Renovation of the *Il Cavallino* art gallery (EXE) / Venice, Italy
–
PRO/1/068
1942 / Renovation and furnishings for the for Pelizzari House (EXE) / w. Luigi Pelizzari / Venice, Italy / (for Luigi Pelizzari)
–
PRO/1/069
1942–3 / Exhibition 'Arturo Martini,' Palazzo Centrale, XXIII Biennale di Venezia (EXE) / w. Mario de Luigi / Venice, Italy / (for La Biennale di Venezia)
–
PRO/1/070
1943 / Villa Grazioli (PAR EXE) / San Pietro in Gu, Padova, Italy / (for Grazioli)
–
PRO/1/071
1943–4 / Interior and furnishings for the living room of the Salvadori House (PRJ) / Venice, Italy
–
PRO/1/072
1943–4 / Capovilla family tomb, cemetery of San Michele (EXE) / San Michele in Isola, Venice, Italy / (for the Capovilla family)
–
PRO/1/073
1943–67 / Gallerie dell'Accademia Renovations (PAR DMD) / Venice, Italy / (for the Gallerie dell'Accademia)
–
PRO/1/074
1944–7 / Renovation and furnishing for the Bellotto fabric store, office and apartment, campo Santi Apostoli (EXE) / Venice, Italy / (for Vittorio Bellotto)
–
PRO/1/075
1944–50 / Renovation and furnishings for the Scarpa (Carlo) House (EXE) / Venice, Italy
–
PRO/1/076
1946 / Cinema with a coffee shop and bar (PRJ) / w. E. Matese and De Toffoli / Valdobbiadene, Treviso, Italy
–
PRO/1/077
1946 / Masterplan for Lido, Venice (COM) / w. Carlo Maschietto and students / Lido, Venice, Italy / (for the Comune di Venezia, Ufficio del Turismo)
–
PRO/1/078
1946 / Exhibition of students' sculpture (PRJ) / Venice, Italy
–
PRO/1/079
1947 / Mixed programme apartment building, Piazza Spalato (PRJ) / Padova, Italy / (for Eugenio Fondelli)
–
PRO/1/080
1947 / Banca Cattolica del Veneto (PRJ) / w. Angelo Masieri / Udine, Friuli-Venezia Giulia, Italy / (for the Banca Cattolica del Veneto)
–
PRO/1/081
1947 / Offices and furnishings for the Volo travel agency (PRJ) / Venice, Italy
–
PRO/1/082
1947 / Study for the offices of the Transadriatica agency (PRJ) / w. Carlo Maschietto / Venice, Italy
–
PRO/1/083
1947 / Lanzillo tomb (PRJ) / Venice, Italy / (for Augustine Lanzillo)
–
PRO/1/084
1947–8 / Exhibition space for mechanical calculators, International Trade Fair (EXE) / w. Mario de Luigi / Padova, Italy
–
PRO/1/085
1947–50 / Giacomuzzi House (EXE) / w. Angelo Masieri / Udine, Friuli-Venezia Giulia, Italy / (for Luciano Giacomuzzi)
–
PRO/1/086
1948 / IX Venice International Film Festival (EXE) / Venice, Italy
–
PRO/1/087
1948 / Exhibition design, including 'Paul Klee (1879–1940)' and 'Arturo Martini; Tre pittori metafisici dal 1910 al 1920,' XXIV Biennale di Venezia (EXE) / Venice, Italy / (for La Biennale di Venezia)
–
PRO/1/088
1948 / Estimate for the renovation of Palazzo Venier dei Leoni, Grand Canal, Dorsoduro (EXE) / Venice, Italy / (for Peggy Guggenheim)
–
PRO/1/089
1948 / Parish Church, Torre da Mosto (EXE) / Conegliano, Treviso, Italy

–
PRO/1/090
1948 / High-rise building complex with coach station (PRJ) / Padova, Italy
–
PRO/1/091
1948 / Entrance for the Casa Nova furniture store (PRJ) / Venice, Italy
–
PRO/1/092
1948 / Study for a bridge, River Brenta (PRJ) / Fontaniva, Padova, Italy
–
PRO/1/093
1948 / Headquarters for the Banca Cattolica del Veneto, Cervignano del Friuli (COM) / w. Angelo Masieri / Udine, Italy
–
PRO/1/094
1948–9 / Temporary pavilion, Print and Propaganda Film Festival, X Venice International Film Festival (EXE) / Lido, Venice, Italy / (for La Biennale di Venezia)
–
PRO/1/095
1948–9 / Banca Cattolica del Veneto, Tarvisio (EXE) / w. Angelo Masieri / Udine, Friuli-Venezia Giulia, Italy
–
PRO/1/096
1948–50 / Renovation and furnishings for the Duse Villa Serena (PRJ) / Venice, Italy
–
PRO/1/097
1948–51 / Interior for the Pedrocchi café (PAR EXE) / Padova, Italy / (for the Soprintendenza al monumenti di Venezia)
–
PRO/1/098
1948–56 / Renovation and furnishings for the Ongania antiques shop and bookstore (DMD) / Venice, Italy / (for Ferdinando Ongania)
–
PRO/1/099
1948–68 / Renovation and interior for the Fondazione Querini Stampalia (EXE) / w. Carlo Maschietto / Venice, Italy
–
PRO/1/100
1949 / Design for the *Il Cavallino* art gallery, Frezzeria (EXE) / Venice, Italy / (for Carlo Cardazzo)
–
PRO/1/101
1949 / Exhibition 'Giovanni Bellini,' Palazzo Ducale (EXE) / Venice, Italy
–
PRO/1/102
1949 / Exhibition 'Rassegna d'arte contemporanea,' Correr Museum (EXE) / Venice, Italy
–
PRO/1/103
1949 / Extension of the Hotel Bauer (PRJ) / Venice, Italy / (for SAIGAT)
–
PRO/1/104
1949 / Furnishings for the SFE Friulian Electricity Company (PRJ) / w. Angelo Masieri / Udine, Friuli-Venezia Giulia, Italy / (for SFE Friulian Electricity Company)
–
PRO/1/105
1949 / Apartment building (PRJ) / Feltre, Belluno, Italy / (for Eugenio Fondelli)
–
PRO/1/106
1949 / House with four apartments (PRJ) / Maerdy, Venice, Italy / (for Eugenio Fondelli)
–
PRO/1/107
1949 / Astra Cinema (PRJ) / San Dona di Piave, Treviso, Italy
–
PRO/1/108
1949 / Exhibition of set design, Teatro La Felice (EXE) / Venice, Italy
–
PRO/1/109
c. 1949 / Study for a two-storey house with two apartments (PRJ) / Maerne, Padova, Italy
–
PRO/1/110
1949–50 / Artistic and technical advice on the film *The Rival Empress* (EXE) / Venice, Italy
–
PRO/1/111
1949–50 / Modification to the outdoor arena, Venice International Film Festival (PRJ) / Conegliano, Treviso, Italy
–
PRO/1/112
1949–50 / Renovation of the atrium and reception rooms of the Hotel Danieli (PRJ) / Venice, Italy / (for SACAD, di Venezia)

–
PRO/1/113
1949–54 / Cappellin House, gardener's annexe (PRJ) / Venice, Italy / (for Manlio Cappellin)
–
PRO/1/114
1950 / Modifications to the temporary pavilion and exhibition 'Mostra del libro e del periodico cinematografico,' XXV Venice International Film Festival, Palazzo del Cinema (EXE) / Lido, Venice, Italy / (for La Biennale di Venezia)
–
PRO/1/115
1950 / Exhibition 'Il Lavoro,' Correr Museum and 'Il *Fauves*, Quattro Maestri del Cubismo,' Italian Pavilion, XXV Biennale di Venezia (EXE) / Venice, Italy / (for La Biennale di Venezia)
–
PRO/1/116
1950 / Public telephone centre, Telve (DMD) / Venice, Italy / (for Telefonica Telve)
–
PRO/1/117
1950 / Furnishings for the 'A la Piavola de Franza' clothing store, Bocca di Piazza (DMD) / Venice, Italy / (for Gigi Lanaro)
–
PRO/1/118
1950 / Book pavilion, Giardini di Castello (DMD) / Venice, Italy / (for Charles Cardazzo, *Il Cavallino* art gallery)
–
PRO/1/119
1950 / Staircase for the orchestra pit, Palazzo del Cinema (PRJ) / Venice, Italy
–
PRO/1/120
1950 / Villa Guarnieri (PRJ) / Venice, Italy
–
PRO/1/121
c. 1950 / Brino dealership (PRJ) / Conegliano, Treviso, Italy
–
PRO/1/122
c. 1950 / Sports facility (PRJ) / Venice, Italy
–
PRO/1/123
c. 1950 / Levis apartment (PRJ) / Venice, Italy / (for Guido Levis)
–
PRO/1/124
c. 1950 / Renovation of the Ca' Barbaro (PRJ) / Baone, Padova, Italy
–
PRO/1/125
c. 1950 / Puppo House (PRJ) / Padova, Italy / (for Mario Puppo)
–
PRO/1/126
c. 1950 / Villa Regazzo (PRJ) / Lido, Venice, Italy
–
PRO/1/127
1950–1 / Exhibition 'Abitazione e Camera per un albergo in città,' IX Triennale di Milano (PRJ) / Milan, Italy
–
PRO/1/128
1950–2 / Courtyard garden and windows for the Palazzo Centrale, Italian Pavilion, Giardini di Castello (EXE) / Venice, Italy / (for La Biennale di Venezia)
–
PRO/1/129
1950–2 / Villa Bortolotto, Cervignano del Friuli (EXE) / w. Angelo Masieri / Udine, Friuli-Venezia Giulia, Italy / (for Cesare Bortolotto)
–
PRO/1/130
1951 / Exhibition 'Giovan Battista Tiepolo,' Palazzo Centrale, Italian Pavilion, Giardini di Castello and Ca' Rezzonico (EXE) / Venice, Italy / (for the Comune di Venezia)
–
PRO/1/131
1951 / Modifications to the Hungarian Pavilion (PRJ) / Venice, Italy
–
PRO/1/132
1951 / Renovation of an apartment in the Vianello House (PRJ) / Venice, Italy / (for Vianello)
–
PRO/1/133
1951 / Veritti Tomb (EXE) / w. Angelo Masieri / Friuli-Venezia Giulia, Italy / (for Luciano Veritti)
–
PRO/1/134
1951–2 / Renovation and furnishings for the Hoffer House (PRJ) / Venice, Italy / (for Antonio Hoffer)
–
PRO/1/135
1951–2 / Ticket office and entrance pavilion, Giardini di Castello (EXE) / Venice, Italy / (for La Biennale di Venezia)
–
PRO/1/136
1951–4 / Renovation of the Masieri House and studio (EXE) / Udine, Friuli-Venezia Giulia , Italy / (for Angelo Masieri)

–
PRO/1/137
1952 / Exhibition 'Le Biccherne di Siena,' Biblioteca Marciana (EXE) / Venice, Italy
–
PRO/1/138
1952 / Exhibition design, including 'L'opera grafica di Henri de Toulouse-Lautrec,' Correr Museum, XXVI Biennale di Venezia (EXE) / Venice, Italy / (for La Biennale di Venezia)
–
PRO/1/139
1952 / Exhibition design for the IV Convegno Nazionale, Ca' Giustiniani (EXE) / Venice, Italy
–
PRO/1/140
1952 / Garden of the Guarnieri House (EXE) / Lido, Venice, Italy
–
PRO/1/141
1952 / Archivio Storico delle Arti Contemporanee (ASAC), Ca' Giustiniani (PRJ) / Venice, Italy
–
PRO/1/142
1952–3 / Villa Zoppas (PRJ) / Conegliano, Treviso, Italy / (for Gino Zoppas)
–
PRO/1/143
1952–3 / Correr Museum, first floor renovations (EXE) / Venice, Italy / (for the Comune di Venezia)
–
PRO/1/144
1952–3 / Renovation of the Ambrosini House (EXE) / Venice, Italy / (for Pietro Ambrosini)
–
PRO/1/145
1952–4 / Exhibition 'Antonello di Messina e la pittura del "400 in Sicilia",' Palazzo Zanca (EXE) / Messina, Sicily, Italy / (for the Comune di Messina)
–
PRO/1/146
1952–5 / Romanelli House (EXE) / w. Angelo Masieri and Bruno Morassutti / Friuli-Venezia Giulia, Udine, Italy / (for Italo Romanelli and Annamaria ven den Heuvel)
–
PRO/1/147
1953 / Exhibition 'Lorenzo Lotto,' Palazzo Ducale (EXE) / Venice, Italy / (for the Comune di Venezia, Direzione Belle Arti)
–
PRO/1/148
1953 / Consultant for the construction of the EPT Tourist Information Office (EXE) / Conegliano, Treviso, Italy
–
PRO/1/149
1953–6 / Renovation of the first six rooms of the Uffizi Gallery (EXE) / w. Ignazio Gardella and Giovanni Michelucci / Florence, Italy
–
PRO/1/150
1953–6 / Renovatiom of the Drawing and Print Room, Uffizi Gallery (EXE) / w. Edoardo Detti / Florence, Italy
–
PRO/1/051
1953–64 / Venezuelan Pavilion, Giardini di Castello (EXE) / w. Carlo Maschietto and Valeriano Pastor / Venice, Italy / (for la Biennale di Venezia)
–
PRO/1/152
1953–66 / Palazzo Abatellis renovations (EXE) / w. Roberto Calandra / Palermo, Sicily, Italy
–
PRO/1/153
1954 / Exhibition 'Arte Antica Cinese,' Palazzo Ducale (EXE) / w. Valeriano Pastor / Venice, Italy / (for the Comune di Venezia)
–
PRO/1/154
1954 / Rizzi Tomb (EXE) / Udine, Friuli-Venezia Giulia, Italy / (for Valeria Rizzi)
–
PRO/1/155
1954–6 / Renovation and furnishings for the Council Chamber, Palazzo della Provincia (EXE) / Parma, Italy / (for the Amministrazione Provinciale di Parma)
–
PRO/1/156
1954–77 / Fondazione Masieri renovations (EXE) / w. Carlo Maschietto and Franca Semi (commission first given to Frank Lloyd Wright in 1954) / Venice, Italy / (for the Fondazione Masieri)
–
PRO/1/157
1955 / Interior and furnishings for the legal offices of Luigi Scatturin (EXE) / Venice, Italy / (for Luigi Scatturin)
–
PRO/1/158
1955 / Base for the sculpture *La Partigiana* by Leoncillo Leonardi, Giardini di Castello (PAR DMD) / w. Valeriano Pastor / Venice, Italy / (for the Istituto per la Storia della Resistenza delle tre Venezie)
–
PRO/1/159
1955 / Library for the Museo Civico and Casa di Cultura (COM) / w. Gilda D'Argaro, Valeriano Pastor and Edoardo Detti / La Spezia, Liguria, Italy / (for the Comune di La Spezia)
–
PRO/1/160
1955–6 / Aula Magna renovations, Ca' Foscari (EXE) / Venice, Italy / (for the University of Venice)
–
PRO/1/161
1955–8 / Olivetti Summer Camp (COM) / w. Gilda D'Agaro / Brusson, Valle d'Aosta, Italy / (for Olivetti and C.)
–
PRO/1/162
1955–8 / Manilo Capitolo courtroom (EXE) / w. Valeriano Pastor / Venice, Italy / (for the Tribunale di Venezia)
–
PRO/1/163
1955–61 / Veritti House (EXE) / w. Carlo Maschietto and Marconi / Udine, Friuli-Venezia Giulia, Italy / (for Luciano Veritti)
–
PRO/1/164
1955–57 / Gipsoteca Canoviana Addition (EXE) / w. Valeriano Pastor / Possagno, Treviso, Italy / (for the Soprintendenza alle belle arti di Venezia)
–
PRO/1/165
1956–7 / Exhibition 'Piet Mondrian,' Galleria Nazionale d'Arte Moderna, Rome and Palazzo Reale, Milan (EXE) / Rome and Milan, Italy / (for the Galleria Nazionale d'Arte Moderna, Rome)
–
PRO/1/166
1956–60 / Saliviati & C. glass and mosaic showroom (EXE) / Venice, Italy / (for Saliviati & C.)
–
PRO/1/167
1956–63 / Parish Church of St. John the Baptist (EXE) / w. Edoardo Detti / Fiorenzuola, Piacenza, Italy
–
PRO/1/168
1956–63 / Secondary School (PRJ) / w. Edoardo Detti / Livorno, Italy
–
PRO/1/169
1956–67 / Church at Corte di Cadore (EXE) / w. Edoardo Gellner / Corte di Cadore, Veneto, Italy / (for Enrico Mattei, ENI)
–
PRO/1/170
1957 / La Rinascente store, offices and apartment building, via Etnea (PRJ) / Catania, Sicily, Italy / (for the Duchessa di Misterbianco and Baroni Spitaleri)
–
PRO/1/171
1957 / Tursi tomb with three seats (PRJ) / Conegliano, Treviso, Italy / (for Angiolo Tursi)
–
PRO/1/172
1957–9 / Fusina campsite (EXE) / Fusina, Venice, Italy
–
PRO/1/173
1957–58 / Olivetti Showroom, Piazza S. Marco (EXE) / w. Gilda D'Agaro and Carlo Maschietto / Venice, Italy / (for Olivetti & C.)
–
PRO/1/174
1957–64 / Taddei House (PRJ) / Venice, Italy / (for Piero Taddei)
–
PRO/1/175
1957–71 / Correr Museum, second floor renovations (EXE) / w. Valeriano Pastor / Venice, Italy / (for the Comune di Venezia)
–
PRO/1/176
1958 / Exhibition design, XXIX Biennale di Venezia (EXE) / Venice, Italy / (for La Biennale di Venezia)
–
PRO/1/177
1958 / Exhibition 'Da Altichiero a Pisanello,' Castelvecchio Museum (EXE) / Verona, Italy
–
PRO/1/178
1958 / Renovation of the Salviati & C. shop windows and mosaics (PRJ) / Conegliano, Venice, Italy
–
PRO/1/179
1958–61 / Secondary School (PRJ) / w. Carlo Maschietto / Chioggia, Venice, Italy
–
PRO/1/180
1958–61 / Hotel Minerva (EXE) / w. Edoardo Detti / Florence, Italy
–
PRO/1/181
1958–74 / Castelvecchio Museum renovations (EXE) / w. Carlo Maschietto and Arigo Rudi / Verona, Italy / (for the Comune di Verona)
–
PRO/1/182
1959 / Exhibition 'Un secolo d'arte vetraria muranese,' Palazzo della Gran Guardia (EXE) / Verona, Italy
–
PRO/1/183
1959 / Exhibition 'Vitalità nell'arte,' Palazzo Grassi (EXE) / Venice, Italy / (for the Centro internazionale delle arti e del costume di Palazzo Grasi)
–
PRO/1/184
1959 / Design for the foundation of the Rosso building (PRJ) / Venice, Italy
–
PRO/1/185
1959–61 / Design for the Taddei apartment in the Palazzo Da Mula Morosini (PAR EXE) / Venice, Italy / (for Piero Taddei)
–
PRO/1/186
1959–63 / Vocational school (PRJ) / w. Edoardo Detti / Carrara, Massa Carrara, Italy
–
PRO/1/187
1960 / Exhibition design, XXX Biennale di Venezia (EXE) / Venice, Italy / (for La Biennale di Venezia)
–
PRO/1/188
1960 / Exhibition 'Frank Lloyd Wright,' XXI Triennale di Milano (EXE) / Milan, Italy
–
PRO/1/189
1960 / Interior for the Zilio D'Ambrogio apartment (EXE) / Udine, Friuli-Venezia Giulia, Italy / (for Carla D'Ambrogio Zilio)
–
PRO/1/190
1960 / Lazzari Tomb (EXE) / w. Angelo Masieri / Quero, Belluno, Italy / (for Rinaldo Lazzari)
–
PRO/1/191
1960 / Zilio Tomb (EXE) / Udine, Friuli-Venezia Giulia, Italy
–
PRO/1/192
c. 1960 / Staircase for the Gallerie dell'Accademia (PRJ) / Venice, Italy
–
PRO/1/193
c. 1960 / Bettini (Dante) House (PRJ) / Caviola, Belluno, Italy
–
PRO/1/194
c. 1960 / Torres-Zanuso building (PRJ) / Venice, Italy
–
PRO/1/195
c. 1960 / Display window for the Paul Stefani antiques shop (PRJ) / Florence, Italy / (for Paul Stefani)
–
PRO/1/196
1960–2 / Exhibition 'Il governo delle acque. Il senso del colore,' Italia '61, Veneto Pavilion (EXE) / Turin, Italy / (for the Amministrazione della Provincia di Venezia)
–
PRO/1/197
1961 / Design for a shopping and apartment complex, near the Church of San Lorenzo (PRJ) / Verona, Italy
–
PRO/1/198
1961 / Interior of the M.I.M. furniture shop (PRJ) / Bologna, Italy
–
PRO/1/199
1961–3 / Gavina Showroom (EXE) / Bologna, Italy / (for Gavina)
–
PRO/1/200
1961–3 / Renovation and furnishings for the Scatturin apartment and studio (EXE) / w. Valeriano Pastor / Venice, Italy / (for Luigi Scatturin)
–
PRO/1/201
1961–4 / Palazzo degli Uffici Guidiziari (PRJ) / Massa Carrara, Italy
–
PRO/1/202
1962 / Facade and exhibition design, Italian Pavilion, Giardini di Castello, XXXI Biennale di Venezia (EXE) / Venice, Italy / (for La Biennale di Venezia)
–
PRO/1/203
1962 / Exhibition 'Cima da Conegliano,' Palazzo dei Trecento (EXE) / Treviso, Italy
–
PRO/1/204
1962–3 / Palazzo Centrale renovations, Italian Pavilion, Giardini di Castello (EXE) / w. Tobia Scarpa / Venice, Italy / (for La Biennale di Venezia)
–
PRO/1/205
1962–5 / Replanning of the Giardini di Castello (PRJ) / Venice, Italy
–
PRO/1/206
1963–4 / Design for the wine tasting area of the Centro Enologico dell'Istituto Agrario Provinciale di San Michele all'Adige (EXE) / San Michele all'Adige, Trentino Alto Adige, Italy / (for the Centro Enologico dell'Istituto Agrario Provinciale di San Michele all'Adige)

–
PRO/1/207
1963–4 / Extension for the Hotel Duchi (PRJ) / w. Sergio Los / Spoleto, Perugia, Italy / (for Giuseppe Tulli & Sons)
–
PRO/1/208
1963–5 / Cassina House (PRJ) / Ronco Carimate, Como, Italy / (for Casare Cassina)
–
PRO/1/209
1963–5 / Gallo House renovations (EXE) / Vicenza, Italy / (for Ettore Gallo)
–
PRO/1/210
1963–6 / Exhibition design including 'Giacomo Manzù,' Correr Museum, XXXII Biennale di Venezia (EXE) / Venice, Italy / (for La Biennale di Venezia)
–
PRO/1/211
1963–6 / Secco House (PRJ) / Treviso, Italy / (for Aldo Secco)
–
PRO/1/212
c. 1963–70 / Renovation of the Scarpa House (PRJ) / Venice, Italy
–
PRO/1/213
1963–78 / Renovation of the Museo Revoltella and the Museo del Mare (EXE) / w. F. Vattolo / Trieste, Italy / (for the Comune di Trieste)
–
PRO/1/214
1963–78 / Carlo Felice Theatre (PRJ) / w. Luigi Cross and Marcello Zavelani-Rossi / Genoa, Italy / (for the Comune di Genova)
–
PRO/1/215
1964–5 / Permanent exhibition, Trentino (PRJ) / Venice, Italy / (for the Provincia Autonoma di Trentino)
–
PRO/1/216
1964–5 / Second Palazzo Centrale renovations, Italian Pavilion, Giardini di Castello (PRJ) / w. Sergio Los / Venice, Italy / (for La Biennale di Venezia)
–
PRO/1/217
1964–9 / Base for the *Monument to the Female Resistance Fighter* sculpture by Augusto Murer, Giardini di Castello (EXE) / Venice, Italy / (for the Comune di Venezia)
–
PRO/1/218
1964–9 / Zentner House, Aurora Straße (EXE) / w. Sergio Los and T. Senn / Zurich, Switzerland / (for Savina Rizzi Zentner)
–
PRO/1/219
1964–71 / Renovation of the Balboni apartment (PAR EXE) / w. Sergio Los and Carlo Maschietto / Venice, Italy / (for Loredana Balboni)
–
PRO/1/220
c. 1965 / Furniture exhibition for Dino Gavina, Palazzo Podesta (PRJ) / Bologna, Italy
–
PRO/1/221
c. 1965 / Instituto Universitario di Architettura (IUAV) library (PRJ) / Venice, Italy / (for IUAV)
–
PRO/1/222
c. 1965 / Terrace at the IUAV (PRJ) / Venice, Italy / (for IUAV)
–
PRO/1/223
c. 1965 / Canteen for the IUAV (PRJ) / Venice, Italy / (for IUAV)
–
PRO/1/224
c. 1965 / External staircase to the Aula Magna, IUAV (PRJ) / Venice, Italy / (for IUAV)
–
PRO/1/225
c. 1965 / Mazzariol House renovation (PRJ) / Conegliano, Treviso, Italy
–
PRO/1/226
1965–7 / Renovation and furnishings for the Palazzo Labia, Cannaregio 275 (PRJ) / w. Sergio Los / Venice, Italy / (for the RAI)
–
PRO/1/227
1965–72 / De Benedetti-Bonaiuto House, via Salaria (EXE) / w. Sergio Los, Carlo Maschietto, F. Motterle and E. Vittoria / Rome, Italy / (for Piero De Benedetti-Bonaiuto)
–
PRO/1/228
1966–7 / Exhibition design including 'Giorgio Morandi,' Correr Museum, XXXIII Biennale di Venezia (EXE) / Venice, Italy / (for La Biennale di Venezia)
–
PRO/1/229
1966–7 / Neue Pinakothek (COM) / Munich, Germany / (for Oberste Baubehoerde im Bayer, Staatsministerium des Innern)
–
PRO/1/230
1966–7 / Exhibition 'La Poesia,' Italian Pavilion, Expo Montreal '67 (EXE) / w. Sergio Los / Montreal, Canada / (for the Ministero degli Esteri)
–
PRO/1/231
1966–9 / Expansion of the San Cataldo Cemetery (PRJ) / Modena, Emilia-Romagna, Italy / (for the Comune di Modena)
–
PRO/1/232
1966–9 / Renovation of the piazza del Duomo (PRJ) / Modena, Emilia-Romagna, Italy / (for the Comune di Modena)
–
PRO/1/233
1966–9 / Offices for La Nuova Italia publishing house (EXE) / w. Edoardo Detti / Florence, Italy
–
PRO/1/234
1966–78 / Entrance to the IUAV (PRJ) / completed in 1984 by Sergio Los / Venice, Italy / (for IUAV)
–
PRO/1/235
c. 1967 / Carrer Tomb (EXE) / Conegliano, Treviso, Italy
–
PRO/1/236
1967–8 / Exhibition 'Artuto Martini,' Convent of Santa Caterina (EXE) / w. G. Davanzo and Luciano Gemin / Treviso, Italy
–
PRO/1/237
1967–8 / Villa Gavina-Simoncini (PRJ) / Bologna, Italy / (for Dino Gavina and Mary Simoncini)
–
PRO/1/238
1967–9 / Palazzo Centrale renovations, Italian Pavilion and exhibition 'Linee della ricera: dall'informale alle nuove strutture,' Italian Pavilion, Giardini di Castello, XXXIV Biennale di Venezia (EXE) / w. P. Leone / Venice, Italy / (for La Biennale di Venezia)
–
PRO/1/239
1968 / Transformation of the Calissano Factory into a hotel and offices (PRJ) / Alba, Cuneo, Italy / (for Giorgio Quarneti, Calissano)
–
PRO/1/240
c. 1968 / Design for the Piazza del Municipio, Portogruaro (PRJ) / Conegliano, Italy
–
PRO/1/241
1968–9 / Casa Santini (PRJ) / w. F. Motterle / Lucca, Italy / (for Pier Carlo Santini)
–
PRO/1/242
1968–70 / Exhibition 'I disegni di Erich Mendelsohn,' University of California (UCLA) (EXE) / Berkeley, California / (for UCLA, Berkeley)
–
PRO/1/243
1968–70 / Teatro Communale (COM) / Vicenza, Italy
–
PRO/1/244
1968–73 / Renovation of the Franchetti Gallery, Ca' d'Oro (EXE) / w. Guido Pietropoli / Venice, Italy
–
PRO/1/245
1968–78 / Brion Cemetery (EXE) / w. Guido Pietropoli, Carlo Maschietto and the Porcinai Studio / San Vito d'Altivole / (for Onorina Brion)
–
PRO/1/246
1969 / Exhibition 'Frescoes from Florence,' Hayward Gallery (EXE) / London, United Kingdom / (for British Olivetti Ltd)
–
PRO/1/247
1969 / Opticians (PRJ) / Bolzano, Italy
–
PRO/1/248
1969–71 / Design for lighting and public garden (PRJ) / Castelfranco Veneto, Treviso, Italy
–
PRO/1/249
1970 / Exhibition 'Giorgio Morandi,' Royal Academy of Arts (EXE) / London, United Kingdom / (for The Arts Council of Great Britain)
–
PRO/1/250
c. 1970 / Furniture and flooring for the Bratti House and fountain for the entrance hall (EXE) / Treviso, Italy
–
PRO/1/251
c. 1970 / Caroly Tower House (PRJ) / Asolo, Treviso, Italy
–
PRO/1/252
c. 1970 / Connection to Palazzo Vendramin Calergi (PRJ) / Venice, Italy / (for the Comune di Venezia)
–
PRO/1/253
1970–2 / Country Club, Sant'Urbano (PRJ) / w. F. Motterle and Guido Pietropoli / Montecchio, Vicenza, Italy
–
PRO/1/254
1970–5 / Organ and altar for the church of Santa Maria Gloriosa dei Frari (PRJ) / w. Guido Pietropoli / Venice, Italy / (for the Fondazione Giuseppe Volpi di Misurata)
–
PRO/1/255
1970–6 / Renovation of the Arms Museum at the Castle of Brescia (EXE) / w. Francesco Rovetta / Brescia, Lombardy, Italy / (for the Comune di Brescia)
–
PRO/1/256
1970–8 / External interventions and renovation of the Villa Il Palazzetto (EXE) / w. Carlo Maschietto / Monselice, Padova, Italy / (for Aldo Businaro)
–
PRO/1/257
1971 / Exhibition 'Arte e Venezia,' Correr Museum (EXE) / Venice, Italy / (for the Comune di Venezia)
–
PRO/1/258
1971 / Buonpensieri shop (PRJ) / Bologna, Italy / (for Buonpensieri)
–
PRO/1/259
1971–2 / Renovation of the Palazzo della Gran Guardia (PRJ) / Verona, Italy / (for the Comune di Verona)
–
PRO/1/260
1971–2 / Roth House (PRJ) / Asolo, Treviso, Italy / (for Roth)
–
PRO/1/261
1972 / Museo dell'Opera del Duomo (EXE) / Pisa, Italy / (for Opera della Primaziale di Pisa)
–
PRO/1/262
c. 1972 / Renovation and furnishings for the Scarpa (Carlo) studio (PRJ) / Vicenza, Italy
–
PRO/1/263
1972–3 / Exhibition 'Tancredi,' Rotunda di Via Besana (Consultant) / Milan, Italy
–
PRO/1/264
1972–5 / Exhibition design including 'Quattro Progetti per Venezia,' 'Aspetti della Scultura Italiana 1945–1972,' Giardini di Castello and 'Capolavori della Pittura del XX Secolo,' Correr Museum, XXXVI Biennale di Venezia (EXE) / Venice, Italy / (for La Biennale di Venezia)
–
PRO/1/265
1972–5 / X Quadriennale Nazionale d'Arte, Rome (Consultant) / Rome, Italy / (for the Ente Autonomo Esposizione Nazionale Quadriennale d'Arte di Roma)
–
PRO/1/266
1972–5 / Lupi House (PRJ) / Vicenza, Italy / (for Eugenio Lupi)
–
PRO/1/267
1972–7 / Interiors for the meeting room of the Consiglio della Regione Veneta, Procuratie Nuove, Piazza S. Marco (EXE) / w. Angelo Scattolin and Valeriano Pastor / Venice, Italy
–
PRO/1/268
1973 / Exhibition 'Le Corbusier purista e il progetto di Pessac,' Fondazione Querini Stampalia (EXE) / w. Francesco Rovetta / Venice Italy / (for the Fondazione Querini Stampalia)
–
PRO/1/269
1973 / Exhibition 'Ritratto di Venezia,' Correr Museum (EXE) / w. U. Franzoi and Valeriano Pastor / Venice, Italy / (for the Comune di Venezia, Direzione Belle Arti)
–
PRO/1/270
1973 / Fini Restaurant (PRJ) / w. Carlo Maschietto, F. Motterle and Francesco Rovetta / Modena, Emilia-Romagna, Italy / (for Telesforo Fine S.p.A.)
–
PRO/1/271
1973 / Renovation of the Church of San Filippo (PRJ) / Genoa, Italy
–
PRO/1/272
1973–4 / Exhibition 'Venezia e Bisanzio,' Palazzo Ducale (EXE) / w. U. Franzoi / Venice, Italy / (for the Comune di Venezia, Direzione Belle Arti)
–
PRO/1/273
1973–4 / Exhibition 'Vitalità del Centro Storico e la città nel territorio,' Palazzo Comunale (PRJ) / Ferrara, Emilia-Romagna, Italy / (for the Comune di Ferrara)
–
PRO/1/274
1973–4 / Transformation of the Villa Strozzi into the Museum of Modern Art (PRJ) / w. Alvar Aalto, Ignazio Gardella, Hans Hollein, Alan Irvine, Richard Meier and Giovanni Michelucci / Florence, Italy / (for the Comune di Firenze)
–
PRO/1/275
1973–5 / Design for the Interior Design Club store (Consultant) / Florence, Italy / (for International Design)

–
PRO/1/276
1973–5 / Exhibition 'Carlo Scarpa,' Heinz Gallery (EXE) / London, United Kingdom / (for the Royal Institute of British Architects)
–
PRO/1/277
1973–5 / Renovation and addition to the Convent of Santa Caterina for conversion to a municipal art museum (PRJ) / w. Luciano Gemin / Treviso, Italy / (for the Comune di Treviso)
–
PRO/1/278
1973–8 / Gallerie Nazionale d'Arte Messina (PRJ) / w. Roberto Calandra and F. Lombardo / Messina, Sicily, Italy / (for the Soprintendenza alle Gallerie ed alle Opere d'Arte della Sicilia, Palermo)
–
PRO/1/279
1973–8 / Banca Popolare, Piazza Nogara (EXE) / w. Arrigo Rudi / Verona, Italy / (for the Banca Mutua Popolare di Verona)
–
PRO/1/280
1973–8 / Restoration of the Palazzo Chiaramonte-Steri (EXE) / w. Roberto Calandra, Camillo Filangeris and Nino Vicari / Palermo, Sicily, Italy / (for the University of Palermo)
–
PRO/1/281
1973–8 / Extension for book storage, student accomodation and the Director's apartment, Fondazione Querini Stampalia (PRJ) / w. Amerigo Marchesin / Venice, Italy / (for the Fondazione Querini Stampalia)
–
PRO/1/282
1974 / Renovation of a hotel building (PRJ) / Palermo, Sicily, Italy / (for Baron Pucci)
–
PRO/1/283
1974 / Exhibition 'Carlo Scarpa,' Domus Conestabilis-Palladian Basilica (EXE) / Vicenza, Italy
–
PRO/1/284
1974 / Exhibition 'Gino Rossi,' Ca' da Noal (EXE) / w. Luciano Gemin / Treviso, Italy
–
PRO/1/285
1974 / Simon industrial building (PRJ) / Conegliano, Treviso, Italy
–
PRO/1/286
1974 / Development of the Foresto Nuovo at the Scarpa (Carlo) House (PRJ) / Asolo, Treviso, Italy
–
PRO/1/287
c. 1974 / Renovation of the Villa Morosini (PRJ) / Conegliano, Treviso, Italy
–
PRO/1/288
1974–5 / Renovation and extension of the Villa Matteazzi-Chiesa (PRJ) / w. F. Motterle / Ponte Alto, Vicenza, Italy / (for Giovanni Matteazzi-Chiesa)
–
PRO/1/289
1974–6 / Exhibition 'Carlo Scarpa,' Institut Superior de l'Environnement (EXE) / Paris, France / (for the Institut Superior de l'Environnement)
–
PRO/1/290
1974–6 / Three family houses (PRJ) / w. S. Bagnoli, Toyoda, Zuliani / Quero, Belluno, Italy / (for Louis Faccinetto)
–
PRO/1/291
1974–6 / Monument to the victims of the massacre of Piazza della Loggia and commemorative stele for the second anniversary (EXE) / w. Francesco Rovetta / Brescia, Lombardy, Italy / (for Comune di Brescia)
–
PRO/1/292
1974–8 / Excavation and elevated piazza above the archaeological ruins at Feltre (PRJ) / w. U. Franzoi / Feltre, Belluno, Italy / (for the Comune di Feltre)
–
PRO/1/293
1974–8 / Ottolenghi House (EXE) / w. Carlo Maschietto, Giuseppe Tommasi and Guido Pietropli / Bardolino, Verona, Italy / (for Carlo Ottolenghi)
–
PRO/1/294
1974–8 / Renovation and expansion of the San Sebastiano convent, Faculty of Literature and Philosophy, University of Venice (PRJ) / w. Carlo Maschietto and Guido Pietropoli / Venice, Italy / (for the University of Venice)
–
PRO/1/295
1974–8 / Apartment building, Contrà del Quartiere (EXE) / Vicenza, Italy / (for Giacomo Borgo)
–
PRO/1/296
1975 / Exhibition 'Giuseppe Samonà, 50 anni di architetture,' IUAV (EXE) / Venice, Italy / (for IUAV)
–
PRO/1/297
1975 / Renovation of the Aula Magna, IUAV (DMD) / Venice, Italy / (for IUAV)
–
PRO/1/298
1975 / Environment for the small house at Correr (PRJ) / Venice, Italy
–
PRO/1/299
1975–6 / Room for the Muraro House (EXE) / Venice, Italy / (for Michelangelo Muraro)
–
PRO/1/300
1975–6 / Renovation of the Urbinati House (PRJ) / Pesaro, Marche, Italy / (for Antonino Urbinati)
–
PRO/1/301
1975–6 / Restoration of the Villa Zileri Loschi and adjoining residential complex (PRJ) / w. F. Motterle / Monteviale, Vicenza, Italy / (for Montecastello S.p.A. (Bossi, Broianigo and Motterle))
–
PRO/1/302
1976 / Renovation of the Hôtel Salé for the Musée National Picasso (COM) / w. P. Duboy, P. Saddy and P. Rigoni / Paris, France / (for the Museum of France)
–
PRO/1/303
1976 / Giglio In clothing store (EXE) / Palermo, Sicily, Italy
–
PRO/1/304
1976–7 / Banca Antoniana (PRJ) / w. Paulo Rigoni / Monselice, Padova, Italy / (for the Banca Antonian di Padova)
–
PRO/1/305
1976–8 / Exhibition 'Mario Cavaglieri,' Accademia dei Concordi (EXE) / Rovigo, Veneto, Italy
–
PRO/1/306
1976–8 / New entranceway, San Sebastiano convent, University of Venice (EXE) / w. Guido Pietropoli / Venice, Italy / (for the Facoltà di Lettere e Filosofia, University of Venice)
–
PRO/1/307
1976–8 / Renovation of the Curto House (PRJ) / Quero, Belluno, Italy / (for Alessandro Curto)
–
PRO/1/308
1976–8 / Galli Tomb, Genova Nervi cemetery (EXE) / w. P. Terrassan and Giuseppe Tommasi / Sant'Ilaria, Genoa, Italy / (for the Galli Family)
–
PRO/1/309
1977 / Exhibition 'Alberto Viani,' Ca' Pesaro (EXE) / Venice, Italy
–
PRO/1/310
1977 / House with two apartments (PRJ) / Lugo, Ravenna, Italy / (for Ornella Marabini)
–
PRO/1/311
1977 / Church of Santa Maria delle Rose (EXE) / w. Guido Pietropoli / Rovigo, Veneto, Italy / (for the Parish of Santa Maria delle Rose)
–
PRO/1/312
1977 / Mixed programme building of shops, offices and apartments (PRJ) / w. Luciano Gemin and Carlo Maschietto / Treviso, Italy / (for Benetton)
–
PRO/1/313
1977 / Luzzo antique shop (PRJ) / Bologna, Italy
–
PRO/1/314
1977 / Arrangement for an archaeological site in the Palazzo Forti (PRJ) / Verona, Italy
–
PRO/1/315
1977 / Furniture store (PRJ) / Guastalla, Emilia-Romagna, Italy
–
PRO/1/316
c. 1977 / Renovation of a cinema, and an office and apartment building (PRJ) / Ravenna, Italy
–
PRO/1/317
1977–8 / Mobilfiorente Hotel (PRJ) / w. S. Bagnoli / Scarperia, Florence, Italy / (for Mobilfiorente Cinelli Romano & C.)
–
PRO/1/318
1977–8 / Renovation of the library at the Scuola Normale Superiore, Palazzo della Gherandesca (PRJ) / w. Edoardo Detti and P. Terrassan / Pisa, Italy
–
PRO/1/319
1977–8 / Golin apartment (PAR DMD) / Montecchio, Vicenza, Italy / (for Golin)
–
PRO/1/320
1977–8 / Zoppi apartment (PAR EXE) / w. Guido Pietropoli and P. Terrassan / Vicenza, Italy / (for Annamaria and Domenico Zoppi)
–
PRO/1/321
1978 / Exhibition 'Carlo Scarpa,' (EXE) / Madrid, Spain
–
PRO/1/322
1978 / Altar and pavement of the church of Santa Maria del Torresino (EXE) / Padova, Italy
–
PRO/1/323
1978 / Apartment building (PRJ) / Oneglia, Imperia, Italy
–
PRO/1/324
1978 / Banca Popolare di Gemona headquarters (EXE) / Gemona, Friuli-Venezia Giulia, Italy / (for the Banca Popolare di Gemona)
–
PRO/1/325
1978 / Simoncini apartment (PRJ) / Bologna, Italy
–
PRO/1/326
1978 / Alessi shop (PRJ) / Bassano del Grappa, Vicenza, Italy / (for Alessi)
–
PRO/1/327
1978 / Large villa (PRJ) / Riyadh, Saudi Arabia / (for Prince Fahd Ibn Abdul Aziz Al Saud)
–
PRO/1/328
1978 / Restoration of the Castel Grande (Consultant) / Bellinzona, Switzerland / (for the Canton Ticino, Office of Historical Monuments)
–
PRO/1/329
Date Unknown / Design for the booth of the ERCA company, Milan (PRJ)

SELECTED BIBLIOGRAPHY

EDITED BY ROBERT MCCARTER

–

Albertini, Bianca and Sandro Bagnoli, *Carlo Scarpa: Architecture in Details* (Cambridge: MIT, 1989)

–

Albertini, Bianca and Sandro Bagnoli, *Scarpa. I musei e le esposizioni* (Milan, 1992)

–

Barovier, Marina, *Carlo Scarpa: I vetri di Murano, 1927–1947* (Venice: Il Cardo, 1991)

–

Barovier, Marino, *Carlo Scarpa: Glass of an Architect* (Milan: Skira, 1998)

–

Beltramini, Guido, Kurt Forster and Paola Marini, *Carlo Scarpa: Mostre e Musei, 1944–1976, Case e Paesaggi, 1972–1978* (Milan: Electa, 2000)

–

Beltramini, Guido and Italo Zannier, *Carlo Scarpa nella fotografia* (Venice: Marsilio/Regione del Veneto, 2004)

–

Beltramini, Guido and Howard Burns, eds., *Andrea Palladio e la villa veneta: da Petrarca a Carlo Scarpa* (Vicenza: CISA, 2005)

–

Beltramini, Guido and Italo Zannier, *Carlo Scarpa: Architecture and Design* (New York: Rizzoli, 2006)

–

Beltramini, Guido, ed., *Carlo Scarpa e la scultura del '900* (Venice: Marsilio/Regione del Veneto, 2008)

–

Bettini, Sergio, 'L'architettura di Carlo Scarpa,' *Zodiac* 6 (1960)

–

Biadene, Paolo, *Edoardo Gellner e Carlo Scarpa: La Chiesa di Corte di Cadore* (Venice: IUAV Archivio Progetti, 2000)

–

Boccato, Marilena, et. al. eds., *Carlo Scarpa: Il progetto per Santa Caterina a Treviso* (Treviso: Vianello, 1984)

–

Bottero, Mario, 'Carlo Scarpa; lo spazio poetico del Cimitero Brion,' *Abitare* 272 (1989)

–

Bresolin, Elia, ed., *Carlo Scarpa: La tomba Brion* (Comune di Altivole, 2008)

–

Brusatin, Manlio, 'Carlo Scarpa Architetto Veneziano,' *Controspazio* (March–April, 1972)

–

Cadwell, Michael, 'Swimming at the Querini Stampalia Foundation,' *Strange Details* (Cambridge: MIT, 2007)

–

Carmel-Arthur, Judith and Stefan Buzas, *Carlo Scarpa: Museo Canoviana, Possagno* (Stuttgart: Axel Menges, 2002)

–

Ceccarelli, Paolo, *Fondazione Angelo Masieri* (Venice: Masieri Foundation, no date)

–

Ceccarelli, Paolo, Sergio Los, Giuseppe Mazzariol, Italo Zannier, *Verum Ipsum Factum* (Venice: IUAV, 1985)

–

Ceiner, Giovanni and Maria Dan, eds., *Carlo Scarpa e il museo Revoltella* (Trieste, 2006)

–

Codello, Renata and Alberto Torsello, *Architetture veneziane di Carlo Scarpa* (Venice: Marsilio, 2009)

–

Crippa, Maria Antonietta, *Carlo Scarpa: Theory, Design, Projects* (Cambridge: MIT, 1986)

–

Dan, Maria Masau, ed., *Il museo Revoltella di Trieste* (Vicenza, 2004)

–

Dal Co, Francesco and Giuseppe Mazzariol, *Carlo Scarpa: The Complete Works* (New York: Rizzoli, 1984)

–

Dal Co, Francesco, *Villa Ottolenghi: Carlo Scarpa* (New York: Monacelli, 1998)

–

Dal Co, Francesco and Sergio Polano, *Carlo Scarpa: la Fondazione Querini Stampalia a Venezia* (Milan: Mondadori Electa, 2006)

–

Detti, Edoardo, 'Scarpa et la ville,' *Architecture, Mouvement, Continuite* 50 (1979)

–

Di Lieto, Alba, *I disegni di Carlo Scarpa per Castelvecchio* (Venice: Marsilio/Regione del Veneto, 2006)

–

Duboy, Philippe and Patrice Noviant, ed., 'Le annees 70 de Carlo Scarpa,' *Architecture Mouvement Continuite* 50 (December 1979)

–

Duboy, Philippe, 'Carlo Scarpa: Banca Popolare di Verona, Verona, Italy, 1973–1981,' Yukio Futagawa, ed., *GA Global Architecture* 63 (1983)

–

Eccher, Andrea de, and Giulia Del Zotto, *Venezia e il Veneto. L'Opera di Carlo Scarpa* (Milan, 1994)

–

Finelli, Luciana, *Carlo Scarpa tra storia e mito* (Rome, 2003)

–

Fonati, Franco, *Elemente des Bauens bei Carlo Scarpa* (Vienna: Akademie der bildenden Kunste, 1984)

–

Forster, Kurt and Paola Marini, eds., *Studi su Carlo Scarpa, 2000–2002* (Venice: Marsilio/Regione del Veneto, 2004)

–

Frampton, Kenneth, 'Carlo Scarpa and the Adoration of the Joint,' *Studies in Tectonic Culture* (Cambridge: MIT, 1995)

–

Frampton, Kenneth, 'Notes on the Fragmentary Architecture of Carlo Scarpa,' Barry Bergdoll and Werner Oechslin, eds. *Fragments: Architecture and the Unfinished* (London: Thames & Husdon, 2006)

–

Frascari, Marco, 'Carlo Scarpa in Magna Graecia: The Abatellis Palace in Palermo,' *AA Files* 14 (1985)

–

Frascari, Marco, 'The Body and Architecture in the Drawings of Carlo Scarpa,' *Res* 14 (Autumn 1987)

–

Frascari, Marco, 'A Deciphering of a Wonderful Cipher: Eleven in the Architecture of Carlo Scarpa,' *Oz* 13 (1991)

–

Frascari, Marco, 'The Tell-the-Tale Detail,' *The Building of Architecture*, VIA 7 (Cambridge: MIT, 1984)

–

Frascari, Marco, 'The True and the Appearance: Italian Facadism and Carlo Scarpa,' *Daidalos* 6 (December 1982)

–

Gellner, Edoardo and Franco Mancuso, *Carlo Scarpa e Edoardo Gellner. La chiesa di Corte Cadore* (Milan, 2000)

–

Ghizzoni, Gianna ed., *Carlo Scarpa a Possagno* (Possagno: Fondazione Canova, no date)

–

Giovanardi, Renata, *Carlo Scarpa e l'acqua* (Venice: Massimo Dona, 2006)

–

Hoh-Slodczyk, Christine, *Carlo Scarpa und das Museum* (Berlin, 1987)

–

Lampugnani, Vittorio, *Carlo Scarpa Architektur* (Stuttgart: Axel Menges, 1986)

–

Lanzarini, Orietta, *Carlo Scarpa: L'architetto e le arti* (Venice: Marsilio/Regione del Veneto, 2003)

–

Lootsma, Bart, 'Architectre and poetry of Carlo Scarpa,' *De Architect* 4 (1990)

–

Los, Sergio, *Carlo Scarpa: architetto poeta* (Venice: Cluva, 1967)

–

Los, Sergio, *Carlo Scarpa* (Köln: Taschen, 1993)

–

Los, Sergio, *Carlo Scarpa: An Architectural Guide* by S. Los (Venice: Arsenale, 1995)

–

Magagnato, Licisco, 'Il museo di Carlo Scarpa,' *Lotus International* 35 (1982)

–

Magagnato, Licisco, ed. *Carlo Scarpa a Castelvecchio* (Milan, 1982)

–

Manzelle, Maura, ed. *Carlo Scarpa. L'opera e la sua conservazione Volumes I-V* (Venice: Fondazione Querini Stampalia, 1998–2002)

–

Marciano, Ada Francesca, *Carlo Scarpa* (Bologna: Zanichelli, 1984)

–

Marinelli, Sergio, *Museo di Castelvecchio, Verona* (Venice, 1983)

–

Marinelli, Sergio, *Carlo Scarpa: Il museo di Castelvecchio* (Milan: Electa, 1991)

–

Marinelli, Sergio and Girogio Marini, eds., *Museo di Castelvecchio: disegni* (Milan, 1999)

–

Mazza, Marta, ed., *Carlo Scarpa alla Querini Stampalia. Disegni inediti* (Venice: Fondazione Querini Stampalia, 1996)

–

Mazzariol, Giuseppe, 'Opere di Carlo Scarpa,' *L'Architettura Chronache e Storia* (March 1955)

–

Mazzariol, Giuseppe, 'Soria e genesis dell'intervento nella Fondazione Querini,' *Quaderns d'arquitectura e urbanisme* 184 (1983)

–

Mazzariol, Giuseppe, ed., *Banco Popolare di Gemona: Luciano Gemin Architetto* (Treviso: Vianello, 1986)

–

Miotto, Luciana, *Carlo Scarpa et la Musee de Verone* (Paris: Insitut Culturel Italien de Paris, 1984)

–

Miotto, Luciano, *Carlo Scarpa. I musei* (Turin, 2004)

–

Morello, Paolo, *Palazzo Abatellis* (Treviso: Vianello, 1989)

–

Mulazzani, Marco, *I padiglioni dell Biennale* (Milan, 1995)

–

Murphy, Richard, *Carlo Scarpa and the Castelvecchio* (London: Butterworth, 1990)

–

Murphy, Richard, *Querini Stampalia Foundation: Carlo Scarpa* (London: Phaidon, 1993)

–

Nakamura, Yoshio, ed., 'Carlo Scarpa, Extra Edition,' *A+U, Architecture and Urbanism* (October 1985)

–

Nakamura, Yoshio, ed., 'Carlo Scarpa, 1906–1978,' *A+U, Architecture and Urbanism* 229 (1989)

–

Nicolin, Pierluigi, 'L'incompiuta: La Banca do Carlo Scarpa,' *Lotus International* 28 (1980)

–

Noever, Peter, *The Other City: Carlo Scarpa: Die Andere Stadt* (Berlin: Ernst & Sohn, 1989)

–

Noever, Peter, *Carlo Scarpa: The Craft of Architecture* (Ostfildern-Ruit: Hatje Cantz, 2003)

–

Olsberg, Nicholas et. al., Canadian Centre for Architecture, *Carlo Scarpa Architect: Intervening With History* (New York: Monacelli, 1999)

–

Pierconti, J.K. Mauro, *Carlo Scarpa e il Giappone* (Milan: Mondadori, 2007)

–

Pietropoli, Guido, 'L'invitation au voyage,' *Spazio e Societa* 50 (1990)

–

Polano, Sergio and Marco Mulazzani, 'Forgotten works of Carlo Scarpa,' *A+U Architecture and Urbanism*, special edition 204 (1987)

–

Polano, Sergio, *Carlo Scarpa: Palazzo Abatellis* (Milan, 1989)

–

Portoghesi, Paolo, 'In ricordo di Carlo Scarpa,' *Controspazio* 3 (1979)

–

Portoghesi, Paolo, 'The Brion Cemetery by Carlo Scarpa,' *GA Global Architecture* 50, Yokio Futagawa, ed. (1979)

–

Radice, Barbara, 'Carlo Scarpa: un' architetto a regola d'arte,' Moda 16 (January-February 1979)

–

Ragghianti, Carlo Ludovico, 'Le Crosera di Carlo Scarpa,' *Zodiac* 4 (1960)

–

Roiter, Fulvio, *Carlo Scarpa* (ex-Olivetti Showroom) (Venice: Piazza San Marco 101, 1997)

–

Rudi, Arrigo, 'Conclusion: Scarpa as educator,' *Progressive Architecture* (May 1981)

–

Rudi, Arrigo, 'Il riordino e l'ampliamente della Banca Popolare di Verona,' *Architetti Verona* (April–May 1980)

–

Rudi, Arrigo and Francesca Fenaroli, eds., 'Carlo Scarpa Frammenti 1926–1978,' *Rassegna* 7 (1981)

–

Rudi, Arrigo and Valter Rossetto, eds., *La Sede Centrale della Banca Popolare* (Verona: Banca Popolare di Verona, 1983)

–

Saito, Yutaka, *Carlo Scarpa* (Tokyo, 1977)

–

Santini, Pier Carlo, 'Three model operations in ancient contexts,' *GA Global Architecture* 51, Yokio Futagawa, ed. (1979)

–

Santini, Pier Carlo and Giuseppe Mazzariol, 'Un'opera di Carlo Scarpa: Il restauro di un antica Palazzo Veneziano,' *Zodiac* 13 (1964)

–

Scarpa, Carlo, 'Incontri a cura di Gastone Favero: Un'ora can Carlo Scarpa,' Radiotelevsione Italiana documentary, 1970

–

Scarpa, Carlo, 'Monumenti in memoriam Iosephi Brion, ab Honorina uxore fillisque facti, his chartis continentur imagines,' *Memoriae Causa* (Verona, 1977)

–

Scarpa, Carlo, 'Volevo ritagliare l'azzurro del cielo,' *Rassegna* (July 1981)

–

'Scarpa monographisch,' *Quaderns d'arquitectura e urbanisme* 158 (1983)

–

Schultz, Anne-Catrin, *Carlo Scarpa: Layers* (Stuttgart: Axel Menges, 2007)

–

Semi, Francesca, 'Le dessin dans l'oeuvre de Carlo Scarpa,' *Le Cahiers de la recherché architecturale* 19 (1986)

–

Soroka, Ellen, 'Point-Counterpoint: The Art of Interface in the Work of Carlo Scarpa,' *Modulus* 19 (Princeton: Princeton University Press, 1989)

–

Soroka, Ellen, 'Restauro in Venezia,' *Journal of Architectural Education* (May 1994)

–

Steward, David, 'Carlo Scarpa, Casa Ottolenghi, Bardolino, Italy 1975,' *GA Houses* 10 (1982)

–

Tentori, Francesco, 'Un Padiglione di Carlo Scarpa alla Biennale di Venezia,' *Casabella Continuita* 212 (1956)

–

Tentori, Francesco, 'Progetti di Scarpa,' *Casabella Continuita* 222 (1958)

–

Terenzoni, Erilde, *Carlo Scarpa. I disegni per la Tomba Brion. Inventario* (Milan: Electa, 2006)

–

Valente, Esmeralda and Vitale Zanchettin, eds., *I teatri di Carlo Scarpa* (Milan: Elacta and MAXXI, 2010)

–

Toyoda, Hiroyuki and Tadashi Yokoyama, eds. 'Carlo Scarpa: A Special Celebration,' *Space Design* 153 (June 1977)

–

Toyoda, Hiroyuki, 'The Drawings of Carlo Scarpa, Special Issue,' *Space Design*, No.328 (January 1992)

–

Watari, Koichi, *Carlo Scarpa: Villa Palazzetto* (Tokyo, 1993)

–

Yokoyama, Tadashi, 'Carlo Scarpa: Savina Zentner House, Zurich, Switzerland,' *GA Houses* 1 (1975)

–

Zambonini, Giuseppe, 'Process and Theme in the Work of Carlo Scarpa,' *Perspecta* 20 (Cambridge: MIT, 1983)

–

Zambonini, Giuseppe, 'Notes for a Theory of Making, in a Time of Necessity,' *Perspecta* 24 (New York: Rizzoli, 1987)

–

Zanchettin, Vitale, *Carlo Scarpa: il monumentale Brion* (Venice, 2005)

–

Zevi, Bruno, 'I premi nazionali di Architettura e urbanistica a Carlo Scarpa e Ludovico Quaroni,' *L'Architettura Chronache e Storia* 15 (1957)

–

Zevi, Bruno, 'Padiglione del libri d'arte,' *Metron* 38 (1950)

INDEX

PAGE NUMBERS IN *ITALIC* REFER TO ILLUSTRATIONS

A

B

C

D

F

G

AUTHOR'S ACKNOWLEDGEMENTS

I first began to study Scarpa's work shortly after graduating from undergraduate school more than thirty-five years ago, around the time he died. Like Scarpa, I was from an early age fascinated by the works of Frank Lloyd Wright, who, along with Louis Kahn, has been a source of inspiration in both my teaching and practice. While the works of these two architects have monopolized my writing efforts during the past twenty-five years, recently I have also begun to write about some of the other architects who shared Wright and Kahn's distance from the narrowest interpretation of mid-20th century 'International Style' modernism. Several of these architects, such as Alvar Aalto and Aldo van Eyck, were included in the late Colin St John Wilson's 1995 book, *The Other Tradition of Modern Architecture*. While Scarpa was not included in this book, his fundamentally experiential and historically grounded works are exemplary of the characteristics, qualities, and values that St John Wilson argued were essential to a more humanist evolution of modernism.

As I have endeavored to make clear in my text, the work of Carlo Scarpa can really only be understood by being there. It is therefore appropriate that I recognize, in retrospect, that I have likely visited several of Scarpa's relatively few buildings more times than I have visited any single building by another architect. My first visits to Scarpa's works occurred in 1981, during a six-month trip to Europe undertaken prior to enrolling in the post-professional graduate architecture program at Columbia University in New York. While at Columbia, I was privileged to win the SOM Traveling Fellowship, with which I lived in Rome during 1983–4, and my repeated visits the Veneto, to the works of Scarpa, and to the Brion Cemetery in particular, were assisted by the contacts made with the Brionvega company by my friend the architect Lisa Ronchi, the Fulbright contact in Rome, who is a native of the Veneto and family friend of Scarpa. Ronchi also put me in contact with the late Roberto Calandro, Scarpa's associate for his two projects in Palermo, who graciously provided the kind of tours that only someone who worked on a building can give.

When I first arrived to Columbia University as a graduate student in 1981, I also met Kenneth Frampton, with whom I worked for the next ten years, first as a graduate student and teaching assistant (when I read the first drafts of what would later become *Studies in Tectonic Culture*), and, beginning shortly after I graduated, as a faculty colleague and office mate. Frampton and my shared interest and enthusiasm for the works of Scarpa now spans more than thirty years, and, as I hope is clear in this text, I remain deeply indebted to Frampton both for his penetrating insights into the work of Scarpa, and for being a role model as to research method – always going back to the things and places themselves.

In 1991, I was appointed Director of the School of Architecture at the University of Florida, which since 1982 has had a study abroad program for its students based in Vicenza, Italy. I still recall my amazement at finding University of Florida students working in a studio in the top of Palladio's Basilica in 1983. Dean Wayne Drummond agreed to support my proposal that the Vicenza Institute of Architecture (VIA), originally only operating in the summer, be re-established as an academic year program, which we accomplished in 1992. For the next fifteen years, until 2007, when I left the University of Florida for my current appointment, I taught in Vicenza almost every year, ranging from two-week workshops to two-month studios. In 1994, Franca Stocco became the Director of VIA, and, among her other amazing talents, she has been instrumental in helping gain access to a number of the buildings of Scarpa for the faculty and students, and I remain deeply indebted to her for arranging for, as well as accompanying the students and I on, many of my repeated visits to Scarpa's works in the Veneto and other regions of Italy.

In the mid-1990s, in addition to my teaching appointments in VIA, I initiated a series of continuing education tours for Florida architects that involved visiting many of Scarpa's public buildings. In 1997, Frampton joined me in leading these tours, which also included presentations by Scarpa's assistants such as Arrigo Rudi and Sergio Los, local architects whose work has been inspired by Scarpa, historians such as Wilma Barbieri, and by Scarpa scholars such as Kurt Forster and Frampton, as well as visits to the workshops of the craftsmen who worked with Scarpa, such as the master woodworker Lino Contin of Thiene. A particularly memorable 'Scarpa Tour' occurred in 1998, when Frampton, ten architects, two professors, thirty-six students and I spent a day measuring the Brion Cemetery.

All my visits to the Brion Cemetery since the late 1990s have been accomplished with the kind assistance of Giuseppe Marcolin, the Brion family member who has agreed to act as caretaker for the cemetery since it was vandalized in the late 1980s. During the 2000 version of the 'Scarpa Tour,' the architects, students and I were able to attend the opening of the largest exhibition of Scarpa's drawings, 'Case e paesaggi 1972-1978' in Vicenza, and 'Mostre e musei 1944-76' in Verona. While teaching in VIA in 2004, I was also able to attend the opening of the exhibition, 'Carlo Scarpa nella fotografia: racconti di Architettura 1950-2004,' held at the Centro Internazionale di Studi di Architettura Andrea Palladio (CISA) in Vicenza, which holds the largest collection of photographs of Scarpa's works.

Since joining the faculty at Washington University, I have continued my visits to Italy and the Veneto, including the MAXXI Architecture Foundation in Rome, where the drawings of Scarpa are being cataloged and digitized, and where Director Margherita Guccione and Esmeralda Valente have been of the utmost assistance; as well as the Centro Carlo Scarpa in the Archivio di Stato di Treviso, where most of Scarpa's drawings are held, and where the curators Miriam Ferrari and Elisabetta Michelato have been most helpful.

Scarpa's drawings are published with the permission of his son Tobia Scarpa, to whom I am most grateful. My friend Franca Stocco has provided me with occasional but critically important assistance and information in these more recent endeavors. I also want to acknowledge the insightful research into Scarpa's works, as well as the enthusiastic class discussions of the Washington University architecture students enrolled in my spring 2008 seminar, 'The Architecture of Carlo Scarpa;' Huang Chien-Lin, Zachery Kimberling, John Kleinschmidt, Krista Lombardi, Kimberly Newcomer, Christopher Rehwoldt, Michele Richards, Shayne Sobell, Sarah Stanton, Duncan White, Xiao Xiang, and Yao Defei.

Since I began working with Phaidon Press in 1991, I have enjoyed the support of Richard Schlagman, the publisher at the time, Amanda Renshaw, and, in more recent years, David Davies, who, together with their superb staff, are responsible for making what I, and many others, consider the most beautiful architecture books in the world. This book was commissioned by Karen Stein, with whom I was honored to undertake several projects during her time at Phaidon. I have enjoyed working on this book with Emilia Terragni, who has been my commissioning editor since 2006, as well as with the project editors Sara Goldsmith and Joe Pickard, early on, and Tom Wright, who expertly shepherded the book through to publication.

Finally, during my early years of living in New York, I became close friends with the architect Giuseppe Zambonini, author of two of the most insightful essays on his teacher Scarpa's works. From 1985–7, Zambonini and I discussed forming a professional architectural partnership, to be based in New York City. However, before we could finalize our plans, in 1988 Zambonini took the position of Director at the Georgia Institute of Technology School of Architecture in Atlanta, where he tragically passed away only two years later. This book is dedicated to his memory.

PICTURE CREDITS

© 2012. Photo Scala, Florence: 12; ©2007 The Josef and Anni Albers Foundation / Artists Rights Society (ARS), New York: 166bl; Archivio Fotografico © La Triennale di Milano: 29; The Architectural Archives, University of Pennsylvania/Gift of Richard Saul Wurman: 184; © Aldo Ballo: 71t, 86, 89, 90–91, 185tl, 185bl, 185br, 197b, 203, 204–5, 206; courtesy Archivio Barovier: 16, 17t, 17b, 18tl, 18tr, 18bl, 18br, 19l, 19r, 20–1, 22, 23t, 23b, 24, 25l, 25tr, 25br, 30; Gianantonio Battistella © CISA- A. Palladio: front cover, 26–7, 33b, 34, 35, 37tr, 357r, 39l, 39r, 43, 44b, 49, 40, 51t, 51b, 52t, 53l, 53r, 56, 58, 58–9, 60l, 60tr, 60br, 87tr, 87br, 88tl, 90, 92r, 95l, 108, 167, 168, 175t, 181, 191br, 243cl, 243r, 256, 257l, 260, 262, 270b; © Lino Bettanin - CISA A. Palladio- Regione Veneto: inside cover, 4l, 274; © Paolo Biadene: 94t, 94b, 95r; La Biennale di Venezia – Archivio Storico delle Arti Contemporanee: 40, 41, 45, 54t, 54c, 54b, 85tl, 85tr, 85bl, 194l, 194tr; © Richard Bryant / arcaidimages.com: 66r, 67, 70r, 99bl, 99br, 100t, 100b, 102t, 102b, 103t, 105, 106l, 106r, 109, 110, 110–1, 175; © Busato: 215l; Photograph by Stefan Buzas: 251b; Stefan Buzas © CISA- A. Palladio: 4r, 101, 148, 179, 252–3, 255t, 265l, 269t; Photograph by Walter Campara 219r; Photograph by Giorgio Casali: 194br; ORCH_Orsenigo Chemollo: 44t, 66l, 82, 93, 116–7, 119, 120, 124r, 127b, 153, 160–1 165t, 175b, 176–7, 178, 180b, 272; © Elio and Stefano Ciol: 33t, 236b; Collection Centre Canadien d'Architecture/ Canadian Centre for Architecture, Montréal: 57, 112–3, 158l, 243tl, 245, 246–7, 257r, 261, 263b; Drawing courtesy Marcel Croxon: 42, 80b, 92l, 99tr, 163 (original drawing by Richard Murphy), 212, 213tl, 213bl, 213tr, 213cr, 213br, 241b; courtesy of Francesco Dal Co: 275r © Eugenio De Luigi - CISA A. Palladio - Regione Veneto: 221t, 221r, 227l; Fondazione Querini Stampalia: 166tl, 166r; © Klaus Frahm/ARTUR IMAGES: 5l, 5r, 36, 107, 124l, 131b, 132–3, 134tl, 134bl, 134r, 135, 145, 146, 149t, 150, 150–1, 152c, 155l, 155br, 157l, 157r, 158tr, 159, 164, 165b, 170, 171l, 171r, 172l, 172tr, 172br, 173, 189b, 192, 193, 195c, 207r, 210–1, 220tl, 220bl, 222, 223, 226, 228l, 228r, 229, 238–9, 243bl, 258, 264, 268, 269b, 270t, 271, 273l; Fratelli Alinari Museum Collections-Leiss Archive, Florence: 84; © The Gallery Collection/Corbis: 11; © Richard Goy: 14tr; © Pino Guidolotti - CISA A. Palladio: 9b, 10, 103b, 202, 207l, 218, 231; © Maria Ida Biggi 162; © Kunstmuseum Bern, Schenkung Livia Klee: 76t; Private collection, Switzerland, on extended loan to the Zentrum Paul Klee, Bern: 76b; © Antonio Martinelli: 221c; MAK - Austrian Museum of Applied Arts / Contemporary Art, Vienna: 128t; © Miotto, Luciana / Archivio Carlo Scarpa / Museo di Castelvecchio / Comune di Verona: 140, 141l, 141r, 144; Photography by Ugo Mulas: 149b; Photograph by Guido Pietropoli: 195t; © Andrea de Poda: 255b, 267b; Photography by Walter Popp 147; © photograph Sarah Quill: 13t, 13c, 14l, 14br, 191tr; RIBA Library Drawings Collection: 115, 263t; Rosengart Collection Museum Lucerne: 77; © CISA A. Palladio: 8, 9t; Carlo Scarpa Archive: 28, 31t, 31b, 32, 38t, 55t, 55b, 56b, 62l, 62r, 71b, 87l, 88bl, 88r, 99tl, 129l, 129r, 152b, 158br, 166tl, 166r, 187b, 196, 230, 232c, 232b, 237b, 267t, 270c, 273r, 275l; Carlo Scarpa Archive, MAXXI Architecture Collection, © MAXXI, Museum of the XXI Century Arts, MAXXI Foundation, Rome: 38b, 52b, 61, 74–5, 78, 78–9, 80t, 81, 131t, 185tr, 187t, 197t, 201, 219l, 232–3, 233, 234–5, 236t, 237t, 241t, 242, 250, 251t, 254, 265r, 266t, 266b, 267t; © Carlo Scarpa Archive / Museo di Castelvecchio / Comune di Verona: 139t, 143, 156bl (drawing by Richard Murphy), 156br (drawing by Richard Murphy); Vaclav Sedy © CISA- A. Palladio: 46–7, 63, 64, 65, 68–9, 70l, 72–3, 73, 128bl, 128br, 130, 139b, 142, 152t, 155tr, 156t, 180t, 180c, 186b, 186t, 189t, 198–9, 208–9, 214, 216, 217, 220r, 224–5, 227r; Masaaki Sekiya © CISA A. Palladio - Regione Veneto: 244, 248–9, 259; © Mark Smith: 8–9, 96–7, 104, 118, 121, 122, 123, 125t, 125b, 129t, 136–7, 168–9, 234; © Anne-Catrin Schultz: 215r; © Frederic Soltan/Sygma/Corbis: 13b; © Emilio Suetone/Hemis/Corbis: 15; Tips Images / SuperStock: 138; © Paolo Utimpergher: 182–3, 188, 195b, 232t; Courtesy The Frank Lloyd Wright Foundation Archives (The Museum of Modern Art | Avery Architectural & Fine Arts Library, Columbia University, New York). © The Frank Lloyd Wright Foundation, Scottsdale, AZ.: 37l, 191l

Every reasonable effort has been made to acknowledge the ownership of copyright for photographs included in this volume. Any errors that may have occured are inadvertent, and will be corrected in subsequent editions provided notification is sent in writing to the publisher.

Front cover: Carlo Scarpa, Brion Cemetery, San Vito d'Altivole, 1969–77; Brion Cemetery; chapel entryway, pool and subterranean pump room to the left of the chapel vestibule's portal

Inside cover: Period photograph, 1978; Carlo Scarpa (C) with Michele 'Lino' Contin (L), during the construction of Scarpa's *Valmarana* table, in Contin Srl, the woodworking shop where many of his furniture pieces were fabricated

Phaidon Press Limited
2 Cooperage Yard
London E15 2QR

Phaidon Press Inc.
111 Broadway
New York, NY 10006

phaidon.com

First published 2013
Reprinted 2014, 2015
Reprinted in paperback 2017, 2018
Classic format edition published 2021
Reprinted 2024

ISBN 978 1 83866 292 9

A CIP catalogue record for this book is available from the British Library.

Commissioning Editor:
Emilia Terragni

Project Editor:
Tom Wright

Production Controller:
Laurence Poos

Design:
Béla Stetzer

Printed in China